The *Lusitania*

NOTICE!

TRAVELLERS intending to embark on the Atlantic voyage are reminded that a state of war exists between Germany and her allies and Great Britain and her allies; that the zone of war includes the waters adjacent to the British Isles; that, in accordance with formal notice given by the Imperial German Government, vessels flying the flag of Great Britain, or of any of her allies, are liable to destruction in those waters and that travellers sailing in the war zone on ships of Great Britain or her allies do so at their own risk.

IMPERIAL GERMAN EMBASSY

WASHINGTON. D. C., APRIL 22, 1915.

The *Lusitania*

The Life, Loss, and Legacy
of an Ocean Legend

Daniel Allen Butler

STACKPOLE
BOOKS

Copyright © 2000 by Stackpole Books

Published by
STACKPOLE BOOKS
5067 Ritter Road
Mechanicsburg, PA 17055
www.stackpolebooks.com

Printed in the United States of America

10 9 8 7 6 5 4 3 2 1

First Edition

Library of Congress Cataloging-in-Publication Data
Butler, Daniel Allen.
　The Lusitania / Daniel Allen Butler.— 1st ed.
　　p. cm.
　Includes bibliographical references and index.
　ISBN 0-8117-0989-2
　1. Lusitania (Steamship) 2. World War, 1914–1918—Naval operations, German.
　3. Shipping—Government policy—Great Britain—History—20th century. I. Title.
　D592.L8 B88 2000
　940.4'514—dc21
　　　　　　　　　　　　　　　　　　　　　　　　　　　　　　00-036520

FOR TRISH,

who will always hold the key

CONTENTS

Introduction, ix

CHAPTER 1
The *Lusitania, 1*

CHAPTER 2
The Submarine, *17*

CHAPTER 3
The War, *35*

CHAPTER 4
The First Lord and the Admiralty, *57*

CHAPTER 5
The President and the Secretary, *79*

CHAPTER 6
The Diplomats and Spies, *97*

CHAPTER 7
The Warnings, *109*

CHAPTER 8
The Last Voyage, *129*

CHAPTER 9
The Day the *Lusitania* Died, *147*

CHAPTER 10
The Rescue, *167*

CHAPTER **11**
The Outrage and Excuses, *179*

CHAPTER **12**
The Inquiry, *201*

CHAPTER **13**
The Aftermath, *229*

CHAPTER **14**
The Questions, *245*

Author's Note, 259

Appendix I,
Facts about the Lusitania, *263*

Appendix II,
The Cargo Carried on the Lusitania's *Last Voyage, 267*

Notes, 271

Glossary, 277

Bibliography, 281

Index, 287

INTRODUCTION

SHIPS ARE OFTEN BETTER REMEMBERED FOR THEIR PASSING THAN FOR THEIR existence. The name *Titanic* is said to be the third most readily recognized name in the world (after "God" and "Coca-Cola"), but how many people know that she had a sister ship that sailed the North Atlantic for twenty-five years, building such a reputation for being solid and dependable that she became known as "Old Reliable"? Her name was *Olympic*. Even the rawest naval buff knows the story of *Hood* and *Bismarck*, and how *Bismarck* met her fiery end, but who can recall the names and fates of the two British battleships who pounded her so mercilessly that her crew was forced to scuttle *Bismarck*? *Rodney* went to the scrapyard in 1948, *King George V* a decade later. *Arizona* was sunk at her moorings, having barely fired a shot in her own defense, but she became a war memorial—and yet who remembers that her sister, *Pennsylvania*, survived Pearl Harbor to earn an admirable combat record in the Pacific, fought in the last engagement ever between battleships, and was finished off at last as a target for the Bikini Atoll A-bomb tests?

The *Lusitania* was one of these ships. She was an engineering marvel, revolutionary in her day for her size and speed. While perhaps not a beautiful ship outside, her interiors and accommodations established new standards for elegance and luxury aboard passenger liners, standards that were often imitated, rarely equaled, and seldom surpassed. She and her sister, the *Mauretania,* became the yardsticks by which the accomplishments of every passenger ship to come after them were measured. But today few people know little more about the *Lusitania* than some vague recollection from their school days about how she was torpedoed by a German submarine in World War I—or was it II?

Few single incidents in history are as thoroughly misunderstood as the sinking of the *Lusitania* on the afternoon of May 7, 1915. An act of war that shocked and outraged the world, the *Lusitania* disaster served as a rallying cry for armies, a morality play, and a lesson in international law gone awry and diplomacy gone bad, and it has often been perceived as one of the central causes for the entry of America into World War I, the product of German barbarity and the result of British conspiracy. Eighty-five years after the event, a shroud of mystery still clings to the entire incident, as questions are raised about how the *U-20* and the *Lusitania* came to be in the same spot in the Irish Sea at the same moment, and how the single torpedo the *U-20* fired at her could have been responsible for the *Lusitania's* sinking in less than twenty minutes. Charges and countercharges of conspiracy and cover-up, duplicity and deliberate falsehood have abounded over the decades, as pro- and anti-German partisans have clashed with their pro- and anti-British counterparts in print and the electronic media. Yet over all the verbal and printed sparring hovers the brooding presence of the 1,198 men, women, and children who were killed aboard the *Lusitania.*

The Lusitania tells the story of a great and beloved ship that *made* history from the day her keel was laid but is remembered *by* history more for her loss than for her life. The story of the destruction of the *Lusitania* is like an onion, with multiple layers each taking its shape from the one beneath it and giving shape to the one above. Not only is there the terrible human drama of those incredible eighteen minutes when the *Lusitania* sank to the bottom of the St. George's Channel, but there are also the stories of how the *U-20* found itself sitting astride the *Lusitania's* course that May afternoon; of how the U-boats became effective—possibly even decisive—weapons in Germany's naval war against Great Britain; and of the enormous political consequences of the sinking for Germany and the Allies alike. There are admirals, diplomats, ministers and cabinet members, presidents, kings, and kaisers, all of whom were part of the convoluted dance that led to the destruction of the *Lusitania.* That it was a torpedo fired from a German U-boat that sank the *Lusitania* there is no debating. After that point, almost every aspect of the disaster, the events both before and after, are in dispute to some degree.

Were there aspects of the *Lusitania's* design, as well as the provisions for the Admiralty subsidy that paid for her, that contributed to the ship's destruction? Were the charges made by the German government that the ship was carrying an illegal cargo of high explosives based in fact? Did the Germans actually warn passengers that they were going to sink the *Lusitania?* Was there an attempt by the British Admiralty to deliberately expose the *Lusitania* and other ships carrying American passengers to U-boat attack? Was there cooperation or even collusion between members of the American government and the British military to bend American neutrality laws in Great Britain's favor?

After the disaster, the story becomes even more disturbing, for there were diplomatic protests filed, threats issued, careers—military, political, and civilian—made or ruined. The Court of Inquiry into the disaster raised more questions than it answered and left behind suggestions that its proceedings and findings were manipulated for personal as well as political ends. In the United States, the President, the Secretary of State, and the Assistant Secretary of State all cordially and mutually despised each other and so could not form a coherent policy to deal with the outrage of the *Lusitania*'s sinking. German and British agents practically stumbled over one another in their efforts to influence American public opinion after the disaster, while the German Foreign Minister tried to make sense of the American diplomatic protests, and a blustering Kaiser tried to save face while he frantically sought to keep another such disaster from occurring. All the while, the British Admiralty worked hard to gain whatever advantage it could from the public antipathy toward Germany, both in Great Britain and in the United States. It all would have been so funny if it hadn't been so tragic.

Three threads tie all of these varied subjects together, and they interweave throughout the story until they are finally drawn together at the moment the *U-20*'s torpedo strikes the *Lusitania*'s side. First there is the story of the ship itself—the great pride, loyalty, and affection she created in her lifetime, sailing from a glorious peacetime career into a war in which she was destined to become both pawn and symbol. Then there is the military struggle between Germany and Great Britain, as each tried to gain a decisive edge in the naval war on the Atlantic ocean, the outcome of which would determine the course of the Great War. And finally, there is the struggle between Germany and Great Britain to sway both the American public and government to one side or the other and compromise the United States' neutrality for their own gain.

Yet was the sinking of the *Lusitania* really so important that it still deserves analysis more than eight decades after the event? The answer to this question lies in several others. Why are the British Admiralty files about the *Lusitania* still classified? Why does the British government still officially maintain that the *Lusitania* was carrying no munitions, when the manifest showing she was has been available to the public for twenty-five years? Why does the Admiralty still deny that the *Lusitania* was armed, even though professional diver John Light may have found a gun on the wreck in 1961? Is it possible that a German sabotage campaign against American industry in 1914–15 had a direct effect on the loss of the *Lusitania*? Did the captain of the *U-20* actually know he was firing his torpedo at *Lusitania*? Did the Germans actually warn the American public that the *Lusitania* would be sunk? Why did the Germans acknowledge that the sinking of the *Lusitania* was an accepted part of their submarine campaign and seek to justify it to the rest of the world? Why did the American government refuse to act against Germany after the disaster? Why did the American Assistant Secretary of State decide that he would determine which diplomatic communications the Secretary of State and the President would be allowed to see? And why was the Assistant Secretary's best friend the British naval attaché to the British Embassy in Washington, D.C.?

It's quite true that the *Lusitania* disaster was a turning point in world history, but not as is often perceived or is usually taught in American classrooms. It was far from being a primary cause of the United States' entry into World War I, though that is the usual story, for when President Wilson went before Congress in April 1917 to ask for a declaration of war against Germany, not once in the thirty-four minutes he spoke did he mention the *Lusitania.*

What made the destruction of the *Lusitania* a turning point in history is that it forever blurred the line between combatant and noncombatant, a line that soon became obscured altogether. The idea of total war, where there were no front lines and no distinction between the men and women who wore uniforms and those who did not, began with the sinking of the *Lusitania.* Forced labor of Belgian civilians by the Germans; a starvation blockade by the British against Germany; the bombing of Guernica, Rotterdam, and London; the rape of Nanking; the fire bombings of Dresden, Hamburg, and Tokyo; the atomic destruction of Hiroshima and Nagasaki; the ultimate expression of total war during the Cold War, when entire populations were held hostage to nuclear threats—all were part of the spiraling legacy of violence of the twentieth century that began the day the *Lusitania* died.

CHAPTER 1

The Lusitania

TEN MILES SOUTH OF THE OLD HEAD OF KINSALE, AT THE BOTTOM OF THE Irish Sea, lies a tomb, a 43,000-ton steel coffin that broods silently over the remains of 1,200 men, women, and children. It was once a ship, now lying on her side, her torn superstructure and shattered bow mute testimony to the agony of her destruction. For more than eighty years, the decaying hulk has been there, 300 feet down, in a shadow-filled world never brighter than the dimmest twilight. The whiteness of her upperworks, once pristine but now marred by decades of rust, silt, and the refuse of the sea, sometimes still give off a faint phosphorescent glow, while the black hull gently blends into the dark water. It's just possible, on a good day, to make out the name the wreck once carried: On the bow, just forward of the bridge, are the letters *Lusitania.*

When she was conceived and constructed, the *Lusitania* and her sister *Mauretania* were the epitome of the British shipbuilders' art. They were the largest, most imposing, most luxurious vessels ever to have sailed the North Atlantic—or any other ocean, for that matter. They physically embodied Great Britain's pride in her maritime supremacy, while at the same time reinforcing it, and they set daunting new standards by which every subsequent passenger liner would be judged. But most important of all, they brought back the Blue Ribband to Great Britain.

The quest for the Blue Ribband, the mythical appellation that went to the liner that made the fastest Atlantic crossing, east- or westbound, was by the end of the nineteenth century a competition filled with nationalistic and jingoistic overtones, becoming far more than a simple commercial rivalry between shipping firms. When the Cunard Line's *Campania* captured the Blue Ribband with a speed of nearly twenty-one knots in 1896, the title had been in British hands for nearly two decades, usually being handed off between White Star and Cunard ships. Despite a slow start, however, two German shipping firms, Hamburg-Amerika and Norddeutscher-Lloyd, began gathering momentum and prospering from the burgeoning immigrant trade, and soon German ships began to establish a style all their own on the North Atlantic.

Before long, the directors of Norddeutscher-Lloyd decided that their ships should also set the pace. Approaching the Vulkan shipyard of Stettin, East Prussia, they had a simple proposal: "Build us the fastest ship in the world and we'll buy it; anything less and you can keep it." The result was the mean-looking, imposing, unmistakably German *Kaiser Wilhelm der Grosse.* In the words of John Malcolm Brinnin, she ushered in "a period of steamship history when the landscapes of Valhalla enscrolled on the walls and ceilings of grand saloons would all but collapse under their own weight, as well as a period when Teutonic efficiency united with matchless engine power would give Germany all the honors on the northern seas. And when the wits of the first decade of the [Twentieth] Century began to say something was 'hideously' or 'divinely' 'North German Lloyd' they meant, according to one American contemporary, 'two of everything but the kitchen range then gilded.'" Her pretentiousness slowed her not a whit, for the *Kaiser Wilhelm der Grosse* romped across the North Atlantic on her maiden voyage in early 1897 at nearly twenty-two knots.

Great Britain was aghast. "In that jubilee year, England was not feeling modest," wrote Humphrey Jordan. "She despised all foreigners without troubling to conceal the fact; she recognized herself, with complete assurance, as a great nation, the head of a mighty empire, the ruler of the seas. But with the jubilee mood still warming her citizens with a fine self-satisfaction in being Britons, England lost, and lost most decisively, the speed record of the Atlantic ferry to a German ship. The *Kaiser Wilhelm der Grosse* was a nasty blow to British shipping; her triumphant appearance on the North Atlantic came at a moment particularly unacceptable to the English public."

Not content in merely besting the British, the Germans embarrassed them by next introducing the *Deutschland,* which belonged to the Hamburg-Amerika Line, crossing the "Big Pond" at a speed of nearly twenty-three knots. Long, low, with a sleek, four-funneled superstructure, the *Deutschland* looked the part of the Atlantic greyhound. Yet her preeminence was to last less than a year as, adding insult to injury, the new *Kronprinz Wilhelm* set a new record at 23$\frac{1}{2}$ knots, and the year after that, the *Kaiser Wilhelm II* proved a shade faster still. This Teutonic monopoly on the Blue Ribband was more than Great Britain could stand: A head-to-head showdown was approaching between these upstart Germans and the established maritime power of the British. France and the United States, once serious contenders, were soon left in the wakes of these two great rivals.[1]

A key to German success was that the German shipping lines were being heavily subsidized by the German government, with loans and grants for construction costs as well as operating subsidies, a course of action the British government was loath to follow. Conversely, only with government funding and naval design expertise could the British hope to overtake their German rivals. The race for the Blue Ribband would become a vicious cycle of building ever bigger, faster, and, most important to Her Majesty's Government, more expensive ships that Parliament refused to be drawn into.

What the British government hadn't counted on was the Americans, specifically one John Pierpont Morgan, who had the green gleam of money in his eye. Morgan, the greatest of a generation of trust builders, had conceived of a vast freighting monopoly that would control the shipping rates of goods and the fares of passengers being transported from Europe, from the moment they left the Old World till they arrived at their destination in the New. Since the American rail barons, and especially Morgan, had already monopolized the American railroads, all that remained for Morgan's dream to become reality was to gain control of the North Atlantic shipping lines.

Morgan's first move in that direction came in 1898, when he acquired the financially troubled Inman Line. Thomas Ismay, chairman of the White Star Line, had attempted to form a consortium of British shipowners that would keep Inman out of Morgan's hands, but the attempt fell apart because too few of Ismay's colleagues believed Morgan was serious. One of the few failures in his career, Ismay rued it till his death in 1899, foreseeing a fierce rate war on the North Atlantic. He was right. The same year Thomas Ismay died, Morgan was able to purchase a controlling interest in both Hamburg-Amerika and Norddeutscher-Lloyd. A year later, he had gained ownership or control of the Leyland Line, the Dominion Line, and the Red Star Line. Setting his sights on both White Star and Cunard, Morgan began cutting fares until his lines were offering a Third Class passage to America for as little as £2.

J. Bruce Ismay, who had succeeded to the directorship of the White Star Line after his father's death, was every bit as determined as his father to resist Morgan. Morgan, though, received help from an unexpected ally: Lord Pirrie, chairman of the board of Harland and Wolff, the Belfast shipyard that built all of the White Star's passenger liners. Realizing that a rate war would leave White Star with little capital for new ships, and having made Harland and Wolff heavily dependent on White Star for new shipbuilding orders, Pirrie began to pressure the younger Ismay to accept Morgan's offer to buy the line. Thomas Ismay would have told Lord Pirrie to be damned and fought the "Yankee pirate" tooth and nail, but Bruce didn't have his father's innate ruthlessness. Rather than stand up to Pirrie, Ismay eventually caved in, and in 1902, Morgan's shipping combine, now known as International Mercantile Marine (IMM), acquired control of the White Star Line.[2]

Cunard, meanwhile, had skillfully exploited Morgan's attempt to purchase that other great British shipping line. Admittedly, Parliament had been alarmed at IMM's acquisition of White Star and had frantically passed a bill requiring that White Star's ships remain under British registry, so there was a certain sympathy within the House for the idea of government intervention to keep Cunard out of Morgan's hands. Nonetheless, Cunard was taking no chances: Lord Inverclyde, the grandson of one of the line's founders and its current chairman, stayed true to his Scots heritage and played a canny game. When Morgan's representatives approached Cunard with an invitation to either join the combine or let IMM purchase a controlling interest, Inverclyde countered with the proposal that IMM buy the line outright and suggested that IMM make an offer. What Morgan's people didn't know was that Inverclyde was keeping the British Government informed of every new turn in the developing negotiations, determined to play one side against the other.

Now Lord Inverclyde was a genuinely patriotic Briton, but he was first and foremost a businessman, with an obligation to create the best possible situation for Cunard and the company's stockholders, so he was careful to make it clear to the Government that if they chose not to subsidize Cunard, he would be willing to accept Morgans's offer—if the price was right and Inverclyde decided it was in the best interests of the company. He made it perfectly clear that he believed only the Government possessed the resources necessary to keep Cunard out of Yankee hands. At the same time, however, Inverclyde studied IMM's initial offer of £18 per share for fifty-five percent of the company's stock and decided it wasn't generous enough. The Government, thinking it had Inverclyde's measure—that he was merely trying to raise the level of any possible government subsidies—informed Inverclyde that whether or not to join Morgan's combine was entirely his decision.

There were three possible courses of action, as outlined to Inverclyde by Lord Selborne, the First Lord of the Admiralty and the Cabinet minister with whom Inverclyde had been communicating. Those alternatives were to allow Cunard to join or be bought by IMM; to remain independent of IMM and fight Morgan's fare war with Government assistance; or to join a British anti-combine designed to counter IMM. As Lord Selborne outlined it, the Government was adamantly opposed to the first, less than enthusiastic about the second, and very favorably disposed to the third. Lord Inverclyde decided that the time had come to get tough. By making it clear that if the Government was not willing to assist and underwrite Cunard in a manner similar to that in which the German government underwrote Norddeutscher-Lloyd and Hamburg-Amerika, he would sell the line to Morgan, he was ultimately able to wring considerable concessions from the British Government to allow the company to remain in British hands.

That he was successful was due to the sudden and unexpected intervention of the British Admiralty. The Admiralty stepped in because there was another role that the fast German liners could play, one that involved the

Admiralty directly. That role was to function as auxiliary cruisers in wartime. Auxiliary cruisers were a slightly addle-brained fad that enjoyed considerable vogue in most of the world's larger navies in the last part of the nineteenth century and the early part of the twentieth. Essentially, they were fast ocean liners that had been built with reinforced platforms for mounting a number of medium-caliber guns (some as large as six inches) along with compartments that could easily be converted into magazines and storage rooms, as well as shell hoists, handling rooms, and mountings for range-finding equipment. In the event that a war was declared, the belligerent navy would bring these fast liners into drydock, mount their guns and load their ammunition, then man them with crews of reservists, leavened by a handful of regular seamen and petty officers. Their officers would all be reservists. Their mission would be to go out onto the high seas and hunt down enemy shipping, using their superior speed to catch enemy merchant vessels or, if cornered by proper warships, run away.

The Admiralty was suspicious of IMM's motives in acquiring controlling interests in several of Britain's shipping companies, since the cartel also held controlling interests in Hamburg-Amerika and Norddeutscher-Lloyd. Tension was growing between Great Britain and Germany over the rapid and—to the British—unnecessary expansion of the German Navy, which was perceived as a threat to Britain's maritime supremacy. The Admiralty fretted over the possibility that in the event of a war between Great Britain and Germany, IMM could be manipulated by the Germans into denying large numbers of auxiliaries to the Royal Navy, in effect depriving the British of what amounted to a second fleet. The fast German liners, in their guise of auxiliary cruisers, seemed to present a grave danger to British merchant shipping. Without similar ships that could be used to hunt them down, the Royal Navy's only possible response would be to deploy large numbers of the fleet's cruisers for that task, which would be costly in terms of men, resources, and money, and would indefinitely tie up ships that might be desperately needed for other duties.

The Admiralty quickly pressured Parliament into forbidding the transfer of IMM's newly acquired White Star ships from British to American registry, while at the same time forcing increases in the naval budgets and some rudimentary subsidies to the larger shipping lines. That was not enough to satisfy the Royal Navy, however, and when it began to press its own case for fast British liners that could be used as auxiliary cruisers, there was no way for Parliment to resist, given the popular sentiment of the day. When H. O. Arnold-Foster presented a paper to the Cabinet declaring that the posture of the German Navy was one of aggressive intent toward Great Britain, and emphasizing that the fast German liners were specifically designed for swift conversion into auxiliary cruisers so that they could be sent out to prey on British shipping, the Government decided to radically reverse its position with Cunard.

Realizing that the sentiment of not only the public but also that of the Royal Navy was now on his side, Lord Inverclyde pressed home his case with the Government in the autumn of 1902. Members of the Royal Institute of Naval Architects were, at the Admiralty's request, invited to help Cunard form the basic outlines of the design of a pair of new liners that would surpass anything afloat in size, luxury, and most of all, speed. The Admiralty expressed a desire to have these ships be capable of sustained speeds of twenty-four to twenty-five knots, and to be able to do so would require a power plant larger than any that had ever been installed in a ship before. This, in turn, necessitated a longer and larger hull than had ever been built, which would carry naval architecture and design far beyond their existing limits. Likewise, the cost of building these ships would be greater than anyone had ever imagined: Each liner would cost well in excess of £1,200,000, while the annual operating subsidy would be on the order of £200,000.

When Lord Selborne balked at these figures, Inverclyde informed him that it was simply a matter of "annihilation or absorption" for Cunard if the Government did not intervene. The British press was having a field day with the story of how Morgan was trying to acquire Cunard, rousing public sentiment against the "Yankee pirate" and wondering if there was no end to the man's avarice. On street corners in London and Glasgow, "Licenses to Remain on Earth," complete with a reproduction of J. P. Morgan's signature, were being sold for a penny apiece. Over and over editorials asked, Who was to rule the waves—Morgan or Britannia? After he had taken control of the Atlantic, it was postulated, Morgan would begin stripping Britain of her national treasures and reducing the island empire to insignificant vassalage to the might of his omnipotent dollars. John Malcolm Brinnin summed up this sublimely hysterical situation in *The Sway of the Grand Saloon:* "Its hands and wrists fettered, its beautiful white body tied to the tracks while the glinty eyed locomotive from Wall Street came bearing down the line, Cunard cowered and blinked in the mock terror of those who know they are going to be snatched to safety."[3]

The upshot of the whole affair was an almost total capitulation by His Majesty's Government. Under the terms of the agreement between the Government and Cunard signed in October 1902, the Admiralty would finance the construction of the two new ships, the sum of nearly £2,600,000 to be repaid over a ten-year period at 2.75 percent interest, while an annual subsidy of £75,000 would help defray the operating expenses. In return, Cunard guaranteed that control of the line would never pass from British hands, thus thwarting IMM in one deft stroke, and pledged that in wartime the ships would be placed at the disposal of the Royal Navy, while in peacetime a certain percentage of their crews would consist of naval reservists, who would form the nucleus of their wartime crews, should they ever be needed. An additional clause that seemed innocent enough to all parties at the time provided for the entire resources of Cunard to be made available to the Admiralty in the event of war. But probably the most significant provision of the contract was that on questions of the design of the new ships, Cunard was obligated to defer to the Admiralty's wishes.

The design brief was given to a combined civilian and Admiralty design team, headed by one of the foremost naval architects of the day, Leonard Peskett, in the summer of 1903. Peskett and his staff were faced with a herculean task, for while the ships had to meet the requirements laid down by the Admiralty offices in Whitehall, they also had to be able to create a profit for Cunard. As the Admiralty outline ran, these ships had to be capable of sustained speeds of up to twenty-five knots, carry an armament of not less than twelve 6-inch guns, and have their vital machinery spaces protected on a scale similar to that of the cruisers of the Royal Navy. Peskett then had to find a way to provide accommodations for enough passengers to keep the ships operating in the black. As if that weren't enough, Cunard compounded the poor man's problems by decreeing that the accommodations in all three classes were to exceed in comfort and convenience anything ever seen before on the North Atlantic. So Peskett was faced with the challenge of creating what amounted to a floating hotel, capable of holding 2,300 passengers and 900 crew, that could double as a warship if needed.

The design of the *Lusitania* and *Mauretania* was so revolutionary that it deserves to be examined in some detail. The sheer size of the two ships would push naval architecture and marine engineering into completely uncharted territory. The application of new technologies that, though hardly unproven, had never been applied on such a scale before meant that Peskett and his fellow designers could not always depend on past experience as a guide for solving new problems. That they succeeded at all is remarkable; that they succeeded as well as they did is a tribute to their considerable talents.

The result of two years of design work was a tour de force in naval architecture and an aesthetic nightmare. Peskett produced a long, narrow hull, 768 feet in length, with a beam of only 88 feet, with a fully laden draft of 33 feet. The designed displacement of these ships was 41,400 tons fully laden, making them the first ships to pass the 40,000-ton mark in size. Peskett's designs were pushing shipbuilding into the realm of the unknown: His ships were almost 18,000 tons heavier than the largest of the German liners they were meant to best, the *Kaiser Wilhelm II.* Some indication of how rapidly ships were growing in size can be gained by recalling that the last British ship to hold the Blue Riband, the *Campania,* had displaced just 18,000 tons—only ten years earlier! Perched atop this hull was a ventilator-cluttered superstructure that bore more than a passing resemblance to a Queen Anne's mansion, with an after section that looked like an afterthought. Towering above it all were four massive, ungainly funnels that vented the huge boiler rooms below, the whole creating a not incorrect impression of top-heaviness. The two liners, to be called *Lusitania* and *Mauretania*, would be the largest and most powerful passenger ships yet built. They were undeniably impressive, but there was no way they could be called beautiful. Taken overall, they created a sense of ponderous bulk, as opposed to the slim grace of the two ships that would be the White Star Lines' reply, the *Olympic* and *Titanic.*

Their less-than-inspired aesthetics in no way detracted from Peskett's achievement, however. The most outstanding features of their design were their power plants and the choice of high-speed turbines for propulsion, a decision that marked the beginning of a new era in passenger ship construction. The first really large ship ever powered by turbines was the Royal Navy's revolutionary battleship HMS *Dreadnought,* a ship of 21,500 tons launched in 1905 and capable of nearly twenty-two knots—more than 3 knots faster than any contemporary battleship. She was soon followed by a quartet of even larger battle cruisers designed to reach speeds of more than twenty-six knots. The economy and reliability of the turbines that powered these ships were so impressive that the Royal Navy decided that all subsequent capital ships would be powered by turbines, a conclusion that weighed heavily in Cunard's decision making.

Cunard had looked into the feasibility of installing turbines in passenger liners when the *Carmania* and the *Caronia* entered service in 1905. These two ships were identical in every respect save for the engines. The *Caronia* was propelled by conventional reciprocating engines, while the *Carmania* was powered by turbines. The lower operating costs, reduced crew requirements, and reliability of the *Carmania's* power plant decided the issue for Cunard, and turbines were specified for the *Lusitania* and *Mauretania.*

Four sets of Parsons turbines would power the *Lusitania* and *Mauretania,* each set, which included one forward and one reverse turbine, driving one propellor shaft. The total output of the four was over 68,000 shaft horsepower (shp), nearly double that of the *Kaiser Wilhelm II.* The turbines were remarkable engineering achievements, each rotor nearly fifteen feet in diameter and weighing ten tons, containing thousands of individual vanes or blades, each meticulously positioned and balanced, machined to tolerances measured in thousandths of an inch, and spun at such high speeds that a drop of water striking one of the blades would cause the blade to shatter. Gone were the huge pistons, crankshafts, and valve gear of the reciprocating engines, along with all of their pounding and vibration.

While adopting a turbine power plant saved weight and space in the engine room, huge amounts of steam were needed to spin those turbines, more steam than had ever been generated aboard ship before. Twenty-three coal-burning boilers, divided between four boiler rooms, numbered one through four from the bow aft, provided the steam. Twenty-one of the boilers were double ended—that is, they had fireboxes at each end of the boiler casing, while two were single ended. Each end held four fireboxes, so that the *Lusitania* had a total of 176 furnaces, each of which had to be constantly fed coal, one shovelful at a time. It would be backbreaking work; together the boilers consumed over 600 tons of coal a day, more than 3,000 tons on each crossing, in order to generate the steam necessary to speed the ship at over 26 knots.[4]

Although the *Lusitania* was first and foremost a passenger liner, her potential role as an auxiliary cruiser was a very real consideration. In addition to the high speed provided by her turbines, there were several features of the design of the *Lusitania* and her sister that were mandated by the requirements of the Admiralty contract that were not found on most passenger liners. The first of these requirements was a provision for twelve specially reinforced platforms, six on each side of the ship, eight on D Deck, four on C Deck. These platforms were to be the mounting points for the armament of the *Lusitania*, should she ever be called upon to don her guise as an auxiliary cruiser. The specification called for 6-inch guns to be mounted, giving her more firepower than many of the Royal Navy's light cruisers. Specific compartments on the ship, most notably an auxiliary coal bunker forward of the first boiler room, were designated for swift conversion into magazines and shell handling rooms, while other areas—including some passenger accommodations—were specified to be reserved for use exclusively by the Royal Navy in the event of a war or a national emergency.

Some of the specific provisions of the Admiralty contract imposed certain limitations on Peskett's design team, leading to peculiarities in the design of the ship. Since the *Lusitania* would not carry any armor at all, in order to provide a measure of protection from enemy shellfire for the turbines and boilers, both engine rooms and all four boiler rooms were situated below the waterline. Likewise, the movable structure of the rudder and the steam-powered steering gear engine were located below the waterline, although the profile of the *Lusitania*'s stern was contoured along the lines of the traditional ocean liner's counter stern. Watertight subdivision was achieved by adopting a system used successfully in several classes of Royal Navy cruisers. Ten watertight bulkheads ran laterally across the ship, effectively dividing the lower hull into eleven major compartments. Wherever possible, in the boiler rooms for example, each compartment was further subdivided.

Drawing further on Royal Navy experience, Peskett had worked in two longitudinal watertight compartments—one on each side of the ship, running outboard of the boiler rooms for their full length, from the forward bulkhead of Boiler Room Number 1 to the aft bulkhead of Boiler Room Number 4. These compartments served as coal bunkers and were also intended to provide protection for the boiler rooms, as the experience of the Royal Navy had shown that bunkered coal could slow or even stop the penetration of shells as well as dampen the effects of the blast when those shells detonated. There was a certain practical problem to using these longitudinal compartments as coal bunkers, however, as the scuttles had to be opened in their inner bulkheads in order to allow the trimmers and stokers to get to the coal.

In service, it was found that coal dust and debris, not to mention the weight of the bunkered coal itself, soon made the doors of the coal scuttles difficult, often impossible, to close. This meant that the watertight integrity of both the longitudinal bunkers and the boiler rooms could be compromised. If the bunker was opened to the sea by collision, mine, shell, or torpedo, there were three apertures on each side of each boiler room where the sea could enter unchecked and flood the boiler rooms. Peskett also apparently overlooked the incredible capacity of coal to absorb water. Should one of the longitudinal bunkers be opened to the sea, the remaining coal in the bunker would draw up a tremendous amount of seawater, the added weight possibly inducing a dangerous list.

The stability of the *Lusitania*'s design was a concern of Peskett's. He included a caution in the ship's manual that advised her captain to abandon ship should the *Lusitania* ever take on and hold a list of more than twenty-two degrees. Try as he might, Peskett could not produce a more stable design that fulfilled both the Admiralty's requirements and those of Cunard, and the righting moment—the tendency of a ship to return upright after she rolls—couldn't be increased, hence the warning. The restrictions placed on her design by Admiralty requirements, coupled with the long, narrow, fine-lined hull, meant that in order for the *Lusitania* to be able to carry enough passengers to be a paying proposition, Peskett was forced to build high. The *Lusitania* had seven main decks, designated by the letters A through F, from highest to lowest, with the Hold Deck as the very bottom deck of the ship. A Deck was sometimes referred to as the Boat Deck and the two terms were used interchangeably. This meant that the topmost deck was more than sixty feet above the waterline. Atop all of that were the four huge funnels, whose height and diameter were dictated by the necessity of creating a strong enough draft through the boilers.

Cunard then added to Peskett's headaches by deciding that the *Lusitania*'s passenger accommodations would be more comfortable and luxurious than those on any previous ship to sail the North Atlantic. Accessories and amenities in all classes were added, and with them came added topweight, that is weight on the ship that was above her center of gravity. In the most simple terms, the more topweight a ship has, the less stable it becomes, and the *Lusitania*'s stability was rapidly becoming a concern. At the same time, while it created still more problems for Peskett and his fellow designers, it was a shrewd business move on Cunard's part.[5]

For decades Cunard had been symbolic of safe, sedate, rather pedestrian ships that crossed the Atlantic reliably, if not spectacularly. That the *Campania*, the last British ship to hold the Blue Ribband, was a Cunard ship was a happy coincidence, but it was not the consequence of a deliberate policy by the line. Reliability and safety had become the company's hallmarks, and indeed, it was a point of pride that the line could boast—in complete truth—that "Cunard had never lost a life." It was with as much truth as wit that Mark Twain summed up Cunard's attitude when he observed:

> The Cunard people would not take Noah as first mate until they had worked him through the lower grades and tried him for ten years or such matter. . . . It takes them about ten or fifteen years to manufacture a captain; but when they have him manufactured to suit at last they have full confidence in him. The only order they give a captain is this, brief and to the point: "Your ship is loaded, take her; speed is nothing; follow your own road, deliver her safe, bring her back safe—safety is all that is required."

And until the advent of the fast German liners, safety *was* all that was required; the accidents and disasters that seemed to befall the line's British and American rivals never seemed to come Cunard's way. Cunard seemed to believe that the public would esteem safety and reliability over speed and luxury, but the public proved to be a fickle lot, and soon the opulent offerings of Hamburg-Amerika, Norddeutscher-Lloyd, and the White Star Line began making serious inroads on the number of passengers that Cunard ships were carrying. Cunard had no choice but to follow suit and match luxury for luxury, speed for speed. With the *Lusitania* and *Mauretania,* the line was determined to soundly trump the Germans and White Star on both counts. Consequently, it was not only necessary for Peskett's design team to produce an extremely fast ship, but they also had to produce a fabulously luxurious one.

The First Class public rooms aboard the *Lusitania* demonstrated how well the design board fulfilled both Cunard's and the Admirality's requirements. They included a dining saloon, reception room, restaurant, lounge, reading and writing room, smoking room, and veranda café and were served by a pair of elevators—a novelty in 1907. Ensuite cabins were provided, as well as a pair of elegantly appointed "Regal Suites" that were clearly meant for the *crème de la crème* of transatlantic society, each of these suites consisting of a dining room, drawing room, two bedrooms, a bath and toilet, and adjoining rooms for valets or maids. The ship also offered a barbershop, a darkroom for photographers, a clothes pressing room, a special dining room for maids and valets, a lending library, even a telephone system that allowed passengers to place calls from one cabin to another. Everything had been done in fitting out the First Class accommodations to make them more than equal to the finest hotels in Europe.

The centerpiece of the *Lusitania*'s decor was her magnificent, two-tiered First Class Dining Saloon, with its enormous gilt and white-enameled alabaster dome, done in a Louis XVI style. It was the largest such room yet seen in a ship, over ninety feet in length, running the full width of the hull. With a 500-seat capacity, it presented a vast sea of gilt-topped Corinthian columns, overstuffed swivel chairs, and polished mahogany tables set with glittering crystal and gleaming silver.

The First Class Smoking Room, located on A Deck, was an equally eloquent testimonial to the care and expense lavished on the *Lusitania*'s interior. Sitting under a huge, ornate, wrought-iron skylight inset with leaded glass and etched panels, it was decorated in the style of the late Georgian period, a symphony of mahogany and walnut-paneled walls, handsomely carpeted flooring, and massive leather-covered armchairs, beside which sat exquisitely carved, marble-topped tables. The First Class Smoking Room was an unbreachable bastion of carefully blended masculinity and affluence. The entire atmosphere immediately evoked images of silk waistcoats, gold watch chains, expensive cigars, and the deep baritones of rail barons, shipping magnates, international publishers, and millionaire businessmen.

The staterooms and suites for the First Class passengers were, of course, on a scale in keeping with the other First Class amenities. Instead of the usual bunk or berth typical of the transatlantic liner of the day, each stateroom had its own full-size, wrought-iron bedstead, as well as a washstand with hot and cold running water. If a passenger was willing to spend the extra money, whole suites of three, four, or five rooms could be booked, in decors that included Louis XIV, XV, and XVI; Georgian; and Regence (as the British insisted on spelling "Regency" for years).

The craftsmanship and meticulous construction were carried over fully into Second and Third Classes as well. Indeed, Second Class rooms, public and private, could have been mistaken for First Class on almost any other ship on the North Atlantic, including the Dining Saloon, Smoking Room, and Library, and while the Second Class staircase may not have been as grand as that of First Class, it was still an exceedingly handsome structure.

Third Class was a story unto itself. A great many myths have built up around the flood of immigrants that flowed to the shores of the New World at the end of the nineteenth century and the beginning of the twentieth, aided by a spate of romanticized reporting, photographs, and artwork from the period. All too often these "steerage"—as Third Class was commonly known—passengers are portrayed as "tired, poor . . . huddled masses," as babushka- and shawl-beclad mothers gripping the hands of small, wide-eyed children, or as young men in ill-fitting clothing clutching their few belongings in loosely tied bundles, all hoping to find their fortunes in such exotic locales as New York, Pittsburgh, or Chicago.

The truth, as with so many subjects of the journalism of that day, was a good deal more mundane. Despite the increasing numbers of central and southern Europeans emigrating to America, the majority of those leaving the Old World for the New were still Anglo-Saxon. Many were Germans, whose fatherland was undergoing a bewilderingly rapid transformation from an agrarian society to an industrial juggernaut, with all the attendant social dislocations; many others were Britons, often skilled or semiskilled workers, sometimes craftsmen, occasionally members of the professions, forced to seek employment in America as Britain began her slow industrial and economic decline. To these people, a ship was transportation, its sole purpose to take them from Southampton (or Cherbourg or Queenstown) to New York. Passengers like these were not influenced by Grand Staircases, electric elevators, swimming baths, or Smoking Rooms. Their interests lay in clean quarters and decent food. In this respect the *Lusitania* served them admirably.

Third Class berthing was concentrated in the forward end of the ship, with appropriate arrangements for single men and women, married couples, and families. The cabins were spacious, spotless, and if a bit austere, were by all reports comfortable enough. The unmarried men or women shared a room with three to five other passengers of the same sex, while married couples and families had rooms to themselves.

Third Class accommodations included a large number of permanent cabins, as well as large sections of berths formed by movable wooden partitions, so that the numbers and sizes of cabins could be adjusted to the number of passengers, and the unused space given over to open common areas. The days of the cramped, dark hold, reeking of unwashed humanity and bilge, had long been a thing of the past in British and German liners, but as in so many other ways, the *Lusitania* set new standards. The Third Class galley provided a fare that, though unspectacular, offered good food and plenty of it; in some cases, especially those from the more impoverished Irish counties, the steerage passengers ate better aboard ship than they ever had at home. All in all, it was a good deal more than most would be expecting when they paid for their passage.

There was one curious element of decor that ran throughout the ship, which, more than anything, gives an idea of the thought that went into the design of the *Lusitania*'s interior furnishings. Throughout the ship, wherever columns were used, their capitals were always done in the elaborately detailed Corinthian style in First Class, the more subdued but still elegant Doric style in Second Class, and the clean and simple Ionian motif in Third.[6]

The *Lusitania*'s keel was laid on September 15, 1904, at the Glasgow shipyard of John Brown and Sons, Ltd., on the banks of the River Clyde. In the last decade of the nineteenth century and the first decade of the twentieth, the River Clyde had become the center of world shipbuilding, gaining such a reputation for quality engineering and construction that simply declaring a vessel to be a "Clyde-built ship" was sufficient testimonial to her soundness. The *Lusitania* was no exception.

It took more than eighteen months to frame and shell plate the hull, then install the engines, shafts, and screws. On June 7, 1906, as a crowd of over 100,000 people watched from both banks of the Clyde, the *Lusitania* was launched. The next thirteen months were spent fitting her out in the Clydebank Shipyard Basin, as her boilers and uptakes were installed, her interior completed, her superstructure finished, and her funnels and masts stepped. By the end of August, she was ready for a week of intensive sea trials, which would prove whether all of the time, effort, and money invested by Cunard and the Admiralty were well spent—or hopelessly wasted.

The *Lusitania* was a marvel. She exceeded every expectation that anyone had held about her ability to better—and do so decisively—the best speeds the German liners could produce. In four runs from Gourock, Scotland, to Land's End in England between July 29 and August 1, 1907, she averaged nearly 25 1/2 knots, and at one point she reached a speed of over 26 1/2 knots. Despite this remarkable speed, vibration was amazingly mild, proving beyond argument the wisdom of adopting the turbine power plant.

The next month was spent finishing preparations for the *Lusitania*'s maiden voyage from Liverpool to New York. The results of her sea trials were hardly a secret, and it was only a question of by how much would she beat the *Kaiser Wilhelm II*'s record, not whether she would. She departed Liverpool at noon on September 8, 1907, and when she arrived off Sandy Hook, she had shaved six hours off the *Kaiser Wilhelm*'s record. The *Lusitania* returned the Blue Ribband to Great Britain on September 13, 1907. It happened to be a Friday.

The Big Lucy, as she became known with genuine affection, would trade speed records with her sister *Mauretania* for the next seven years. No other ships of the day could even come close to them, the German ships being left far back in the wake of the friendly sibling rivalry. Eventually the *Mauretania* would prove to be marginally faster—in fact, it would be twenty years before the Atlantic would see a ship faster than she—but the *Lusitania* lost none of her popularity. She always had a waiting list—everybody loved the *Lusitania*.[7]

On June 28, 1914, in a street in Sarajevo, Serbia, a young man named Gavrillo Princzip shot and killed the Archduke Franz Ferdinand, heir to the throne of Austria-Hungary, along with his wife. The assassination served as the trigger that released tensions that had been building in Europe for nearly a century. A little more than a month after the shootings, a tragedy of errors saw Russia, Germany, Austria-Hungary, France, and Great Britain go to war. The Great War would eventually claim over ten million lives and leave more than twice that number wounded and maimed. A vicious war at sea would send more than twenty-five million tons of shipping to the bottom of the world's oceans. One of those ships lost was the *Lusitania*, sunk by a German U-boat. No submarine's victim has ever been more celebrated, and no sinking has ever been more shrouded in mystery.

CHAPTER 2

The Submarine

THERE ARE LEGENDS DATING AS FAR BACK AS THE TIME OF ALEXANDER THE Great that tell of various kinds of underwater devices and apparatus, usually some form of diving bell that was lowered into the water to give a person the opportunity to observe the underwater world or, in the case of some of the larger equipment, actually perform some salvage and recovery work on shipwrecks. Alexander himself was lowered into the Aegean Sea in an open-bottomed construct made of pitch-covered wooden staves with small glass ports in it.

Relatively more recent and much more intriguing are reports of some curious experiments done on the Thames River just below London in the seventeenth century. There, an expatriate Dutch doctor named Cornelis Drebble built a submersible boat that was made of leather stretched over a wooden frame and propelled by twelve oarsmen. Ben Jonson described some mysterious fluid that enabled the inventor to purify the air as the craft traveled underwater. James I apparently found the vessel intriguing enough to request and be given a short trip under the river. How Drebble's craft submerged and surfaced, how it was navigated underwater, and what employment Drebble saw for it are all unknown, as no drawings or detailed descriptions of it still exist.

A submersible was used in the American Revolution, when David Bushnell built an egg-shaped craft called the *Turtle*, which made an abortive attack on the British squadron blockading New York harbor in 1776. While several of Bushnell's ideas were visionary, and the *Turtle* functioned flawlessly during her one attempt at sinking an enemy warship, her weakness lay in the fact that the only method of attack available to her was to try to attach a mine to the underside of the enemy's hull—an undertaking that proved to be far more difficult in practice than Bushnell imagined. Still, the *Turtle* does deserve a significant place in history for being the first underwater craft to attack an enemy warship.

During the Napoleonic Wars, Robert Fulton tried to interest first the English, then the French in an underwater craft he called the *Nautilus*. The Royal

Navy, with its overwhelming superiority in conventional warships, saw no need for a submersible and wasn't interested, but Napoleon was. After watching Fulton's curious craft blow up an anchored hulk, the Emperor decided to purchase the *Nautilus,* intending to wreak havoc on the blockading British fleets. In typical Napoleonic fashion, though, the Emperor welched on the deal, and Fulton never received a sou. Fed up, Fulton went back to America to try his hand at other, ultimately more successful, ventures.

During the American Civil War, the Confederacy constructed a class of several submersibles, called Davids (as in David versus Goliath), in an effort to defeat the Union blockade that was slowly strangling the Confederate economy and war effort. The Davids (they were never individually named) weren't true submarines in that being steam powered, they could not submerge completely, but had to run with their rudimentary conning towers awash to allow the engine to draw air in and smoke from the boiler to vent. Only one of these odd craft ever made an attack on a Union warship, in October 1863, and that was unsuccessful.

It was a Confederate submersible, the CSS *Hunley,* that garnered the honor of being the first submarine to ever sink an enemy warship. The *Hunley* was a long, thin, cigar-shaped machine, propelled by a single screw turned by a dozen crewmen turning a crankshaft. Her vertical and horizontal movements were controlled by a set of rudders that were remarkably similar to the diving planes used on modern submarines. The *Hunley's* method of attack was to drive an explosive charge, called a torpedo, mounted on a long spar projecting from the front of the submersible, into the side of an enemy warship, set a timer fuse, and then back away from the target, making her escape underwater and, preferably, under cover of darkness as well.

The *Hunley's* victim was the ironclad USS *Housatonic,* part of the Union force blockading the harbor at Charleston, South Carolina. In the middle of the night on February 27, 1864, the *Hunley* crept up undetected on the *Housatonic* and drove her torpedo deep into the bowels of the Union ship. What happened next is uncertain, for while the explosive charge went off as planned and the *Housatonic* sank, something happened to the *Hunley,* and she never returned to the safety of Charleston Harbor.

As time passed, it gradually became clear that all of these would-be underwater warships had two things in common, one doctrinal, the other operational. Doctrinally, the submarine was the weapon of a numerically inferior navy, where the capability to strike silently and invisibly—and hence unexpectedly—at an enemy fleet would go far to offset an opponent's superior numbers. The second, operational, theme was the rather ineffective nature of the weapons that were available for the submarines to use. All of the methods tried required the submersible to physically carry an explosive device of some kind to the target ship, which dramatically increased the chances of the submarine being detected and also exposed it to the hazard of being damaged by the blast of its own weapon. Until a more reliable and less dangerous method of striking at an enemy vessel was developed, the submarine would remain a nautical novelty but never become the weapon of a first-class naval power. In the last half of the nineteenth century, Sweden, France, and Russia all spent considerable time, effort, and money in building underwater craft of various types. They were all notable for one thing only—their singular lack of success.[1]

The man regarded as the father of the modern military submarine was a character straight out of a Victorian three-decker novel: the eccentric genius inventor. John Phillip Holland was an Irish-born schoolteacher who had emigrated to the United States in 1873. While by all accounts a good teacher, outside of his classroom he was a genuine Irish patriot and passionately anti-British. He was also clever and soon began to look for ways to put his creativity to military uses against the British oppressor. Keenly aware of the fact that Britain's domination of Ireland was dependent on the Royal Navy and that the Irish revolutionaries of the Sinn Fein movement had no chance whatsoever of being able to challenge Britain's naval supremacy by conventional means, he began sketching ream after ream of detailed design drafts for submarine boats, which he believed could offer the Irish patriots a relatively inexpensive means of paring down British maritime strength.

Early on in his work, his genius manifested itself, for he hit on solutions to almost all the problems that had been plaguing submarine designers for centuries. This was partly luck, but it was also due in great measure to his ability to see how seemingly unrelated technologies could be combined to produce a practical underwater warship. First, and most fundamental of all, was his use of water ballast to change the displacement of the submarine, making it lighter to surface, heavier to submerge, combined with a system of horizontal and vertical rudders that would control the craft's course and attitude, a system that remains in use unchanged to the present day. He then designed a dual propulsion system, using a gasoline engine to power his submarine when it was surfaced and battery-powered electric motors to drive it underwater, a system that remained an integral part of every submarine until the advent of nuclear power.

Just as significant was his choice of weapon. He designed his "boats" to be armed with one torpedo tube. It was that torpedo tube that gave Holland's submarines their credibility as real warships. By allowing a self-propelled torpedo carrying an explosive charge to be launched at a target from a relatively safe distance, the necessity for an underwater craft to approach its intended target vessel closely enough to physically place an explosive device on the target's hull, then attempt to withdraw before it went off, was effectively eliminated.

The "automobile torpedo" had been invented in the 1860s by a captain in the Austrian Navy. Until that time, the term *torpedo* had been applied to what were merely kegs of gunpowder fitted with percussion or contact fuses, functioning much like latter-day underwater mines. It was to this type of device that Admiral Farragut was referring in the Battle of Mobile Bay when he cried "Damn the torpedoes! Full speed ahead!" The "automobile torpedo" was designed to take the explosive warhead to the intended target rather than wait passively in the hope that the target came to the warhead.

An Englishman named Robert Whitehead, who worked for the Austrian Navy, took the basic design, which ran by clockwork, and developed an improved version that ran on compressed air, with a range of 250 yards and reasonable accuracy. Encouraged by the Royal Navy, Whitehead returned to Britain and opened a factory to produce his torpedoes (by now the "automobile" had been dropped) in the fall of 1872. Progressively introducing gyroscopic stabilization, longer ranges, and larger warheads, he was able to vastly increase the torpedoes' accuracy and striking power. By the end of the nineteenth century, torpedoes were capable of carrying warheads weighing over a quarter of a ton, to ranges of more than a mile. The British were quick to appreciate the potential of the torpedo and began mounting torpedo tubes on all of the Royal Navy's battleships and cruisers. They also began building several classes of high-speed torpedo boats to serve with the main battle fleet of the Royal Navy, as well as an entirely new class of ships, known as "torpedo boat destroyers"—soon simply shortened to "destroyers"—to protect the British fleet from enemy torpedo boats.

John Holland, though, was one of the first to conceive of the torpedo as the ideal weapon for the submarine, since a submerged submarine so armed could approach an enemy warship undetected and fire a torpedo capable of doing serious, even fatal, damage to it, then safely withdraw. So the marriage of Holland's submarine and Whitehead's torpedo resulted in a submersible weapon that was not only technically feasible, but tactically practical as well.

Not that the world's navies were quick to beat a path to Holland's door. When Irish nationalists couldn't come up with the money necessary to produce any of his boats privately, Holland went to the U.S. Navy with his designs, hoping that by selling them he could raise enough capital to build one for his comrades in Ireland. He was flatly refused by the Secretary of the Navy, who declared emphatically that it would be impossible to find crewmen to volunteer for service in such an absurd vehicle.

Scraping together what money he could, and using $6,000 supplied by the Irish revolutionaries, the Feinnians, Holland was able to build two boats, which he rather unimaginatively christened *Holland I* and *Holland II*. When the Feinnians stole the second boat, Holland broke with them completely, but he didn't give up on developing his submarine designs. By now he had his sights firmly fixed on the U.S. Navy, and twice he entered and won competitions sponsored by the navy for the best submarine design. But the navy was unrealistic in its design specifications, and the submarine built to that design—the aptly named *Plunger*—promptly sank upon launching. Holland knew he could build a better boat without outside interference, and in 1898, he finally produced the boat that he called the *Holland III,* known to history as simply the *Holland.*

This time around, the U.S. Navy was so impressed by what Holland had wrought that it purchased his *Holland III* for $150,000 and then awarded him a contract for three more improved "Holland boats" to be built for $175,000 apiece. The little submarines were 68 feet long, 12 feet in beam, and displaced (surfaced) 104 tons. These Holland boats contained all of Holland's inventions and innovations: Each had an inner hull that contained the crew and all of the submarine's machinery; external ballast tanks that could be filled with seawater to decrease the boat's displacement, making it sink beneath the surface, or pumped out, increasing the displacement and making it rise again; and a dual propulsion system, using a gasoline engine to drive the craft when it was surfaced and a battery-powered electric motor to propel it underwater. The boats were very maneuverable underwater, if a bit slow, their top speed while submerged being just two knots. They were armed with one torpedo tube apiece. One often overlooked characteristic was that they had an exceptional range for their size—over a thousand miles.[2]

By 1900, America, France, Greece, Turkey, and Russia, nations whose fleets differed vastly in quality and quantity, all had submersibles of one sort or another, usually built to Holland's designs, or a close approximation thereof, of varying degrees of usefulness. What was curious, even remarkable, at the time was that neither of the world's two greatest naval powers, Great Britain and Germany, were displaying any enthusiasm for this new weapon system. The reason for this lack of interest was primarily doctrinal, and though the doctrines were deeply rooted in each nation's history, it was, oddly enough, an American sailor who gave them voice.

In 1890, a rear admiral retired from the U.S. Navy, Alfred Thayer Mahan, published a brilliant book called *The Influence of Sea Power on History.* Beginning with the Punic Wars between Rome and Carthage two centuries before Christ, Mahan forcefully and convincingly argued that the decisive factor in the most important wars in history, those that changed the flow of civilization's development, had been sea power—that is, the ability of one nation's navy to control strategic waterways and deny their use to the enemy, primarily through blockade. Mahan's thesis culminated in his representation of the decisive nature of the French blockade at Yorktown precipitating Cornwallis's defeat by

Washington in 1783, and his demonstration that the Royal Navy was the one opponent Napoleon Bonaparte was never able to decisively defeat, while the Royal Navy's blockade of Europe had strangled the Continent's economy until Europe rose in anger to bring down Napoleon's empire.

In some ways, Mahan was a seagoing von Clausewitz, who maintained that strategy was the method by which one nation imposed its will upon an enemy. Mahan's reasoning was logical, his examples persuasive, and his presentation eloquent. (Even today, when many works contemporary with Mahan's seem stilted and make for awkward reading, Sea Power is still informative and, in the best sense of the word, entertaining.) There was one basic flaw in Mahan's work—oversimplification—but given the brilliance of his presentation and the obvious nature of the conclusions drawn from the examples he gave, this was easily overlooked, and so Mahan's theories had profound effects on the British and German Admiralties.

Mahan's ideas were so well received in London and Berlin because they could be interpreted to allow each nation's navy to draw exactly the conclusions that it wanted, offering historical justifications for each nation's naval policies. For the British, Mahan's work was scholarly proof of what the Royal Navy instinctively had known for centuries, that a fleet superior in numbers and training to any and all possible opponents ensured command of the sea, with all the consequent strategic and economic benefits that command entailed. Throughout the nineteenth century, the Royal Navy had held to a policy of maintaining a fleet as large as the combined strength of any two possible enemies' navies (usually France and Russia were the suspected culprits) in order to execute a strategy of blockading the enemy's coast while simultaneously maintaining a battle fleet at sea. The Royal Navy had never actually developed that policy as a result of political or strategic analysis, even when it had been adopted as the Navy's strategic doctrine. Mahan's work made this article of faith—for that's what it really was—seem to be premeditated, an act of remarkable foresight on the part of their Lordships in Whitehall. Consequently, whenever awkward questions might arise in Parliament over the cost of a given year's naval estimates, Mahan's book would be trotted out and used to justify the Admiralty's position.[3]

In Germany's case, though, it was painfully obvious that Mahan's conclusions highlighted the inability of a small navy to effectively intervene against a larger fleet, especially if the larger fleet was intent on merely maintaining a blockade rather than seeking battle. Consequently, the more ambitious Continental navies—Russia, France, and in particular Germany—began to explore ways of breaking the power of the blockade. The Russians were never able to develop a coherent naval policy, since the nation was in the midst of widespread social and economic upheaval while the army was given priority in reform, reorganization, and reequipment. In France, Mahan's ideas resulted in the *Jeune École,* the New School, a sort of doctrinal trip into a naval Never-Never Land of torpedo boats, quick-firing guns, and submarines that were often more dangerous to their crews than to the enemy. Before it had run its course, this school of strategic thought reduced the French Navy to third-rate status, a blow from which it never recovered.

In Germany, as might be expected, the method by which German naval doctrine developed was considerably more well thought out, though not necessarily more correct in its conclusions. Within Mahan's theorems about the necessity of a nation to maintain a credible battle fleet in order to exert sea power, and thus influence world events, was the corollary of the "risk fleet." A risk fleet, in short, was a navy that was not large enough to decisively defeat a numerically superior opponent, but ship for ship was qualitatively the better fleet and so could threaten to inflict unacceptable losses on its foe, should the two fleets meet in battle, and at the same time could utilize the superiority of its individual ships to erode its enemy's numerical superiority through attrition tactics in smaller engagements. The effectiveness of the smaller navy is then dramatically increased, since a blockading fleet must avoid large-scale actions, as it cannot risk the possibility of losses that reduce the effectiveness of the blockade; hence the term "risk fleet." With Imperial Germany's colonial ambitions necessitating a blue-water navy to support it, and the growing assumption that Britain and Germany would find themselves on opposing sides of any coming European war, the attractions of such a navy for Germany were considerable.

The Kaiser, Wilhelm II, incorrigibly belligerent—one observer remarked that "Wilhelm was always playing at war"—and suffering from a severe inferiority complex regarding his English cousins, was determined to build a High Seas Fleet that would command respect for his newly created empire. Unarguably, the strength of the Royal Navy lay in her great battleships—by 1914 it would have over seventy in commission—so the German High Seas Fleet would need battleships. It sounded very simple; in fact, it was not.[4]

In 1890, when Mahan published *The Influence of Sea Power on History,* the German Navy was little more than a joke. As late as 1854, it had not even existed, but it was in that year that the Prussian king, Friedrich Wilhelm IV, created a Prussian Admiralty and appointed his brother, Prince Adelbert, to command it. The Prussian Navy played no part in the succession of wars Prussia fought against Denmark, Austria, and France in order to create the German Empire. In fact, Prussian naval officers and seamen who served during the Franco-Prussian War were not permitted to list their service during that time as war service in their personal records. The Admiralty was actually commanded by a general who reported first to the army general staff and then to the Admiralty. In the two decades after the Franco-Prussian War, the German Navy was nothing more than a coast defense force, with little capability of projecting German sea power.

For the vast majority of the German people, this was a perfectly acceptable state of affairs. It was the army that was popular both with the public and with the German aristocracy. After all, it had been the army, not the navy, that had fought three victorious wars and unified the German Empire. With a perennially hostile France, hell-bent on revenge for the humiliations of 1871, to the west, and the hulking menace of the Russian army to the east, every pfennig invested in the army seemed to be money well spent. There seemed to be no sense in wasting money on warships that would almost certainly have little or no influence on the course of any future war that Germany might find herself caught up in. Despite Wilhelm's ambitions, the whole idea of a powerful German Navy rarely met more than a lukewarm reception among the German people.

But the German people were wrong and the Kaiser was right, although in a fashion typical for him, he went overboard in his determination to build a strong navy. As the German economy began to grow in the last quarter of the nineteenth century, Germany suddenly found herself as the second-largest maritime power in the world—only Great Britain's merchant marine was greater. Suddenly Germany's economic interests were worldwide, and it was only sensible that some measure of protection be available to them and to the hundreds of German ships that were carrying cargoes to and from every corner of the globe.

This was an essential part of Mahan's thesis about sea power, and it became painfully obvious that Germany's huge merchant fleet was vulnerable to attack by even a third-rate navy. For decades, the German merchant marine had enjoyed the tacit understanding that it was under the protection of the Royal Navy, an understanding that had its foundation in the days of Waterloo, when the British and Prussians had formed the alliance that defeated Napoleon once and for all. The Germans began to doubt the durability of that understanding, however, as the British began methodically settling old quarrels with France and Russia, Germany's traditional enemies. Should a war break out with Germany and Britain on opposite sides, the German merchant fleet would be essentially defenseless and likely be swept from the world's oceans in a matter of a few weeks by the Royal Navy. Even if Germany were to be involved in a war that found Britain neutral, the Royal Navy would still be compelled under international law to withdraw its protection of Germany merchant shipping, leaving it easy prey to whatever naval forces Germany's foe might possess.

Wilhelm listened as his economic and naval advisors explained these facts of life to him, and the conclusion he came to was, given his bombastic personality and martial prejudices, inevitable. He was determined to accomplish one of two objectives, if not both: Germany would coerce Britain into a formal alliance, while at the same time building a fleet that, while not superior in numbers to the Royal Navy, would be of such quality that the British would be afraid to bring it to battle.

The first task was the responsibility of the diplomats, while the second belonged to the navy. There was only one officer in the entire German Navy whom the Kaiser believed could accomplish such a task, a maverick officer who had for years been demanding that Germany build exactly such a fleet as the kaiser now envisaged, Adm. Alfred von Tirpitz.

With his bald head, hard eyes, and forked beard creating an unforgettable image, von Tirpitz has rightly come to be regarded as the father of the German Navy. He was appointed Naval State Secretary (the German equivalent of the U.S. Secretary of the Navy or the British First Lord of the Admiralty) in the summer of 1897. He immediately began formulating a policy for expansion of the German Navy that would allow it to become a powerful tool in formulating and executing German foreign policy. With the explicit blessing of the Kaiser, von Tirpitz presented the German Reichstag with a series of Navy Bills in 1897, 1900, and 1903 that wrote the expansion of the navy into German law, and then rammed them through. The Kaiser had wanted battleships; Tirpitz had given him battleships.

In fact, von Tirpitz demanded a fleet so powerful that the greatest naval power in the world would think twice before challenging it. Realizing that even the immense Krupp shipyards at Kiel and Wilhelmshaven could never match Britain's building capacity hull for hull, von Tirpitz required ships that were bigger, faster, better protected, and better crewed than their British counterparts. Not surprisingly, since he was focused on powerful surface ships, von Tirpitz was not terribly quick to grasp the potential of the submarine, but then, he wasn't alone, for the British had no better idea of how to employ their submarines than von Tirpitz did his; indeed, the scope of the possibilities for submarine warfare would be demonstrated almost by accident. Von Tirpitz regarded the submarine, as did most level-headed senior naval officers (that is, everyone but the French), as an effective coastal defense weapon, but hardly a worthy adjunct to a seagoing battle fleet.[5]

The High Seas Fleet actually acquired its first submarines almost as an afterthought. In early 1903, both Russia and France placed orders for nearly identical submarines to be built by Krupp's sprawling Germaniaweft shipyard at Kiel. The German Naval High Command thought it best to keep an eye on what its neighbors to the east and west were doing, and so ordered a few submarines of its own, built to a similar design. In October 1904, the first German submarine, unimaginatively christened the *Unterseeboot-1* ("Undersea Boat-1," or *U-1* for short), joined the kaiser's fleet. Looking for all the world like a mad scientist's mechanical shark, she was 110 feet in length, displacing just under 500 tons, and mounted a single 75-millimeter deck gun forward of her conning tower. Hidden behind sliding plates in the bow and stern of her rivet-covered hull were four torpedo tubes, two forward, two aft. She carried a crew of thirty-seven enlisted men and four officers.

Admittedly, by getting into the game rather late, the Germans were able to avoid some of the technical mistakes of the French, Russian, and United States' navies. For example, from the first, the High Seas Fleet avoided using gasoline engines, with all their attendant dangers from fires and fumes, employing instead heavy oil, then later diesel motors, in their submarines. Likewise, they avoided the folly of steam-powered submarines, which continued in service in some navies until long after the World War I had ended. And since the finest optical engineers in the world were found in Germany, the optics of the U-boats' periscopes, painstakingly crafted by Zeiss, were markedly superior to those of any other navy.

Yet however methodical and well thought out the designs of the U-boats were, it would be a grave error to assume that the High Seas Fleet's interest in submarines was anything more than the nautical equivalent of "keeping up with the Joneses." The focus of the Naval High Command remained locked, and would continue to be, on the great clash of dreadnoughts that British and German naval staffs alike predicted would come. Though they had their submarines, the Germans had no idea what to do with them. As Edward Horton put it in his magnificent book *Submarine*:

> The Germans were not developing any sinister master plan, they were not consciously developing "the ultimate weapon". They were getting into the swim with everybody else and they built the type of submarine they did for the logical reason that it was the only one that could be of any use to them. . . . As Europe hurtled toward war, Germany was not looking to the submarine as her salvation any more than Britain was looking to it for her ruin.[6]

Like its technological stablemate, the aeroplane, the submarine was in 1914 certainly primitive by modern standards, but it embraced all the latest advances in technology and, together with the airplane, would undergo a very rapid evolution in the coming conflict. In some ways, the lack of an established doctrine worked in the submariners' favor, since they were left pretty much on their own to develop their own tactics and operational procedures, rather than being subject to the rigid doctrinal philosophies of some deskbound bureaucrat disguised in a sailor's uniform. At the same time, the submariners began to develop their own eccentricities and traditions, and as so often happens to any small organization within a military body that is devoted to some obscure, not to say arcane, mission, or finds itself armed with a new, untried weapon system, the submarine crews began to regard themselves as something special, almost elite, and began to look for ways to prove it.

The British, while never doubting the supremacy of the dreadnought battleship, had begun their own cautious development of a submarine force: With the French, Russians, and Germans all building them, the Royal Navy simply couldn't afford to ignore them. The result was the A-1 class, the Royal Navy's first submarines, larger and more powerful versions of the American Holland boats. British submarine development then proceeded apace: 1906 saw the introduction of the diesel-powered D-class, large boats of 500 tons. The E-class of 1914 displaced 700 tons, carried four 18-inch torpedo tubes, and was capable of speeds up to 96 knots on the surface and about 10 knots submerged. August 1914 saw plans in hand for an additional sixty boats to be added to the fleet within the next year.

On the other side of the North Sea, though, Germany was taking a tremendous technical lead. Her U-boats were generally larger than the contemporary British classes, their diesels more powerful, their optics better, and their torpedoes larger, faster, and more accurate. While the speeds of the German and British submarines were comparable, the U-boats' range was nearly twice the 1,500-mile range of Britain's newest submarines, the E-class. On the eve of war in 1914, Germany possessed nearly twice as many modern submarines as Great Britain.

So it was on the morning of September 22, 1914. that the submarine came of age as a weapon of war. Like ducks in a shooting gallery, three British armored cruisers, *Hogue, Aboukir,* and *Cressy,* were torpedoed and sunk by the *U-9.* They were not the first British warships to be sunk by a German submarine; that unhappy distinction belonged to HMS *Pathfinder,* a light cruiser torpedoed and sunk in the North Sea on September 3 by the *U-21.* But the implications as well as the magnitude of the disaster that befell the three cruisers far overshadowed the loss of a single light cruiser.

Assigned to, of all things, an antisubmarine patrol in a section of the North Sea known as the Broad Fourteens, the three cruisers—sister ships, all of the *Bacchante* class—were big (12,000 tons) and heavily armed with twelve 6-inch guns each, but they were all nearly fifteen years old, slow with nearly worn-out engines, and very poor, almost nonexistent underwater protection. Moreover, their armament made them totally unsuitable for antisubmarine duties—there wasn't a truly effective antisubmarine weapon among the three of them.

This vulnerability, along with their advanced age, had barred the three cruisers from the rigors of duty with the Grand Fleet in Scapa Flow. Even in their current assignment, they were regarded by certain sections of the Admiralty as something of a liability. They were manned mostly by married reservists and had been assigned the Broad Fourteens patrol because initially it had been regarded as relatively safe duty. After the loss of *Pathfinder* in waters not too far from their patrol area, the Admiralty had reconsidered this, and the three cruisers were to be transferred to less hazardous waters in the English Channel, but before the orders reassigning the ships reached them, the three creaking cruisers ran afoul of the *U-9*.

The *U-9* wasn't all that much more impressive than her three victims. Built in 1910, she displaced just under 500 tons and was one of the last U-boats to be powered by kerosene engines rather than diesels. She was cramped even by submarine standards and mounted just four torpedo tubes, two forward and two aft. There were problems with her diving planes, and at times it was almost impossible to keep the boat trimmed on an even keel. She carried a crew of twenty-nine, commanded by a twenty-four-year-old kapitanleutnant named Otto Weddigen. Weddigen was just three days out of Wilhelmshaven on his first war patrol when he sighted the three cruisers and realized with some surprise that their course would take them almost directly across the *U-9*'s bow.

Aboukir was the first to go. Just after 6:30 A.M., Weddigen put a torpedo into her port side. It was a lucky shot, striking one of the cruiser's forward magazines, which exploded when the torpedo's warhead detonated. *Aboukir* broke in two and sank in just minutes, taking a large part of her crew with her. The captains of *Hogue* and *Cressy* thought the stricken *Aboukir* had hit a mine, and the immediately turned around to come to the sinking cruiser's aid. *Hogue* stopped less than 400 yards from *Aboukir* and began lowering her boats.

For Weddigen, this was too good to be true. Carefully maneuvering the tiny *U-9* around the two motionless cruisers, he fired two more torpedoes, hitting the *Hogue* in her starboard side. Constructed with longitudinal bulkheads that served as coal bunkers, the old ship began to list sharply. The coal in the bunkers began sucking up inrushing seawater like a gigantic sponge, and the *Hogue* rolled until she was nearly on her beam ends, lying on her side in the water. While *Aboukir* had vanished in a few minutes, it took more than twenty minutes for *Hogue* to sink, and hundreds of her crewmen were able to reach the water and swim away from the sinking ship.

By now the captain of *Cressy* knew that the other two cruisers hadn't run afoul of a minefield, but had been torpedoed by a submarine, and he reacted accordingly. He ordered full speed ahead, zigzagging as he went, while *Cressy*'s gunners began firing at anything that looked even vaguely like a submarine.

Dawn had just broken, and there were still patches of fog on the water, making the most mundane objects look sinister. *Cressy's* guns let fly at wreckage, life rafts, shadows, trying in vain to hit the U-boat.

Weddigen meanwhile had crash-dived and badly depleted his batteries trying to avoid the mad-bull rushes of the *Cressy.* Nursing the *U-9* back to the surface—he had to chase his crew like a bunch of chickens back and forth, fore and aft, to get the boat to rise or dive—Weddigen waited and watched through his periscope until *Cressy* crossed his bows, then put his last two torpedoes into her. The warheads detonated deep in the old cruiser's boiler rooms, and like *Hogue,* she began to roll over on her side as her longitudinal bunkers filled with seawater. After a few minutes, one or more of *Cressy's* boilers exploded, and the cruiser turned turtle, slowly sinking in the morning sunlight. Within the space of two hours, all three cruisers had gone to the bottom, taking with them more than 1,400 British sailors and the legend of British naval invincibility.[7]

It would be incorrect to say that the Royal Navy was stunned. It was just plain spooked. As Winston Churchill, First Lord of the Admiralty at the time of the disaster, wrote in *The World Crisis:*

> The Grand Fleet was uneasy. She could not find a resting place except at sea. Conceive it, the *ne plus ultra,* the one ultimate sanction of our existence, the supreme engine which no one had dared to brave, whose authority encircled the globe—no longer sure of itself. The idea got round—"The German submarines were coming after them in their harbours. . . ." Now, all of a sudden, the Grand Fleet began to see submarines in Scapa Flow. Two or three times the alarm was raised. The climax came on October 17. Guns were fired, destroyers thrashed the waters and the whole gigantic armada put to sea in haste and dudgeon.

The *London Chronicle* called the triple sinkings "a disaster the importance of which would be foolish to minimise." As depressing as the loss of the three cruisers was to the Admiralty, what was truly mortifying was the knowledge that they had been sunk by a weapon that almost the whole of the Admiralty, from Churchill on down, had scorned.

Not that the German Naval High Command was particularly quick on the uptake in understanding the significance of the *U-9's* exploit. The strategy, planning, doctrines—indeed the very hopes and dreams—of the German admirals were so firmly fixed on the idea of one great cataclysmic clash of fleets, a sort of ironclad Trafalgar, that they were at first oblivious to the fact that Weddigen had given them the key that would release German naval power from its North Sea prison.

For it was an unavoidable reality that despite all their toasts to *"Der Tag!,"* their confidence in the ability of their crews to best the Grand Fleet and the magnificent quality of the ships they commanded, the German Naval High Command was utterly unable to force the Royal Navy to do battle with them. Since the turn of the century, when Germany and Great Britain began vying for naval supremacy after von Tirpitz had begun his massive building programs, the whole course of the naval race had been determined by two overriding factors—one industrial, the other geographic. In both instances, Germany came out second best.

First, of course, was Britain's enormous numerical superiority in capital ships, coupled with the industrial capacity to maintain it. While it was true that Britain's industrial output had declined relative to Germany's since the Franco-Prussian War ended in 1871, it was still the largest in the world, and Britain boasted nearly twice as many slipways capable of building battleships as Germany. Just as important was the necessity of Germany to maintain a huge standing army, which required the majority of Germany's iron and steel production to equip and maintain, a burden Great Britain's foundries and arsenals never had to bear.

The second, geographic, factor was in some ways even more important to bringing about the impotence of the High Seas Fleet. Simply put, Great Britain sat astride the only access the High Seas Fleet had to the high seas. The only two routes that the German Navy had to the North Atlantic were either down through the English Channel or up through the North Sea and around Scotland. Neither proved to be practical, since the Channel, a natural choke point, would have been too easily sealed off by Royal Navy mines and sub-marines (indeed, this was one of the few uses envisioned by the Royal Navy for its submarines before the war). The long journey through the North Sea and around Scotland would have merely meant that the High Seas Fleet was steaming into the waiting arms of the Grand Fleet, moored at Scapa Flow in the Orkneys, at the entrance to the North Sea. As Grand Adm. Karl Doenitz, a destroyer captain in the Great War, wrote in his memoirs, "The High Seas Fleet was denied its normal radius of action—to steam into the North Atlantic, where alone a decision was possible. Only [when it was] in the North Sea our fleet presented no danger to the Grand Fleet. The Royal Navy then had but to put into operation the war plans envisioned before 1914."

What Doenitz was referring to was that the Royal Navy, wholeheartedly embracing the concept of the blockade as the definitive expression of sea power according to Mahan, had adopted the strategy of a strategic blockade of North Sea, cutting off all imports into Germany—including food, since Germany was not able to produce enough for her own needs, and nitrates, which were essential to the manufacture of explosives, of which Germany possessed no natural sources. Originally the Royal Navy's operational planning had called for light units of the Grand Fleet to cruise a few miles outside German waters, while the van of the fleet would be keeping station in the North Sea. The Germans had anticipated this and countered by devising a number of stratagems that would lure only part of the Grand Fleet into an engagement with the whole of the High Seas Fleet, gradually eroding the Royal Navy's numerical superiority until the High Seas Fleet could contest a breakout into the Atlantic, defeating the blockade and in turn threatening Britain's shipping lanes.

The Admiralty threw a spanner in the High Seas Fleet's works even before the war broke out, when it realized that the Grand Fleet need only prevent the Germans from breaking out of the North Sea. By stationing the Grand Fleet at three anchorages in Scotland—at Rosyth in the Firth of Forth, in Cromarty Firth, and at Scapa Flow, all mutually supporting and within short steaming distance of each other—the Royal Navy effectively sealed off the North Sea, catching, as the Duke of Wellington would have put it, "a damned big rat in a damned small bottle!" That the Grand Fleet would have ample warning of any sortie by the High Seas Fleet only made the task of maintaining the blockade easier. That it was the Germans themselves who were unwittingly providing the warning was probably the best-kept secret of the war. And thereby hangs a tale, for the ability to read German ciphers would have a decisive effect on the course of the war, and especially the Admiralty's campaign against the U-boats.[8]

In the early hours of August 4, 1914, before the sun rose, a small British cable ship, the *Telconia,* was cruising back and forth in the waters near Emden, where the German and Dutch borders meet at the North Sea. Dragging a grappling hook behind her, the cable ship dredged up five underwater telegraph cables and, one by one, cut them. These were the German transatlantic cables, Germany's secure links with her overseas embassies and consulates. Now Germany would be forced to rely on wireless to communicate with her agents and diplomats overseas, depending on the security of her codes and ciphers to prevent prying enemy ears from listening in. It seemed a reasonable assumption, for the German cipher systems—there were ciphers for naval, military and diplomatic usage—were among the most complex in the world, and repeated tests by the Germans themselves had assured Berlin that they were impenetrable.

That may have been true, but they were not beyond being compromised. In an incredible string of bad luck for the Germans, in the first three months of the war the British were able to recover copies of three of the most widely used German codebooks. The diplomatic cipher was recovered from the wreckage of a light cruiser sunk in the North Sea while trying to run the

British blockade and deliver the codebook to the German Embassy in the United States. The cipher for German zeppelins, merchant vessels, and small ships was taken from a freighter captured by the Royal Australian Navy in the Pacific. But the greatest prize of all was a copy of the German High Seas Fleet naval cipher, which contained all the codes used by the German capital ships as well as the U-boats, captured by the Russians when two of their cruisers destroyed the German light cruiser *Magdeburg* in the Baltic. While busy picking up survivors, the Russian sailors happened upon the body of a German signal officer, who was clutching the lead-weighted copy of the naval cipher to his chest in a death grip. Showing rare good sense, and even rarer generosity for the Russians in those days, the Imperial Russian Navy sent the codebook to London by fast cruiser, reasoning that the Royal Navy could put it to the best possible use.

The cipher books were rushed to Room 40, Old Building (Rm 40 OB), the cryptographic department of the Office of Naval Intelligence (ONI), where they came under the authority of the Director of Naval Intelligence (DNI), Capt. William Reginald Hall. Captain Hall had arrived at his post of DNI fresh from the bridge of a battle cruiser, and he continued in the same quaint fashion that had made his ship one of the most efficient in the Royal Navy, namely by running his department under the assumption that there was a war to be fought, which meant peacetime standards and habits were no longer acceptable. When he came to the office of DNI, Hall knew next to nothing about cryptography or intelligence gathering, but with typical thoroughness, he had within a few short months mastered his new profession as few ever have. It wasn't long before he was building an intelligence network that had few rivals and no peers. From working hand in glove with Scotland Yard chasing German spies to keeping the Foreign Office informed about Middle East intrigues, Hall had a finger in every shadowy pie that threatened the Empire. As Barbara Tuchman put it in *The Zimmerman Telegram,* "Like God in the British national anthem, Hall was ready to confound the politics and frustrate the knavish tricks of Britain's enemies. He was ruthless, sometimes cruel, always resourceful."

With the three codebooks in his hands, Captain Hall found his department in a position unlike any other before in history: The ONI had the capability to decode and read German communications in "real time"—that is, just as quickly as the recipient. All the while, the Germans remained blissfully ignorant that their signals were compromised and so continued to chatter merrily over the airwaves to one another, while British listening stations faithfully copied each message and forwarded them by secure landline to Room 40. The results were remarkable, for they allowed the Grand Fleet several hours', sometimes days', notice when the High Seas Fleet planned a sortie, so that the Royal Navy was never taken by surprise, reducing all of von Tirpitz's "risk fleet" theories and stratagems to ashes.[9]

What the Office of Naval Intelligence didn't realize at first, any more than the rest of the Admiralty, was that the cipher books held the key to eliminating the threat of the German U-boats, who would be giving their positions away every time they communicated with the Naval High Command in Wilhelmshaven. This isn't all that surprising, since Captain Hall, like every other British—and German—naval officer was still thinking in terms of a great Trafalgar-like clash of battle fleets. The sinking of *Aboukir, Hogue,* and *Cressy* obviously badly shook the Admiralty, but the mental leap necessary to arrive at the conclusion that the U-boat might be able to accomplish the mission of the High Seas Fleet—neutralize the Grand Fleet and attack Britain's shipping lanes—was just too great for most of the Admiralty to make.

The German Naval High Command was a little quicker on the uptake than their British counterparts, but not by much. Gradually it dawned on them that while the High Seas Fleet was a prisoner of geography, the submarine wasn't, by virtue of its ability to travel underwater and hence undetected, and it would allow the Germans to outflank the Royal Navy technologically. Both the Grand Fleet and Britain's merchant shipping were proven to be vulnerable to underwater attack, while the Royal Navy's antisubmarine measures were limited at best, pathetic or nonexistent at worst. In Berlin and London, there was a growing appreciation—one hopeful, the other apprehensive—that the U-boat might well become a decisive weapon in the naval war.

CHAPTER 3

The War

MORE THAN EIGHTY YEARS LATER, IT IS ALL BUT IMPOSSIBLE TO TRULY COM-
prehend how enthusiastically the peoples of Germany, France, Austria-
Hungary, and Russia rushed to war, the ecstatic crowds thronging the Unter
den Linden, the Champs Élysées, the Ringstrasse, or Red Square cheering as
their respective governments declared war, or how readily the young men
were prepared to march off to the sound of the guns, to the strains of
"Deutschland uber Alles," "Le Marseillaise," or "God Save the Tsar." What
should have been an isolated quarrel between Austria-Hungary and Serbia
instead became the means to an end for settling old scores, asserting new
hegemony, or confirming existing preeminence.

For Germany, this war was a God-sent opportunity to settle scores with a
revivified France and secure German dominance—economic, political, and
military—of the Continent for generations. For France, it was a chance at fulfilling the national dream of *revanche* on the despised Boches and reclaim the
"lost" provinces of Alsace and Lorraine. Russia was presented with an opportunity to restore the international prestige she had lost in the Russo-Japanese
War in 1905, and by championing little Serbia in her dispute with Austria-
Hungary, Russia could solidify her self-appointed role as protector of all Slavic
peoples in Europe. The aging, creaking Austro-Hungarian Empire, whose confrontation with Serbia had snowballed into the continentwide conflict, was
determined to crush once and for all the nationalistic aspirations of the tiny
Balkan states while reasserting her status as a Great Power.

But for one nation, the coming of war was an agony. Watching intently,
but having no real interest in becoming part of this growing conflagration,
Great Britain desperately tried to mediate a peaceful settlement, but to no
avail. True, there was an increasingly dangerous and bitter naval race going
on between the Royal Navy and the High Seas Fleet, as the British perceived
the Germans to be a threat to the Royal Navy's dominance of the world's
oceans, on which Britain's economy depended—a perception that the Germans were only to happy to reinforce. It was also true that there had been
extended staff talks between the French and British armies to coordinate a

response should Germany invade France. And it was further true that Britain had been signatory to an international treaty signed in 1839 that guaranteed the integrity of a neutral Belgium. But so far, by the first day of August 1914, the German Navy hadn't stirred from its berths in Kiel and Wilhelmshaven, German troops had not crossed the French border, and Germany, as heir to Prussia's diplomatic obligations, had also been a signatory to that 1839 treaty and had always honored it. So while there was concern in Whitehall that Britain would be drawn into the war against her will, there seemed to be little cause for believing it would actually happen. After all, there was no reason for His Majesty's Government to become involved in what essentially was a quarrel in eastern Europe that posed no threat to Great Britain or her national interests.

That was to change, abruptly and irrevocably, that afternoon, when word reached the Foreign Office that at 3:00 that morning, German troops had invaded Belgium, surging forward in a huge mass of field-gray toward the fortress city of Liege. Swiftly, Lord Grey, the Foreign Secretary, was directed to send a formal protest to Germany over this violation of Belgian neutrality and further issue an ultimatum to Berlin, announcing that if German troops had not begun their withdrawal from Belgium by noon on August 4, a state of war would exist between Great Britain and Imperial Germany. The officials in Berlin's foreign ministry on the Wilhelmstrasse were aghast: The Chancellor, Bethmann-Hollweg, had assured everyone that Britain would never go to war over an eighty-year-old treaty that was hardly more than "a scrap of paper."

The Germans didn't even bother to respond. Instead, they kept pouring more and more troops into Belgium, along with mammoth cannon specially designed years before by Krupp and Skoda to reduce the Belgian forts that ringed Liege and blocked their advance. For the Germans were bound by that strategic dogma that has become enshrined in the lexicon of popular history as the Schlieffen Plan: the rigid and inflexible deployment of Germany's armies, designed to crush France in six weeks, before the mobilization of Russia's huge army could be completed, allowing the whole of German might to be massed in the east to face the expected Russian onslaught, eliminating Germany's worst nightmare—fighting a two-front war.

The provisions of the plan necessitated the violation of Belgian neutrality to guarantee the success of the German Army, allowing three-fourths of the German forces—one and a quarter million men—to swing behind the French armies positioned along the Franco-German border and descend on them from the north, rolling up the French lines like a bloody carpet. Twelve noon passed on August 4 without word of any intention of a German withdrawal, and so the orders went out, dispatching the British Expeditionary Force (BEF) to Belgium, there to take up positions on the left of the French Seventh Army and prepare to meet the German juggernaut.

To the German *Generalstab* (general staff), the BEF, Britain's "red little army," was so small as to be almost not worth consideration in their plans—indeed, Kaiser Wilhelm II had referred to it as a "contemptible little army." Amused, the officers and rankers of the BEF adopted this sobriquet as a badge of honor and styled themselves "The Old Contemptibles." German derision notwithstanding, those seven divisions were the finest troops Europe had ever seen or ever would see, and when they met the oncoming waves of field gray on August 22, they handed the advancing Germans setback after bloody setback for the next month, retreating only when their exposed flanks were threatened, their numbers slowly but irrevocably dwindling, as the supporting French armies, bleeding and demoralized, reeled from the shock and surprise of the German assault.

Fatal delays were inflicted on the unforgiving timetable of the Schlieffen Plan's schedule for advance, and when the German Second Army was within sight of Paris, a hastily assembled French army, not letting the time bought so dearly by the BEF go to waste, made a desperate stand on the River Marne, then launched a devastating counterattack that threw the now-weary Germans back some forty miles, with the exhausted armies finally coming to a halt on September 22.

But by now Britain's "red little army" was fast becoming a "dead little army," and while reinforcements from the distant garrisons of the Empire finally began to reach France, it was clear to everyone that the BEF had been decimated. At the same time, it slowly dawned on the generals and politicians alike, and even more slowly on the general public, that something had gone terribly wrong in the calculations that had been made and the assurances given before the troops marched off to war. A slightly discordant note began to slip into the melodies the *soldaten, poilus*, and Tommies heard as they left for the front, for beneath the strains of *"Die Wacht am Rhein,"* or *"Le Marseillaise,"* or "Tipperary" could be heard, albeit faintly, the murmurings of those to whom victory had been entrusted and now wondered when—or even if—that victory would materialize.

It would all be so easy, they had said, it would be over in six weeks, eight at the most. The troops, everyone was assured, will be home before the leaves fell. But when the leaves fell, they only covered the fresh graves of the dead, or swirled into the newly dug graves of those still dying. Then the cry was that the war would be over before Christmas, but Christmas came and went and there was no end in sight, either of the war or the casualty lists. The winter of 1914–15 was one of the bitterest ever recorded, certainly the coldest in memory, and the thinly clad German, French, and British troops suffered as much from frostbite as they did from enemy shells and bullets.

After the first clash of arms in Belgium and on the French frontier had swept the Germans to the gates of Paris, and the aptly named "Miracle of the

Marne" had pushed the advancing *feldgrau* tide back, a series of sidestepping maneuvers westward had begun, as each army sought to work its way around the other's flank. By the end of 1914, the opposing armies had reached the English Channel, and the "Race to the Sea" had ended, with neither the Allies nor the Germans able to execute a decisive maneuver and roll up their opponent's lines.

Already a thin, snakelike line of trenches, growing more and more elaborate with each passing week, had been dug from the Swiss border to the Channel, depriving each side of the opportunity to maneuver, as the opposing armies strengthened their positions and began looking for a way to break the enemy's lines. And soon entire military traditions were being overthrown, as it began to dawn on the Germans that here was a problem no amount of *Generalstab* intellect could think its way out of; as the French realized that no amount of elan could defeat well-laid-out patterns of German artillery fire; and as the British saw that their tiny BEF, so tragically mauled in the battles in Belgium when facing overwhelming odds, could never be resurrected, and that to build an army of the size required to honor her obligations to Belgium and France, the entire resources of the Empire would need to be mobilized.

Meanwhile, at the front, by the spring of 1915, the armies were beginning to learn the rudiments of trench warfare and develop modes of living that could only find parallels in the darker passages of Jules Verne or H. G. Wells. The trenches, originally little more than shallow ditches or foxholes just a few feet deep, loosely connected by a rough dirt parapet and supported behind a few hastily strung strands of barbed wire, began to evolve into far more sophisticated systems and defensive positions, with listening posts, dugouts, bunkers, and communication trenches.

Bruce Bairnsfather, who lived through the worst years of the Western Front as an infantryman, encapsulated the life in the trenches when he wrote this only slightly tongue-in-cheek description of it for his friends:

> Select a flat ten-acre ploughed field, so sited that all the surface water of the surrounding country drains into it. Now cut a zig-zag slot about four feet deep and three feet wide diagonally across, dam off as much water as you can so as to leave about a hundred yards of squelchy mud; delve out a hole in one side of the slot then endeavor to live there for about a month on bully beef and damp biscuits, while a friend has instructions to fire his Winchester at you every time you put your head above the surface.

What he didn't describe was the intermittent but ceaseless shelling, as the Germans, during their retreat from the Marne, had generally seized the high ground, the better to keep a wary eye on developments on the Allied side of the lines, and began to evolve ever more elaborate defensive positions, content to lob artillery shells into the enemy trenches and leave any offensive action to the Allies.

It was a grim prospect. The Allies really had no choice: As long as the Germans occupied Belgium and parts of France, peace was impossible—they had to be forcibly ejected. It was a bloody and rather hopeless undertaking, as time and again the French and British armies surged forward against the waiting German defenses—and each time found some hellish new innovation that cut them down by the thousands. Machine guns proliferated, giving even small units incredible amounts of firepower, what J. F. C. Fuller called "the concentrated essence of infantry."

Huge entanglements of barbed wire appeared, with barbs the size of a man's thumb, the better to catch on uniforms, accoutrements, and flesh, pinning the hapless victims long enough for the chattering machine guns to find them. Mine throwers made their debut, hurling packages of explosives into enemy trenches, often wrapped with a covering of metal shards, watch springs, cogwheels, or nails.

Soldiers began to learn that sounds could be dangerous—the steady mechanical rattle of the Spandau machine gun, which made a weird, half-human, half-metallic sighing as spent shell casings were ejected; the hissing roar of the *flammenwerfer,* the flamethrower, Germany's newest weapon of terror; the unforgettable "click-clack, clack-click" of a round being chambered in a Lee-Enfield rifle; the short, sharp scraping of the primer cord being drawn from the handle of a potato masher hand grenade. And always the shells. There were shells that whistled, shells that warbled, some that chugged like freight locomotives, others that whined like banshees, and some that whispered in flight. There were shells that whistled before they exploded, shells that exploded then whistled, and shells that whistled and moaned but never seemed to explode. And then there was always the one the soldiers never heard—the one that got them.

Even the colors were lethal: red Very lights at night signaling corrections to artillery bombardments; green or yellow mists snaking along the ground, the terrible tendrils of phosgene or mustard gas; white on a man's gums or blue on his feet announcing the presence of trench mouth or trench foot; black on a wounded soldier's body declaring that gangrene had already set in.

Medal- and decoration-bedecked generals, so often depicted—and not always inaccurately—with their glittering staffs and retinues of sycophants setting up headquarters in parquet-floored chateaus or carefully constructed concrete *Kommandantur* bunkers miles behind the lines, would push bright-colored pins across clean, unsmudged maps as they massed their forces for what they would grandiosely announce to the press as a "Big Push" or a "hammerblow" at the enemy's position, certain that this would be the great offensive that would crack the front wide open and rout the enemy. The cost in lives may have seemed prohibitive, but it was an article of faith that the enemy would always suffer the worst. The French were especially good at this, for with that peculiarly Gallic talent for self-deception, the French General Headquarters formulated the absurd idea that for every two Frenchmen who died in action, three Germans had been killed.

But the slaughter was appalling for both sides: In the First Battle of Ypres, in October 1914, where wave after wave of German infantry, many of them university students advancing arm-in-arm singing patriotic songs, were cut down by the deadly accurate British rifle fire, one German division lost over 9,300 men out of a strength of 12,000—*in a single day*. In the massive disillusionment of the postwar years, it became popular to pillory the commanding generals on both sides as mindless brutes who could conceive of no alternative but to feed endless masses into a vast killing machine, in the hope that the enemy would run out of troops first. It was actually all very simple to the generals, the popular refrain went, just supply them with enough troops so that the enemy couldn't kill them fast enough and victory was assured.

Given the predictable outcome of almost all the offensives that the Allies launched, such an attitude is easy to understand. What happened time and again was that, after an artillery bombardment that lasted for hours, sometimes days, or even weeks, the Tommies and *poilus* would clamber over the top of their trenches and crawl to their jump-off tapes, lying in the mud until the second hands of their officers' watches touched zero hour. Then they would stand up, the British to the sound of the officers' whistles, the more romantic French to bugles blaring the *Pas de Charge,* and begin their methodical advance across the shell-torn mudscape that stretched between the opposing lines of trenches and became known as No Man's Land. The Germans, having weathered the barrage in the relative safety of their deep dugouts, would emerge to assume their prepared positions and bring down a withering hail of rifle, machine-gun, and artillery fire on the advancing troops.

The results were inevitable. More often than not, there wouldn't be enough soldiers left alive among the attackers to take the objective and hold it, or if the Allied troops did reach their goal, the cost was prohibitive—one advance of barely 700 yards took three weeks at a cost of nearly 30,000 lives. Even when there were no titanic battles being fought, nearly 5,000 men were being killed every day by sniper fire and random shelling, though on such days the communiqués issued to the public would read "All quiet on the Western Front." The British, methodical as ever, referred to such losses as "normal wastage."

What makes it all so incomprehensible three generations later is that the soldiers accepted it so willingly—even cheerfully. True, there were those horribly disillusioned few, more mutilated in soul than in body, who recoiled from the horror. Some, like Siegfried Sassoon, an English officer despite his name, were sensitive and literate enough to give voice to their feelings. It was after he had flung his Military Cross into the sea that Sassoon penned the words:

> Pray to God you'll never know
> The hell where youth and laughter go.

And it was Wilfred Owen who wrote just weeks before he was killed in 1918:

> Where are the passing bells
> For these who die like cattle?

Yet the Siegfried Sassoons and the Wilfred Owenses were the exceptions. Countering them were the millions who fought stoically, with a quiet, unassuming belief in the essential rightness of their nations' causes that has long since vanished. Somehow, even after all the absurdities of World War II, Korea, and even Vietnam (though none would be remembered for being as absurd as World War I), there is still a rose-tinged nimbus of romance that surrounds the Great War. It was the songs—"Keep the Home Fires Burning," "Pack Up Your Troubles," "Till We Meet Again," and everyone's favorite, "Tipperary." It was the traditions—in England, newly commissioned subalterns visiting an armourer to have their swords sharpened before leaving for France, much as Henry V had done; the French *cuirassier* regiments and squadrons of German *uhlans* looking as if they had just stepped out of a Phillipoteaux painting of the Napoleonic Wars. It was black and silver saber knots, and spiked *Pickelhauben* helmets, and French gunners resplendent in black and gold tunics. It was the grandeur of an age that was in fact its shroud.

France and Germany had armies of conscripts, it is true, but conscription had been a national institution for generations. What made these conscripts conspicuous was how few tried to evade their responsibility. In Great Britain, the situation was even more astonishing: Not until 1916, when Britain would be compelled to field the largest army the Empire had ever mustered to carry out the Somme Offensive, would the British Army have to resort to a draft to fill its ranks. These young men, rightly called the flower of European youth, were the most idealistic the world would ever see, untainted by the cynicism and affected, postured disdain of later generations. Instead they steadfastly believed in *Ein Kaiser, ein Volk, ein Reich,* or *Liberté, Égalité, Fraternité!* and *Vive le Republique!,* or fighting for King and Country. What Europe was killing, no matter how willing the victims, was the vitality that would leave later generations listless and disillusioned, the fire that had driven the Continent having been quenched forever.

And in truth, the generals, much maligned as incompetents as they are, and many of them deservedly, really didn't intend to slaughter the finest generation of young men their nations would ever produce. The hard, painful truth was that they were unprepared for the war they found themselves given the responsibility of fighting. For years, it had been a tenet of military faith, and correctly so, that the day of the frontal assault was over—the American Civil War and the Franco-Prussian War had first demonstrated that, and the Russo-Japanese War of 1905 and the Balkan War of 1912 had only reinforced the lesson. Modern firepower made frontal assaults too costly, for infantry in even a hastily prepared defensive position could hold off several times their number of attacking troops, inflicting unacceptable losses in the process. So for decades, the emphasis had been placed on conducting wars of maneuver, which gave an army the opportunity to turn a foe's flank and achieve a decisive result in battle without having to resort to the terrible waste of frontal attacks.

Every aspect of European military thought was devoted to the pursuit and exploitation of mobility, which gave the capacity to maneuver, from the German *Aufmarch* (mobilization) plan and the railroad timetables of the German troop trains to the design of French artillery equipment. What no one clearly foresaw, though von Schlieffen came closer than anyone, was that the sheer mass of modern armies would negate the advantages of mobility. When von Schlieffen muttered (and he really did), "Let the soldier on the farthest right brush the [English] Channel with his sleeve," he was acknowledging that only by engaging in sweeping maneuvers on a scale never before dreamed of could mobility be decisive, for on a narrow front, the sizes of the two armies would prohibit any kind of war of maneuver.

But even von Schlieffen, whose creativity was more the result of hard work than real genius, never conceived of a war where maneuver would be impossible. Maneuver, to the generals of the Great War, was decisive—by definition, it had to be. And in truth it was, for when the Schlieffen Plan failed in September 1914, a decisive result had been reached, though no one knew it at the time. The decision was that the Germans would not take Paris this time and so knock France out of the war. That had been the objective of the Schlieffen Plan, and it failed, and hard on the heels of its failure came one of the greatest general staff blunders of all time, for the Germans had no contingency plan to fall back on should the vaunted Schlieffen Plan not deliver Paris into their hands. Even worse, as a direct result of the plan, Germany now had to number Great Britain among her enemies, a consequence of the invasion of Belgium.

What this meant was that the series of sidesteps toward the Channel that became known as the Race to the Sea were hastily improvised and executed, rather than part of a thought-out strategy. When the race was over, the result was two sets of opposing armies, organized, trained, and equipped to fight wars of maneuver, deprived of any opportunity to do anything but bludgeon away at each other in an endless series of bloody frontal assaults. For the generals, it was a nightmare: They literally had no idea what else to do. The Western Front was a scenario outside all of their experience, German, French, or British, and in a desperate attempt to do *something,* the only course of action left to them was to continue to pound away at the enemy, hoping against hope that someone, somewhere, might break through and return mobility to the battlefield.

For the Germans, of course, there was no need to attempt to force a breakthrough of the Allied lines; as long as they occupied Belgium and northern France, they were winning, and so they could let the Allies beat themselves bloody against their defenses. In fact, the only time between the fall of 1914 and the spring of 1918 that the Germans conducted any offensive in the West was in February 1916, when the chief of the general staff, Gen. Erich von Falkenhayn, persuaded the Kaiser that they could "deprive England of her best sword" by bleeding the French Army white in "a limited operation" around a series of run-down forts that ringed an insignificant city called Verdun.

At the same time, the Germans were determined that there would be *ordnung* (order) in the occupied parts of Belgium and France and immediately set about demonstrating to the civilian populace exactly what the German concept of "order" embraced. Almost from the first day of the war, the German troops had systematically begun rounding up in every village and town they passed through the local leading citizens, the doctors, the schoolteachers, the mayor and other local officials, holding them hostage to ensure the docility of the French and Belgians living behind Germans lines. Acts of violence against German soldiers, the locals were duly informed, would result in the summary execution of one or more of the hostages.

Soon word of how the Germans were enforcing their rules of occupation leaked out, raising a deafening outcry of protest from the Allied powers as well as some of the larger and more influential neutrals. Wholesale punishment of civilians for acts of resistance to an occupying army was a new and, in that day and age, sinister development in the conduct of war. Not that the Germans weren't provoked or lacked precedent. The idea of civilians resisting a foreign army wasn't new—indeed, it harked back to the Napoleonic Wars. There was even a name for civilians who committed acts of violence against uniformed troops in occupied territory, fittingly enough a French one: *franc-tirailleurs.* In point of fact, it was the French who had first dealt with a hostile, armed civilian populace when the Emperor Napoleon invaded the kingdom of Spain in 1808 and attempted to put his brother Joseph on the

Spanish throne. The resultant spontaneous uprising by the Spanish people created the "Spanish Ulcer" that bled Bonaparte's empire dry and gave the world a new word to add to its martial dictionary: guerilla.

The French response to the unseen assailants who lurked in the shadows with knife, gun, or garrote in hand had been much the same as that of the Germans a century later: execution of randomly selected hostages; wholesale slaughter of villages; rape, pillage, and plunder of any town or city foolish enough to resist a French army. The conduct of the French so infuriated the Spanish peasants who were the usual targets of French vengeance that the eight years of French occupation of Spain saw an ever-increasingly violent cycle of reprisal and atrocity that ended only when the British Army under Wellington expelled the French for good in 1814.

What made the conduct of the French in Spain between 1809 and 1813 sufficiently different from that of the Germans in Belgium and northern France in 1914 was that the actions of the French armies were not the products of an established policy, but were the result of spontaneous outbursts of anger and frustration. Not so the Germans in the occupied territories—they were carrying out a policy that had been formulated before the war began, and commenced doing so almost as soon as their armies crossed the borders: Captured German records would show that Belgians who were "disrespectful" of their German invaders were stood before firing squads as early as the second day of the war. Their gravestones can still be found, with weathered inscriptions reading: "*1914: Fusille par les Allemands*"—"Shot by the Germans."

German vengeance was not limited to acts of retaliation against the individuals who assaulted them, either. On August 21 and 23, the Prussian 101st Grenadiers, one of the elite units of the German Army, carried out a series of systematic executions in the city of Dinant. A total of 639 civilians were killed in cold blood, seven of them less than two years old, the youngest the three-week-old Mariette Fivet, who died in her father's arms. The "offense" against the Germans that had provoked the massacre was never revealed.

The Germans even had a word for it: *Schrecklichkeit* "frightfulness," a living terror. They had learned it from their great mentor, von Clausewitz, who taught that cowing a civilian population into passive cooperation or at least docility would shorten wars by ensuring the security of the rear areas. There would be many attempts by Allied propagandists to exploit this brutal side of the German character through the most lurid falsehoods, such as the corpse factory legends of 1917, but beneath the rumor mongering and myth making there lurked a central core of truth—the Germans were behaving brutally, so that, in Barbara Tuchman's memorable phrase, "Suddenly the world became aware of the beast beneath the German skin."

As the carnage began to mount on the Western Front, the Russians in the East were reeling under successive attacks in Poland and Galacia by German and Austro-Hungarian armies. Later generations would find it convenient to portray the Imperial Russian Army as pitifully armed, incompetently led, and riddled throughout its ranks with revolutionaries, who preached defeat and the overthrow of the monarchy, sapping the will of the Russian soldiers to fight. While such depictions contained an element of truth, they are a far cry from reality. Russia's peasants, her aristocracy, and her tiny middle class, just beginning to emerge as Russia was taking her first real strides toward industrialization, embraced the declarations of war in July and August 1914 with as much wild enthusiasm as any shown in Germany or France. For the peasantry, the war was a call to defend Holy Mother Russia, the ultimate expression of that semimystical bond between the *muzjik* and his land; for the aristocracy, it was the opportunity to demonstrate the superiority of their bloodlines and their culture over those of the hated German (to a Russian noble, to be called a "German" was a mortal insult); and to the middle class, the war was almost a godsend, presenting broad vistas of opportunity for investing in and expanding Russia's fledgling industries, while at the same time enhancing the prestige and reputation of the Russian parliament, the Duma.

At the same time, the organization, equipment, and small to midlevel unit tactics of the Russian Army were every bit as good as those of the French or even the Germans. The individual Russian soldier, though usually poorly educated and often illiterate, could be a formidable fighter, while the discipline, drill, and professionalism of the Russian NCOs were positively Prussian in nature. True, the Russian Army lacked artillery in the same numbers as the Western European armies, but given the rather stark nature of the Russian road system and the very limited Russian railway network, it is understandable that the Imperial Staff decided that the limited number of heavy guns that the army deployed was not necessarily a disadvantage. Given the vast distances any Russian army would have to maneuver in, it was clear that a lot of heavy artillery would be a clear impediment to mobility. On the other hand, the Russian Army had far more readily embraced the machine gun than any other European army, even the German.

Much had been expected of the Russian Army, if only for its immense resources in manpower. But the Russians possessed another quality that neither the French nor the Germans had counted on: loyalty. In September 1914, as the German First and Second Armies were lunging toward Paris, the French government, desperate for any succor, appealed to the Russian Imperial Staff to launch an attack into East Prussia that would cause the Germans to withdraw some of the divisions that were pressing so hard against the French forces. Tsar Nicholas and his senior officers, though well aware that the Russian mobilization was only half completed, felt honor bound to come to their ally's aid and so ordered Field Marshal Samsonov to attack immediately into East Prussia from Poland. Samsonov protested that his armies weren't ready: Some of his units were still in transit from their depots, what artillery he did have was not yet adequately supplied with ammunition, and no operational planning had been done. Nonetheless, the Tsar insisted, and Samsonov obeyed.

At first the Russian forces made rather remarkable progress as they advanced steadily into East Prussia, brushing aside the light screen of defending units the Germans had deployed along the border. The advance continued unchecked for more than a week, until Samsonov ran into the German Third Army, commanded by then-general Paul von Hindenburg. The result was the Battle of Tannenburg, an unmitigated disaster for the Russians.

Samsonov's army, along with General Rennenkampf's, which had been assigned to support Samsonov's offensive, were encircled and almost completely destroyed. Samsonov did his best to extricate as many of his troops as he could, then, once he became aware of how hopeless the debacle was, rode off into a small wood and blew his brains out. A huge hole had been torn in the Russian front, and had von Hindenburg had the troops available to exploit it, the magnitude of this disaster for the Russians would have been unimaginable. As it was, a crisis was created on the Eastern Front, from which the Russian Army would never wholly recover.

That von Hindenburg lacked the troops to properly exploit his victory had been merely a matter of timing, however. Though it would ultimately end in disaster, Samsonov's offensive had thrown a serious scare into the breasts of the German General Staff, and they hastily packed up two army corps from Belgium aboard a few dozen troop trains and rushed them to East Prussia, a process that, all told, took just under two weeks. When they arrived, though, the Battle of Tannenburg was over, the surviving Russians having stopped their headlong retreat and re-formed a stable front. Yet, in a curious way, their arrival was still decisive, for those two corps would be absent from the Western Front when the French launched their counterattack at the Marne on September 9. The German First and Second Armies, nearly exhausted after six weeks of constant advance, reeled under the French assault and, lacking the fresh reinforcements those two corps would have provided, fell back, leaving Paris in Allied hands, deprived of the last chance for a decisive German victory on land in the West.

The cost to the Russians, though, was staggering: Nearly half a million men were lost in the Battle of Tannenburg alone, while Samsonov's suicide, understandably the act of a sensitive man pushed by circumstances beyond the brink of despair, deprived the Russians of one of their better field commanders. It was there that the real Russian weakness lay, for Russia's officer corps simply was no match for that of Germany's. Two generations of various influential historical writers with Marxist sympathies, Western politicians who after the war sought scapegoats to explain the success of the Russian revolutionaries, and Soviet propaganda have almost hopelessly besmirched the reputation of the Russian officer corps as corrupt and hopelessly, helplessly inefficient. But the Russian Army had come far after the humiliations of the Russo-Japanese War of 1905: A series of progressive war ministers and the determination of the Tsar, who, though neither a great intellect nor gifted strategist, was determined to erase the shame of that war and eliminate waste, sloth, and corruption. He had imbued the lower and middle level officers with a true sense of professionalism, while the higher levels of command boasted such officers as Grand Duke Michael, whose reputation commanded professional respect among soldiers around the world. At the same time, the Russian armed services had displayed a keen interest in technological innovation, including submarines and aviation. What Russia lacked—and this lack was made glaring on the Eastern Front—was a body of trained professional staff officers like the German Great General Staff, whose collective institutional expertise had no parallel in the world.

As Field Marshal Brusilov would demonstrate in 1916, the Russians were capable of conceiving and executing offensive operations as well as any army in the world. Yet without a Great General Staff to spread its expertise and experience throughout the whole of the army and to develop the planning necessary to cope with the rapidly changing conditions of the battlefield, the Russians could never consistently perform as well as the Germans on either a strategic or an operational level. As a result, on the one front where decision by maneuver would be possible, the Russians would be fighting with a severe handicap. It would prove decisive in many ways.

And yet the Russians had completely, if unwittingly, laid ruin to the carefully formulated Schlieffen Plan, and saved Paris—and most likely France. For this remarkable achievement, Samsonov and his army received little, if any, acknowledgment from the French at the time, while to this day, French schoolchildren are taught that France was saved entirely by her own efforts. The Russian Imperial Staff, in their attempt to come to the aid of a desperate ally, had in turn nearly crippled the ability of their own army to defend the Motherland: Along with some of Russia's finest troops, a large proportion of the heavy and medium field artillery and transport that the Russian Army possessed had been lost at Tannenburg. Though artillery would never play as prominent a role on the Eastern Front as it would the Western, and the infantry would enjoy a mobility that the Western Front armies only dreamed of, the inability to bring artillery support to critical sectors of the front would hamstring the Russians in the months and years to come. Russia was far from beaten, but victory was now a far more difficult prospect than ever before.[1]

When the Russian military delegations in Paris and London made the extent of the Russian defeat at Tannenburg known, it became readily apparent that Russia would be forced to draw upon the resources of her allies to make up for the material losses. The French, not suffering from any qualms of conscience, offered to send assorted aircraft and artillery pieces that her own armies weren't using, mostly obsolescent equipment held in storage for years. The British, on the other hand, recognized the gravity of the situation and realized that if Russia's war effort could be sustained, the sheer numbers of troops she could deploy would eventually wear the Germans down to exhaustion. Consequently, the ability to supply Russia with whatever munitions and equipment she needed became of paramount importance to the British government.

At the same time, the deadlock on the Western Front was dominating the thinking of the men who were developing Allied strategy. The general staffs of both Great Britain and France, along with the government officials responsible for the war effort, were unanimous in their belief that the Western Front would be the decisive theater in the war. The question, the answer to which desperately eluded them, was how to counter Germany's tremendous strategic advantages: She possessed the most important terrain features on the Western Front; she could exploit her interior lines of supply to reinforce any threatened sector of the front by merely adjusting the routing and timetables of a few troop trains; and she was content to remain on the strategic defensive in the West, while expending her offensive resources on campaigns in the East that were driving deeper and deeper into Russia, threatening the Tsar's forces with defeat in detail. The logical, conservative, and orthodox solution, which most of the men responsible embraced, unable to envision any real alternatives, was simply to continue to pour men and materiel into the Western Front until the Allies would be able to crack the German lines through sheer weight of numbers, the ultimate invocation of the philosophy of the big battalions.

There were, however, those minds who had determined that such a fatalistic acceptance of the *status quo bellum* was simply unacceptable. For the most part these minds were British, for the French, obsessed with evicting the hated Boche from the sacred soil of *la Patrie*, while sinking ever deeper into Napoleonic fantasies on a headlong rush to *la gloire* no matter what the cost, would countenance no operations that did not commit ever greater resources to the Western Front. It was that mindset that von Falkenhayn would exploit with ghastly results when he launched his "limited offensive" around Verdun in February 1916. It should not be said that the French were ignorant of the uses of sea power, for by gaining command of the western Mediterranean in the first six weeks of the war, the French Navy allowed the tough, professional colonial divisions that were stationed in North Africa to be safely transported to Marseilles, supplying badly needed reinforcements to the crumbling French lines.

But the lesson was lost on the French *quartier-generale*, lacking as it did the visionaries who could perceive how the Allies' advantage in sea power could be used to negate the Central Powers' ability to use railroads and interior lines. On the other hand, even the most narrow-minded British officers were well aware of how, all throughout British history, the Royal Navy had been able to extend the reach—and hence the power—of the army, from Marlborough, to Wellington in the Peninsula, to the Crimea, to countless colonial wars around the globe. Consequently, there were more than a few visionary officers and senior officials in His Majesty's Government that almost from the first days of the war began to look for ways to exploit the remarkable potential of Great Britain's sea power.[2]

There was a certain inevitability that one of those visionaries would be the First Lord of the Admiralty, Winston Leonard Spencer Churchill. Churchill, more than most politicians, grasped the essential fact of Britain's unique military and geographic position: The Royal Navy could provide Britain's army with the strategic mobility it was lacking on land. Along with the First Sea Lord, Adm. John "Jackie" Fisher, Churchill began in late 1914 to formulate an operation that would land a sizable British army behind German lines, somewhere along Germany's North Sea coast. Construction of specialized ships for shore bombardment was authorized, as well as several unique designs for various support vessels. Churchill hoped the effect on Germany would be twofold: first, to cause a massive redeployment of German forces on the Western Front, decisively weakening them at some sector where a breakthrough could be achieved; and second, to provoke the German High Seas Fleet into action against the landing force, which in turn would be covered by the Grand Fleet, resulting in the great, Trafalgar-like conflagration that both navies so devoutly believed in, but that neither had so far been able to bring about.

What Churchill and Fisher were envisioning was not merely a diversion, but nothing less than opening a new front against the Germans. Admittedly there was more than a little opposition to such an ambitious plan, not least among those officers of the Imperial General Staff, who for various reasons shared the same point of view as the French, being opposed to any operations that did not reinforce the Western Front. But also among some circles in the Royal Navy, there were those who were concerned about such an enormous undertaking in what amounted to the enemy's home waters, virtually on the Germans' front doorstep, as it were. It was already widely known how Churchill had tried to utilize Antwerp, strongly held by the remains of the Belgian Army, as a staging area for large-scale British operations against the Germans in August and September 1914, with a notable lack of success. Neither the army nor the navy wanted any part of another such abortive attempt. The debate that developed in the War Cabinet was not so much over whether an amphibious landing should be attempted, but rather where and on what scale.

But in October 1914, those who had been hedging about committing themselves to an amphibious landing suddenly found their hands forced as the strategic picture changed abruptly. Germany, skillfully exploiting the distrust and repeated insults that the Turks had been subjected to by France and Great Britain throughout the nineteenth century, concluded a military alliance with Turkey. Suddenly, all French and especially British possessions in the Near East were vulnerable to attack by Turkish armies, but even more disastrous for the Allies, by joining the Central Powers, Turkey closed the Straits of the Bosporus and the Dardanelles, the only access from the Mediterranean Sea to the Black Sea, and even more important, the only route by which Britain and France could send supplies to Russia during the winter months, when ice closed Russia's northern ports.

For Russia this was critical: In the first three months of the war, she had lost over a million men, new recruits were being sent to the front without rifles because all the existing prewar stocks had been issued, while troops at the front who had rifles often had no ammunition for them. Artillery units were rationing their shells, some guns being limited to firing three rounds a day. Without the material support of France and Great Britain, Russia's war effort would collapse in a matter of weeks; her industrial capacity was still far too small to be able to meet more than a fraction of her armies' needs. In turn, it was vital to France and Britain that Russia continue fighting, for she was tying down huge numbers of German soldiers that, if they were suddenly available for service on the Western Front, could allow the Germans to overwhelm the Allies by sheer weight of numbers. The Allies were left with no alternative: To keep Russia in the war, they had to reopen the supply route through the Black Sea, and they could only do so by seizing the Straits of the Dardanelles.

The site chosen for the Allied landing was the Gallipoli Peninsula, a barren, rocky promontory on the southern, or Asia Minor, shore of the Dardanelles. Planning went swiftly, and the staff work was completed by early December, with a target date for landing operations to begin in March 1915. Considerable naval resources were allotted to support the landing force, no less than sixteen French and British battleships, including the brand new *Queen Elizabeth*, at the time the most powerful warship in the world, taking part in a series of bombardments against the Turkish defenses all along the Dardanelles that began on February 18 and continued intermittently through March 22.

The Turkish defenses were all but obliterated, as most of their heavy guns were destroyed, along with most of their reserves of ammunition. Had they but known it, the Allied warships could have sailed up to Constantinople and demanded Turkey's surrender at gunpoint. Not that the warships had gotten off unscathed: Several were damaged to greater or lesser degrees by the Turkish guns before they were silenced, and two battleships, the French *Bouvet* and the British *Irresistible*, were lost to mines, but these were older ships, not first-rate units, and the Admiralty had been willing to risk their loss. Unfortunately, there was no way for those aboard the Allied warships to realize that their shelling had succeeded beyond all expectations, and so, when they completed the bombardment, they sailed back to their base in the Aegean off the island of Lemnos, prepared to support the army's landing force.

The problem was that the landing force was far from ready. Despite repeated urgings from Churchill to make haste and strike as hard and as quickly as possible, the commander of the landing force, Gen. Ian Hamilton, dawdled. Churchill's fear was that every day the army tarried in getting troops ashore on the Gallipoli peninsula was another day gained by the Turks to recover from the mauling they had received from the navy. He was right, of course, although there were personal reasons for his anxiety. The whole Dardanelles operation was his brainchild, and while the operation had been endorsed by the whole of the War Cabinet, he had become inextricably linked to it, so he was acutely aware of who would be compelled to shoulder the blame should anything go wrong, thus his repeated urgings to the army to hurry. Hamilton asked Churchill to defer to his greater experience: The Turkish guns were silenced, that was all that mattered. There would be little, if any, opposition to the landings, since without artillery support, the Turks would never be able to put up an effective defense. Despite considerable misgivings, Churchill backed down, and the army continued its preparations.

When the British forces (actually they were ANZACs, the justly famous Australian–New Zealand Army Corps) finally did land on April 25, they met with fierce resistance that caused heavy casualties and made the landings a shambles. Instead of being able to sweep up the length of the peninsula, the ANZACs were forced to dig in on their beachheads, sometimes barely a dozen yards from the water's edge. What had happened was exactly what Churchill had feared. Under the advice and leadership of the German general Otto Liman von Sanders, who was as energetic as Hamilton was languorous, the Turks had reorganized and reinforced the Gallipoli garrison and turned the rubble of their coast defense fortresses into defensive strong points, bristling with machine guns. They didn't need artillery support, since the ANZACs had no way of bringing their own guns ashore and no effective means of coordinating with the naval forces offshore to provide fire support, so Turkish rifles and machine guns were sufficient to contain the ANZAC beachheads. Within days, the Allied position on the peninsula began to look like a microcosm of the Western Front, as the ANZACs began to earn their nickname of "Diggers" by frantically excavating trenches to protect themselves from the constant Turkish fire. The signs were there for anyone who wanted to read them: The Gallipoli expedition was about to become a disaster.[3]

Inevitably, Churchill found himself at the center of the rapidly developing maelstrom of criticism. His political opponents ignored the fact that the whole War Cabinet had approved of the Dardanelles operation and that Churchill had repeatedly urged that the pace of operations be speeded up as well as warned the War Cabinet of the danger of not pressing the amphibious assault immediately after the naval bombardment. Instead, they began clamoring for Churchill's resignation as First Lord, assigning him sole responsibility for the failures of Hamilton. Churchill was handicapped in his efforts to defend himself by the fact that much of the information available to him when he had conceived of the Gallipoli landings was highly secret.

If this had been the only crisis he faced, Churchill might have successfully weathered the storm, once he had been given the opportunity to present the facts in his own defense. Unfortunately, just as the Dardanelles operations were getting under way, the war at sea had taken a new and nasty turn, as the number of British merchant ships being sunk by German U-boats began to increase alarmingly. What Great Britain now faced was not a crisis, but the beginnings of a threat to her survival.

What had happened was simple: On February 15, 1915, Germany issued a declaration that not only changed the course of the war at sea, but also changed the basic nature of warfare forever. The German Foreign Office had sent a cable to every neutral capital in Europe, as well as every country in North and South America:

> The waters surrounding Great Britain and Ireland, and including the whole of the English Channel, are proclaimed to be a War Zone. On and after the 18th of February 1915, every enemy merchant ship found in the said war zone will be destroyed without it always being possible to avert the dangers threatening the crews and passengers on that account. Even neutral ships are exposed to dangers in the war zone, and in view of the use of neutral flags ordered on January 31st by the British government and of the accidents of naval war, mistakes may not always be avoided and they may be struck by attacks directed at enemy ships.

Accompanying the declaration was a list of safe zones in which neutral ships could travel to Europe, none of which, of course, led to a British port. Along with the list came a lengthy, somewhat tedious "memorial," as the Germans called it, in which they stated their reasons and justifications for taking such an unprecedented action. Meticulously legalistic, it stressed the fact that Britain had been the first nation to declare such a war zone, that the British blockade and contraband classifications were illegal, and it urged all neutral nations to take whatever precautions they deemed necessary to protect their citizens and commerce.

Simply put, the British had pushed the Germans too far. Beginning in October 1914, a steady stream of orders had issued forth from the Admiralty to British merchant captains regarding their conduct if they were attacked by a German U-boat. First, it was made a criminal offense for a captain to stop his ship if ordered to do so by a German submarine. Then, merchant skippers were given orders that required them, if they were challenged by a U-boat, to not only refuse to stop, but to attempt to engage the submarine with whatever armament the merchant ship had or, if it was unarmed, to attempt to ram the U-boat. Finally, all British merchant ships were ordered to paint out their funnels' colors and names and to fly false flags whenever possible, to make identification difficult.

The Germans learned of these orders entirely by accident, when the *U-21* put a half dozen shells into the *Ben Cruachan,* a steamer on her way to Liverpool, on January 31, 1915, and her captain decided that discretion was the better part of valor and stopped his ship. When a prize crew from the *U-21* boarded the *Ben Cruachan,* they found the orders along with the ship's papers and promptly confiscated the lot of them before sending the *Cruachan* to the bottom. The German government's reaction was so sharp and swift because the Admiralty orders had made a mockery of the German Navy's attempt to carry out its submarine campaign according to the dictates of the Cruiser Rules.

The Cruiser Rules were a naval etiquette dating back to the days of Henry VIII in the early 1500s. Briefly, the Cruiser Rules governed a warship's conduct toward merchant shipping during wartime. A warship was expected to order an *unarmed* merchant ship to halt by firing a warning shot across the merchantman's bow. Once stopped, the merchant crew was obliged to allow the warship's crew to search the vessel without threat of harm or interference in any way, while in turn the searchers could not threaten or use force against the crew except in self-defense. If the merchant ship belonged to a neutral, it was to be allowed to proceed untouched, even if it was bound for a port belonging to a hostile power.

If the freighter ship belonged to a hostile power, then the warship had two options available to it. A prize crew could be put aboard the merchantman to sail it into the nearest friendly port, where the ship and crew would be interned, or if that proved to be impractical, then both the vessel and cargo could be destroyed—after the crew and any passengers were given time to take to the lifeboats. It was all a very clearly defined, very civilized method of waging war.

However, the protection the Cruiser Rules offered to ships, cargo, passengers, and crew applied only to unarmed freighters and merchant ships, and there were several ways a captain could lose that protection for his ship. Any attempt to run away from the warship that ordered the merchant ship to halt, or a simple refusal to halt when so ordered, allowed the warship to resort to force. Likewise, any overtly hostile act—opening fire on the warship with a deck gun, trying to ram, or assaulting the boarding party—allowed the warship to deal with the freighter in any way the warship's captain saw fit. Finally, any attempt to signal for help allowed the warship complete freedom of action.[4]

This whole convention was obsolete by 1914, especially in the case of submarines. U-boat crews were small, making the capture of enemy freighters impractical, and the advent of the wireless made virtually certain a call for assistance by a merchant ship ordered to heave to. Such a call was dangerous for the submarine, since it would invariably include the U-boat's position and would bring any nearby antisubmarine forces rushing to the scene.

Most critically, though, was the fact that by January 1915, many British merchant ships were "defensively" armed as a measure of protection against submarine attack. Usually this defensive armament consisted of a pair of twelve-pounder guns, as the British called their 3-inch guns, although some ships carried guns with calibers as large as six inches. A single hit from a twelve-pounder could cripple a U-boat, and a hit from a 6-inch shell would blow the submarine out of the water. Surfacing and challenging a ship carrying such an armament left the U-boat dangerously exposed to an attack itself, to which the U-boat would have no reply but to torpedo the merchantman.

The defensive armament had originally been a measure intended to provide a degree of self-defense against surface raiders—the fast German liners, now in their auxiliary cruiser guise, that the *Lusitania* and *Mauretania* had been built to wrest the Blue Riband from in peacetime, and hunt down and sink in wartime. The German liners had indeed rendezvoused with ships of the German Navy in the early days of the war and had mounted deck guns and stockpiled ammunition, then began to prowl the shipping lanes of the North and South Atlantic. For a few weeks, they enjoyed moderate success, but determined action by the Royal Navy soon sent them to the bottom of the ocean or forced the survivors into neutral ports, where the ships and crews were interned. The British didn't stop arming their merchant ships, though, since the Germans persisted—with some notable success—in slipping the odd raider or two past the British blockade to raise hob with Allied shipping in the Atlantic.

It was only after the U-boats began sinking merchant ships in late 1914, however, and after a number of armed merchantmen had forced U-boats to break off their attacks, (with the typical Teutonic passion for legality, the U-boat crews had been scrupulous in observing the Cruiser Rules in the first five months of the war) that the Admiralty realized that the deck guns were very effective defenses against submarines. The U-boats' favorite method of sinking a merchant ship was to surface alongside her, order the ship to stop, then wait for the crew to take to the lifeboats before using the U-boat's deck gun to blow holes in the merchant ship's waterline. Since the U-boats carried a deck gun ranging from 88 to 105 millimeter in size, this usually didn't take more than fifteen or twenty minutes. (U-boat skippers preferred to save their torpedoes for warships, which was sensible, since the submarines could carry only a dozen or so torpedoes but could store hundreds of shells.)

The Admiralty realized that if faced with the prospect of surfacing amid a flurry of 3-, 4-, or even 6-inch shells whistling past their ears, the U-boat crews would choose the better part of valor and attack without surfacing. This would force them to expend their precious torpedoes much more rapidly and reduced the threat each submarined posed. It also meant that the U-boats would be more likely to simply attack without warning as well.

Learning that even unarmed freighters were expected to try to ram U-boats on sight proved to be too much for the U-boat commanders to take (the thought of several thousand tons of enemy merchantman bearing down on a tiny U-boat was enough to give any *Korvettenkapitan* ulcers). They argued with the chief of naval staff, Vice Adm. Friedrich von Pohl, that the British measures had made further adherence to the Cruiser Rules a practical impossibility, and any attempts to do so would cause needless loss of boats and crews. They wanted to be able to sink British ships on sight, without warning, and they wanted neutrals warned that they sailed in British waters at their own peril. Because their lives were on the line, they were persuasive in their arguments, and von Pohl took the suggestion to the War Staff. Von Tirpitz objected strongly, saying that allowing the U-boats to sink ships on sight would have a strongly adverse effect on neutral opinion and would be "more far-reaching in its effect on neutrals than a [surface] blockade, and considerably more dangerous politically."

It was von Tirpitz's opinion that while the world understood and respected the legitimate nature of Britain's blockade of Germany, it would not understand the legitimacy of a German policy of unrestricted U-boat warfare. Officials from the government disagreed, saying that public opinion in Germany demanded a retaliatory gesture to the British blockade, which was already making itself felt in some sectors of the German economy. Von Pohl, listening to the arguments being traded back and forth, came up with what he believed to be a novel solution: Why not mimic the British and declare the waters around the British Isles to be a war zone, much like Britain's announcement of the North Sea as a "military area" in October 1914? Rather than forcing all ships entering the "war zone" into German ports and seizing their cargoes, Germany would simply provide instructions and routes to avoid the war zone. Since this would not interfere with neutral shipping but merely reroute it, there would be no contradiction with Germany's policy that the British blockade was illegal. The Kaiser himself endorsed the idea, and the appropriate memoranda were drawn up and sent out to the German embassies around the world on February 5.

The U-boats wasted no time in putting the proclamation into effect. Between February 18 and March 28, twenty-five ships were sunk by U-boats, sixteen of them torpedoed without warning. Of a total of 712 crewmen from those sixteen ships, 52 were killed, though not a single passenger out of 3,072 involved were even injured. It was a not unenviable record, but it couldn't last forever, and on March 28, the whole complexion of the submarine campaign changed still further.

The 5,000-ton steamer *Falaba*, bound for Liverpool with a cargo that included thirteen tons of high explosives, was ordered to halt by the *U-28*, which fired a shot across the freighter's bow. The two ships were about forty miles from the Smalls lighthouse, the time just after 2:00 P.M. The *Falaba*'s captain, obeying his Admiralty orders, refused to stop, instead turning away from the submarine in an attempt to flee. At this point, even under the Cruiser Rules, the *U-28* could have torpedoed the *Falaba* without warning, but her skipper, Kapitan von Forstner, instead gave chase, eventually forcing the *Falaba* to stop. Von Forstner then gave the *Falaba*'s crew ten minutes to abandon the ship.

At this point, the *Falaba*'s wireless operator began sending frantic calls for assistance, saying his ship was under submarine attack and giving her position. Again the *Falaba* could have been sent straight to the bottom, but again von Forstner restrained himself. The steamer's passengers and crew dawdled as they got into the lifeboats, her captain playing for time, gambling on a patrol vessel appearing to drive the U-boat away. (The *Falaba*'s skipper has to be admired—if need be, he was going to play every trick in the book to keep from losing his ship.) Von Forstner gave the *Falaba* another ten minutes to finish abandoning the ship, then three more minutes' grace after that, while all the while the *Falaba*'s wireless calls for help continued.

Inevitably, an armed trawler showed up and opened fire on the *U-28*. Alternatives and patience exhausted, von Forstner ordered a torpedo put into the *Falaba*'s side. The *Falaba*'s cargo of explosives blew up in sympathetic detonation with the torpedo, sending the ship to the bottom in minutes. Among the 104 lives lost was Leon C. Thresher, an American citizen, the first American to be killed in the war at sea. The Great War had finally crossed the Atlantic.[5]

CHAPTER 4

The First Lord
and the Admiralty

IN AUGUST 1914, THE FIRST LORD OF THE ADMIRALTY WAS A STOOP-shouldered, cherub-faced, slightly balding man just shy of his fortieth birthday—considered young for someone in such a responsible position. He was regarded as intelligent, witty, impetuous, talented, ambitious, visionary, and erratic. He had been a soldier, a war correspondent, a wanted fugitive, a best-selling author, and a politician. Politically he was astute, militarily he was daring. He was one of the most controversial men of his day. A contemporary remarked that with him there was no middle ground: You either admired or detested him. His name was Winston Churchill.

He had been born in Blenheim Palace, the seat of the Dukes of Marlborough, in 1874, his father an English lord, Randolph Churchill, his mother an American socialite, Jennie Jerome. In his youth, he was an indifferent student, though early on he discovered a penchant for using the English language that would someday astound the world. Because his academic performance was so erratic, Oxford and Cambridge were denied him, so he chose Sandhurst, the British West Point, anticipating a career in the army, his first posting being with the Fourth Hussars in India. It was there that he completed his education, on his own terms and in his own time, becoming broadly and deeply read. He discovered that his facility with English could be translated into newspaper and magazine articles and books, providing him with a living independent of his officer's pay. At the same time, he discovered a streak of personal ambition and decided that his future lay in politics rather than the military. He promptly set about making a name for himself, one that would become a household word by the time he was ready to seek a seat in Parliament.

To do this, he exploited one of the more unusual aspects of his family situation. His father had died of paresis a month before he graduated from Sandhurst, and his mother, far from going into mourning, became one of the most accomplished courtesans of her day. In truth, Randolph and Jennie

Churchill had been estranged for years before Randolph's death and had even given up maintaining the pretense of living together. Jennie, who was justly renowned for her astonishing beauty and her equally astonishing sexual appetite, became intimately linked with some of the most powerful men in the British Empire, including the Prince of Wales, the future King Edward VII. Winston set out to use these liaisons to his advantage, urging his mother to press his case to whomever of her lovers, past or present, could do the most to advance his career by getting him to whichever spot in the world the fighting was the fiercest.

Soon London newspapers began carrying articles bylined by Winston Churchill from such exotic locales as Afghanistan, Omdurman in the Sudan, the island nation of Cuba, and South Africa. It was there in 1899, during the Boer War, which he was covering as a war correspondent, that he was captured by the Boers, made a daring escape across a hundred miles of open enemy territory, and returned triumphantly to London, to be elected to Parliament in 1900.[1]

Once in the House of Commons, his rise to prominence astounded everyone. By 1908, he was a Cabinet member, appointed president of the Board of Trade. Along with the Chancellor of the Exchequer, David Lloyd George, Churchill was instrumental in the passage of an unprecedented program of liberal legislation—health insurance, old-age pensions, unemployment compensation—financed by, Churchill's aristocratic origins notwithstanding, taxes on the rich and titled landed gentry. In 1910, he played a major role in the passage of the Parliament Bill, which emasculated the House of Lords and concentrated the whole of legislative authority in the Commons.

It was September 27, 1911, that Churchill became First Lord of the Admiralty. Just five weeks before that, the man he replaced, Reginald McKenna, had been badly embarrassed at a meeting of the Committee of Imperial Defense, an embarrassment that cost McKenna his job. The committee was a joint civilian-military body, consisting of the Cabinet and senior staff officers from the army and Royal Navy, responsible for planning and preparations for the defense of the Empire. For five years, informal military talks had been held between the British and French general staffs, a response to a mutually perceived threat to France and the Low Countries from Imperial Germany, and this meeting was to review the planning of both the army and the Royal Navy. There were profound, fundamental differences between what each of the services believed its proper role to be, as well each one's relationship to the other. The morning was given to the army, the afternoon to the navy. The army's presentation was lucid, clear, well thought-out, and practical. By contrast, the navy's planning seemed to be incoherent, ill formed, and impractical. The Prime Minister, Herbert Asquith, informed

McKenna that the whole of the Cabinet had agreed to adopt the army's pro-posals for war planning, based in no little part on the navy's inept perfor-mance that afternoon. McKenna tried to argue, but Asquith's mind was made up. McKenna would have to go.

Choosing his successor was not exactly simple. Richard Burdon Haldane, the Minister of War who had successfully reorganized and reformed the British Army a few years previously and who was in large part responsible for the army's excellent preparations and presentation, approached Asquith with the idea that he should become First Lord, and apply the same skills to the Royal Navy that he had to the army. There was merit to his case, but Asquith, who was infamous for making decisions by not actually making them, temporized. Churchill put his candidacy forward: A week before the committee met, he had sent a memorandum on military planning to Asquith that had anticipated the army's planned operations, and Asquith had been impressed. Finally, the Prime Minister, believing that it would be better to have the First Lord in the Commons rather than the House of Lords (where Haldane, about to be elevated to Viscount Haldane, would sit), decided to give the Admiralty to Churchill.

Churchill took office on October 25, 1911, and made his presence felt almost immediately. There was more than a little apprehension about his appointment, both within the navy and without. His admirers saw an energetic young man (at thirty-six, Churchill was nine years younger than the next youngest Cabinet member) who was brilliant, self-confident, eloquent, and full of new ideas; his detractors saw in equal measure an erratic young man who was self-absorbed, overly ambitious, opportunistic, and unpredictable. Both points of view were equally correct, as events over the next four years would show.

However, the immediate effects of Churchill's appearance at the Admi-ralty were both startling and beneficial. Immediately the Admiralty began tracking and plotting the position of every German warship, whether at sea or in port, while the sea lords, four admirals who acted as executives for the First Lord, began keeping watches so that one of them was always at the Admi-ralty. Orders for new ships that had been authorized but not placed were quickly put in hand, while detailed war plans were developed. Work on new heavy guns that would outrange and overpower anything the German High Seas Fleet possessed was begun.

Winston regarded the ships and men of the Royal Navy as his own, and he quickly took a very proprietorial attitude toward them. He wanted to know everything about everything, and since he had the Admiralty yacht *Enchantress* at his disposal, he could easily turn up anywhere. He was as inter-ested in submarines as he was battleships, in wireless as in guns, and had to know how everything worked. His curiosity was insatiable.

At the same time, he paid as much attention to the welfare and well-being of the ordinary sailors as he did the condition of the ships they served on. The pay for seamen, which hadn't changed in sixty years, was raised; petty disciplinary offenses were eliminated; inadequate leave was improved; and slow promotions were sped up. Food, clothing, and quarters were all examined, altered, and improved as necessary.

To many of the Royal Navy's officers, especially the senior ones, these intrusions of Churchill's were regarded as heavy-handed meddling. The Royal Navy had become accustomed to a series of First Lords who were merely ornamental, the actual administration and day-to-day running of the navy being done by the four sea lords, each of whom were responsible for a specific aspect of the service: The First was in charge of operations, the Second, shipbuilding and procurement; the Third, personnel; the Fourth, supply. The sea lords had become accustomed to running their branches of the Admiralty as they saw fit, giving advice to the First Lord for him to rubber stamp. Churchill turned this whole concept on its ear. He regarded the Sea Lords as his subordinates and gave them orders rather than following their suggestions. From the first day of his tenure, the Royal Navy knew who was in charge. Churchill effected no revolution in ship design, radical strategies, or bold new tactics, but what he changed in the Royal Navy was its attitude: He fully believed that the navy's sole responsibility was to be ready for war, at any time, and systematically set about bringing the whole fleet around to that same point of view. His energy and drive became infectious, especially among the ratings and younger officers.

He could be ruthless when he needed to be, as well. When some of the senior admirals, including all four sea lords, confronted him one day, declaring that his methods were detrimental to the traditions of the Royal Navy, he rounded on them with the reply: "And what are they? I shall tell you in three words. Rum, sodomy, and the lash. Good day, gentlemen."[2]

But Churchill had to work with these men, and he knew it, so he decided that making peace with the admirals was necessary if he was to be effective in his post. Adm. Sir Arthur Wilson, the First Sea Lord, who had so badly represented the navy at the Imperial Defense Committee meeting, was unceremoniously removed from his post after Churchill took office. Wilson's replacement would have to be a unique individual; it would have to be someone that the entire Royal Navy respected, but who was open to new and exciting ideas. Churchill sent for Lord Fisher.

Adm. Sir John Arbuthnot Fisher had retired four years previously. Called "the greatest admiral since Nelson," known to the public—who adored him—as "Jackie," Fisher had been born in Ceylon in 1941, the son of an infantry-officer-turned-plantation-owner. Fisher had entered the Royal Navy as a midshipman at age thirteen and had worked his way up through the offi-cer ranks, commanding his first ship at thirty-five, his first battleship at thirty-six. As he progressed through various fleet commands, his finest hour was between 1904 and 1910, when he was First Sea Lord. In those six years he reorganized the Royal Navy, most significantly by first establishing a Reserve Fleet and then concentrating the whole of the fleet's battleship and battle cruiser strength into the Home Fleet, which was then redesignated, appropriately enough, the Grand Fleet. He scrapped or sold old, obsolescent ships, freeing up experienced men and money for new units; conceived and built the dreadnought battleship; introduced submarines and the 13.5-inch gun; overhauled the navy's education and training programs; and oversaw the construction of 161 warships, including twenty-two new battleships. It was an astonishing performance.

Fisher was fiery tempered, passionate, given to great angers and great kindnesses. With dark, almost black, eyes and a curiously Oriental face, he characterized himself as "ruthless, relentless, and remorseless." He certainly was unforgiving when dealing with officers who crossed him professionally, seeing to it that their careers were effectively ended. He had the advantage of almost always being right; consequently, few officers, or civilians for that mat-ter, dared to cross him. He was usually right because he was a genius, and it's worth noting that he was one of the first British admirals to grasp the poten-tial of the submarine.

In 1911, Fisher was seventy years old, and while the fire still burned within him, it no longer burned as bright. Unarguably a genius but an erratic one, he had become more eccentric as he got older. By 1911, he was irascible, impulsive, and prejudiced, and a streak of intolerance and narrow-mindedness that had not been evident before was starting to appear. But he seemed to be as dynamic as ever, and it was that energy that Churchill wanted to once again harness. Fisher returned to the Admiralty as First Sea Lord in June 1912, and by all accounts, the relationship between the old sea dog and the youthful politician was one of mutual respect and admiration. They seemed to make an excellent team, Churchill bursting with ideas about how to increase the pre-paredness of the Royal Navy, Fisher with exact knowledge of how to accom-plish them. Only a very careful observer could have seen that a collision of wills between these two headstrong men was inevitable and would have disas-trous consequences for both of them.[3]

The one significant change that Churchill made in Great Britain's prewar naval strategy was how the blockade of Germany would be maintained. Since the eighteenth century, the blockade of an enemy's ports was the fundamental strategic concept of the Royal Navy: The British exercised sea power in wartime by denying their enemies the opportunity to do the same, and the method of doing so was to blockade the enemy, both naval and merchant ships, in his home ports. The foe's economy would wither, the fighting ability of his warships would decline, and the enemy's morale would suffer, until the whole edifice of the enemy's nation would begin to totter and topple or until he sued for peace. It had worked against the Spanish, it had worked against the Dutch, it had worked against the Danes, and most importantly, it had worked against Napoleon. It had even worked for the Union against the Confederacy in the American Civil War. Two hundred years before Captain Mahan had articulated the concept of sea power, the Royal Navy had been exercising it in the most practical terms.

The essential soundness of the idea of the blockade was so self-evident that even into the twentieth century, no equally effective alternative had ever been devised, although several weapons, notably the torpedo boat and the submarine, had been developed with the idea of being able to defeat—or at least seriously disrupt—a blockade. Until Churchill's arrival at the Admiralty, the basic scenario envisioned by the Royal Navy's planners was that in the event of a war between Germany and Great Britain, a possibility whose likelihood seemed to grow with every passing month, the Royal Navy would immediately establish a blockade of Germany's North Sea ports. At the same time, the Straits of the Skagerrak between Denmark and Norway would be closed, sealing off the Baltic Sea and rendering Germany's Baltic ports useless. In what was termed a "close blockade," meaning that the blockading ships kept station relatively close to the enemy's ports, light units—cruisers and destroyers—would patrol the coastal waters of Germany while the capital ships—the battleships and battle cruisers—would wait patiently over the horizon, waiting for the word from the smaller ships that the High Seas Fleet was coming out to do battle, and the naval war would be decided in a great, Trafalgar-like confrontation.

This task was made easier for the Royal Navy because of a quirk of geography that placed Germany and the High Seas Fleet at a perpetual disadvantage. For the High Seas Fleet to be able to exercise sea power of its own—that is, to be able to successfully interdict and disrupt Britain's merchant shipping—it would have to be able to reach the shipping lanes of the North Atlantic. The only routes to the Atlantic that the High Seas Fleet had available were either through the English Channel or up through the North Sea and around Scotland. The Royal Navy sat firmly astride both of them. Almost by default, then, for the Royal Navy and High Seas Fleet, the North Sea was perceived to be the decisive theater.

The Germans had anticipated this and planned accordingly. Tacitly admitting that it was decisively outgunned and outnumbered by the Royal Navy, the German Naval High Command devised a number of stratagems by which a part of the Grand Fleet would be drawn into an engagement with the whole of the High Seas Fleet and crush it, gradually eroding the Royal Navy's numerical advantage, until the German fleet could fight its way into the Atlantic, defeating the British blockade and in turn cutting Britain's shipping lines.

Unfortunately for German planning, Churchill foresaw this possibility and realized that a High Seas Fleet bottled up in the North Sea was just as ineffective as if it were bottled up in its ports, and that consequently maintaining a close blockade, with all of its attendant risks of exposing parts of the Grand Fleet to piecemeal destruction, need not be put in hand at all. A "distant blockade," which simply denied the German Navy the chance to even reach the Atlantic, was just as effective and far less hazardous to the ships of the Grand Fleet. Grand Adm. Karl Doenitz, who commanded a U-boat in World War I, summed up the situation: "The High Seas Fleet was denied its normal radius of action—to steam into the North Atlantic, where alone a decision was possible. Only in the North Sea our fleet presented no danger to the Grand Fleet. The Royal Navy had but to put into operation the war plans envisioned before 1914."

In order to make the doctrine of the distant blockade work, a massive new fleet anchorage was built at Scapa Flow, in the bleak Orkney Islands off the north coast of Scotland, where the North Sea opens into the Atlantic. There the Grand Fleet would wait, steam up, while the cruisers and destroyers watched close to the German shore, ready to flash the signal that the German fleet had sortied. An additional advantage to the fleet anchorage at Scapa Flow was that it was believed to be safe against submarine attack. In one fell swoop, the Royal Navy had frustrated the German strategy: Keeping the Grand Fleet concentrated at Scapa denied the Atlantic to the High Seas Fleet, ensured that the Germans would never catch part of the Grand Fleet and defeat it in detail, and protected the fleet in a safe anchorage.

By the time the crisis of July 1914 had arrived, Churchill had mastered the Admiralty and had prepared the fleet for war with Germany. As fortune would have it, when the crisis came for Great Britain, and His Majesty's Government had to decide whether to come to the defense of beleaguered Belgium, the Grand Fleet was just completing its summer maneuvers in the North Sea and hadn't yet put into port. Prince Louis Battenberg, the Second Sea Lord, correctly divining Churchill's intentions, ordered the fleet to remain concentrated at sea, ready to go into action on a few hours' notice. Churchill approved, and Battenberg's initative paid remarkable dividends: When war broke out between Germany and Britain on August 4, the Royal Navy was prepared and in position to protect the transfer of the BEF across the English Channel to France, which was the decisive strategic move of the beginning of the war. The High Seas Fleet wasn't ready to try to interdict that movement, and what could have been the German Navy's greatest opportunity to decisively intervene in the war was lost forever.

For Churchill, this was at once a triumph and a disappointment. All of his efforts had paid off in one decisive stroke, his critics for once not able to challenge his actions or his perceptions. At the same time, having so effectively neutralized the High Seas Fleet, and then conducted a campaign of hunting down and destroying the handful of German warships and surface raiders that were at sea when the war broke out (among them most of the fast German liners that the *Lusitania* and *Mauretania* had been designed to seek out and destroy), there was little for him to do. The thousand and one administrative details that constituted the day-to-day running of the Royal Navy were beneath someone of his talents, or so he seemed to believe. What was more, there was little glamour and no glory in it, and for a young man not yet forty, those were concepts that still held some attraction. It hadn't been with the intention of becoming a paper-shuffling bureaucrat that he had come to the Admiralty.

One of the problems created by Churchill's energy and drive was that he had created an overcentralized command structure at the Admiralty, frequently described as "monolithic." One of his earliest acts as First Lord had been to reorganize the operations of the Royal Navy so that almost every decision required his authorization. Such a system could produce amazing results, for when Churchill worked, he really worked. In a letter Fisher wrote to Adm. Sir John Jellicoe, commanding the Grand Fleet, he commented that "Winston has so monopolized all initiative in the Admiralty and has fired off such a multitude of purely departmental memos (*his power of work is absolutely amazing*) that my colleagues and I [the four Sea Lords] are no longer superintending *Lords* but only *the First Lord's registry!*"

Unfortunately for Churchill, this bustle of activity earned him a reputation as a meddler, wanting to have a finger in every pie. His command structure at times actually impeded Admiralty operations, for few staff officers were willing to make command decisions in his absence on their own initiative. (One of the few who would, Prince Louis of Battenberg, the Second Sea Lord, had been forced from office in a shameful political intrigue over the fact that although he was a member of the British Royal Family, he had been born in Germany, and therefore his loyalties were politically suspect. Churchill, dismayed and ashamed, could do nothing to prevent Battenberg's removal.) Winston's "in" basket might contain such wildly dissimilar items as a requisition for toilet paper for one of His Majesty's cruisers, lying atop the latest intelligence reports on a new class of German battleship. Churchill had replaced lethargy with frenzy.

One of the first people to appreciate this was Fisher. At first it seemed that the two men complemented each other, though it would be difficult to imagine a more oddly matched pair. Adm. Sir David Beatty, Jellicoe's second in command and Churchill's formal naval secretary, wrote, "The situation is curious, two very strong and clever men, one old, wily, and of vast experience, one young, self-assertive, with a great self-satisfaction but unstable." Even their work habits were diametrically opposed: Fisher would rise at dawn and work until midafternoon, while Churchill would rarely appear at his desk before noon but would work far into the night. Fisher would arrive to find the results of Churchill's night's work waiting on his desk in the morning, while Churchill could expect a lengthy memo or report in response when he arrived, signed at the bottom with Fisher's famous "F" in green ink. Of them, Alan Moorehead wrote:

> Together they were a formidable team. Fisher had but to produce a plan and Churchill would put it through the cabinet and the House of Commons. In this way together they had got Jellicoe the command of the Grand Fleet, they had secured the navy's supply of [fuel] oil by inducing the government to finance the Persian wells, and then had embarked on a shipbuilding program which had made Britain the strongest maritime power in the world.

Fisher had specialized in naval gunnery and had been the driving force behind the design and construction of the all-big-gun battleship, the dreadnought, and its half-sister, the battle cruiser. This did not mean, though, that he was blind to other innovations in naval weaponry. Earlier in his career, Fisher had commanded the Royal Navy's torpedo school, and he was deeply aware of that weapon's growing potential. As a result, he was the only senior admiral who anticipated the threat that the submarine could pose to Great Britain, not only to her warships but also as a commerce raider—something that even Churchill, with his ever-active imagination, had missed. In fact, the two quarreled sharply over how submarines would be used in any future war, Churchill maintaining that "no civilized nation would ever resort to such barbarous action"—that is, using the submarine to prey on civilian merchant shipping. He had missed the basic truth of Fisher's pithy comment that "Violence is the essence of war, and moderation in war is imbecility!" Fisher understood long before anyone else in the Admiralty, or in Great Britain for that matter, that in any future war, considerations of civilized behavior would be tossed aside in the quest for victory.

The first inkling of the true military potential of the submarine came on September 9, 1914, when the light cruiser *Pathfinder* was torpedoed by the *U-21*. What was alarming about the sinking was not the material loss to the fleet, which was insignificant, but rather that it had happened in open waters, away from the coastal areas and shores where British doctrine had held that submarines were most effective. One keen observer was Commodore Roger Keyes, one of the Royal Navy's most imaginative and promising officers. Keyes drew Churchill's attention to the deployment of three *Bacchante*-class cruisers, manned mostly by reservists, in the North Sea near where *Pathfinder* had been sunk. A recent Admiralty report, he reminded Churchill, had declared that class of cruiser to be particularly vulnerable to torpedo attack, primarily because of their long, unprotected longitudinal coal bunkers; in fact, the fleet had derisively nicknamed the trio the "Livebait Squadron." Horrified, Churchill issued orders on September 17 for the three ships to be transferred to less hazardous stations. Not realizing the urgency of the orders, the new assignments didn't reach the three cruisers in time. They were *Hogue, Aboukir,* and *Cressy.*

The tragedy of the Broad Fourteens was a wake-up call to the Admiralty in general and Churchill in particular, both as a threat to the Royal Navy and as a menace to British merchant shipping. Admittedly, Churchill and the rest of the Admiralty had been obsessed with catching the fast German surface raiders, which they believed represented the major German threat to Britain's shipping lanes, but it's still difficult to understand why they had failed to appreciate the potential menace of the submarine. The Admiralty had plenty of warning: In May 1913, A. J. Balfour, a former Prime Minister, had written a lengthy letter to Fisher, outlining the vulnerability of Britain's merchant fleet to submarine warfare. The most significant passage of the whole document was Balfour's prescient speculation, "The question that really troubles me is not whether our submarines could render the enemy's position untenable, but whether their submarines could render our position untenable." Fisher—the sole exception among senior British naval officers, the rest of whom had scorned the submarine—summed up his feelings in a paper he submitted to Churchill the following month, saying, "The submarine menace is truly a terrible threat to British commerce. . . . It is freely acknowledged to be an altogether barbarous form of warfare . . . [but] the essence of warfare is violence and moderation in warfare is imbecility."

Fisher's paper shocked the Admiralty. Churchill replied in January 1914, noting there were some points where he did not share Fisher's convictions: "Of these the greatest is the use of submarines to sink merchant vessels. I do not think that this would ever be done by a civilized power." More specifically, the consensus of informed opinion, both political and military, was that it would be impossible for the submarines to conduct a campaign against merchant shipping within the framework of international law—the Cruiser Rules—and that no civilized nation would even consider violating that body of law. The then Second Sea Lord, Prince Louis of Battenberg, concurred, while the Assistant Director of the Operations Division, Herbert Richmont, maintained that the submarine was of "the smallest value of any vessel for the direct attack on trade." It was a point of view that still prevailed in the Admiralty when the war began.[4]

Yet the U-boats gave lie to that concept within weeks of the outbreak of hostilities. They had been acting as commerce raiders since the beginning of the war and were taking a steadily mounting toll of British merchant shipping, doing their best to abide by the accepted practices of international law and trying to observe the Cruiser Rules as closely as possible. Their success, at first almost as little remarked upon in Berlin as in Whitehall, slowly became apparent to the German Naval High Command, and with it came an understanding of the opportunities the submarine offered. The whole of prewar German naval strategy had been directed at breaking through the British blockade and cutting off Britain's supply lines: Should the High Seas Fleet fail to do so, and the British maintain their blockade, then Germany would be forced out of necessity to seek an alternative strategy. None was apparent, because of the cruel trick geography had played on Germany and her navy. But as the U-boats began striking successfully at British merchant ships, it began to dawn on the Germans that here was Germany's opportunity to outflank the British technologically. If geography would deny the High Seas Fleet the opportunity to carry the war to Great Britain, then German technical skill would provide an alternative. No one in the British Admiralty, save Fisher, foresaw the submarine as that alternative. Unfortunately for Britain, Fisher was right.

This pitiful lack of comprehension on the part of the admirals in Whitehall of the strategic implications of submarine warfare, and of the capabilities of the U-boats themselves, is best illustrated by the Admiralty's first defensive measures. Not realizing that the U-boats had the range to sail across the Atlantic without refueling, the Admiralty thought that it could deny them entrance to the Western Approaches and the Irish Sea by stretching a net- and mine-behung boom across the English Channel. Not only was the idea ludicrous, but the execution was an abysmal failure. The U-boats avoided the "Channel Barrage," as it was called, by simply sailing into the North Sea, rounding the Scottish islands, and running down the west coast of Ireland. The only other methods the British had of combating the German submarines were armed patrols and extensive mining.

The armed patrols were Churchill's first response, although at this point, their value was more psychological that tangible. The patrols themselves were usually second-line ships manned mainly by reservists and led by antiquated admirals. For the most part, they were inadequately equipped, ineptly led, and inevitably ineffective. The most potent weapon against the U-boat, the destroyers, were desperately needed to protect the Grand Fleet up in Scapa Flow, or else screen the fleet as it made one of its periodic "sweeps" of the North Sea.

Mining was another story altogether. Great Britain had long made it a policy to oppose mining open waters, one of the most vigorous opponents being Churchill, who rightly called mines "a pollution of the seas," threatening friend, foe, and neutral alike. The Germans, though, had mined the approaches to several of Britain's larger ports in the opening days of the war, essentially presenting the British with a *fait accompli* where mining was concerned. The British responded with a vengeance, the Royal Navy laying nearly 4,000 mines in the waters around the largest German ports. The purpose of these minefields, both German and British, was to discourage merchant ships, friendly or neutral, from using the harbors that the mines obstructed. The British mines, though, were sometimes an embarrassment to the Royal Navy: They didn't seem to be quite sure exactly whose side they were on. Several British minelayers had been damaged when mines went off prematurely after having been laid, and a number of larger German warships sported "dud" British mines on their fo'c'sles or quarterdecks as souvenirs. A more acute problem was that the mines had a tendency to drift, some in the North Sea by as much as twenty miles, justifying Churchill's appellation of "pollution."[5]

The introduction of the large, sometimes overlapping British and German minefields in the Channel and the North Sea caused the implementation of the British blockade to take on a new and sinister twist. Clearly these minefields presented a very real danger to merchant ships sailing in the North Sea, and the British cleverly exploited this danger, using it to tighten the blockade of Germany. As early as mid-August 1914, the Royal Navy had begun stopping neutral ships on the high seas, often seizing their cargoes if the ultimate destination of the goods was Germany, regardless of where the ship was actually bound and without consideration to the ship's nationality. This rather high-handed and arbitrary policy (the decision to seize a ship's cargo or allow it to continue on its way unhindered was entirely at the discretion of the captain of the warship), which the British called the concept of "continuous voyage," brought a squawk of protest from the government of the United States. The American government pointed out that such searches and seizures in international waters were, under international law, utterly illegal, citing the concept that "the flag covers trade"—that is, if a ship carrying cargo belonged to a neutral power, then the cargo was considered neutral until the ship reached port and the cargo unloaded.

At first the British government blithely ignored the American protests, invoking as justification an Order of Council passed by the Cabinet on

August 20, 1914, which ruled that it was the ultimate destination of a cargo—Germany or her allies—and not the destination of the ship carrying it, that determined the right of the Royal Navy to seize it. The order was based on a 1912 report to Parliament by the Imperial Defense Committee that defined the doctrine of "continuous voyage," which was diametrically the opposite of "the flag covers trade" concept within international law. "Continuous voyage" held that the ultimate destination of a cargo determined whether it could be seized, not the destination of the ship; it was a concept that had its origins back in the interminable wars between the French and British during the seventeenth and eighteenth centuries, but it was not universally recognized or accepted. It was definitely not accepted by the government of the United States, and when the American squawk turned into a snarl, His Majesty's Government hurriedly backed off, not wanting to provoke a confrontation with the United States that Britain could ill afford. At the same time, letting all that Yankee shipping sail unhindered through the North Sea was making a mockery of the British blockade, for while the ships were usually bound for ports in Denmark, the Netherlands, or Sweden, the cargoes were more often than not ultimately consigned to Germany.

The North Sea minefields provided the British with the pretext they needed to put the teeth back into their blockade. So on October 12, 1914, the British government, citing the danger to neutral shipping from the errant minefields, declared the whole of the North Sea to be a "military area" and required all ships, regardless of nationality, that intended to enter that area to first report to a British port for instructions on avoiding the minefields. Ships refusing to voluntarily put into a British port would be intercepted by the Royal Navy and escorted in. Once there, the British had every legal right to search the ships, and most cargoes were seized on the spot, because they fell into one or more categories of contraband.

Contraband was a term that the British took considerable liberties with in 1914, and their definitions were of considerable importance to the enforcement of their blockade of Germany. Churchill's role in this, though never clearly defined, had to have been significant, since the implementation of the blockade was his responsibility as First Lord of the Admiralty, while the interpretation and application of international law was very much a political decision, which again placed him at the center of the issue, since his position in the Cabinet as First Lord was a political one. Likewise, the declaration of the North Sea "military area" was both political and military in nature—the announcement of the "military area" was a tacit admission that a blockade of Germany was in effect, although it was not formally announced as such for another month. The blockade was one of the most coldly calculated decisions ever made in modern warfare, and its intent was frighteningly simple: Since

Germany was not self-sufficient in the production of foodstuffs, but rather had to import much of her grain and beef, the Royal Navy was going to starve Germany into submission. Thus the definition of contraband, whether in military or political terms, was of critical importance to the British blockade.

Traditionally, there are three classes of contraband: The first is absolute contraband, the materials of war—munitions and weapons; the second is conditional contraband, goods that have both military and civilian applications, food and cloth being two obvious examples; and the third is noncontraband, items that have no significant military application whatsoever, such as paper and soap. Immediately upon declaring the North Sea a "military area," the British government announced that foodstuffs would be considered absolute contraband, on the grounds that in the event of a food shortage within Germany, troops would be given preference over civilians in the distribution of what food stocks there were. As the war progressed, the list of materials considered to be conditional or noncontraband would continually shrink, as more and more materials were classified by the British as absolute contraband.[6]

But while the mining of the North Sea had allowed the British to put even sharper teeth in their blockade of Germany, it was not an effective method of defense against the U-boats; the German subs simply avoided the areas that were known to be mined. As the rate of merchant sinkings grew, Churchill initiated research into ways of countering the U-boats' technological advantages, although none held any promise of immediate results. Underwater detections systems in 1914 were primitive at best and highly unreliable, so hunting submerged U-boats was a hit-or-miss proposition. Likewise, few weapons were available that were effective underwater that could be used against the submarines—the depth charge was still some two years away.

It had quickly became the standard tactic for U-boat commanders to save their precious torpedoes for warships or unusually large targets and to rely on surface attacks using their deck guns and scuttling charges to dispatch any merchantmen they intercepted and stopped. Typically, the U-boat would approach its intended victim submerged, then suddenly surface close enough that its deck gun couldn't miss, and order the merchantman to stop. Without some means of retaliating, the merchantman would be at the U-boat's mercy. It was at this same time, however, that the U-boat was most vulnerable as well, for the advantages were not all on the side of the U-boat.

The German submarines were small, most of them less than 700 tons, while the average merchant ship weighed about 5,000 tons. The U-boats were far less steady, meaning that their gunnery was far more erratic and, most important of all, damage that would seem negligible to a surface ship could wreak havoc on the submarines' relatively fragile pressure hulls. Simply put, if the merchant ships had some means of striking back at the U-boats, the submarines would quickly find themselves on the defensive. Fortunately for the British, just such a solution was at hand, though it had origins in an unexpected source.

So seriously had the Royal Navy taken the threat of the German surface raiders that in 1913, Churchill had ordered a program started to mount a rudimentary "defensive" armament of two to four medium-caliber guns, along with their associated magazines, shell hoists, and rangefinding apparatus, on a number of British merchant ships that were earmarked as auxiliaries for the fleet in wartime. Other ships had their internal arrangements modified so that conversion to auxiliary cruisers or surface raiders could be accomplished in a matter of days, should war come unexpectedly. Among the ships taken in hand for this was the *Lusitania,* which in May and June 1913 had gun rings, shell hoists, and handling rooms installed and the coal bunker forward of Boiler Room No. 1 converted into a magazine.

Ships that had guns mounted under this program were termed to have been "defensively" armed, and when compared with the possible armament of their German opponents, it was a fair description. The usual complement of guns given to a "defensively armed" merchant ship was a pair—sometimes two pairs—of either 3-inch or 4-inch guns, though occasionally a 6-inch gun might be mounted. Compared to the 4.1-inch and 5.9-inch guns carried by the German raiders, these 3- and 4-inch guns were comparative popguns, and would at best only serve to hold the raider at bay while help from units of the Royal Navy were summoned. But when put up against the single 3.4-inch gun a U-boat mounted, a quartet of 3-inch guns was a formidable battery. Indeed, a single hit from a U-boat's deck gun wouldn't be able to do fatal damage to a merchantman, but a single hit from a 3-inch gun could fatally rupture the U-boat's pressure hull, and a hit from a 6-inch gun would simply blow the submarine out of the water.

Not long after it became recognized that the surface attack was the preferred tactic of the U-boat skippers, it was noticed by some astute junior officer at the Admiralty that ships carrying a "defensive" armament were usually able to force a U-boat to break off its attack, although some U-boat commanders would then simply torpedo the merchant ship. It didn't take long for the Admiralty to realize that if faced with the prospect of surfacing alongside a merchantman, only to find a flurry of 3-, 4-, or even 6-inch shells whistling about their ears, most U-boat crews would either not attack at all or else try to put a torpedo into the side of the offending cargo ship. This would mean that the U-boat would have to attack the merchant vessel without warning and would run a real risk of accidentally attacking a neutral ship.

Naturally, Churchill assumed the credit for this. In his six volume history of the Great War, *The World Crisis,* he wrote: "The first British countermove [against the U-boats], made on my responsibility . . . was to deter the Germans from surface attack. The submerged U-boats had to rely increasingly on underwater attack and thus ran the greater risk of mistaking neutral for British ships and drowning neutral crews and thus embroiling Germany with other Great Powers." While more than a little bit self-serving, since the whole idea of defensive armament was never intended to be an antisubmarine measure, it does sum up Churchill's grasp of the situation, and the program of arming merchant ships was rapidly accelerated. It also hints at the fact that the effort to neutralize the growing U-boat threat brought out darker sides of Churchill's multifaceted character.

From October 1914 onward, a steady stream of orders to British merchant captains issued forth from the Admiralty offices in Whitehall, each of which first had to be approved by Churchill. These orders required the merchant skippers to comply with instructions that systematically deprived their ships of the protections afforded them by the Cruiser Rules, which the Germans had been doing their best to observe. One of the most significant was the ram-on-sight instruction, which made the merchant ship fair game for any method of attack the U-boat chose, and which would make any U-boat commander seriously consider attacking without warning rather than take the risk of being run down.[7]

That the ram-on-sight orders were no idle threat, and why they deprived a merchant ship of its immunity to attack were compellingly demonstrated by the small (500-ton) British steamer *Thordis* on February 28, 1915. Carrying coal to Portsmouth, she was steaming along the south coast of England when she was barely missed by a torpedo that had been fired at her without warning. Apparently deciding that the little freighter wasn't worth a second torpedo, the U-boat surfaced, and the *Thordis* turned toward it and ran it down, severely damaging the submarine's hull, though the U-boat was able to limp back to Wilhelmshaven. The *Thordis's* skipper was promptly rewarded with a Distinguished Service Cross and a commission as a lieutenant in the Royal Navy Reserve, while the sum of £200 was awarded the officers and crew of the little ship. The maritime journal *Syren and Shipping,* which had offered £500 for the destruction of a U-boat by a merchant ship, promptly paid the crew of the *Thordis* as well. That the U-boat survived was unknown to the British, but sight of its crushed conning tower and bent hull taught the Germans a lesson that was profound—if the *Thordis* had been a larger ship, she would have simply ground the U-boat under her keel. The British ram-on-sight orders were no bluff.[8]

This meant that the Germans had to take the other orders they had discovered among the papers captured on the *Ben Cruachan* on January 30, 1915, just as seriously. Among them were two orders that were—and still are—considered so barbaric that it was difficult for the Germans, once they had published their copies of the orders, to convince the world that they were genuine. Coupled with the instructions to ram any U-boat on sight was a memorandum advising on how to deal with prisoners, should any be taken: "Survivors should be taken prisoner—or shot, whichever is more convenient." As for the possibility of a U-boat attempting to surrender rather than risk wholesale destruction: "In all actions, white flags should be fired on with promptitude."

The reasoning behind these orders, which even today causes a shudder of revulsion to run through anyone reading them, has never been explained. It can be reasonably assumed that there was a political aspect to them, since Churchill had made it clear that he had considered the political implications of having armed merchant ships fire on German submarines, forcing the U-boats into an increasing risk of attacking a neutral ship by accident. But the political motives behind the instructions to shoot prisoners or ignore attempts to surrender is far less comprehensible.

Here the whole issue begins to move into murky waters, for it begins to involve not Churchill the First Lord of the Admiralty, but Churchill the politician and Churchill the maker of strategy, roles that to him became easily blurred as to become indistinguishable. Again, in *The World Crisis,* Churchill described how he saw his position as First Sea Lord gave him a particular perspective on how the war was to be fought:

> The distinction between politics and strategy diminishes as the point of view is raised. At the summit, true politics and strategy are one. The maneuver which brings an ally into the field is as serviceable as that which wins a great battle. The maneuver which wins an important strategic point may be less valuable than that which overawes or placates a dangerous neutral.

Churchill's position as First Lord gave him a seat on the War Cabinet, the committee organized by the Prime Minister, Herbert H. Asquith, to formulate strategy for the British armed forces and direct the British war effort. It was not necessarily successful, for Asquith, who was an excellent peacetime Prime Minister, left something to be desired as a wartime leader—specifically, leadership. Asquith's ministerial style was to essentially let the various ministries pursue their own policies and then report to him with results. In peacetime, it was a workable system, but as a way of waging war, it created havoc, as the various ministries competed for priority in resources and materials, and the lack of an overall coordinating strategy meant that Britain's war effort was never sharply focused.

It also meant that Cabinet members like Churchill could formulate policies and implement them without having to have them approved by the whole cabinet first. Certainly it wouldn't be difficult for Churchill to see his position as First Lord as the "summit" he spoke of and begin to combine strategy and politics. The significance of Churchill's observation is that in 1914 there was only one "dangerous neutral" in the world: the United States.

The danger that the United States presented was a very real one to Great Britain, not as a military threat, but rather an economic one. The sheer magnitude of the war had never been anticipated by the British military planners, and not only had Britain's prewar stocks of ammunition proved to be hopelessly inadequate, but her industry lacked the capacity to meet the demand, especially for artillery shells and heavy guns. The War Cabinet had hastily improvised a purchasing committee, composed mainly of civilians, to acquire the necessary materials from manufacturers in the United States or, if necessary, to negotiate contracts for the production of munitions and supplies for the British war effort. Here the British were exploiting a loophole in American neutrality laws, which permitted the sales of arms and munitions to private individuals and businesses, but not to the governments of belligerent powers.

Churchill was well aware of the fact that the British blockade had severely curtailed America's trade with the Scandinavian countries, and of course, Germany was lost as a market to American businesses. He also knew that powerful business interests that were well represented in Congress deeply resented this loss and were entertaining ideas of calling for a ban on the sales of munitions and war materials to anyone, business or government, from any of the warring nations. Should that happen, Britain would be crippled.

But he also knew that the American public in general, and President Wilson in particular, regarded the submarine as a barbaric weapon and were affronted by attacks on neutral ships, especially American ones. Churchill realized that if the Royal Navy could force the U-boats to wage their antishipping campaign in a manner that ran contrary to the accepted rules of warfare—with a little help from suitable British propaganda—then that attitude could be exploited. The Wilson Administration, responding to what was sure to be a rising wave of anti-German indignation among the American people, who would little care about the niceties of international law, would be able to brush aside the protests of the American business interests and ensure the continued flow of supplies to Great Britain. It's important to note here that Churchill wasn't thinking of the United States as a potential ally, but as a constant source of supply for Britain's war effort. It was an important distinction.[9]

The first step, then, was to make sure the German U-boats did not frighten away neutral shipping from the British Isles; instead, the British must strive to do the exact opposite. On February 25, 1915, just ten days after the Germans declared the waters around Great Britain to be a war zone, Churchill had written the president of the Board of Trade, Sir Walter Runciman, "It is most important to attract neutral shipping to our shores, in the hope of embroiling the United States with Germany." In that event, he remarked, "Britain's position for enforcing the blockade would be greatly enhanced" and he "looked forward to a sensible abatement" of the protests from Washington.

The implications of Churchill's statement were staggering: He was favoring, if not actively working toward, creating circumstances where neutral ships—and neutral lives—would be deliberately exposed to destruction in the waters surrounding the British Isles, hoping their destruction would create a rift between Germany and the United States. Yet one of his primary charges as First Lord of the Admiralty—indeed, of the Royal Navy—was the protection of any merchant ship bound for Great Britain, regardless of whether the ship was neutral or British. In truth, the ability to exercise that protection was the essence of sea power, and the raison d'être of the Royal Navy for four hundred years. Setting that responsibility aside in order to achieve a political end—which attempting to incite a confrontation between America and Germany clearly was—was a blending of strategy and politics exactly in the manner Churchill described as appropriate for someone at "the summit," but it also implied a startling, even disturbing, willingness to subordinate the responsibilities of his office to greater ambitions. Even more unsettling, it implied that same callousness toward human life that would cause Sir Edward Henry Carson, the Attorney General, to remark, when referring to the losses on the Western Front, that "the necessary supply of heroes must be maintained at all costs." It was the same attitude that would term the loss of 5,000 men a day during the periods when the communiqués read "All quiet on the Western Front" as "normal wastage."

It wasn't just ships that were being threatened by this attitude, which was well on its way to becoming an informal policy; it was the lives of the sailors manning them. Here the use of nautical and naval terminology may have turned Churchill's head aside from the reality of what he was saying: Admirals and naval planners, shipbuilders and architects, all spoke in terms of "tonnage" and "bottoms" when debating how to best deal with the growing U-boat menace, and the numbers were important. When Balfour wrote questioningly to Fisher "whether [the U-boats] could make our position untenable," he was referring to the possibility that the submarines could sink ships faster than Britain could replace them—sooner or later Britain would run out of ships sufficient to keep her population fed and her armies fighting. But lives were being risked as well, not just the lives of British merchant seamen, which, it could be argued, Churchill had the right to risk by deliberately exposing them to the U-boats: Any vessel of the British merchant marine was subject to Admiralty orders, so it could be said that Churchill was within his legal rights in placing them at risk if he believed it was in the best interest of the British war effort. But also at risk were the lives of the men manning the neutral vessels, who believed that they were being protected by the Royal Navy when they sailed into British waters, but for whom that protection was being slowly and methodically withdrawn in order to achieve a political end.

Nor was it simply the lives of sailors being risked on the ships that were being so cruelly exposed. Passengers—civilians, neutral and belligerent alike —were threatened by the U-boats, and by being systematically forced to sink ships without warning, the U-boats were becoming a larger threat to those civilians with each passing day. Apparently Churchill sensed that there was a threshold to the destruction beyond which no neutral power, and in particular the United States, could be pushed without confronting Germany. It was a dangerous rationalization, for while it was not the same as German *Schreck-licheit*, it was perilously close, as it did amount to using unwilling civilians for military purposes. It was only a few small steps away from being the very thing that Great Britain had said she had gone to war to combat.

The consequences, real and potential, of this idea of deliberate exposure, as well as just how willing the Admiralty was to distort the truth in order to influence American opinion, were clearly demonstrated by Whitehall's handling of what became known as "the *Gullflight* incident." On May 1, 1915, the British patrol ships *Filey* and *Iago* intercepted the American tanker *Gull-flight* off the Scilly Isles, near the western tip of England at Land's End. Something about the tanker made the captain of the *Filey* suspicious—there had been a German submarine patrolling the area, and he suspected that the *Gullflight* had secretly rendezvoused with the U-boat and refueled it. The tanker was ordered to accompany the *Filey* and *Iago* into the nearest port, St. Mary's. The *Filey* took station ahead of the *Gullflight*, the *Iago* falling in on the tanker's port quarter. At this point, the *Gullflight* became a ship under convoy, nominally a British ship—a seemingly fine point, but as such, she could be attacked without warning by a U-boat. Less than an hour later, the *U-30*, under the command of Kapitan von Rosenberg-Grusczynski, spotted the trio of ships, and seeing the White Ensign of the Royal Navy flying from the *Filey's* mast, he mistook the tanker to be British and under convoy—a legitimate target that did not require warning under the Cruiser Rules. Nevertheless, von Rosenberg surfaced and ordered the trio of ships to halt. The *Filey* put her helm over and tried to ram the *U-30*, but von Rosenberg crash dived, and the *Filey* missed.

Coming back up to periscope depth, von Rosenberg put a torpedo into the side of the *Gullflight*, then seconds later noticed a small American flag flying at her stern and immediately broke off the attack. The torpedo did relatively little damage—tankers are notoriously tough ships—but in the confusion, two of the *Gullflight's* crewmen jumped overboard and were drowned. Later that night, as the three ships were entering St. Mary's harbor, the *Gullflight*'s captain had a heart attack and died.

The Admiralty was in an uproar. Releasing the full story to the public would make the Royal Navy look incompetent, and it was certainly questionable whether the Americans would take kindly to the suggestion that one of their ships had been suspected of supplying fuel to a U-boat. Adding insult to injury was the finding of a hastily convened board of inquiry within the Admiralty that stated that the *U-30* had acted entirely in accordance with the Cruiser Rules and had every right to torpedo the *Gullflight*, since the ship was technically under convoy by the Royal Navy. If word leaked out that this was the sort of protection the Royal Navy could provide neutrals, no foreign ship would be coming anywhere near the British Isles.

Churchill quickly and quietly buried the inquiry's report and instead had a very highly colored and imaginative version of the events released to the public. It told of the *Gullflight*'s being attacked without warning or provocation, while the *Iago* and *Filey*, who just happened to be in the area, came dashing to the rescue, but not before the *Gullflight* had been engulfed in a hail of shells from the *U-30*. Even more dastardly was the way the U-boat torpedoed the tanker while the crewmen were desperately trying to take to the lifeboats, their captain having been killed by shellfire. The unfortunate American tanker was only saved when the *Iago* and *Filey* drove the *U-30* away, then was escorted by them to safety in St. Mary's harbor. While the whole incident—which did lead to some tense moments between Germany and the United States—would soon be completely overshadowed by even more ominous events, it is instructive in showing how willing the Admiralty was to indulge in pure fabrication to influence public opinion in the United States.[10]

Churchill, meanwhile, was devoting the majority of his attention and energy to the Dardanelles. Since early February 1915, when the plan to force the Turkish straits had been mooted, planning for the attack took up more and more of his time and attention. The U-boat campaign was never far from his mind, but the Dardanelles had increasing priority, especially in March and April, as the naval bombardments took place and the landings began; by the first week of May, the Gallipoli campaign had subordinated every other responsibility Churchill had at the Admiralty, for by then he was not only trying to salvage an operation whose plans were quickly unraveling, but he was also fighting for political survival, as critics of the Dardanelles sought a scapegoat for the failure.

Certainly the *Lusitania* was the last thing on his mind. The last time it is known for certain that he paid specific attention to her was in September 1914, when he met with Leonard Peskett in Liverpool to discuss the usefulness of the *Lusitania* and *Mauretania* to the Royal Navy. Peskett reviewed the work done on the *Lusitania* in May 1913: the entire length of the Shelter Deck (D Deck) had been double plated for additional protection; the reserve coal bunker forward of Boiler Room Number 1 converted into a magazine; a similar conversion to part of the Mail Room; and four gun rings installed, two forward, two aft, on the specially designed deck platforms—all that would be necessary for the guns to be mounted would be for a dockyard crane to lift the guns into position and secure them to the deck. With obvious pride, Peskett detailed the ships' design and construction, concluding with the words, "The Royal Navy hasn't got anything like them!"

"Yes, we have," Churchill retorted. He had been struck by the similarity in the two liners' design to the three cruisers *Hogue, Aboukir,* and *Cressy*—in particular, the vulnerable longitudinal coal bunkers along their sides. "To me, they're each just another 43,000 tons of livebait!" The next day, September 24, the Admiralty informed Cunard that the *Mauretania* would be requisitioned for conversion to a troopship, but that the Royal Navy had no further use for the *Lusitania.*[11]

CHAPTER 5

The President
and the Secretary

By September 1914, there was only one "dangerous neutral" that might need to be "placated or overawed," that being the United States of America. It was a remarkable nation, possibly the most peculiar and idiosyncratic on earth. Certainly, in the beginning of the twentieth century, it was a far different nation than it would be at the end of it.

America was a young nation, at once conscious of its youth and self-conscious because of it. It many ways, the country resembled an adolescent: It was boisterous, crude, compassionate, visionary, suspicious, energetic, and self-righteous. Certainly it was an innocent country, curiously homogenous in its origins, and far from being the "land of opportunity" it would one day become. That would happen after the end of the Great War, as the conflict in Europe had come to be called, along with the beginnings of the great flood of immigrants from eastern and southern Europe that would change the demographics of America's population permanently. In 1914, out of a population of nearly one hundred million people, more than two-thirds of them were descended from northern and western European stock, mainly Anglo-Saxon. The average income for middle-class families was less than $500 a year, for farmers half of that.

Like an adolescent beginning to feel the first physical, emotional, and mental stirrings of adulthood, America was beginning to become aware of the world around her, particularly Europe, and realizing that she could not remain as blithely aloof as she had for nearly a century and a half. It was an awareness that the American people did not necessarily welcome or embrace. Certainly, like most adolescents feel toward their elders, most Americans were very self-conscious and felt a marked sense of inferiority toward Europe and Europeans. These feelings were manifested in different ways, and determined largely by social class. The upper class tried to compensate for their perceived inadequacies by slavishly aping the styles, manners, and mannerisms of the

European aristocracy—particularly that of England—usually carrying the imitation to an excess that became a parody. It was undeniably a time marked by money grubbing and ostentation on the part of the American upper class, when "excess" and "success" became interchangeable. Less than one-tenth of the population of the United States controlled three-quarters of the nation's money, while more than a handful of American millionaires had accumulated fortunes greater than the world had ever seen. These same Americans were better at making money than at spending it. Like most *nouveau riche,* their hallmark was conspicuous consumption, with little discrimination or taste. They had more money than they knew what to do with, and the desire of American plutocrats to spend lavishly, coupled with a sense of insecurity due to the very rapidity with which most of them had made their fortunes, drove them to imitate their European cousins.

It was inevitable that this upstart leisure class should be drawn to the greatest city in the world at the time—London. Finding themselves amidst a kindred people, these wealthy Americans discovered what they craved—and what America as a nation and the humility of their individual births could not hope to give them: the pomp and grandeur of a 1,200-year-old monarchy, with all the stability, nobility, and grace that were its trappings; the company of men and women who carelessly and comfortably wore names and titles that were a part of history; and a society that was relaxed, mature, and secure in its own longevity. The American plutocrats attempted to apply a thin veneer of this civility over their own rough-and-tumble origins in hopes of concealing them. Richard O'Connor commented on this peculiarly American phenomenon, observing that "the newly minted gentlemen had worked with pick and shovel on arrival, and their ladies had bent over their washboards; but all that was crammed into a forgotten attic of the past."

The middle class, for the most part, showed disdain for Europe and the Europeans. Sometimes removed from their immigrant origins by only two or three generations, sometimes by a dozen, they generally regarded Europe as wicked and decadent, the war being fought there just another example of the sort of petty dynastic squabble gone wrong that their ancestors had had the good sense to leave behind. They were the factory managers and supervisors, doctors, craftsmen, small businessmen, bank clerks, accountants, brokers, bookkeepers, merchants, and shopkeepers, who, along with their wives and families, guarded their social station with as much determination as the upper class did theirs. Smugly self-righteous, they were obsessed with respectability—always watchful not to say or do something that even hinted at a lack of good manners or proper breeding, or would somehow suggest that the individual involved was actually nothing more than a puffed-up member of the working class.

As a result, they embraced the values of patriotism, education, hard work, and piety, and took a perverse pride in their propriety. Often they would even be stolid and unimaginative, but they were hardly docile: The Progressive movement, a semiradical wing of the Democratic Party that preached a platform of social reform aimed at curtailing the power of big business and the American plutocrats, had garnered a surprising amount of support from the middle class. The Progressives had demanded changes in the laws setting standards for education, wage controls, regulation of the length of the workday and workweek, more stringent safety and child labor laws, and protection for the American farmers from foreign competition. They inhabited row upon row of neat, tidy houses, each with its own back garden, where in season, narcissus, roses, jasmine, daffodils, and tulips would bloom and their children would play after school.

Then there was the working class, who lived in the industrial cities of the Northeast and the Midwest—Boston, New York, Philadelphia, Pittsburgh, Detroit, Cleveland, Chicago, St. Louis, and Kansas City, where the vistas were of seemingly endless corrugated-iron factory roofs and stockyards, forests of belching smokestacks, gantries and hoists of the pitheads, and endless warrens of sooty red brick or wood frame row houses that gave shelter to the men, women, and children who toiled their lives away in the textile mills, coal mines, or steel works. These cities were the economic backbone of the United States.

In all of these cities, the row houses had deteriorated to slums, where a family of eight might share two beds and a pair of thin blankets among them, with little or nothing in the way of sanitary facilities, and subsist on an inadequate diet that left the children stunted, pale, and apathetic. Few children completed even the most basic education. By the age of eight, they would be working, usually in a textile mill, where their small and nimble fingers were best suited to work amid fast-moving mechanisms. Wages were rarely more than a few dollars a week, and injuries and fatalities involving a child snatched into the maw of a great weaving or spinning machine were commonplace and considered unremarkable by management, since replacements were always readily at hand.

The adults fared little better, often working in mine shafts or before vast, open-hearth steel mills for as little as ten cents an hour, in twelve-hour shifts with no lunch break (lunches were eaten at the workplace), seven days a week. Taking a day off without permission in advance could result in a worker being dismissed without warning. Disease was rife, chiefly tuberculosis, and limited and meager diets often resulted in stunted bodies and minds. What most workers today take for granted were the merest pipe dreams: Paid holidays, health care, pensions, and sick leave were ideas that hadn't yet been formulated, let alone articulated.

The labor unions had made some inroads in alleviating the worst of the workers' lot, but poverty and its accompanying deprivations were still the rule in most industrial workers' lives. A blacklist even existed in some industries: A worker dismissed for labor agitation could be barred from rehire, sometimes just within the industry, sometimes in the entire city. To souls such as these, the war in Europe was of little interest, and though they could be as patriotic as any scion of the middle class, often there were strong anti-British sentiments, especially in cities where there was a significant Irish population, such as Boston, or a large German community, such as St. Louis or Cincinnati.

But far and away the largest segment of the American population was the farming community. In 1914, three out of every four Americans worked in agriculture—the great migration to the industrial cities wouldn't begin for another decade. The farmers' world was the world of the open prairie, endless horizons of gently rolling farmland, the true "amber waves of grain," interspersed with woodlands of white pine, spruce, and beech, stands of birch, walnut, and oak. Here men would listen for the call of the blackbird and the robin, the blue jay and the mockingbird, and sharpen the blades of their reapers in anticipation of the fall harvest. Here life moved to a rhythm little changed for decades, a world of farmers, ranchers, blacksmiths, and tanners— men who rose and retired with the sun. Their work was hard, for the mechanization of the American farmland was only beginning. They worked the land and tended their animals much as their great-great-grandfathers had. Occasionally a stolen afternoon would be spent fishing for trout in a nearby stream, and most evenings would find the men gathered around the kitchen table with their families for dinner, often ended with a reading from the family Bible before the children went out to play for a few hours before darkness fell—but always there would be an ear cocked to the wind, an eye glancing at the sky, for all it took was one of those terrible Great Plains thunderstorms to roll in from the west and wash away an entire spring's planting or sweep away a herd of cattle in a sudden flood. It was a world undisturbed by the comings and goings of the rich and powerful, and it had precious few summers left.

This first decade of the twentieth century was the culmination of a hundred years of the most accelerated rate of change in society and technology that mankind had ever known. Between 1812 and 1912, humanity had gone from transportation, communication, production, and manufacturing methods powered by human or animal muscles, augmented by wind and water, to a world of steam engines, steamships, steam-powered machinery—and more and more frequently, of machines powered by internal combustion engines. The new century was one of electric lighting and communications, though as yet electricity was common only in the cities, and then only in the middle- and upper-class areas.

In less than a century, mankind's rate of travel overland had more than trebled, while at sea it had more than quadrupled. Where in 1812 the best speed a traveler could hope for would be perhaps twenty miles an hour in a horse-drawn coach, a railway passenger in 1912 would routinely reach speeds approaching seventy miles an hour on an express. A trip across the North Atlantic that once took more than a month was now accomplished in a week or less, and with a degree of safety and comfort unimaginable a few generations before.

The accelerating rate of change was most marked in the last decade. In 1900, there had been less than 8,000 automobiles in the entire United States, but by 1910, there were close to a half million. In 1903, the first flight of a heavier-than-air craft lasted twelve seconds and covered 852 feet; in 1909, Louis Bleriot had flown across the English Channel, a distance of twenty-six miles. The years between 1900 and 1910 had seen the introduction of the phonograph, wireless telegraphy, turbine-powered steamships, the electric light, the telephone, the original Kodak "Brownie" camera, heavier-than-air flying machines, motion pictures—all of them as reliable apparatus rather than mere technical novelties. Though they were rarities for most Americans, these devices and inventions were spreading rapidly and would eventually change the face of the nation.

But the real sense of what America was like in the autumn of 1914 lay in the details, in the day to day minutiae of living. A loaf of bread cost ten cents, a newspaper was a penny. The country's favorite motion picture was David W. Griffith's *The Birth of a Nation,* and admission was a nickel. Professional baseball had established itself as the national pastime, the leading teams being the New York Yankees and the Washington Athletics in the American League; the Yankees' cross-town rivals, the New York Giants, behind the pitching of the legendary Christie Mathewson, were contesting the Philadelphia Phillies for top spot in the National League.

While in every city there were still masses of pushcarts, hansom cabs, horse-drawn trolleys, and deliverymen's drays, the number of automobiles and gasoline-engine-powered trucks on city streets and rural roads was growing daily. The automobiles of the day are frequently presented as the playthings of the idle rich, and there is an element of truth in that depiction: An Overland 6 cost $1,475, a Cole tourer went for $1,785, while a Pierce Arrow ("Ask the man who owns one") was a hefty $2,043—more than four times the average annual income of middle-class household. But there were also cars like the Maxwell, sturdy and dependable, if nothing spectacular, which sold for $685, and Henry Ford was unwittingly beginning to transform America into the most automobile-dependent society in the world by selling his Model T for $490 and offering time-payment plans to buyers.

The advertising slogan of the Pierce Arrow was highly illuminating: It didn't say, "Ask the man or woman who owns one." To most Americans, men and women alike, the idea that a woman would actually own an automobile herself, or even have much say in the family decision to buy one, was absurd. Equally absurd was the idea that women were emotionally or intellectually qualified to vote, despite the ardent, sometimes strident, rhetoric of the leaders of the women's suffrage movement. The support for the "suffragettes," as they were called, ran hot and cold with the American public, influenced as much by events as by the merits of the arguments for and against women having the vote. The sinking of the *Titanic* in 1912, for example, had been a sore blow to the suffragettes, as their opponents, playing to the romantic notion of the gallant men standing aside to allow "women and children first" into the lifeboats, declaring that those who wanted the vote for women were "willing to allow men to die for them, but not vote for them." At other times, "votes for women" had attracted the attention of national figures as prominent as former President Theodore Roosevelt.[1]

Roosevelt attracted attention no matter what he did. Though his politics weren't always popular, he was. Having caused a devastating split in the Republican party when he broke with his former protégé, William Howard Taft—a split that cost Taft reelection to the presidency in 1912 and instead resulted in a Democratic victory that put Woodrow Wilson in the White House—Roosevelt continued his "larger-than-life" existence. At the moment, he was adding unexpected life to what should have been a fairly boring libel suit in Syracuse, New York. An upstate New York political boss, William Barnes, Jr., had decided he didn't much care for being called "a crook" by Roosevelt and sued for damages. It was a mistake. Barnes's chief counsel, William M. Ivins, had boasted to Elihu Root, who had been Secretary of State under Taft, that he was going to "nail Roosevelt's hide the fence." Root's reply was a warning to Ivins to "be very sure it's his hide you get on that fence."

Root knew his man: Roosevelt found the witness stand to be as "bully" a pulpit as the presidency had been. He turned his testimony into speeches— good speeches, too—railing against corruption in American politics, expounding on the Progressive movement, deriding President Wilson's diplomacy in Latin America, and advocating America's entry into the war in Europe. Roosevelt always made good copy, and before too long, the libel trial in Syracuse had driven the war off the front pages of the newspapers.

Roosevelt was particularly qualified to comment on the current state of American foreign policy, as he had been instrumental in guiding the United States into the unaccustomed position of a world power. Shielded for a century behind the Monroe Doctrine, which declared that European nations had no right to interfere in the internal affairs of the nations of the New World, the United States had expended the same expansionist energies that drove the British, French, Belgians, and Germans to build world empires in Africa and Asia to spread and sprawl across the American continent. It may or may not have been coincidence that the closing of the American frontier came just a few short years before the United States' first exercise in world power, the Spanish-American War of 1898.

That war, fought equally for enlightened selflessness and economic self-interest, had turned the United States into a colonial, imperial power. (Significantly, Roosevelt had been the Assistant Secretary of the Navy in the crucial months before the war and been one of the most vocal and insistent advocates of military intervention to a reluctant President William McKinley.) Flexing naval and military muscle it never really knew it had, the United States defeated the Spanish in every engagement they fought, land and sea, in a space of four months. The peace treaty with Spain had ceded all of the Spanish possessions in the New World, most importantly Cuba, to the United States, as well as giving over the entire Philippine archipelago in the Pacific. The role of colonial overlord at first didn't sit well with the American people, who recalled that their own nation's history had begun as the result of abuses of power in a handful of colonies by a distant government. When Theodore Roosevelt became president after the assassination of William McKinley in 1901, he provided a new voice and a new vision of the role America would play in the world.

Roosevelt expounded what became known as the "Roosevelt corollary" to the Monroe Doctrine: While no European nation had the right to interfere with events in the New World, the United States did have that right—and as Roosevelt often interpreted it, the duty as well. This new policy allowed him, for example, to support the province of Panama's bid for independence from Colombia in 1904—a revolution that, oddly enough, occurred at the same time that Roosevelt proposed an American-built and controlled canal across the Panamanian isthmus, an idea the government of Colombia was lukewarm toward at best. Roosevelt developed a foreign policy that bore a remarkable resemblance to old-fashioned European imperialism, exploiting the resources of Central and South America and using the United States' economic strength to influence the internal politics of the Latin American nations. When William Howard Taft, Roosevelt's hand-picked, carefully groomed protégé, was elected to the presidency in 1908, this policy was continued, although by this time it was labeled somewhat derisively as "dollar diplomacy."[2]

Woodrow Wilson abhorred "dollar diplomacy"; to him it was imperialism, pure and simple, and imperialism went against every principle that Wilson had. He had plenty of them and was in a position to make them count for more than most people could. Thomas Woodrow Wilson was the twenty-eighth president of the United States. He was born in Virginia in 1856, the son of a Presbyterian minister who later became a professor at Columbia Theological Seminary. By all accounts, he had a reasonably happy childhood, and the clerical and academic influences of his early years would remain powerful motivating forces throughout the rest of his life. He was educated at Davidson College, Princeton University, and the University of Virginia, where he studied law. His legal career was brief, however, as barely a year after he had set up his practice in Atlanta, Georgia, he gave it up to study government at Johns Hopkins University, where he earned his doctorate in government.

Wilson seemed to have found his niche in academics, for he spent the next twenty-five years on the faculty of some well-known college or major university. From 1885 to 1888, he was professor of history and political science at Bryn Mawr College; the next two years he spent as professor of history and political economy at Wesleyan University; and in 1890, he returned to Princeton, this time as a professor of jurisprudence and political economy. It was at Princeton that Wilson began to demonstrate some of the talents and skills that would carry him to the White House: He developed a reputation as a witty and engaging lecturer, and he produced several books and articles on international politics and economics that, while scholarly and respectable, were far from dry and dull. Princeton also allowed Wilson an opportunity to let his administrative abilities show: Chosen president of the university in 1902, he began a series of reforms—not only of the university hierarchy, but also of the curricula—that made Princeton one of the most progressive universities of the day.

It was this talent for meaningful reform that caught the attention of the Democratic party leadership in the state of New Jersey. Wilson had never expressed a preference for either party, Republican or Democrat, but he detested the "machine" system that dominated New Jersey politics. It had been several years since the Democratic party had been able to field a strong candidate for governor in the state, and when the Democrats approached Wilson in 1910 with the idea of running for state office, it was a challenge he couldn't turn down. Campaigning vigorously, Wilson soon outshone the lackluster Republican candidate and won the election for governor by a plurality of 49,000 votes. Though his strongest backing within the party had come from the conservative Democrats, Wilson soon demonstrated that he disliked being beholden to anyone and guided a liberal reform program through the New Jersey legislature. Provisions of the program made it clear how broad Wilson's vision was: They included a direct-primary law, a corrupt-practices act, an employer's liability act, the creation of a public utilities commission, and the regulation of trusts.[3]

His impact on New Jersey, both political and economic, made him a contender for the Democratic nomination for president in 1912, though by no means the leading candidate. Wilson's reputation carried only so much weight in the Midwest, where William Jennings Bryan was regarded as the champion of the farmers and the working class. Consequently, when the convention met in June 1912, it soon became hopelessly deadlocked over its choice of candidate. The deadlock continued for a week until Bryan finally put his support behind Wilson, who was then quickly nominated.

The presidential election campaign of 1912 was one of the more curious in history and wouldn't have a parallel for another eighty years. Theodore Roosevelt and William Taft had split the Republican party—Taft had grown tired of simply being Roosevelt's puppet, and Roosevelt had little, if any, confidence in Taft's ability to think and act for himself. Both men stood as candidates for the presidency, Taft as the Republican nominee, Roosevelt for the newly created "Bull Moose" party. The split broke up what had been a formidable block of voters. Had the Republicans maintained their unity, Wilson would have had little chance of being elected. As it was, although he won a landslide in the electoral college, 435 votes to the combined total for Taft and Roosevelt of 96, he received almost a million fewer votes in the popular vote totals than did his two opponents. It was a weakness he was acutely aware of.

All the same, that didn't prevent Wilson from pursuing a reform program in Washington as aggressive as the one he had championed in New Jersey. The legislation Wilson would introduce or sponsor was as varied and wide ranging as the Federal Child-Labor Law, the Clayton Anti-trust Act, repeal of the Panama Canal tolls, the La Follette Seaman's Act, and the establishment of the Federal Trade Commission, along with the Federal Reserve. His administration also negotiated and signed thirty treaties establishing equitable trade relationships, mainly with Latin American countries that Wilson felt had been exploited by his predecessors' manipulative policies.

The burgeoning American industrial juggernaut that had driven Roosevelt's and Taft's policy of "dollar diplomacy," which Wilson so deplored, presented the Allies with the solution to a looming crisis of their own but in the process created diplomatic ones for Wilson. The war had strained the industries of Britain, France, and Russia to the breaking point, as the demand for shells, guns, rifles, and every conceivable kind of military equipment outstripped the capacity of Allied factories to meet it. The United States' economy was already growing at a fantastic rate—within half a century its potential output would dwarf the entire production capacity of Western Europe. In 1914, its untapped reserves could be used to make up the deficiency that French and British industries, straining at every fiber of their being, simply could not remedy. That the Allies would turn to American industry was inevitable.

That they did was a diplomatic nightmare for Wilson's administration, as it created a very real possibility that America's neutrality could be compromised. Neutrality was fundamental to Wilson's developing vision of the United States becoming the arbitrating power in the European war, and he was determined to conduct American neutrality according to the precepts of international law as he understood them. Strict neutrality, at least as Wilson believed it should be practiced, was, simply put, quite impossible: The relative industrial strengths of the Central Powers and the Allies, as well as the peculiar nature of the war at sea, had put America in a "damned if she did, damned if she didn't" position.

By the time the autumn leaves began falling in 1914, it was painfully evident to the Asquith government that the only way the Allies could make up the shortfall in production of munitions and war materials was to have them manufactured in the United States. The longer the Cabinet studied the problem, the more obvious it became that it would be several months, possibly more than a year, before British industries would be able to supply the demands of Britain's own armed forces, let alone provide assistance to French industries. The need to keep the Russian armies supplied only made the problem worse.

For Germany, there was no such problem. By the time the Armistice was signed in November 1918, the immense arms forges of Krupp of Essen and Austria-Hungary's sprawling Skoda works would provide the German and Austrian armies with more guns, grenades, and ammunition than they could use. Consequently, there was no necessity for Germany to even consider buying war material from the United States. This is where the dilemma began for Wilson: One side needed access to American industry, the other did not, and so selling or not selling munitions to any of the belligerent powers became an issue that threatened American neutrality, along with Wilson's hopes for a role in arbitrating a peace settlement.

Under international law, a neutral state wishing to sell weapons and supplies to warring powers must make them available to all belligerents; otherwise, that nation could not maintain its neutral status. Choosing who it would and would not sell to was tantamount to taking sides, and the would-be neutral could be regarded as a belligerent power even though no declaration of war had been made or hostile act had taken place. In the case of the United States, should President Wilson decide to permit the sale of arms, the only benefactors would be Britain, France, and, indirectly, Russia. Even if Germany had wanted to purchase munitions, the annihilation of the German merchant marine in the opening weeks of the war meant that no American-made war material would have reached the Fatherland.

The other side of the coin presented similar difficulties for Wilson: Should he forbid the sale of any and all war materials, Germany would clearly benefit, as the Allied war effort would be crippled by a lack of supply. The upshot of the situation was that either alternative would observe the letter of international law, while at the same time rendering the spirit of the law meaningless—and compromising American neutrality. To Woodrow Wilson, maintaining both the spirit of the law and American neutrality were just as important as observing the letter of the law. To find a workable solution to the dilemma, Wilson turned, however reluctantly, to his Secretary of State, William Jennings Bryan.[4]

It's been said that politics makes for strange bedfellows, and if that is true, then Wilson and his Secretary of State may have been the strangest political bedfellows in American history. In complete contrast to Wilson, with his neat, analytical mind and methods, William Jennings Bryan was an emotional, even passionate man who often let his feelings dictate his actions. He was the leading Populist politician in the country, championing the cases and causes of the farmers and the working class against big businesses and banking interests. Three times he was nominated as the Democratic candidate for President, and though he was defeated all three times, he remained a powerful figure in the Democratic Party. In some parts of the country, especially the Midwest, Bryan was considered to be just as important a figure in the Wilson administration as the President himself.

Bryan was born in Salem, Illinois, in 1860, and studied law at Union College in Chicago. He built a remarkably successful legal career, first in Illinois, then later in Nebraska, achieving a reputation as a brilliant courtroom lawyer. His political career began in 1891, when he first went to Washington, D.C., as a congressman from Nebraska. In the capital, his remarkable rhetorical gifts soon attracted attention, and he began to become a force to be reckoned with among the Democrats.

Bryan first achieved national prominence in 1896, when he was a delegate to the Democratic National Convention for the state of Nebraska. Speaking in favor of a currency reform called bimetallism, which would have greatly benefited the working class and farmers but was strongly opposed by business interests for various arcane economic reasons, Bryan took an aggressively Populist stand. Addressing the delegates, Bryan at one point threw his arms open and cried out, "You shall not crucify the common man on this cross of gold!"—and created an instant sensation. The speech was immediately dubbed "the Cross of Gold speech" and printed in full in every major newspaper in the country. Bryan's popularity, both within the party and with the public, skyrocketed, and Bryan found himself the Democratic nominee for president. He lost to William McKinley—the mood of the country was overwhelmingly Republican at the time—but he had firmly established himself on the American political landscape.

Bryan would again be his party's standard-bearer in 1900 and 1908—he knew better than to run in 1906 against Teddy Roosevelt, who was the only man who could be rightly said to be a better speechmaker than Bryan—but lost both times as well. In 1912, he played a decisive role in the nomination of Woodrow Wilson. The convention had gone through forty-six votes to find a nominee without success and seemed hopelessly deadlocked. Bryan suddenly announced that he was willing to shift his support to Wilson and instruct the delegates committed to him to vote for Wilson instead. The deadlock was broken, Wilson was nominated, and when he was elected, he owed Bryan a huge political debt. He offered Bryan the post of Secretary of State, which Bryan accepted with alacrity.

In so many ways, Bryan was the complete antithesis of Wilson. While Wilson was correct and austere, Bryan was warm and engaging; Wilson was always impeccably turned out, while Bryan often appeared slightly rumpled; Wilson was reserved, meticulous, and tidy, while Bryan was emotional, often unconcerned with details, and usually surrounded by a wealth of clutter. The two men were the physical embodiment of their origins—the aristocratic Wilson the scion of the eastern establishment, the passionate Bryan the product of the American Midwest.

The war in Europe eventually opened up an irreparable rift between Wilson and Bryan, but at the beginning of the conflict, both men sought to maintain America's position as a neutral power. What set Bryan apart from Wilson, and indeed from the majority of his fellow politicians, and what would ultimately cost him his office, was that he was a dedicated pacifist who believed that war was humanity's ultimate horror, one to be avoided at any cost, not just when it was politically or economically expedient. Bryan was a man with deeply held Christian beliefs, which he brought to bear in carrying out his duties as Secretary of State.

He believed along with Wilson that it was America's duty to be as impartial as possible, adhering to the letter and spirit of international law. But Bryan was careful to avoid the pro-Allied leanings to which Wilson seemed to be susceptible, and he took pains to repeatedly point out to Wilson that Great Britain's violations of international law were as least as frequent and flagrant as Germany's. The two men agreed that it was America's duty to occupy the moral high ground in its aloofness from the war, allowing the United States to be able to approach both sides as an "honest broker" and bring about a negotiated peace. But Wilson also believed that many of Germany's actions, most pointedly Germany's methods of subduing the civilian population in occupied Belgium, were a threat to the moral foundation of Western civilization, and that Germany should somehow be reprimanded or punished for her conduct.

To Bryan, this was not America's responsibility, at least not until warring powers agreed to stop fighting and accept a negotiated peace. Bryan argued that the only way the United States could be acceptable to all of the warring powers was if the American government was scrupulous in observing complete neutrality: Passing judgment on the actions of one side or the other would only weaken American credibility. Though Wilson essentially agreed with Bryan's position, he could never embrace it wholeheartedly, as his own pro-Allied bias caused him to view Germany's actions with far greater suspicion than those of the Allies.

In producing a working interpretation of American neutrality laws, though, Wilson was more than satisfied with Bryan's solution. Bryan's approach was, to say the least, novel: By eliminating governments as agents for the purchase of war materials, any transactions for supplies or munitions would have to be carried out as private business ventures. This was what Bryan proposed—that no agency of any of the warring powers be allowed to acquire any kind of war material from suppliers in the United States. Instead, private individuals or businesses could purchase munitions and supplies as if they were ordinary business transactions. The American government would not be involved in any way except to enforce the appropriate laws regarding shipping and handling of dangerous munitions—otherwise, government participation by any of the belligerent powers, as well as that of the American government, was prohibited. It was to be understood that the American government assumed no liability for the rights of the purchaser, shipper, or the contents of any cargo. Contraband cargoes could be seized by the Royal Navy in the course of enforcing the British blockade of Germany, while ships bound for Britain were vulnerable to being intercepted and sunk by German raiders. In neither case would the American government be in any way responsible, since the cargoes were technically private property.

Unique as this interpretation was, in all respects it stood as a truly neutral decision. It removed the American government from any complicity in the sale of arms and munitions, while it theoretically allowed the Germans the same access to American supplies that the French and British had. Admittedly, this equality was abstract, since the destruction of the German merchant marine made it practically impossible for the Central Powers to import American arms. Even so, when Wilson endorsed Bryan's interpretation and this decision was communicated to the capitals of the warring nations in mid-September 1914, the German government accepted the arrangement for what it was, an attempt to preserve America's neutral status, and regarded it as legal and proper. As for the British, they had demonstrated in their August 20, 1914, Order of Council that they regarded the convolutions of American neutrality laws as merely minor obstacles, to be evaded, sidestepped, or defied as need be, but clearly this decision was perfectly acceptable to them.[5]

There was, however, a joker in the pack, an individual who would influence events in ways beyond which he ever anticipated or desired, ruthlessly manipulating people to satisfy his own ambition and greed, while never realizing that he was being manipulated himself: the American Assistant Secretary of State, Robert Lansing. Lansing was one of those peculiar individuals, fortunately rare, in whom some redeeming quality is desperately sought and never found. He was a lawyer who had specialized in the settlement of territorial and boundary disputes. He first came to be noticed within the State Department when, in the early 1890s, he negotiated a series of boundary settlements for several European and American trading ports on the Chinese mainland. His entry into the circles of Washington power and politics was eased by his marriage in 1892 to Eleanor Foster, the daughter of John W. Foster, who had been the Secretary of State under President William Harrison. His father-in-law provided introductions to several of the corporations he had joined since leaving public office, introductions that in turn lead to Lansing becoming acquainted with several Wall Street brokerages. A key to understanding his character can be found in his overwhelming Anglophilia, going so far as to habitually wear tweeds and taking "elocution lessons" to develop an "English" accent. His papers—especially his diaries—give an inescapable impression of someone who was always slightly phony, always looking for the main chance and the sharp practice, while trying to maintain a facade of propriety and respectability. He was a man who could always be counted on to do what was best for the United States *and* Robert Lansing, though not always in that order.

Lansing's appointment in a Democratic administration was rather unusual—he was, after all, a Republican. It had been made as a favor to Sen. Elihu Root of New York. Bryan, suspicious of Lansing from the beginning, opposed Lansing's appointment, citing as grounds that "there are substantial reasons to believe Mr. Lansing has been guilty of impropriety in receiving financial benefit from commercial interests" while still a junior lawyer in the State Department. Root intervened directly with Wilson, who overrode Bryan's objections, and Lansing was duly appointed. Lansing, for his part, cordially detested Bryan and secretly coveted his position.

Bryan did find Lansing useful, if not likable. By temperament, the passionate Bryan was often unsuited to the task of drafting diplomatic notes and memoranda, filled as they were with circumlocutions and subliminal meanings. This was something Lansing excelled at, having learned the subtleties of negotiation and diplomatic language while settling boundary disputes in China. Lansing also frequently prepared memoranda for Bryan and Wilson that they used to formulate policy: It was Lansing who had provided Bryan with the legal basis for his interpretation of American neutrality laws when he informed Bryan that "the President possesses no legal authority to interfere in any way with the trade between the people of the United States and the nationals of belligerent countries." This allowed Bryan to absolve the American government of any responsibility for the actions of private businesses buy-ing or selling munitions. Despite—or perhaps because of—Bryan's respect for his work, which he regarded separately from his dislike for Lansing as a man, Lansing took a perverse pleasure in writing memoranda that pointed out legal or practical flaws in Bryan's policies, usually after those policies had been announced publicly, a ploy that frequently made Bryan look foolish within the administration.

Where Lansing's true loyalties lay are best illustrated by his actions in late October 1914. Lansing had developed close ties with vice presidents of two major New York banks, Thomas W. Lamont of Morgan and Company and Samuel McRoberts of National City Bank. Both banks were anxious to begin floating loans to France and Great Britain, something that Wilson was not prepared to do, since it might jeopardize American neutrality just as seriously as might selling war materials. McRoberts wrote a long letter to Lansing, explaining the dangers to the American economy if the New York banking community was forbidden to do business with the Allied powers: Countries like Canada, Australia, and Argentina would make the loans to the Allies instead, and would profit accordingly, while American bankers could only deal with minor nations.

Lansing saw the letter as another opportunity to upstage Bryan, so he copied it almost word for word, making subtle changes to give the impression that it was his work. Careful not to let Bryan know of McRoberts's letter or the memorandum he had prepared from it, Lansing took the memorandum to President Wilson on the evening of August 23, presenting it in such a way that Wilson believed that Bryan knew and approved of the document. In less than an hour, Lansing had secured Wilson's approval for permitting American banks to make loans to the Allied powers. Bryan learned of Wilson's decision when he read about it in the *New York Times*.

What Lansing was doing was single-handedly changing American foreign policy from the "strict neutrality" that Bryan and Wilson were working to achieve to that of "strict legality," and was doing so in ways that he would personally profit from. Wilson was susceptible to Lansing's machinations because Lansing was, quite simply, a more palatable figure to him than was Bryan. Wilson resented the fact that he essentially owed his presidency to Bryan, a fact that Bryan, to his credit, never mentioned to Wilson as far as is known. Nevertheless, every time Wilson found himself in Bryan's presence, it was a forcible reminder that he, the President of the United States, was beholden to Bryan, the Secretary of State. Moreover, Lansing was, like Wil-son, reserved, meticulous, and organized—a complete contrast to Bryan. And best of all, Lansing owed his position to Wilson, which made for a more acceptable superior-subordinate relationship than existed between Wilson and

Bryan. Consequently, whenever Lansing had a suggestion, put forward a position, or offered a paper on any subject within his purview, Wilson was immediately more receptive to him than he would have been to Bryan.[6]

For a variety of personal reasons, Lansing was very pro-British, and he began to use his position, as well as his influence with Wilson, to direct the administration's interpretation of American neutrality in ways that significantly favored the British over the Germans. When the London Orders of Council were issued by the British Cabinet on August 20, 1914, Wilson had been angered by the Royal Navy's assertion of its alleged rights of search and seizure on the high seas, and Lansing drafted the note that Wilson sent to London in protest. At the same time, he was able to convey to Sir Edward Grey, the British Foreign Minister, that the apparent show of belligerence was exactly that—a show.

In contrast, when the Germans declared the war zone around the British Isles in February 1915, Wilson's reaction, prompted by Lansing, was sharp and sudden. Since the beginning of the war, Wilson's perception of America's role—as well as his own—in world affairs had been evolving, as he sensed an opportunity to bring the same sense of even-handed dealing between the Great Powers that he had brought to American relations with Latin America. It was, he said, an opportunity for the United States to gain "great personal glory" by standing "ready to help the world." Even as early as September 1914, Wilson started to see himself as "the great arbitrator," commanding his fellow Americans to be neutral "in fact as well as in name, in thought as well as in action," since the mission of the United States was to "speak the counsels of peace," to "play the part of impartial mediator." Perhaps casting an eye toward the verdict of history, Wilson said he wanted to "serve humanity" by bringing the moral force of the New World to bear on the old, to mediate a peace under the American flag—or, as he put it, "under the flag not only of America but of humanity."

When Germany declared the war zone, the tone of Wilson's rhetoric took a sharp turn away from impartiality. In his reply to the German announcement, which Lansing drafted, he deplored any departure from the accepted practices of the Cruiser Rules, then warned the Germans that "in the event that German submarines should destroy on the high seas an American vessel or the lives of American citizens, it would be difficult for the government of the United States to view the action in any other light than as an indefensible violation of neutral rights." Should such an attack take place, the United States assured the Germans that they would be held to "strict accountability."

Those two words fundamentally and permanently changed the nature of relations between Germany and the United States. To this day, no one knows whether it was Lansing's idea or Wilson's, although it was more likely Lansing's creation. The ominous ring of "strict accountability," at once threatening and fraught with what Lord Morely, one-time member of the British Cabinet, called "an air of senseless animosity," more closely resembled the type of brinkmanship that Lansing seemed to enjoy provoking whenever he wasn't in a position to be held responsible, than it did the measured diplomacy that had characterized Wilson's foreign policy.

The German government was baffled by the implication that Americans traveling on British ships were immune from attack by German submarines—there was no such provision within the accepted body of international law, nor was there any precedent for this assertion. Quite to the contrary—and as a specialist in international law, Lansing should have been well aware of this—there were several instances, the most recent being the Russo-Japanese War in 1905, where it had been made clear to all neutral powers that their citizens traveled on ships belonging to any belligerent power at their own risk. The thinly veiled threat that the United States would go to war with Germany should any American lives be lost to U-boat attacks caused the German Foreign Ministry to completely rethink Germany's policy toward the United States. Von Bethmann-Hollweg, Germany's Chancellor, had suspected Wilson of having a pro-Allied bias ever since late 1914, when it took over a month for the United States to lodge a protest with Great Britain over the establishment of the British blockade of Germany and the Royal Navy's practice of searching and seizing neutral ships on the high seas. When the American reaction to the German declaration of the war zone arrived just five days after the German announcement, the speed with which the reply arrived, as well as its contents, simply seemed to prove to Bethmann-Hollweg that Wilson was already favoring the Allies, regardless of how high-minded his pronouncements about American neutrality sounded.

Secretary of State Bryan had deplored the German submarine campaign as much as Wilson did and agreed that America should take a firm stance in opposing the German declaration. He also suggested to Wilson that, to avoid appearing unnecessarily provocative, it would be a wise move diplomatically to repeat American objections to Britain's blockade and methods of enforcement at the same time as the protest to Germany was issued, but Wilson ignored him. This was the first indication that Bryan's influence with the President was declining, as Wilson, however much he privately disliked Bryan, had always respected his Secretary of State's advice in foreign policy.[7]

It was also the first indication that Lansing's star was on the ascent in the State Department. It's difficult to determine after more than eighty-five years whether Lansing actually thought he was better qualified than Bryan to be Secretary of State or simply coveted his office out of a lust for power. What is obvious is that however thorough and meticulous Lansing might have been in his legal briefs and memoranda for the State Department, it's doubtful that he ever could have mustered the kind of selfless vision necessary to be an effective policy maker. Clearly he possessed none of Bryan's rock-ribbed Christian morality or Wilson's humanitarian principles. Robert Lansing's world was compassed first and last by the interests of Robert Lansing. In the simmering tension over the U-boats, Lansing saw his opportunity to replace Bryan: He would use the crisis created by the sinking of the *Lusitania,* not to resolve a confrontation that would threaten to break into open hostilities between Germany and the United States at any minute, but as a vehicle to embarrass Bryan and drive him from office. His succession to the vacant Secretary's office would be unquestioned.

That would suit Lansing perfectly, for undeniably there were skeletons in his closet, some going back as far as the questions of financial impropriety from his early days in the State Department. Certainly, one aspect of his private life that would not hold up under close scrutiny was the fact that Lansing's best friend was not an American, but an Englishman, and one who was manipulating Lansing as thoroughly as Lansing was manipulating Wilson and Bryan. He was an officer of the Intelligence Division of the Royal Navy, Capt. Guy Gaunt, who was the naval attaché to the British Embassy in Washington, D.C. It was an unusual relationship, made all the more so by the fact that Gaunt was responsible for all British intelligence operations in the United States. The two men were often seen lunching together or meeting at various social gatherings that, even in 1914, were an essential part of the political landscape in Washington. Strangely, no one thought to question the fact that the best friend of the United States Assistant Secretary of State was a British spy.[8]

CHAPTER 6

The Diplomats and Spies

THAT CAPTAIN GAUNT WAS AN INTELLIGENCE OFFICER WOULD HAVE COME AS no surprise to the Washington, D.C., diplomatic community. The naval and military attachés assigned to embassies the world over almost always work for the intelligence department of their particular service, and their acknowledged role is to collect information about the armed forces of their host country. Usually this is done quite openly, by attending military reviews and maneuvers, through discussions and staff talks with the senior officers of the various services, and through gathering information from whatever public sources are readily available.

In the case of Captain Gaunt, not only was he responsible for all the official duties of his office, but he was also the de facto director of all covert British intelligence and counterintelligence activities in the United States. In this, Gaunt was careful not to undertake any actions that might antagonize his hosts, his reasons for this being twofold: First, he genuinely liked the Americans and saw no reason for needlessly antagonizing them; second, Great Britain needed to continue to have access to American industrial capacity or else her war effort would collapse—consequently, Gaunt was not about to do anything that would jeopardize the situation as it stood.

Gaunt was a good-looking, solidly built man, every inch the seaman he appeared to be. He was intelligent and witty, and was on everyone's social list in the diplomatic circles of Washington, D.C. It was during a round of one of those endless social functions that Gaunt met Robert Lansing, the Assistant Secretary of State. Lansing, of course, in his pathetic attempt to appear as urbane and civilized as a natural-born Englishman, almost certainly made himself known to Gaunt. Whatever Gaunt thought of Lansing personally, it was clear to him that in his professional capacity, a friendship with the Assistant Secretary of State would be a significant advantage indeed in tailoring British policy to complement the prevailing attitudes of the American government, as well as influencing American policy whenever possible. Lansing, who not surprisingly had few close friends, began to spend more and more time with Gaunt, the two men usually meeting for lunch on Saturday, then attending a football game together at one or another of the universities around Washington.

For Gaunt, this was a golden opportunity to see inside the workings of the Wilson administration, for apparently Lansing couldn't keep his mouth shut, and Gaunt's reports to London were filled with the details of the increasingly tumultuous relationship between President Wilson and Secretary of State Bryan. It also allowed Gaunt the opportunity to "unofficially" discuss new policy initiatives with Lansing and get a feel for how they would be received by the administration.

Of course, this was not a one-way street—no relationship, personal or professional, ever was with Robert Lansing. Gaunt was in the privileged position of being able to inform Lansing which American companies were about to receive large orders from the British purchasing commissions for munitions and war materials. This information Lansing was able to pass on to his contacts on Wall Street, as well as capitalize on himself. In Gaunt's opinion, it was a small enough price to pay for the invaluable political intelligence he received from Lansing.

Gaunt was privy to this information because he was charged with overseeing the security arrangements for cargoes being shipped to Great Britain from American ports, as well as coordinating the activities of the various purchasing agents who would be coming to the United States—arranging meetings with the appropriate industrialists and corporations, securing bids, and locating new manufacturers. These duties sometimes called for Gaunt to demonstrate that for all of his *bonhomie,* he was still an officer of the Royal Navy and could act like one: The individuals who sought to profit from Britain's near desperation were legion.

One of the best-known examples of how Gaunt could turn a would-be exploiter into a lackey was the case of Alfred Fraser. Fraser was an American "entrepreneur" of somewhat questionable background who, one afternoon in September 1914, walked into the War Office in London with a sheepskin coat under his arm and announced that he could provide as many as the British Army wanted, at thirty-seven shillings ($8.80) each. It was exactly what the War Office, worried about equipping an entire army for the upcoming winter, had been looking for. He walked out with an order for 100,000 of the coats; however, he made one small mistake—he asked for the money in advance. The War Office smelled a rat and, knowing that Fraser was returning to New York, asked Captain Gaunt to look into the matter a little further.

What Gaunt discovered was that sheepskin coats had been manufactured in Boston, then sold to a New York clothing wholesaler named Heckman for the equivalent of fourteen shillings ($3.36) apiece. Heckman, in turn, sold the coats to Fraser on a five percent commission basis. Even allowing for

Heckman's commission, Fraser's profits would have been enormous. In exchange for not being exposed as a fraud—the United States had enacted legislation to prevent profiteering—Fraser agreed to work for Gaunt, becoming a front for shipping critical cargoes to Great Britain. Once Captain Gaunt met with a British financier named George Booth in late October 1914, there would be a definite need for front men like Fraser.[1]

Within days of the United States informing the belligerent powers that the sale of war materials to belligerent governments was forbidden but sales to private individuals and businesses would be permitted, George Booth had booked passage on the *Lusitania* for New York, armed with what amounted to a shopping list of munitions he was authorized to purchase, the list having been prepared by the War Cabinet, the section of the British Cabinet that was charged with the direction, prosecution, and supply of Britain's war effort. Booth's position was interesting—he had no official standing, but was a member of the Committee on War Supplies, an ad hoc body of British businessmen and financiers that had sort of grafted itself onto the War Cabinet. Because it wasn't a formal government agency, the committee could freely purchase munitions and supplies in the United States; at the same time, it acted with the approval and authority of the War Cabinet.

George Booth had actually been instrumental in setting up the Committee on War Purchases. One of the directors of the Bank of England, he had been approached by Sir Walter Runciman, the president of the Board of Trade, to set up an organization that would work through the "old boy network" to acquire supplies and equipment for the British Army. In August 1914, when the rest of Europe was confidently declaring the war would end in a matter of weeks, Field Marshal Lord Kitchener, the Secretary of State for War, in a moment of terrifyingly profound insight, declared that the war would last three or more years and that the reserve stocks of ammunition guns and equipment would be woefully inadequate. Kitchener had urged that the Cabinet take steps to procure the materials needed before the reserves on hand ran dangerously low. As a whole, the Cabinet disagreed with Kitchener, but Runciman felt that the Field Marshal's arguments had merit and decided to act accordingly. Realizing very quickly that it would be several months before Britain's industry would be able to supply the demand of Britain's armed forces, he could only see one alternative: purchase the materials needed from manufacturers in the United States.

His approach to Booth wasn't entirely coincidental. In addition to the contacts in the financial world that Booth's position as one of the directors of the Bank of England provided, George Booth was the cousin of Alfred Booth, the chairman of the shipping and import-export firm of Alfred Booth and Company, a business started by Alfred's father. The company owned one shipping line outright, the Booth Steamship Company Limited, as well as tanneries, factories, and construction companies in Brazil, the United States, and Great Britain; it was tied financially to several other shipping firms, as well as having holdings in a number of storage and wholesaling businesses. Alfred Booth and Company was also the single largest stockholder in Britain's single largest shipping line, Cunard, and Alfred Booth sat as chairman of the board.

Runciman and D. F. Wintour, the Director of Army Contracts for the Board of Trade, asked George Booth to inquire of Alfred Booth whether the company would be willing to arrange the financing of British munitions purchases in America, as well as act as the overall coordinator of the British purchasing missions to the United States. Alfred Booth agreed, realizing that not only was he doing his patriotic duty, but that since all transactions were to be conducted as private business affairs, it was good for business as well. When George Booth went to New York at the end of October 1914, it was to act as his cousin's agent and on his behalf. His crossing on the *Lusitania* had been memorable; he had been miserably seasick for most of it. He was an experienced traveler and was no stranger to the *Lusitania,* but he couldn't recall the ship having rolled and pitched as much as it seemed to on this crossing.

When Booth sought out the *Lusitania's* captain, David Dow, and asked if it was his imagination or if the *Lusitania* really was livelier than she had been before the war, he was surprised by the explanation Captain Dow gave him. The ship *was* livelier, Dow explained: The double plating of the Shelter Deck that had been done in the spring of 1913 had added to the ship's topweight, increasing her already marked tendency to roll, while at the same time, the forward transverse coal bunker had been converted into a magazine, making her bow noticeably lighter and increasing her tendency to pitch. Captain Dow was unhappy with the ship's instability, but there was nothing he could do about it. In a letter to his cousin Alfred, Booth jokingly remarked that if his trip to the United States was successful, the *Lusitania* would sail with a full cargo hold and ride a little better, easing Captain Dow's fears somewhat, at least on the eastbound runs.

Booth was met in New York by Captain Gaunt, who had with him both some last-minute additions to the "shopping list" Booth had brought over from Great Britain, and letters of credit from the British government to Alfred Booth and Company, which in turn would finance the purchases George Booth would make through Morgan and Company. Most of the firms Booth intended to do business with had offices in New York, although Gaunt and Booth did take a short trip to Maryland to place an order with Du Pont, the American chemical manufacturer, for 600 tons of guncotton to be used by the Royal Navy in manufacturing new mines.[2]

The money Booth would eventually spend on supplies and munitions was staggering. In just one year, the banking house of Morgan and Company would handle $1,100,453,950 worth of munitions purchases, earning an $11 million commission for the bank, as well as a hefty dividend for the bank's stockholders—which included Robert Lansing. Before the war would end, that amount would be multiplied nearly tenfold as the Allies drew ever more heavily on the resources of American industry to support their war effort.

Purchasing the supplies was one thing; getting them to Great Britain was another. Over half of all the ships sailing from the United States to Europe departed from New York, among them four-fifths of the ships bound for Great Britain. Inevitably, this meant that New York was fairly swarming with German spies anxious to report to Berlin the details of what cargoes were consigned to which British ships bound for which British port, allowing the German Naval High Command to route the U-boats to intercept the most important ones. A loophole in American maritime regulations made it very easy for German agents to do just that, and the Germans were quick to exploit it.

The regulations required every ship sailing from an American port to file a copy of her sailing manifest—that is, a listing of all cargo being carried, along with a record of provisions and supplies purchased for the voyage—with the Collector of Customs at the Port Authority. Since these manifests were part of the public record and open for public inspection, it required little extraordinary effort on the part of any German agent to determine what cargoes were being transported on which ships and promptly cable that information to Berlin. In New York, it was even easier: The New York Port Authority daily published a listing of the cargoes of ships that had sailed the previous day. It wasn't long before the British realized what a threat this information posed to their merchant shipping: The Germans could pick and choose their targets.

Fortunately for the British, there was a loophole within the loophole, and they were just as quick in their turn to exploit it as the Germans had been. Almost invariably, a passenger or cargo ship would make last-minute purchases of perishable food, particularly fresh vegetables, at dockside before departing. Since these purchases had to be accounted for as well in the ship's sailing papers, a "supplementary manifest" would be filed by the shipping agent after the ship sailed. The British began filing very brief, innocuous manifests for their ships, sometimes only a page or two in length, in order to obtain sailing clearances. Once the ships in question were safely at sea—or in some cases, after they had reached their destination—a supplemental manifest listing the full cargo would be filed. Deprived of easy access to specific information about what cargoes were consigned to which ships, the Germans had to resort to other methods to find out what the British were shipping from the New World to the Old.

The British were just as quick to turn the German's own tactic against them, too: Examining the manifests for ships bound for neutral ports, they were able to learn what ships were carrying cargoes ultimately destined for Germany and forward that information to the Admiralty in London. The Admiralty then made arrangements to have those ships and their cargo seized.

Of course, the supplemental manifest ruse was so patently transparent that it could only have succeeded with the help of a blind eye being turned toward it in the Port Authority of New York at some point. In this case the visually challenged official was Dudley Field Malone, a former Treasury Department lawyer who had been appointed Collector of Customs for the Port of New York by President Wilson in 1912. Despite his Irish roots, Malone was staunchly and vocally pro-Allied in his sentiments, and while he was responsible for ensuring that every ship that left New York sailed in complete compliance with the neutrality laws of the United States, it was also his prerogative to determine exactly what constituted "complete compliance." One provision of American neutrality law that Malone frequently overlooked specifically forbade the shipment of war materials—contraband, especially ammunition—on passenger ships of any nationality or registry.

Malone was able to ignore this provision of the neutrality laws because frantic research by Cunard lawyers in New York and the legal staff of the British Embassy in Washington, D.C., had discovered an obscure exception to the regulation. In 1910, the Union Metallic Cartridge Company, by 1915 a part of Remington Arms, wanted to ship small consignments of sporting rifle cartridges on fast coastal steamers along the Atlantic seaboard. Current shipping regulations prohibited carrying any type of explosive cargo, including ammunition, on steamships carrying passengers. Union Metallic approached the Municipal Explosives Commission of the New York City and arranged a demonstration that would prove that rifle cartridges were not actually explosive, as the term was generally understood, when exposed to open flames or extreme heat.

The demonstration consisted of Union Metallic officials building a pile of rifle cartridges and shotgun shells, along with large quantities of .22-, .38-, and .45-caliber pistol rounds, setting the pile alight, and keeping it burning for twenty-five minutes. Inevitably the cartridges and shells "cooked off," but not being confined to the barrel of a gun, the bullets were harmlessly tossed a few feet and the hot gases from their discharge quickly dissipated. Certainly it was not a scientific test by any standard, but Union Metallic wasn't attempting any duplicity: They were merely trying to simulate the conditions that would be found in the hold of a coastal steamer, where their shipments would rarely approach 1,000 rounds of all calibers. The commissioners who had witnessed the event were suitably impressed by Union Metallic's logic and granted the company permission to ship their ammunition on the coastal passenger steamers, provided the shipments were listed on the manifests as "Non-explosive in Bulk."

What the Cunard lawyers and their colleagues at the embassy learned was that this exemption had been written in such careless manner that any form of ammunition being shipped from New York could be transported, provided it was franked as "Non-explosive in Bulk." Between the subterfuge of the false manifests and the legal mislabeling of explosive cargoes, British purchasing agents in New York were able to ship over a half a million tons of high explosive shells, along with several million rounds of rifle and machine gun ammunition, to Great Britain over the next two and a half years, much of it on passenger liners. What seemed to escape Cunard's lawyers, though certainly the embassy lawyers should have known better, was that by carrying a cargo of ammunition—contraband by any nation's definition—the transporting ships, including passenger liners, were legitimate targets for German warships, specifically the U-boats. It was an oversight—if it *was* an oversight—that would have tragic consequences for the *Lusitania*.[3]

Captain Gaunt wasn't the only attaché in Washington who was a busy man. His military counterpart at the German embassy, Capt. Franz von Papen, of the German Army, was conducting his own espionage campaign as well, though with different methods and different results. Gaunt was working to assist the efforts of the British purchasing agents in the United States, while at the same time influence the attitudes of both American politicians and the public. Von Papen was concentrating on thwarting the British undertakings—he realized early on that Germany stood little chance of winning over American sentiment and so he chose not to waste his time on such efforts.

Von Papen couldn't have been more of a contrast to the square-jawed, devil-may-care Gaunt. Von Papen was a tall, thin, weasel-faced caricature of a Prussian officer. Unlike Gaunt, he thoroughly detested Americans, and in his letters to his wife often wondered what offense he had committed to be consigned to the purgatory of Washington, D.C. Von Papen, who had an unusually high opinion of his own character and abilities, regarded himself as an urbane and sophisticated man, while most Americans were by contrast, in his opinion, unmitigated boors. He had a caustic manner of dealing with people, which caused most Americans he came into contact with to regard him with suspicion and dislike, sentiments he heartily reciprocated. He was often heard to remark that greed was the major motivation for the average American, and he held the opinion that the Americans as a race were still fairly far down the evolutionary ladder. They had only made the transition from walking on four legs to two, he maintained, because someone once suggested that there was more money to be made that way. There were times during the war when German diplomats were their own worst enemy.

Von Papen, however, wasn't interested in making friends with the American people—that was the job of the ambassador, Count Johann von Bernsdorff. Von Papen's brief essentially placed him outside the ambassador's authority and charged him first and foremost with thwarting the efforts of the various British purchasing missions that came to the United States, beginning with George Booth and the others that followed. Though in his memoirs, Captain von Papen took credit for a wide-ranging campaign of sabotage and destruction, including demolishing several Canadian railway lines, blowing up a series of munitions plants in New England, and placing bombs aboard several British steamers that sailed from New York and later sank without a trace, in truth those were the acts of German-American fanatics and Irish immigrants who were giving vent to their anti-British sentiments and were never under von Papen's control. The actions he *was* responsible for putting in hand to counter the British efforts in acquiring arms and munitions were usually far less spectacular, but also far more effective and long ranging.

Given the British love of a good joke, had some other nation been the target of von Papen's activities, they might have seen the humor in many of his actions. When George Booth made his first trip to New York on behalf of the Committee on War Supplies, von Papen correctly judged just what Booth was attempting to procure in the United States and tried to beat him to the punch. To deny the American factories the capacity to manufacture the arms Booth was ordering, von Papen set up a huge arms manufacturing firm, using a German-American businessman as a front and drawing on virtually unlimited funding provided by Berlin. The company promptly placed orders for lathes, forges, presses, and machine tools, essentially acquiring the entire available inventory of the machinery that would be desperately needed by the companies Booth was placing his orders with. This effectively delayed the fulfillment of the British orders by several months, until new equipment could be produced and the American factories begin to retool.

In another operation, von Papen again utilized German-Americans, who set up several small to medium-size companies, giving them each very respectable British-sounding names, that allegedly produced one or more articles of uniform clothing or military equipment of which the British were running short and desperately seeking manufacturers for. These companies existed on paper only, but the British were unaware of this and paid large deposits, sometimes even paying in full in advance, for equipment that would never be produced.

One minor escapade of von Papen's had unforeseen consequences that may have affected the *Lusitania*. When George Booth visited Du Pont to place an order for 600 tons of guncotton (cellulose nitrate) for the Royal Navy, he was informed that while the order could be filled within a matter of months, there was a shortage of the watertight containers used to safely transport the explosive. One of von Papen's dummy companies had purchased from the manufacturer of the containers—a Du Pont subsidiary and the only manufacturer of such containers in the country—the company's entire inventory. While Du Pont could fill Booth's order for guncotton, it couldn't assure him that there would be sufficient containers on hand when the order was ready to ship it all properly. Booth gave Du Pont the go-ahead to complete the order for the guncotton and, when it was ready, to ship it to New York however Du Pont thought best. The guncotton was ready by mid-April 1915 and shipped to New York in the last week of the month. It arrived there on April 29 but disappeared the next day. The *Lusitania* sailed on her last voyage on May 1.[4]

Not all of the diplomats who would play a part in the coming crisis over the destruction of the *Lusitania* were in Washington. Two of them were in London, Col. Henry House, special envoy of the President, and Walter Hines Page, Ambassador to the Court of St. James, the U.S. representative to Great Britain. Both men would play peculiar roles in the drama surrounding the *Lusitania* in the days and months to come.

Col. Edward M. House was a long-time close friend of President Wilson's who became his personal envoy when Wilson was elected President in 1912. Although he held no official position, House's opinions carried great weight with Wilson, who trusted House implicitly. The Colonel, in turn, was careful to not abuse that trust or misuse the influence he had with the President. Much as Richard Nixon used Henry Kissinger in his first term of office, Wilson frequently entrusted House with delivering messages from the President that Wilson believed that for varying reasons should not go through formal channels. House also served as Wilson's eyes and ears in the foreign ministries of the belligerent powers, so that Wilson could better guide America along the path of neutrality. Admittedly, House was passionately pro-Allied, but he did his best not to let his bias affect his performance of his duties, although he wasn't always careful to make his unofficial status clear, sometimes leading officials to mistake his personal beliefs for the official position of the U.S. government. Certainly House was no warmonger: He believed as firmly as Wilson did that America's role in the war should be that of a peacemaker. It was a view that he had held even before the war broke out. Sensitive to the tensions building in Europe in the last few months before the peace was shattered, House had written to Wilson from Berlin in May 1914 that the political situation "is extraordinary. It is militarism run stark mad. Unless someone acting for you can bring about a different understanding there is someday going to be an awful cataclysm."

This blunt realism served Wilson well time and again, and he would soon have a tricky job for House to do in London: In the spring of 1915, House would go and meet with senior members of the British government so that he could give Wilson an independent assessment of how receptive

Britain's leading politicians would be to a negotiated peace settlement. According to Ambassador Page, the idea of a "peace without victory" was completely unthinkable for the Asquith government, but Wilson had his doubts. For some months, the President had been privately questioning how much of Ambassador Page's reports were factual and how much were wishful thinking on the Ambassador's part.

Walter Hines Page enjoyed his posting to London and was genuinely fond of his hosts, the British, which is usually a useful trait for an ambassador. However, it is also a requisite for an ambassadorial post that the ambassador communicate to his capital exactly what the attitudes and opinions of the host nation's leaders are, and divine as far as possible their intentions and capabilities, so that he can provide timely advice and counsel to his own leaders. Page had an unfortunate habit of detailing to Washington not what the members of Asquith's cabinet were thinking, but what he hoped or wished they were thinking. Page's Anglophilia had caused him to become something of a Teutonophobe, and consequently, his hostility toward Germany made itself manifest in his reports on developing British political and military policy.

Sentiment, both within the British Government and with the British public, had not hardened to the point where a negotiated peace was impossible, but the longer the war lasted, the less likely it would be that negotiations could be successful. If Wilson was ever to be "the Great Arbitrator" he envisioned himself to be, he needed clear, accurate assessments of the mood and intentions of the British government. If Page couldn't provide that, then Wilson needed someone on the scene who could. That someone would be House.[5]

Beneath all the maneuverings and postures of House, Page, Gaunt, von Papen, and the others ran an undercurrent of tension, a constant realization that while they shuffled papers and made telephone calls, wrote diplomatic reports, and had luncheons with close friends and mortal enemies, men were dying miserably every day by the thousands, far from their comfortable offices and homes. Despite the veneer of civility that most of them covered themselves with as they conducted their business, they were all aware that it was a deadly business and that more men would die as a result of decisions they made or didn't make, actions they took or didn't take. They were waging war in the shadows, but it was war nonetheless. At the same time, there was an even darker war being waged that none of them were aware of, but that would affect each of their lives and their offices drastically, as it would reveal secrets that would change the complexion of the war in its entirety.

In Room 40 of the Admiralty Building in Whitehall, down in the basement, lurked a group of wireless and cypher experts under the command of Capt. Reginald Hall. Their existence was completely unknown to the outside world, their activities the best-kept secret of the war. Systematically, they sifted through signals collected by listening stations scattered across the British Isles, looking for intercepted cypher messages sent by wireless to German submarines at sea, along with diplomatic cables sent to German embassies and legations overseas. Once such a signal was found, several of the experts would sit down with the cyphered text and one or more very large, thick books and begin comparing groups of numbers in the cyphered message with similar groups of numbers in the books. Had the German Army and Navy, not to mention the German government, known what this handful of men under Captain Hall were doing, they would have been appalled: The British were reading the German codes.

Through a combination of ruthless action and good luck, the British had almost from the beginning of the war been able to read the German naval cyphers. Great Britain had declared war on August 4, 1914. The very next day, Royal Navy destroyers were dispatched to points all along the coast of Europe, including neutral countries, to cut the transoceanic telegraph cables that Germany had depended on to maintain contact with her embassies and agents overseas. This forced the Germans to utilize wireless to send their diplomatic dispatches, allowing the British to eavesdrop on them. Ships at sea, of course, were already dependent on wireless to send and receive reports and orders.

Though at the time the cables were cut the British weren't able to decipher the German diplomatic or naval codes, they were confident that they would eventually be able to do so. Code breaking is something of a British tradition, dating as far back as Sir Robert Walsingham under Elizabeth I in the early sixteenth century, right through to World War II, when the codebreakers at Bletchley Park, building on the fundamental work of French and Polish cypher experts, were able to crack the Enigma system and often read top-secret German orders to field commanders before their recipients did.

The first break in the cypher war came for the British in October 1914. The German cruiser *Magdeburg* had run aground in the Baltic Sea and was attacked by several Russian warships. As the cruiser was being pummeled, the signal officer decided to throw the ship's codebooks overboard in case the ship should fall into enemy hands. Before he could do so, a shell burst nearby and killed him, his body toppling overboard. The next day, when the Russians recovered the body and prepared it for burial, they discovered the codebooks clutched to his chest. Realizing that possession of the German naval cyphers would be far more useful to the British than to themselves, the Russians put the codebooks on one of their fastest cruisers and sent them to Great Britain.

It was a gift beyond price, and worth every gun, bandolier, and round of ammunition Britain had sent or would send to Russia. The Germans had learned that the *Magdeburg's* signal officer had intended to destroy the books, and when they found that he had been killed and his body lost, they assumed that the books had gone to the bottom of the sea with him. The Russians never informed the Germans otherwise, so the Naval High Command in Berlin never suspected that their signals were hopelessly compromised.

The advantage this gave the British was phenomenal. Within one of the codebooks was a diagram of the German grid square system that the High Seas Fleet used to determine the position of their ships. Each square was broken down into successively smaller squares, so that a German warship could signal its exact position within two or three miles simply by informing Berlin that it was at such and such a grid square, giving the combination of letters and numbers that identified that specific section of the map. A full-size copy of the German map, ten feet on a side, was quickly produced for the Operations division of the Admiralty and soon became known as "the Plot." Since position signals were sent daily by every German warship at sea, U-boat and surface ship alike, by reading these signals and marking the positions given on the Plot, the Royal Navy knew from day to day the exact location, within one or two miles, of every German ship at sea.

This allowed the British the luxury of being able to route vessels at sea, whether ships or the Royal Navy or civilian merchant shipping, away from areas where U-boats were known to be operating. Thus ships carrying cargoes of particularly high priority or special significance could be kept well clear of any threat from the submarines. Which ships would be diverted where was a decision left to the First Lord, Winston Churchill. Put another way, this code-breaking capability meant that the only way any large British ship could run afoul of a U-boat was either through sheer bad luck—or if the Admiralty wanted it to.

The cypher boffins in Room 40 were also making great strides in breaking the German diplomatic cipher. A variety of technical reasons led the cryptologists to believe that the naval code and the diplomatic code came from the same basic cypher system; consequently, the naval code would prove to be the key to the diplomatic code. Breaking that code would eventually provide the key to one of the turning points of the war, America's declaration of war against Germany. In the meantime, British knowledge of German submarine movements provided by the daily position reports would prove to be decisive— though in a way no one intended—in determining the fate of the *Lusitania*.[6]

CHAPTER 7

The Warnings

EXACTLY ONE MONTH AFTER THE ADMIRALTY INFORMED CUNARD THAT THE Royal Navy would have no further use for the *Lusitania,* she left Liverpool on her first wartime crossing. The intervening four weeks had been spent preparing the liner for the realities of war: Blackout curtains were installed at every porthole and window throughout the ship; she was extensively repainted, her four funnels completely black, her upper superstructure a muted buff, and her name and port of registry painted over on both sides of her bow and at her stern; and since nearly a third of her prewar crew had been Royal Navy reservists, new crewmen had to be hired and familiarized with the ship or, in some cases trained from scratch.

The return of the *Lusitania* to passenger service was greeted with sighs of relief in the Cunard boardroom, for though the transatlantic trade had fallen to barely two-thirds of its prewar volume, the loss of the *Lusitania, Mauretania,* and the newer, larger *Aquitania* to service with the Royal Navy had severely crimped Cunard's ability to meet even the deflated demand for accommodation. With the *Lusitania* back on her old run, Cunard's directors now felt they could maintain their share of the transatlantic trade.

This didn't mean that the Royal Navy was quite finished with her. Alfred Booth was reminded of several of the clauses in the contract between the navy and Cunard, in particular those that specified that the *Lusitania's* cargo capacity was to be available at any time should the Royal Navy have need to use it, as well as the Admiralty's right to issue orders changing the *Lusitania's* course, speed, or destination at any time. The *Lusitania* wasn't the only ship these conditions applied to; the Admiralty contract had required all of Cunard's ships to be placed at the Royal Navy's disposal during wartime, to be used when and how the navy saw fit.

Also, the Admiralty had the authority to issue orders to all ships of British registry, making those ships, in effect, auxiliaries of the Royal Navy. General instructions for all British registered merchant ships, as well as special orders for specific vessels on particular crossings, were drawn up and issued by the Director of the Admiralty's Trade Division, Capt. Richard Webb. Webb's department was entrusted with the safety of every British merchant ship—and in particular, their cargoes—at sea. Once Webb's instructions were cleared by the Intelligence and Operations sections, they were transmitted to the Senior Naval Officer (SNO) in every British port. In major foreign ports, the function of the SNO was taken over by the British consul, which in the case of the *Lusitania* would be Sir Courtenay Bennett in New York.

There were actually two forms of communications that Captain Webb's division sent to merchant ships. The first was the Admiralty Instruction, which carried the full authority of a direct order from the Admiralty, and which a merchant captain disobeyed at the peril of facing stiff fines, suspension, or loss of his Master's Ticket, and possibly a prison term. The second was the Admiralty Advise, a collection of documents concocted by the assortment of superannuated admirals that Lord Fisher kept on at the Admiralty in an advisory capacity. Compliance with the Advises was entirely voluntary, and most merchant skippers ignored them completely. In truth, the Admiralty Advises can only be charitably described as ludicrous. A sampling of their contents shows why: One maintained that submarines rarely operated within sight of land, while another said precisely the opposite; another contended that torpedoes were not a serious threat to merchantmen, yet another said that the best method of avoiding a torpedo was to execute a high-speed ninety-degree turn toward it, a tactic with a high probability of success for a destroyer, but highly unlikely—not to mention unsafe—for a 33,000-ton ocean liner.

It was during that first crossing that George Booth noticed that the *Lusitania* seemed to be somewhat of a different ship than he had known before the war. For one thing, the level of service didn't seem quite up to prewar standards, although that was easy enough to explain: Many of the ship's best men had been reservists and were called up to serve with the Royal Navy, while many others had found berths on other Cunard ships during the two months that the *Lusitania* had been laid up. As for her newfound tendency to roll and pitch when the seas were anything rougher than a gentle swell, Booth resigned himself to accepting it. There was nothing that could be done about it without taking the *Lusitania* out of service again to rework the modifications made in the fall of 1913, and that was something Cunard couldn't afford to do.[1]

Booth was able to conclude his business in the United States in time to return to Great Britain on October 20, the *Lusitania's* second eastbound crossing of the war. It had been a remarkably successful trip, for with the unfortunate exception of the unobtainable watertight cases for shipping the guncotton, Booth had accomplished everything the War Cabinet had hoped he would: The arrangements for financing the British purchases had been successfully established through Morgan and Company, the orders for ammunition and guns placed, and the network of contacts between the British Embassy, the consulate in New York, and the Cunard offices set up and running soothly.

The lack of watertight containers for the guncotton was nothing more than a minor annoyance to Booth and Gaunt, but it's unfortunate that they didn't look into the situation more closely. If they had, they might not only have discovered one of Captain von Papen's more clever ploys for frustrating British efforts in the United States, but they may well have been able to follow a trail that would have led them to some of von Papen's less sophisticated, more violent activities. The German military attaché hadn't confined himself to business maneuverings and financial manipulations, though he vastly preferred such nonviolent ploys, if for no better reason than they gave him an opportunity to display how clever he could be. Still, he was not above resorting to violent methods if the results promised to be worth the risk. Von Papen began infiltrating German agents and German-Americans with strong ties to the Fatherland into the workforce along docks and piers of the New York waterfront. Several of his agents were able to provide important information about critical cargoes being sent to Great Britain; others were able to smuggle time bombs or incendiary devices into the holds of ships carrying cargoes bound for Great Britain. Timed to go off when the ships were on the high seas, these bombs, it would be learned after the war, were responsible for over a score of ships vanishing without a trace.

The climax of von Papen's sabotage campaign wouldn't come until July 29, 1916, when one of his agents named Kurt Thummel would set fire to the Lehigh Valley Company's freight terminal in the lower New York Harbor. Lehigh Valley handled ammunition shipments bound for Great Britain from Remington Arms. In one spectacular blast, thirty-seven loaded freight cars, twelve barges, and a warehouse and pier, along with the terminal complex, disappeared, and over sixty lives were lost. Six months later, Thummel set fire to the Lehigh's Kingsland Assembly Plant in Kingsland, New Jersey, destroying the facility and causing $17 million worth of damage.

That some of von Papen's people might be working on the Cunard docks was a very real worry for both Captain Gaunt and Sir Courtenay Bennett, the British Consul in New York. Once Booth had the working arrangements between Cunard and the Consulate established, Gaunt had a desk set up for himself in the Cunard offices at Pier 54, where he could not only keep an eye on the workforce and hopefully spot any suspicious activity, but also monitor cargoes bound for Great Britain. One of George Booth's priorities when he arrived in New York was to take care of the legal arrangements whereby all of the British ships that would be carrying munitions to Great Britain would be cleared as being under charter to Cunard. This allowed Gaunt to keep the Admiralty apprised of which cargoes were bound for what ports and arrange for escorts for especially critical or sensitive shipments.

Captain Gaunt and Sir Courtenay soon ran afoul of Charles P. Sumner, the manager of Cunard's operations in New York. Described as a "good steamship man," who was respected up and down the East Coast by other shipping lines for his business acumen and straightforwardness, Sumner took a dim view of Captain Gaunt, Sir Courtenay, false manifests, and their blind acceptance by Dudley Malone. When the intricacies of various British ruses were explained to him, along with the fact that Cunard would be shipping cargoes of high explosives on passenger liners, in violation of American neutrality laws, Sumner, a proper Bostonian, was outraged.

His exact words are lost, but apparently Sumner was vehement enough in his protests to both Gaunt and Bennett that Sir Courtenay cabled Sir Eyre Crowe, the Assistant Undersecretary of State at the Foreign Office in London, that "Sumner must be in the pay of the Germans" since he had been "very offensive . . . in his refusal to ship munitions on any Cunard passenger ship. . . . He sees neither the logic nor the necessity in shipping government supplies in bottoms of British registry, even when those supplies are under contract to the Admiralty." The most immediate result of Sumner's stand was that when the *Lusitania* sailed for Liverpool on November 4, she carried a mixed cargo but no munitions, the only eastbound crossing she ever made without explosives in her hold. Another result was that after Sir Eyre spoke to Alfred Booth about Sumner, his salary was promptly doubled to £5,000 ($24,000). Sumner, all objections suddenly overcome, took the money and lapsed into silence.[2]

Alfred Booth was a man who knew the value of a pound, and while he considered the salary paid to Sumner money well spent, he couldn't see why the *Lusitania* should lose money for Cunard on every crossing she made. On November 16, 1914, Cunard's accounting office informed Booth that the ship was losing an average of £2,000 ($9,600) each voyage, because of the inevitable decline in the number of passengers crossing in wartime, along with an increase in the price of coal. Booth considered suspending the *Lusitania*'s operations for the winter, but the Admiralty requested that she remain in service, so the decision was made to cut her operating expenses. To do this, some 260 crewmen were released, including 85 stokers and trimmers. This resulted in an immediate savings of £1,350 ($7,480) on each crossing, as well as a reduction in coal consumption of 1,600 tons. The savings in coal were realized by shutting down the six boilers of Boiler Room Number 4, since there were no longer enough stokers and trimmers to keep all twenty-three boilers lit. This meant that the *Lusitania*'s maximum speed was cut from twenty-six to twenty-one knots, and her cruising speed reduced to eighteen knots.

It was not a popular decision. The *Lusitania*'s vaunted speed had for months been promoted as her best protection against submarine attack— with her top speed nearly twice that of the fastest U-boat, it was believed she could simply run away from any threat. Now her cruising speed was barely faster than the top speed of a fast merchantman, and the German submarines were sinking far too many of those for her crew to feel safe. When the *Lusitania* left Liverpool for New York on November 26, twenty-five of the seventy-seven able-bodied seamen of her complement refused to sign on for the crossing. When she reached New York, forty-five stewards jumped ship.

Charles Sumner cabled Booth demanding to know what had happened and why the *Lusitania* was no longer taking her full load of coal. Booth explained about the decision to shut down Boiler Room Number 4, and turned down Sumner's suggestion that she carry full stokeholds in case of an emergency. Even so, when the *Lusitania* sailed for Liverpool on December 7, she did so with full bunkers; Captain Dow had refused to set sail unless he had a full load of coal. What won the day for him, though, was a memo to Booth that coal was cheaper in New York than in Liverpool. It was the last time she sailed with full bunkers.

While Captain Dow never explained why he thought carrying a full load of coal would be useful in an emergency (it would have taken nearly twenty hours to light the six cold boilers and build up a head of steam in them), he had reason to be concerned for the *Lusitania*'s safety. On her first crossing to Liverpool afer Christmas 1914, she was nearly caught by the German raider *Karlsruhe*, one of the few German surface raiders still at large. Slipping in and out of the fog of the Grand Banks off Newfoundland, the *Lusitania* made good her escape, but it had been close. Leaving Liverpool on February 20, as she was crossing the Bar across the Mersey River, the *U-30* sank two merchantmen less than ten miles away. On the return crossing, she was just entering the mouth of the St. George's Channel when the *U-20* (the submarine that, by a strange twist of fate two months later, in almost exactly the same spot, became the *Lusitania*'s nemesis) torpedoed a cargo ship almost within sight of the liner.

Captain Dow was not a timid man, but enough was enough. On March 8, 1915, he informed Alfred Booth in no uncertain terms that while he was willing to command a merchant ship in hazardous waters, he was no longer willing to command a passenger ship carrying munitions under such conditions. Booth politely heard Dow out, then relieved him of command of the *Lusitania*, appointing Capt. William Turner as her new skipper.[3]

They called him "Bowler Bill" because of his habit of wearing a bowler hat at all times save for when he was on the bridge of his ship. He was broad shouldered and square jawed, with an honest, open face. Stocky and solid, he had a foursquare look about him that gave the impression—correctly—that he suffered neither fools nor stupidity gladly. He had gone to sea at the age of twelve as a cabin boy in 1863 and worked his way up through the officer grades. When he joined Cunard in 1883, he was one of those rare true sailors—a breed long since vanished—who was equally at home under sail or steam. He had earned his Master's and Extra Master's Tickets for both square-rigged sailing ships and steamships. His first command had been a square rigger on the Australian run, and when he joined Cunard, he rose steadily in the company's esteem until, before the war, he had been captain of both the *Lusitania* and *Mauretania,* the most prized position on the North Atlantic run.

He has been described as both something of a martinet and taciturn by nature, but both descriptions are unfair. In truth, he was a captain who gave orders expecting them to be obeyed, and when they weren't, he would accept reasons but not excuses. He was distinctly uncomfortable with the social role that modern steamship captains, especially those on the crack transatlantic liners, were being called to play with increasing frequency. But if he withdrew from all unnecessary socializing with the passengers aboard the vessels he commanded, it was because he was painfully aware that he lacked the refinement and the social graces that such mingling demanded. In many ways, he was still that twelve-year-old cabin boy who had gone to sea for the love of ships more than fifty years before. He had worked his way from the forecastle to the bridge—anywhere else, he was almost painfully shy and insecure—but he was happiest when he was on his bridge, his command rolling gently beneath his feet.

Just how seriously he took his responsibilities was made clear as soon as he took command of the *Lusitania.* He inspected the ship from stem to stern on March 10, and then issued a blistering report of his findings to the head office, refusing to set sail until the deficiencies he noted were corrected to his satisfaction. Not content with filing a report with Cunard, he also sent a copy to the Board of Trade Surveyor in Liverpool. Since the Surveyor had the authority to pass on the fitness of all ships to sail from Liverpool, Turner knew that he would get action. Will Turner took the responsibilities of being a ship's master very seriously.

Foremost among Turner's complaints was the quality of the crew; he found many of them ignorant of their jobs and undisciplined. The lifeboats were adequate in number, but the condition of their davits and the extra equipment each boat carried—oars, oarlocks, masts, spar, and sail—was decidedly poor, while the ship's trim tanks were faulty and the performance of the turbines was not up to prewar standards. Since few men in the employ of Cunard could be as intimidating as Will Turner when his wrath was kindled, the line immediately set about correcting as many of the faults as it could.

Obviously there was little Cunard could do about the quality of the crew, so many of the line's best men having been siphoned off by the Royal Navy; the company had made up the deficiency as best it could. The trim tanks were serviced, and every single item of lifesaving equipment was inspected by the Board of Trade representative in Liverpool, Captain Barrand, who had every defective item replaced, including three lifeboats. Turner was informed that nothing could be done for the turbines without putting the *Lusitania* into drydock, taking her out of service for some months. All of this took some time, but when she left Liverpool on April 17, 1915, she was in first-rate order and carried an A-1 insurance rating from Lloyd's of London.[4]

The *Lusitania's* arrival in New York on April 24 was, like the crossing, unremarkable. That same day, Vice Adm. Sir Horace Hood hoisted his flag aboard the elderly armored cruiser *Juno,* moored in Queenstown Harbour, along the coast of southern Ireland. Hood was given command of the anti-submarine patrols in the Irish Sea and the approaches to the St. George's Channel. His flagship, as well as the three other cruisers that made up his squadron, *Isis, Sutlej,* and *Venus,* were all, as he was bitterly aware, based on the same design as that unfortunate trio, *Hogue, Aboukir,* and *Cressy.* It was an unsettling thought.

On the morning of April 26, Captain Gaunt received a call at his Washington, D.C., office from Morgan and Company in New York. Du Pont had just notified Morgan that the order for 600 tons of guncotton placed by George Booth the previous October was completed, and lacking the special containers used for transporting guncotton, they were requesting shipping instructions. Gaunt took a train to New York that evening and spent the next morning at Du Pont's Christfield, New Jersey, facility. It was decided to pack the guncotton in ordinary burlap bags, then place each bag in a separate cardboard box, each box weighing about forty pounds. The guncotton was packed accordingly and shipped to Cunard's Pier 54, where it arrived on April 29. By May 2, it had vanished, but no record of it ever leaving New York has ever been found.[5]

The same day that the guncotton arrived in New York, the lean, gray shape of a U-boat slipped out of the harbor at Wilhelmshaven and headed into the North Sea. The *U-20* had been scheduled to sail on April 25, but faulty packing on the watertight seal of her main periscope delayed her by four days. Her commander was Kapitan-Leutnant Walther Schwieger, thirty years of age, the scion of an old and respected Berlin family. Handsome in a big-shouldered, blond, blue-eyed sort of way, educated and urbane, Schwieger had joined the U-boat service before the war began and had acquired a remarkable wealth of knowledge about the limitations and capabilities of German submarines, enough so that he was consulted on more than one occasion by Admiral von Tirpitz. Schwieger was popular with both his officers and his crewmen and was respected by them for being a careful and conscientious skipper. He was successful too: This was his fourth war patrol, and he was already credited with sinking over 50,000 tons of Allied shipping. At the same time, there was a certain element of ruthlessness in his character: While he would never be accused of deliberately shooting helpless survivors in their lifeboats or swimming in the water, he had a reputation for firing his torpedoes first and not always asking questions later. On his previous patrol, in February, he had fired a torpedo at—and missed—the British hospital ship *Asturias,* though whether it was due to bad aim or a faulty torpedo was never determined. He later claimed he thought the *Asturias* was an ordinary freighter, an excuse that didn't hold up under official scrutiny and for which he received a mild reprimand.

All the same, Schwieger was a commander who believed that his first priority was the safety of his ship and crew, and he acted accordingly. His attack on the *Asturias* had been prompted by the increasing number of British ships that were carrying heavier and heavier deck guns. If there was the slightest doubt in Schwieger's mind that a target could present a threat to the *U-20,* he wasn't willing to take that chance. This attitude gave his crew confidence in him, and more than one former crewman of the *U-20* has described the submarine as a "happy boat."

Built in 1913 by the Germaniawerft shipyard, owned by Krupp, the *U-20* was just under 200 feet in length and displaced 750 tons. Her top speed on the surface was fourteen knots; submerged it was cut back to eight. She mounted four 18-inch torpedo tubes in her bow, and an 88-millimeter (3.5-inch) deck gun in front of her conning tower. Her crew was made up of four officers and thirty-two ratings, all bound together by the camaraderie almost always found among men who are the pioneers of a new technology. Contemporary photographs of the interiors of the U-boats graphically demonstrate the craftsmanship and care that went into their construction, with carefully turned brass and steel fittings, meticulously fitted optics and instruments, and various pieces of equipment clearly handmade for each boat, all maintained by the crew with equal care and pride. While at sea, the cramped interiors of the U-boats would become cluttered and unkempt; in port, they were always kept smart and spotless, never showing signs of the neglect and desuetude that would eventually overcome the Kaiser's surface ships.

There were no eerie notes reminiscent of Captain Nemo aboard her: The *Nautilus* never captured a ship laden with 20,000 cases of champagne or served as a seagoing kennel—two dachshunds and an indeterminate mutt called the submarine home. Nor was there a mournful pipe organ playing dirges. The *U-20*'s pride and joy was her "orchestra"—a violin, a mandolin, and a sqeezebox played by a "red-headed gnome" who was a member of the engineering crew. It was a crew close knit by the bonds of professionalism, each man knowing that his life depended not only on how well he did his own job, but also on how well each of his shipmates did his.

The *Lusitania* arriving at Cunard's Pier 54 in New York on September 13, 1908. She has just completed her maiden voyage and captured the transatlantic speed record, with an average speed of over 25.75 knots.

Taken just a few minutes earlier, this photo gives a good impression of the imposing bulk of the *Lusitania* and how she seemed to tower out of the water.

From bow on, the fine lines of the *Lusitania*'s narrow hull are evident. This gave her impressive speed but made her noticeably unstable.

The *Lusitania*'s Boat Deck, starboard side, looking aft. It is interesting to note that this photo was probably taken shortly after the *Titanic* disaster in April 1912: The three lifeboats halfway along the deck are merely sitting in chocks, but not slung from davits, indicating that they were added rather hastily. Later davits would be added for these boats an Englehart collapsible boats stored beneath each of the conventional lifeboats.

Capt. William Turner, standing on the bridge of the *Lusitania*. Turner was a captain of great experience, who before the war had commanded some of the most prestigious liners on the North Atlantic run, including the *Lusitania, Maurentania,* and *Aquitania.* He is wearing, most unusually, a proper captain's cap rather than the bowler he was accustomed to wearing, which gave him his nickname, "Bowler Bill."

First Lord of the Admiralty Winston Churchill (*left*) and First Sea Lord Admiral Sir John Fisher (*right*). Churchill was young, energetic and ambitious; Fisher was old, crafty, and devoted to the Royal Navy. At first they got along famously; later they would almost destroy each other.

Left to right: Col. Edward House, special envoy for the president of the United States; Robert Lansing, assistant secretary of state; and Woodrow Wilson, president of the United States.

Secretary of State William Jennings Bryan (*left*) and Assistant Secretary of State Robert Lansing. Bryan was a dedicated public servant, moral and scrupulously honest. Lansing was a political opportunist who never let the best interests of the United States get in the way of what was best for Robert Lansing.

Capt. Guy Gaunt, naval attaché to the British Embassy in Washington, D.C., during the Wilson administration. He ran a highly successful espionage operation in the United States during the Great War—and may have had the assistant secretary of state as one of his agents.

Capt. Franz von Papen, military attaché to the Imperial German Embassy in Washington, D.C., during the Wilson administration. Von Papen also ran some remarkably successful spying and sabotage operations in America. His later career included becoming the last chancellor of the Weimar Republic.

Kapitan-Leutnant Walther Schwieger, commander of the *U-20*. Early in his career as a U-boat skipper, he established a reputation for shooting first without bothering to make sure of the identity of his target.

The *U-20*. Small, less than 200 feet in length and displacing only 750 tons, she and her sisters had the capability of sending the largest, most powerful ships to the bottom of the sea.

Lord Mersey (*right*) on his way to preside over the Board of Trade Inquiry into the loss of the *Lusitania*. Only by chance was Mersey prevented from wrongly blaming Captain Turner for the loss of the ship.

Mrs. Paul Crompton of Philadelphia and her six children. The oldest was seventeen, the youngest nine months. Mother, father, and all six children were lost in the disaster.

Crowds gather in Liverpool on May 8, 1915, outside the Cunard offices, awaiting the news of the disaster. Learning from the White Star Line's mistakes in 1912, Cunard released as much information as it could as quickly as it came out. Usually the news was bad.

A far cry from the smiling, confident days before the war, Captain Turner was photographed in Queenstown the day after the disaster. He appears to be bewildered, almost dazed, understandable after the trauma of the previous day. He is wearing a borrowed fisherman's cap, and his uniform jacket appears to have shrunk, a result of his spending nearly six hours in the water before being rescued.

Escorted by a military honor guard, the first of over 100 unidentified victims are carried to Old Church Cemetery outside Queenstown.

Sectarian differences are put aside as an all-faiths service is held before the mass grave of the unidentified victims.

The obverse face of the Goetz medal. Intended as a satire of German submarine warfare, it bears the inscription "No Contraband Goods!" below a representation of the *Lusitania*. Goetz actually began designing the medal before the disaster: He was certain—though he never explained why—that a U-boat would sink the ship, but he got the date wrong. I reads "5 Mai (May) 1915."

The reverse face of the Goetz medal, showing passengers lined up at a Cunard ticket window, where their fares are taken by a Death's Head. The sign under the window reads, "Business as usual." Goetz made forty copies of the medal, some of which fell into British hands. Three hundred thousand duplicates were made for propaganda purposes, as the British claimed the medal celebrated the sinking.

The *U-20* sailed up the North Sea, past Scotland on her way around the British Isles. By May 1, she was off the Orkney Islands and began shaping a course westward, one that would take her down the west coast of Ireland to her assigned patrol area off the southern Irish coast near the mouth of the St. George's Channel. Schwieger expected the hunting to be particularly good in these waters, because the British landings at Gallipoli would have to be supplied by sea, many of the ships bound for the Mediterranean passing through the St. George's Channel. The landings had taken place on April 25, but the Turks had put up an unexpectedly fierce resistance, abetted by an almost total lack of cooperation between the landing force and the Royal Navy. Among the troopships that would be rushing reinforcements to the Dardanelles would be a trio of big four-funneled steamers: the *Lusitania*'s former White Star rival, the *Olympic*; her Cunard stablemate, the almost new *Aquitania*; and her sister ship, the *Mauretania.* Any of the three would be a target no U-boat skipper could pass up.[6]

While the *U-20* was heading out into the North Sea on her way to the south coast of Ireland, hundreds of people from all over the United States, as well as some of the Canadian provinces, began making their way to New York, converging in Cunard's Pier 54, where the *Lusitania* was to set sail for Great Britain on May 1. Charles Plamondon and his wife, Mary, arrived in New York on the last day of April, having come from Chicago. Mr. Plamondon owned a company that manufactured brewing equipment, and with Prohibition looming on the horizon, he was forced to find buyers outside of the United States. He was finally making a long-postponed trip to Dublin, Ireland, to close a deal with Guinness. He was met at Pennsylvania Station by his son Ambrose, who was a law student at Columbia University. The three of them spent the night at the Waldorf-Astoria before leaving early on the morning of May 1 for the Cunard docks.

Like the Plamondons, Elizabeth Duckworth arrived in New York on April 30, although to her, spending a night at the Waldorf would have seemed like the height of folly. Then again, the Plamondons were traveling first class; Elizabeth was traveling third. Taking the train from her home in Taftville, Connecticut, she spent the night with friends in Brooklyn. A sturdy woman of fifty-two, twice a widow, Elizabeth was returning for good to England, to Blackburn, Lancashire, where she had been born. A plain but pleasant-looking woman, she had spent many long years working in a textile mill and looked forward not only to her homecoming, but also to the prospect of relaxing for a week aboard the *Lusitania*: Relatively spartan though Third Class may have been, it did offer the luxury of requiring her to do absolutely nothing except show up for meals.

A bookseller from Boston, Charles Lauriat, was on his way to London, where his company had offices. Accompanying him was Lothrop Withington, a genealogist of some note. For a seasoned traveler like Lauriat, this crossing, his twenty-third, promised to be just another voyage, a dull if necessary part of his job. At least he was able to travel in the comfort of First Class.

For eighteen-year-old Leslie Morton, the voyage on the *Lusitania* promised to be anything but dull. He and seven shipmates, among them his elder brother, John, had jumped ship off the square-rigger *Naiad* to sign on to the *Lusitania* for this one crossing and so gain a quick passage home to England. Leslie was determined to enlist in the British Army and couldn't wait to experience his first action under fire.

Florence Padley had come to New York all the way from Vancouver, British Columbia. She was on her way to Liverpool to visit friends. Other Canadians making the crossing on the *Lusitania* included Capt. Richard Matthews and his wife. Captain Matthews was an officer of the 6th Winnipeg Rifles and was returning to France after taking a well-earned leave. His wife had decided to join him on the voyage and stay in England until the war was over and Captain Matthews could come home.

One passenger who was going home was Madame Dr. Marie De Page. Her husband, Dr. Antoine De Page, was the director of the La Panne Hospital in the tiny corner of northwest Belgium not occupied by the German Army. Madame De Page, dark-haired, dark-eyed, and beautiful, had spent the last six weeks in the United States raising funds for the La Panne facility. As charismatic as she was lovely, Madame De Page had been hugely successful and was now anxious to return to her husband, her work, and her country, all of which she loved equally.

A friend of Madame De Page, Theodate Pope, was also traveling to Great Britain. A tall woman, attractive in a rather severe way, Theodate was an architect and interior designer who had made a reputation for herself designing libraries. She was also intensely interested in spiritualism and psychic phenomena, and in England was to be the guest of Sir Oliver Lodge, Britain's leading spiritualist. Traveling with her was Edwin Friend, another authority on psychic phenomena, who hailed, like Miss Pope, from Farmington, Connecticut.

Allen Loney and his wife were Americans, but they were going home to Britain. They had moved there some years before, and their daughter, fourteen-year-old Virginia Bruce, was growing up to be a proper young Englishwoman. Mr. Loney had gone to France in late 1914 to work as a volunteer ambulance driver with the International Red Cross, and Mrs. Loney, becoming homesick in his absence, had gone back to New York with Virginia for a few months. Now Mr. Loney had collected his wife and daughter, and all three were looking forward to returning to the England they all loved.

Stoughton Holbourn was going home as well, although home for him—and his position in it—were a bit unusual. A professor of classical literature who lectured around the world, Holbourn had the distinction of being the laird of a small Scottish island in the North Sea called Ultima Thule—sometimes called "Foula," though nobody knows why one tiny island had two different names. The two hundred–odd residents of his island were his nominal "vassals," and Holbourn was well known and popular on his private little fiefdom. He had just finished a lecture tour in the United States and Canada, and was anxious to return to his beloved island.

And there were also newlyweds who were beginning their honeymoons with a voyage on the *Lusitania*. Leslie and Stuart Mason had been married on April 21, Stuart coming all the way from Ipswich, England, to wed Miss Leslie Lindley, daughter of one of Boston's wealthiest and most influential families. Now he was talking his new bride home. Margaret Mackenzie and James Shineman were wed on April 19, and now they were going home to Margaret's native Scotland to break the news to her parents. For both couples, it was a happy, giddy time.

Not everyone was happy, though. In Boston, just about the time when he and his wife should have been catching the train for New York, Edward Bowen was telephoning the Cunard agent instead, instructing the agent to cancel the passage on the *Lusitania* that Bowen had booked for himself and his wife. As he later explained it to his friends, "A feeling grew upon me that something was going to happen to the *Lusitania*. I talked it over with Mrs. Bowen and we decided to cancel our passage, although I had important business engagements in London." Bowen never understood what it was that made him decide not to sail on the *Lusitania*, but whatever it was, it most likely saved his and his wife's lives.[7]

Kapitan-Leutnant Schwieger was always amused by the effort the British had put into constructing the mine- and net-behung boom across the English Channel that had become known as the Channel Barrage, never more so than when he transmitted his daily position report to the German Naval High Command in Wilhelmshaven and Berlin. Designed to deny the U-boats easy access to the Atlantic by forcing them to go around the northern end of the British Isles, the Channel Barrage was effective in ways that Schwieger failed to comprehend. By forcing the U-boats to spend three or four days in transit to and from their patrol areas, it reduced the amount of time each boat could spend on station by at least a week. British Intelligence let it be known that the Admiralty didn't believe that the German submarines actually had the range to sail all the way around Great Britain and Ireland, though this was really a patently false rumor intended to lull the Germans into a sense of false security regarding British knowledge of the U-boats' capabilities.

Schwieger would have been appalled had he known that not only did the Admiralty know full well the range and performance of his submarine, but that they were keeping track of his progress around Scotland and Ireland on a day-by-day basis. The cryptographers in Room 40 in the basement of the Admiralty Building in Whitehall were decoding the *U-20*'s daily position reports almost as fast as their counterparts in Wilhelmshaven and Berlin, and the Plot in the Admiralty operations room was carefully updated with the latest information about the *U-20*'s movements, as well as every other U-boat at sea. Significantly, his progress around the British Isles was being monitored by the Admiralty, though no action was being taken against him other than a few vague warnings about submarine activity off Ireland being issued. It was a vital advantage if the British chose to use it properly, for it could allow them to divert ships away from waters where the U-boats were on patrol. The decision to warn which ships and when to do so was left to the discretion of the First Lord, Winston Churchill, or in his absence, that of the Director of the Trade Division, Captain Webb. Over the next few days, as the courses of the *U-20* and the *Lusitania* would bring them both into the waters off the south coast of Ireland, that responsibility would shift between the two men, as neither seemed to see the peril that the *Lusitania* was steaming toward, or if they did, neither was willing to act, each wanting the other to make the decision.

That the peril to the *Lusitania* was real enough seemed to be fully confirmed the morning she sailed. On May 1, 1915, a curiously worded notice, with the signature of "The German Embassy" at the bottom, appeared in a number of American newspapers across the country. The most startling was the appearance of the notice in the travel section of the *New York Sun*. There, right next to the Cunard advertisement for the *Lusitania*'s departure that afternoon, was a black-bordered announcement with the word "NOTICE!" across the top in boldface. It read:

> Travellers intending to embark on the Atlantic voyage are reminded that a state of war exists between Germany and her allies and Great Britain and her allies; that the zone of war includes the waters adjacent to the British Isles; that, in accordance with formal notice given by the Imperial German Government, vessels flying the flags of Great Britain, or any of her allies, are liable to destruction in those waters and travelers sailing in the war zone on ships of Great Britain or her allies do so at their own risk.
>
> Imperial German Embassy
> Washington, D.C., April 22, 1915

Despite what it said, the notice did not come from the German Embassy at all, nor did it originate with the German Foreign Ministry in Berlin. It was the product of a meeting of some of the leading citizens of New York's German-American community. On April 20, George Viereck, editor of the German-American daily *The Fatherland,* called the meeting in an attempt to avert a serious breach in the relations between Germany and the United States over the German submarine campaign. It was clear to them that as far as Germany was concerned, for all practical purposes the United States had already chosen sides and was openly favoring the Allies. What could be done to keep the U-boats from further antagonizing the United States, to keep the Americans from making a whole-hearted commitment to the Allied cause? After reviewing the *Falaba* incident and Washington's reaction to it, Viereck remarked to his friends, "Sooner or later some big passenger boat with Americans on board will be sunk by a submarine, then there will be hell to pay."

An open breach, and the prospect of war, between the country where these men were born and their newly adopted homeland was something they did not want to contemplate, so they debated how to draw the American public's attention to the German point of view. Dr. Karl Fuhrer suggested emphasizing the starving children in Germany who were wasting away as a consequence of the blockade, then making the point that the submarine campaign was an attempt to force the British to raise the blockade and end the suffering in Germany. It wasn't a bad idea, and it might have worked but for one flaw that was spotted by Dr. Bernhard Dernberg. "The American people," he said, "cannot visualize the spectacle of a hundred thousand, even half a million, German children starving by slow degrees as a result of the British blockade, but they can visualize the pitiful face of a little child drowning amidst the wreckage caused by a German torpedo."

Eventually it was decided that a warning be published, addressed to American passengers, reminding them that they traveled at their own risk, not because they were the intended targets for German torpedoes, but because Germany and Great Britain were at war, and they could lose their lives if a German submarine sank the British ship they were traveling on. Such an action by a U-boat would be all very legal and proper and correct, and the Americans would simply have to understand. As the warning was being drafted and the list of newspapers in which it was to be published was being decided, Dr. Dernberg's comment about the child aboard the torpedoed ship jarred Viereck's memory, and he asked what the next sailing date for a large British passenger ship would be. When he was told that the *Lusitania* was scheduled to sail from New York in ten days, an even deeper sense of urgency overcame Viereck. "Publish this thing," he demanded, "*before* the *Lusitania* sails!"

Once the draft of the warning was complete and the papers that would carry it agreed upon, Viereck telephoned the German Embassy and asked for official approval of the text. The Ambassador, Count von Bernsdorff, was out, but by chance, Viereck was connected to Captain von Papen. Von Papen refused to endorse the warning in his name, the name of the Ambassador, or that of the German Foreign Minister, von Jagow. Instead, he suggested that it simply be signed "The Imperial German Embassy" and hung up. Within hours, copies of the warning, along with appropriately endorsed checks, were sent out to the newspapers Viereck and his compatriots believed to be the most influential. The majority of them went out by mail, but those going to New York papers were delivered by hand to ensure that the deadline on Friday, April 23, was met.

The copy of the warning sent to the *New York Sun* went to the night editor, who, when he read it, sensed a deeper story. He called the U.S. State Department for advice on whether to print it or not, and was told that printing it without confirmation from the German embassy first could be dangerous, as the warning could be construed as libelous. Hearing this, the night editor put a "black" on the warning so that no other paper could publish it, then called United Press and asked the news service to circularize any of its subscribing papers that the State Department had contacted the *Sun* and ordered that no copy from any belligerent embassy be carried by any paper without the prior approval of the State Department. This was obviously untrue, but United Press failed to verify the editor's claim, and soon the warning began to take on a life of its own, far different from what Viereck and his colleagues intended it to be.

When the warning failed to appear in the Friday papers, Viereck wondered why, but it wasn't until Monday morning, April 26, that he was able to find out. Once he did, he called Washington and urgently requested a interview with Secretary of State Bryan.

Bryan agreed to see him that afternoon, and so Viereck caught a train to Washington and shortly after lunch sat down with the Secretary of State. Bryan listened dumbfounded as Viereck described the reasons for creating and publishing the warning, then went on to explain how, on all of her eastbound crossings but one, the *Lusitania* had carried cargoes of munitions bound for Great Britain. He supported his contention by producing copies of the *Lusitania*'s supplementary manifests. He then informed Bryan that there were 6 million rounds of rifle ammunition sitting on Cunard's Pier 54, waiting to be loaded aboard the *Lusitania*. (How he knew was a question Captain von Papen probably could have easily answered.) Bryan immediately cleared the warning for publication and later that evening went to the White House and repeated everything Viereck had told him to President Wilson. Wilson heard Bryan out but expressed considerable scepticism about Viereck's truthfulness and motives, essentially telling Bryan not to bother with the whole affair any further.[8]

The 6 million rifle rounds Viereck spoke of (it was actually just under 5 million rounds) were only part of a very unusual cargo the *Lusitania* would carry on this crossing. For four days, her forward cargo hold was being loaded with a curious assortment of goods. The hold went all the way down to the Orlop Deck, the lowest deck of the ship. It was situated just forward of Boiler Room Number 1, separated only by the now-disused transverse coal bunker, a distance of some 30 feet. Included in the cargo were 1,639 copper ingots; 1,300 pounds of sheet brass; 4,927 boxes of .303 rifle cartridges, 1,000 cartridges per box; 1,248 cases of 3-inch shrapnel shells, described by the manufacturer, Bethlehem Steel, on the waybill as 3-inch shrapnel shells, filled, the total weight of the shells being 52 tons; 3,863 boxes of burlap-wrapped cheese, each box weighing approximately 40 pounds; 323 bales of unprocessed furs; and a few score tons of various sundries, foodstuffs, and miscellaneous cargo. Interestingly enough, over half the *Lusitania's* cargo for this voyage was, under the British definition, one form or another of contraband. The total value of the cargo when its loading was finished on the morning of May 1 was $735,000, while the ship and her furnishings were valued at $10 million. She was insured for only $7.5 million, at the regular 5 percent premium, with an additional 1$\frac{1}{4}$ percent wartime premium. The insurance rates were unusually low because of the *Lusitania's* reputation for speed and safety.[9]

At 8:00 A.M. on the morning of May 1, 1915, a rather drab, overcast Saturday, two masters-at-arms, Peter Smith and Billy Williams, took up positions at the head of the main gangway between the *Lusitania* and the pier, prepared to greet the boarding passengers. What they weren't prepared for was a bevy of reporters and photographers milling about at the end of the gangway. One of the reporters came up the gangway and, spotting Third Officer John Lewis, asked to speak to Captain Turner. When Lewis refused, the reporter showed him a copy of that morning's edition of the *New York Sun*. In the travel section, right next to the Cunard advertisement announcing the sailing of the *Lusitania* at noon that day, was the German warning notice written by George Viereck and his associates. The notice had actually appeared in most of the New York papers Viereck had submitted it to, but none of them were placed in a position that seemed so provocative—or sinister. The reporters were waiting to "buttonhole" prominent passengers as they boarded, to get their reaction to the warning notice. Lewis decided that this was not a matter for Captain Turner to deal with and instead called the Cunard offices, asking that Charles Sumner come down to the dock to talk with the reporters. Sumner said he would be there within the hour. When he arrived, he made light of the warning, gesturing to the crowd of passengers boarding the *Lusitania*.

"You can see how it has affected the public," he said, emphasizing that no bookings had been canceled in response to the notice.

The reporters did manage to get some good copy. Charles Bowring, part owner of the Bowring Brothers shipping line, derided the notice, saying, "In my opinion it was a very silly performance of the German Embassy." Justus Miles Foreman simply dismissed it by saying, "I have no time to worry about trifles." Sir Hugh Lane, former director of the Irish National Gallery, called the notice "too absurd for discussion."

Alexander Campbell, the general manager of John Dewar and Sons of London, was the most categorical in his derision of the warning notice. "I think it's a lot of tommyrot for any government to do such a thing, and it is hard to believe that the German ambassador dictated the advertisement. The *Lusitania* can run away from any submarine the Germans have got and the British Admiralty will see the ship is looked after when she arrives within striking distance of the Irish coast."

As he watched Sumner deal with the reporters, Third Officer Lewis felt satisfied that he had handled the situation adequately. He turned to the purser and asked, "Who's the quality sailing with us?" The purser, in a magnificent display of English condescension, replied, "We have no quality people sailing with us, only monied people." The purser was being a little too parochial in his judgement. It didn't mean that there weren't any interesting people making this crossing. On the contrary, the *Lusitania's* passenger list could have been described as rather colorful.

For those intrigued by political controversy, there was Margaret Mackworth, Lady Rhondda, who was one of England's leading militant suffragettes. She had actually gone to prison for her political beliefs and her activities, including smashing shop windows and disrupting public meetings, and was inordinately proud of it. Her father, D. A. Thomas, a Member of Parliament from the Rhondda Valley in Wales, was traveling with her.

The theatrical world was remarkably well represented. Making the crossing was the lovely actress Rita Jolivet, her brother-in-law, actor George Vernon, and Vernon's friend, playwright Charles Klein. One of Klein's plays, *The Lion and the Mouse*, had been a big hit for producer Charles Frohman, who was also making this passage, on his way to London to scout for talented new actors and writers.

Frohman was a legend in the theatrical world, and one of the best-known and best-loved men in New York. Coming up the gangway, a short, stout figure, looking much like "a Napoleon with a Hebraic nose," he leaned heavily on his "wife" as he walked—his "wife" being the nickname he had given his cane, its support a constant necessity because of painful rheumatoid arthritis in his knees and hips. Shy and soft-spoken, he was the soul of kindness:

Being one of the shrewdest businessmen in America had never convinced him of the need to abandon good manners or common courtesy. Frohman was credited loudly and widely, and quite truthfully, as single-handedly raising the American theater from the mire of disdain and disrepute that John Wilkes Booth had plunged it into fifty years before, and giving it a status equal to that of its European counterpart. Originally compelled to bring actors and actresses to the United States from Europe when no suitable American talent could be found, now Frohman was reversing that trend, as the popularity of American stage performers grew on the other side of the Atlantic.

One of the keys to Frohman's success was his insistence on quality. Well-written, intelligent, and entertaining plays, actors who would really act, and performers and stage crew who kept their private lives clean of scandal allowed him to raise the profession of acting and the world of theater in the United States to a level of respectability usually only enjoyed by the professions. The rising popularity of the motion picture was a concern for him, but he was convinced that he would never live to see the day when the "movies," as they were called, became more popular than the stage in the United States.

The other key was his charm. James Barrie, the playwright, in eulogizing Frohman, said, "I have never known anyone more modest and no one quite as shy. He seemed to be born afresh every morning." Frohman never ceased to smile, never raised his voice, never broke his word. His loyalty to his friends and business associates was legendary, and it was returned in kind.

And in some ways, Frohman was ahead of his time. Evincing a tolerance that ran against the grain of growing American sentiment, Frohman had decided to produce a play written by forty-one-year-old Justus Miles Foreman, a novelist who had recently turned to writing for the stage. Foreman was crossing with Frohman, hoping to find a producer in Britain for his work. The name of his play was *The Hyphen,* and it was scheduled to open in Boston in one week. It was about German-Americans.

As he came up the gangway, the reporters descended on Frohman, who received them patiently and responded as best he could while he made his way to his cabin. At one point, one of them asked straight out, "Are you afraid of the U-boats, Mr. Frohman?"

"No," he replied with a smile, "I'm only afraid of the IOUs." And with that he ushered them out of his cabin and sat down to enjoy the company of his friends.

One man who never had to worry about IOUs—indeed, in his thirty-seven years he had never known any kind of material want, let alone debt was Alfred Gwynne Vanderbilt. Heir to the immense Vanderbilt fortune begun by Cornelius Vanderbilt in the second quarter of the nineteenth century, he was one of the last of a generation of fabulously wealthy men whose death knell had sounded on the decks of the *Titanic* three years before. Vanderbilt had actually canceled a reservation on that ill-fated ship the day before she sailed. Did that mean that he led a charmed life? he was frequently asked. He would answer with a shake of his handsome head. Wealth didn't always blind a person to reality, and Vanderbilt held few illusions about life. Happily married— the former Margaret Emmerson McKim was his second wife—with two sons to whom he was utterly devoted, he knew what it was to be utterly unhappy. His first marriage had been a disaster, the divorce ugly, and one of the consequences traumatic: A married St. Louis socialite who had been named in the suit had taken her life, and the tragedy cast a pall over Vanderbilt he never quite shook off.

He escaped the reporters as quickly as he could, after commenting on the warning notice in the *Sun* with a quick "Why worry about submarines? We can outdistance any submarine afloat!" and made his way to his cabin on A Deck, starboard side. He didn't feel like discussing his trip to Great Britain with the press. He was on his way to a meeting of the International Horse Show Association. Vanderbilt had been instrumental in reviving the sport of road-coaching and was acknowledged to be one of the best four-in-hand drivers on either side of the Atlantic, but the announcement would be made at the association meeting that there would be no racing for him this season. There was a war on, and while giving up four-in-hand racing wasn't going to win the war for the Allies, it was a gesture, however symbolic.

Vanderbilt was fond of the *Lusitania* and had crossed on her a number of times over the years. In September 1907, he sailed down to Sandy Hook to meet her at the end of her maiden voyage, when she won the Blue Ribband. He always took the same cabin on A Deck and usually kept to it for most of the voyage; despite the popular image of a multimillionaire, he was not a cigar-smoking, party-going extrovert. In fact, he was almost painfully shy—he shunned crowds because he hated being pointed out. In that way, as in many others, he was the complete opposite of Elbert Hubbard.

Elbert Hubbard, who along with his wife, Alice, was boarding the *Lusitania* that morning as well, was a virtual unknown in Europe, but in America his homespun humor and philosophies had made him something of an institution. An author and lecturer, Hubbard had a way of expressing his observations and opinions in homely little stories and wry quips that always contained a kernel of thought-provoking truth. He published a series of small books, *Little Visits to the Homes of. . .,* where he would re-create afternoons, sometimes real, sometimes imaginary, spent in the homes of people as diverse as farmers, shopkeepers, bankers and steel tycoons. One pamphlet he had written, the antiwar *A Message to Garcia,* had sold 40 million copies. From his home in East Aurora, New York, he spouted aphorisms that many of his admirers considered verse, and he was considered news wherever he went. He had just written an article that had been published in every major newspaper in the country, entitled "Who Lifted the Lid off Hell?" a rhetorical question he then answered, "William Hohenzollern." Now he was about to venture off to Europe, where, he told the reporters, "I intend to interview the Kaiser. If he refuses I'll wait until after the war and interview him on St. Helena."

At dockside, a brass band appeared and began playing—nobody knew who sent for them or why—and the drizzle began to ease up. By now a steady stream of passengers, along with friends and relatives who had come to see them off, were making their way up the gangway to the deck of the big Cunard liner. The band seemed to lighten everyone's mood, and soon the usual festive air that normally surrounded the *Lusitania's* sailing began to be felt.

At 10:00, though a curious incident occurred. Five telegrams were delivered to the *Lusitania,* with Vanderbilt, Frohman, and Hubbard among the recipients. All five were similarly worded, each being a warning not to sail on the *Lusitania,* as the Germans intended to destroy her. The ship's senior wireless operator, Robert Leith, took the messages through the ship's land line and promptly notified Charles Sumner. Sumner, shaking off the reporters, promptly confiscated all five telegrams and asked Leith to try to find out who had sent them and why. It took Leith nearly an hour, but he eventually learned that all five had been sent from the Western Union office in Providence, Rhode Island, by John Rathon, editor of the *Providence Journal,* a newspaper long noted for its anti-German sentiments. What Rathon hoped to accomplish by sending the messages was never made clear.

Sumner returned to his office, accompanied by Captain Tuner, where the two men attended to the details of transferring forty passengers and the cargo from the Cunard liner *Cameronia,* requisitioned that morning by the Royal Navy. Sir Courtenay Bennet appeared, informing Turner that no new sailing instructions had been received from the Admiralty, then handed him a weighted and sealed bag from the embassy in Washington to the Foreign Office and went through the formality of reading the instructions that the bag was to be thrown overboard in the event of enemy attack. Finally, Bennet told Turner about the most recent attack on a British ship in the Irish Sea, the *Gullflight.*

Sumner quickly explained the telegram incident to Bennet, informing him of their content and origins. Bennet agreed with Sumner and Turner, both of whom believed the messages were nothing more than a journalistic stunt done in extremely poor taste. Returning to the *Lusitania,* Turner had the dock quickly cleared of reporters, strode up the gangway and told the masters-at-arms to begin shooing the visitors ashore, then made his way to the bridge. The *Lusitania's* steam whistle gave a huge blast, and at 12:30

Turner ordered the lines mooring the *Lusitania* to the pier cast off. A trio of tugboats began easing the big ship out into the Hudson River, while the crowds on the pier cheered and waved good-bye, the cheers and waves returned by those aboard. The brass band continued to play, barely heard now over the bellow of steam whistles and the shouts of farewell. Slowly the *Lusitania* eased away from Pier 54, growing clouds of smoke rising from her funnels as her bow swung around and she began to ease forward, down into New York Harbor, through the Narrows, and out to sea. Before long, all anyone could see of her was a smudge of coal smoke on the horizon; then, after a bit, even that was gone.[10]

So the crowds cheered and the passengers waved and threw their *bon voyage* streamers at those standing on the pier, as the *Lusitania* steamed out of New York Harbor and into the North Atlantic. Everyone on board, and everyone who had watched her leave the pier, thought she was sailing to Liverpool. Instead, she was sailing to eternity.

CHAPTER 8

The Last Voyage

CAPTAIN TURNER WAS GLAD TO FINALLY BE BACK ON HIS BRIDGE AND BACK AT sea, both places he felt that he really belonged. Swiftly putting New York behind her, the *Lusitania* had stood well out to sea before nightfall on Saturday, and by noon Sunday she had put 500 miles behind her. As Turner puffed on his pipe and studied the noon position report, he was satisfied that any German U-boats or surface raiders that may have been lurking off the American coast were now well behind him. He had conducted Divine Services that morning, one of the few social duties he truly enjoyed. In his fifty-one years at sea, Turner had seen the world's oceans at their most beautiful and most terrifying, and consequently needed no prodding to humble himself before the Almighty. Once the worship service was over, however, he went back to the bridge and returned to the business of being a captain.

He didn't like the role that had been thrust onto the captain of a passenger liner: Not only was he supposed to command the ship, but he was also expected to entertain the passengers, exhibit flawless manners as an example to the other officers, make sure that all those whose social stations entitled them to the privilege were seated at the captain's table at luncheon or dinner, and have a kind word and a smile for everyone on board. It was not a life that his experience or training had prepared him for.

The days were long gone, and Turner knew it, when all a captain had to do to please the owners was bring his ship safely and smartly into port. At that, Will Turner was an acknowledged master. The son of a sea captain, Turner had had little liking for his father's wish that he become a minister. Instead, in the best seagoing tradition, he had run away from home to become a cabin boy. He had fallen in love with sailing ships and had circumnavigated the globe several times under canvas before finally acknowledging what every aspiring young officer knew—that the future lay in steam. He studied hard and took every exam he could as soon as he felt qualified, gradually working his way up among the steamships of the North Atlantic and Australian runs, finally acquiring the coveted Master and Extra Master Tickets (Any Vessel, Any Ocean, Sail or Steam). His last days under sail were spent in command of the bark *Star of the East,* a berth he took to fulfill a peculiar requirement of the Cunard line: They would never give command of one of their vessels to someone who hadn't earned a command in another line first.

His rise within the Cunard ranks seemed slow; it wasn't until 1903, twenty years after he joined the line, that he was given a ship of his own, the little *Aleppo.* Clearly he impressed someone with his handling of the small Mediterranean steamer, for after that his rise within the company was meteoric. Within seven years, he had skippered the *Carpathia, Ivernia, Umbria, Caronia,* and *Carmania.* In 1910, he took over the *Lusitania* for the first time and drove her to some of her fastest crossings. The next year, he was given command of the *Mauretania,* the prize posting of the Cunard fleet, making headlines when he took her to the rescue of the passengers and crew of the burning steamship *West Point.* His ship handling in that venture had been at once so daring and so impeccable that he was awarded the Shipwreck and Humane Society's medal for heroism. When a new queen was launched in 1913, the *Aquitania,* he was given the honor of commanding her on her maiden voyage. His crews admired and respected him, a rarity among merchant seamen, some men following him from ship to ship. He was a disciplinarian, but he was fair, something that couldn't be said for every captain. Among merchant skippers, Will Turner ranked with the best.

It hadn't been without cost, though. His wife had left him in 1912, for reasons that were never explained. He had two sons, Percy and Norman, but they were both grown men now. Norman was serving in France, an officer in the Royal Regiment of Artillery. Percy had followed the family's seagoing tradition and was an officer in the British Merchant Marine. Whether it was loneliness or something else entirely that caused Turner to keep to himself, no one could say he hadn't earned the right to do so. Socializing could be left to others.

His officers understood Turner's reluctance to mingle socially with the passengers, and so they humored him. Most of the social duties were handled by Staff Capt. J. C. Anderson, with whom Turner had a friendly, if not particularly close, relationship. Turner's best friend on board was the Chief Engineer, Archibald Bryce, a big, strapping man with an overpowering walrus mustache. Like Turner, Bryce had been with Cunard for thirty-two years, all of them in Engineering. In a way, working as an engineer for Cunard was something of a tradition in Bryce's family: His father had been an engineer on one of Cunard's old paddlewheel steamers not long after the company began its transatlantic service.

While Bryce commiserated with Turner over the passing of the "good old days"—as an engineering officer, Bryce was spared the burden of mingling with the passengers—he could at least assure the captain that the ship was sound. She had trimmed out nicely, thanks to the work on the trim tanks

Turner had demanded in March, and the engines were as good as they could be, short of a complete overhaul of the turbines. Turner could have confidence in his ship.[1]

By Monday, May 3, the *Lusitania* was off the Grand Banks, and her passengers were settling into a comfortable shipboard routine. Several new friendships had been started. Dr. Howard Fisher, a Washington, D.C., physician who was on his way to France to join his brother, where together they would set up a volunteer hospital, was traveling with his sister-in-law Dorothy Connor. By chance, they met Charles and Mary Plamondon and discovered that they had several mutual acquaintances. Elizabeth Duckworth was particularly enjoying herself: She had quickly become fast friends with Mrs. Alice Scott and Alice's young son, Arthur. Together the three of them amused themselves by exploring the big ship.

The *Lusitania* was in many ways a paradise for a curious boy like Arthur —big, powerful, full of exciting new sights, sounds, and smells. For children traveling First Class who were less adventurous than he (or whose parents were less adventurous than Alice Scott) there was a big playroom on B Deck that was also their dining room. In Second Class, a special section of the dining saloon was reserved as a play area for children when meals were not being served. There was no designated play area in Third Class, but if Arthur Scott's explorations were any indication, this may have simply meant that the Third Class children were likely to have more fun than their First and Second Class counterparts, confined as they were to their respective playrooms.

Another shipboard friendship, this one rather more unlikely, sprang up between Professor Holbourn and twelve-year-old Avis Dolphin. Avis was traveling to Great Britain, where she would be staying with her grandparents while she attended school. A particularly intelligent, somewhat serious child, she seemed fascinated by the professor and his knowledge, especially his ability to tell the stories of classical literature in a way that a twelve-year-old could understand. Holbourn, in turn, was intrigued by this precocious young lady and her thirst for knowledge.

While there seemed to be very little gambling on board, there was some ferocious card playing. In addition to the ship-sponsored whist competitions being held in each class, the Second Class Lounge was the scene of a seemingly nonstop ongoing game of contract bridge. One of the players was Archibald Donald, a young, Scottish structural engineer who had left a good job with Truscon Steel in Boston to join the British Army. He was on his way to officer's training at Edinburgh University. Two other regulars in the game were his cabin mates, John Wilson, a chemist who had gone to Cambridge with Donald, and George Bilbrough. Admittedly, the young men were spending as much time as they were in the lounge because there were a surprising number of attractive young ladies in Second Class, and also because their cabin was almost stiflingly hot. The Second Class Lounge was, for a number of reasons, an altogether more pleasant venue for passing the time.

The final member of the foursome must have had a difficult time finding a good game of bridge in Calgary, Alberta. The Reverend H. L. Gwyer was returning to his native Scotland with his wife of just three weeks, Margaret, another child of the heather and Highlands, but he was spending precious little of his waking hours with her. It seemed that every free moment he had he was sitting in the lounge with Donald, Wilson, and Bilbrough, bidding, trumping, and finessing. Mrs. Gwyer unhappily saw far less of her husband than she wished she would.

Very early on May 4, the *Lusitania* passed the halfway point on her journey across the Atlantic, making an average speed of a steady if disappointing fifteen knots. On most ships, this would have been considered excellent, but for her, it was positively torpid. In her first twenty-four hours at sea, she had made a respectable 501 miles, but by the next day, that had dropped to 468 miles and remained in the 460s for the rest of the voyage. Charles Lauriat was particularly disappointed by this: Having been accustomed to the *Lusitania*'s speed before the war, every day he picked a high number for her progress in the ship's pool, and each time he lost. To Lauriat, this was inexplicable, but he consoled himself with the thought that when the ship was within sight of the Irish coast, Captain Turner would pour on the steam and really show some speed.

Lauriat, of course, was blissfully unaware of the six cold boilers of Boiler Room Number 4, which guaranteed that the days of twenty-six-knot runs were over. Even so, a sort of peacetime atmosphere had prevailed so far. The ship had left New York nearly as full as could be expected in wartime, with 1,257 passengers aboard, the largest number carried on a single crossing since the war began. There were 290 in First Class, 600 in Second, and 367 in Third. British and Canadian citizens accounted for 944 of the total, while 159 were Americans.

There were five musicians aboard, who played in the First Class Dining Saloon at luncheon and dinner, and in the First Class Lounge in the afternoon and evenings. They had what to Europeans was a disconcerting habit of breaking into "The End of a Perfect Day" or "Just a-Wearyin' for You" or some other Carrie Jacobs Bond tune whenever Elbert Hubbard entered the dining saloon, but it was their way of greeting him, a greeting that always drew an affectionate smile of thanks from Hubbard.

An unexpected musical treat came from the Royal Welsh Male Chorus, returning to Britain after touring the United States and Canada. The Welsh have long been known as a race of singers, and the chorus did its best to confirm that belief, giving concerts in both First and Second Class Lounges almost every night after dinner. Third Class passengers were invited to the concerts in the Second Class Lounge.[2]

On the morning of May 4, there was, as required by law, a lifeboat drill. Originally the *Lusitania* had carried sixteen lifeboats, the number specified by the Board of Trade regulation then in force, but only enough to carry 1,040 people, less than two-fifths of the total she could accommodate. After the *Titanic* disaster and the scandal of her insufficient lifeboats, the regulations had been revised to require enough boats to hold the ship's entire capacity. To meet this new requirement, Cunard had increased the number of conventional hard-sided lifeboats to twenty-two, each of which were numbered, the odd numbers carried on the starboard side of the ship, the even numbers to port. Underneath the conventional boats were stored twenty-six Englehardt "collapsibles," folding boats that were made up of a shallow wooden keel with canvas sides that could be raised before the boat was launched or after it had been put in the water; the sides were held in place by wooden pins and folding iron stays. The conventional boats were all slung from davits, while the collapsibles were stowed in cradles underneath them, the idea being that the collapsibles could be slung from the same falls as the conventional boats once the regular boats had been launched, or they could simply be allowed to float off the deck if the ship were *in extremis*.

Cunard had discovered that when the *Lusitania* rolled, the lifeboats would swing from side to side in their davits like giant pendulums. On their inward swings, the keels of the boats would crash against the sides of the collapsibles, damaging the latter's canvas gunwales. To stop this, a six-foot-long chain was secured to the deck and attached to each boat by means of a wooden peg. This restricted the arc the boat could swing in, protecting the collapsibles. If the boat had to be lowered, the peg holding the chain was to be knocked free with a wooden mallet stored in each boat.

The davits from which the boats were slung did not have any sort of compensating gear that would have allowed the boat to be lowered on a relatively even keel regardless of the severity of the trim the ship had taken on. Instead, they were simply heavy metal arms with simple block-and-tackle affairs, each davit working independently of its mate at the other end of the lifeboat. Trying to keep a lifeboat reasonably level while it was being lowered if the ship were to sink rapidly by the bow or stern would require great skill on the part of the men at the falls, the lines holding the boat. Inexperienced crewmen would most likely find it nearly impossible. One other potential defect was that if the ship took on a list greater than seven degrees, the davits on the side opposite the list wouldn't be able to swing the boats out far enough to clear the side of the ship.

In any case, at 7:00 A.M., the crew designated to carry out the boat drill appeared on the Boat Deck alongside the designated lifeboat, in this case Number 13. The supervising officer blew his whistle, and the crew quickly donned their lifebelts, then ran to the boat, stripped off the cover, and climbed in. Then they sat there. There was no attempt to fit the oars in the oarlocks, or even count the oars to see if the correct number was there. Nobody checked the auxiliary mast, spars, or sail, and no one checked to see if the freshwater tins were topped up. The boat wasn't swung out, nor, since the ship was under way, could any attempt be made to lower it to see if the falls were working properly. A second whistle blow, and the crewmen climbed out of the boat, replaced the canvas cover, took off their lifebelts, and went back to work. The whole drill lasted perhaps ten minutes, and while it may have been somewhat entertaining for those few passengers brave enough to rise at such an early hour to watch it, it had been far from instructive.[3]

On the morning of May 4, the *U-20* was cruising to the northwest of Ireland, just beginning her long run down the west Irish coast. Much like the passengers on the *Lusitania*, Schwieger and his crew had finally settled into a comfortable daily routine. As he and other U-boat captains were demonstrating, the submarines had a destructive potential out of proportion to their small size, and that small size dictated most every aspect of shipboard life on the *U-20*. The interior of a U-boat was, in a word, cramped, and space was at a premium everywhere. The ingenuity that the crew displayed in making the most of that space was remarkable.

The typical U-boat war patrol was three to four weeks long: one week outbound from Emden to the assigned parol area, one or two weeks on station, and one week spent returning. During this whole time, the U-boat was entirely on its own: There were no friendly ports to replenish supplies or make repairs, so each U-boat had to be as self-sufficient and self-contained as possible. Spares, extra equipment, and food would be stored everywhere, in the magazines, the torpedo room, the captain's cabin, even the head. The refrigerated space was tiny, so fresh meats, bread, and vegetables would be consumed first; by the time the patrol was over and the U-boat on its way back to Emden or Wilhelmshaven, the crew would be eating meals prepared entirely from tinned food.

Next came the torpedoes. The *U-20* carried a full load of eight torpedoes, which were stowed wherever room could be found. This meant that at the beginning of the patrol, the space normally used by the torpedomen's bunks was occupied by spare torpedoes, the sailors being forced to sleep on the deckplates or cobble up makeshift bunks across the "tin fish," as the long, deadly weapons were called. Two were slung overhead by chains in the engine

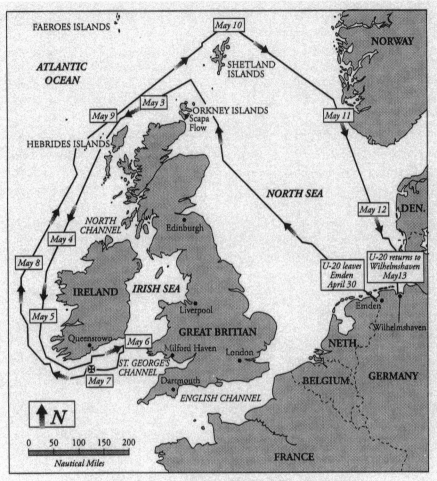

Cruise of the *U-20*, April 30–May 13, 1915

room and pulled forward through the ship on a special overhead railing when the time came to load them into the tubes.

Thirty-six men shared a single toilet (the "head") and lived for a month or more at a time, twenty-four hours a day, inside a space about the size of a small, single-story house. In such an environment, there was little time for formalities such as saluting, but self-discipline was a necessity. Every man aboard soon learned the strengths and weaknesses of each of his shipmates, as well as those of his officers. The camaraderie that resulted, the sense of being a service apart, an elite within the High Seas Fleet, had no parallel anywhere in the rest of the German Navy. The U-boat crews were professionals, and proud of it.

As the *U-20* made her way toward Fastnet, Schwieger reviewed his orders. One of the last signals he had received from the High Seas Fleet had read: "Large British troop transports expected starting from Liverpool, Bristol, Dartmouth . . . get to stations on the fastest route possible route around Scotland; hold them as long as supplies permit . . . submarines are to attack transport ships, merchant ships and warships." What, if any, verbal instructions he had been given prior to leaving Emden will never be known. The day before, he had sighted a small freighter, perhaps 2,000 tons, just as he was passing the Hebrides. He fired one torpedo at it, which missed. It was only then that Schwieger noticed the Danish flag flying from the little freighter's stern, and once he did so, he broke off the attack. A small incident, but highly illuminating.

May 4 passed uneventfully for the *U-20*, and by daybreak she was cruising off Fastnet. Schwieger had no idea that his submarine had been spotted for the first time that morning and a report of the sighting was on its way to the Admiralty in Whitehall. He did know that he was less than a day's sailing away from his assigned patrol area. The next few days should prove to be very exciting for him and his crew. He had no idea just how exciting they would be.[4]

The report from Fastnet that a U-boat had been spotted there that morning swiftly made its way to the Admiralty's Operations Section, where it was evaluated as a reliable report and was placed in the stack of position updates that were ready to be added to the Plot.

The Plot was the result of the sterling work done by Captain Hall's Room 40. Hall's intelligence operations had such deep and far-reaching effects that some of the work done by Room 40 has been classified for all time. But the masterpiece of the war had to have been "the Plot." Working from information in the captured German naval codebooks given to the British by the Russians, the cryptographers in Room 40 recreated an exact replica of the map the German Naval High Command used to keep track of the daily movements of all of the German ships at sea, including the German grid square system that allowed the U-boats to inform Berlin and Wilhelmshaven of their portions without having to resort to giving longitude and latitude coordinates that were easily deciphered. Each day, the U-boats, along with any German surface ships, would update their portions, not realizing that they were keeping the British informed of their movements as well.

Superimposed over the German grid was the standard British map grid, a system that allowed the Operations Division of the Admiralty to be able to instantly correlate the position of a German submarine or surface raider to the British position reference system. On this map would be placed small silhouettes of all the British, Allied, and German ships and submarines at sea.

Atop the silhouette of each surface ship was a disc, sized to scale for the map, that indicated the lookout radius of the ship the silhouette represented. The larger the ship and the taller her masts, the greater the distance her lookouts could see, and so the larger the disc. Submarines were represented by red squares thirty-two scale miles to a side, believed to represent the maximum area a U-boat could search during daylight hours. Projected from each silhouette was the last known course of the ship it represented, along with an extrapolation of that course for the next twenty-four hours. On the morning of May 5, the largest ship at sea was the *Lusitania,* still nearly 900 miles west of Fastnet, where the *U-20* had just been sighted.

May 5 was to be an unusual day all around for the Admiralty, as Churchill was leaving that morning for the Western Front to meet with Field Marshal John French, the commander in chief of the BEF. Ostensibly Churchill was going as a representative of the War Cabinet to observe the British assault on Aubers Ridge on May 6, but as usual with Churchill, there was more going on. He was also going to spend part of his time with French plotting the removal of Field Marshal Lord Kitchener as Secretary of War and replacing him with French. The price of Churchill's support for French in the cabinet was to be French's nomination of Churchill as his replacement. It was all very muddled and very Churchillian—Winston always seemed to believe that no matter how good a job he was doing in his present position, he could always do a better one in someone else's place.

Arriving at the for-him-unheard-of hour of 8:00 in the morning, Churchill was immediately briefed on all overnight developments, as well as the movements of all ships at sea. Studying the Plot closely, he saw that the battleship *Colossus,* returning from patrol, would run dangerously close to Fastnet and the *U-20* if she held her present course. A signal was quickly sent out instructing *Colossus* to take a more westerly course as she passed up around Ireland. For some reason, even though he could clearly see that the *Lusitania's* projected course took her right across the latest reported position of the *U-20,* Churchill said nothing about her.

Why he failed to do so has become the stuff of myth and legend. Had he been trying to create just such a combination of circumstances, where a British passenger liner carrying a considerable number of American citizens would be attacked by a German U-boat? Had it all been a part of a considered and thought-out policy? Why had he ordered an accelerated program of arming merchant ships, the provocative "ram-on-sight" orders, and the instructions to disregard the Cruiser Rules? Why had he issued instructions to shoot captured U-boat crewmen and to fire on white flags? Why had he allowed the illegal shipment of cargoes of munitions on passenger vessels—and with Germany's knowledge of it? Had it all been part of a plan to sting

the Germans into blindly shooting at any target, regardless of the consequences, knowing that sooner or later one of those targets would be a passenger ship full of innocent men, women, and children? Such an attack, even if
the ship wasn't sunk, would seem certain to provoke an anti-German outrage
in the United States that no amount of pacifism or principle on the part of
Bryan and Wilson could overcome. While it would be unlikely that America
would go so far as to declare war on Germany as a consequence of such an
attack, it would certainly bring a swift end to any thoughts Congress might
have had about stopping the sale of munitions to any of the belligerent powers, as well as silencing the awkward questions some influential Americans,
Secretary of State Bryan among them, were asking about the British conduct
of their blockade of Germany.

Or was it simply the oversight of a man who had been daily carrying the
burden of running the world's largest navy, who was being unfairly saddled
with the responsibility for the failure of the Dardanelles campaign by the very
people who had approved of it, who was fighting for survival amid personal
and political attacks made by men who had only a fraction of his vision and
ability? Churchill once remarked that Admiral Jellicoe was "the only man
who could lose the war in an afternoon." He was wrong—there was another
such man, and it was Churchill himself. No single naval triumph, no matter
how great, could have won the war for Britain. But a single serious defeat
would have meant disaster; it was much to Churchill's credit that the Royal
Navy never came close to such a defeat while he was in office.

Whether his decision was determined by a policy intended to create a
confrontation between Germany and the United States or was simply a consequence of oversight will probably never be known for certain. Nonetheless,
the failure to either divert the *Lusitania* away from the *U-20*'s position or
specifically warn her of the danger she was standing into was Churchill's own
fault. He had taken over such a huge part in the day-to-day running of the
Admiralty that the initiative of many of his subordinates had atrophied. For
others, it was the ideal situation for that peculiar brand of individual found
everywhere in any bureaucracy, those dedicated to protecting themselves and
their careers and avoiding responsibility at all costs. In this situation, with
Churchill making most of the decisions, such evasions were easy. Likewise,
deliberately exposing a British passenger liner carrying American citizens to
almost certain attack would have been easy to accomplish in an environment
where everyone took orders but never questioned them.

Whichever the case may have been that morning, when Churchill viewed
the Plot one last time before departing for France, he allowed the existing situation to remain unchanged. No one bothered to point out to him—and he
either overlooked or ignored—that unless her course was changed and she
was diverted elsewhere, the *Lusitania* was headed straight for the waters off

the Irish coast where the *U-20* was operating. When Churchill left Whitehall, he took with him the Admiralty's last chance to save the *Lusitania*. Now her fate was in the hands of Captain Turner and Kapitan-Leutnant Schwieger.[5]

On the morning of May 5, an agent for Cunard's New York office appeared at the Port Authority of New York. With him was a copy of the *Lusitania*'s supplemental manifest to be filed with the Collector of Customs office. Listed on the manifest among a seemingly innocuous collection of dry goods and sundries were 4,200 cases of rifle ammunition, totaling over 5 million rounds, and a 51-ton consignment of 1,248 cases of filled 3-inch shrapnel shells, along with their fuses. Like all such manifests, it was available for public inspection, and could be examined by anyone who asked to see it.

By 2:00 P.M., the *U-20* was well east of Fastnet, following the south Irish coast at a distance of roughly twenty miles. Around 5:30, Schwieger spotted a small schooner and ordered her to stop. She was the *Earl of Lathom,* a pretty little ship of just ninety-nine tons, out of Limerick in ballast bound for Liverpool. Schwieger told the crew to abandon her and bring him the schooner's papers. His crew placed two grenades in her hold, which blew out her bottom when they went off, and the *Earl* sank in a matter of minutes. Leaving the schooner's crew to their long pull for the shore, Schwieger ordered the *U-20* to move slightly farther to the east. Fog enveloped the submarine a short while later, and she spent the night standing well out to sea, away from the shipping lanes, charging her batteries.[6]

When Churchill arrived in Paris that afternoon, he cabled the American Ambassador in London, Walter Page, expressing his regrets for not being able to attend a dinner party Page was giving on Friday evening, May 7. His responsibilities in France, Churchill said, would in all likelihood keep him there through Friday night. Page was giving the dinner in honor of Colonel House, President Wilson's special emissary. Although his mission had failed, Page was determined to give the Colonel as good a sendoff as London society could provide in the spring of 1915. Included among the invited guests were Sir Edward Grey, the foreign secretary; George Booth; Wickham Steed, the foreign affairs editor of the London *Times*; Captain Hall of the Admiralty's Intelligence Section; and Lord Mersey, the Commissioner of Wrecks for the United Kingdom.

Colonel House had gone to Europe to promote President Wilson's "Freedom of the Seas" concept. In essence, the idea was for both Germany and Great Britain to abandon their blockades, exempting all merchant traffic from attack or harassment. This would mean the two powers could trade wherever and with whomever they chose, leaving their navies to fight each other rather than shipping. If adhered to, the policy would have led to a general armistice within months, for it would have basically institutionalized the stalemate on the Western Front. The Germans naturally wholeheartedly embraced it, since such an armistice would have been much to their advantage. The British, however, knew that the German war effort must eventually collapse because of the blockade; if nothing else, the German Army would starve along with the German nation. Sir Edward Grey informed House that the idea was politically and militarily unacceptable in Great Britain: In a rare agreement between the two men, Lord Kitchener and Winston Churchill opposed Wilson's proposal, since its consequences would leave Britain at a grave strategic disadvantage when the peace talks began. House had an appointment with King George V at noon on Friday, May 7, and if he couldn't win the Crown's endorsement of Wilson's plan, Page's dinner Friday night would be his last opportunity to present it to a sympathetic and influential audience.[7]

At dawn on May 6, a subtle change came over the *Lusitania.* Sometime during the night, she had entered the German war zone, and precautions were being taken that hadn't been thought necessary before. The lifeboats were swung out in their davits, while, as the passengers began waking and moving about the ship, stewards started rigging blackout curtains at portholes and doors. Lookouts were doubled, then trebled. Captain Turner was taking no chances. Visibility was good, as the day promised to be as beautiful as the previous three had been, with cool breezes and lots of sunshine. The North Atlantic, normally the most fickle of oceans, was behaving herself for once.

Though he was still nearly 400 miles from Fastnet, the westernmost point of Ireland, Turner was well aware that he was rapidly approaching dangerous waters and was determined to spend as little time in them as possible. As soon as he made landfall, he would take a fix to be absolutely certain of where he was and begin working out his course and speed to Liverpool to make port on the morning of May 8. The *Lusitania* could only cross the Bar across the mouth of the Mersey River leading to Liverpool at high tide. If he missed that tide, he would be forced to wait for almost twelve hours, steaming back and forth in confined waters, a virtual sitting duck for any U-boat on the prowl.[8]

Thursday, May 6, was a good day for the *U-20.* Before dawn, Schwieger moved his submarine closer to the Irish coast, to a spot about twenty-five miles southeast of the Old Head of Kinsale, a prominent headland and frequent landfall for ships crossing the Atlantic from America or coming up from the Mediterranean bound for the St. George's Channel. At 7:00 A.M., the Harrison Line steamer *Candidate* emerged from a fogbank less than a half mile from the *U-20.* Schwieger quickly called his gun crew up on deck, and they rapidly put two shots across the freighter's bow. Rather than heaving to as ordered, the

Candidate began to pick up speed and dodge away from the U-boat. Schwieger knew the rules as well as anyone, and as far as he was concerned, the *Candidate* was now fair game. The steamer darted back into the fogbank and the *U-20* followed.

Half an hour later, the fog shifted, exposing the *Candidate* with the *U-20* sitting fifty yards off her port bow. The steamer was carrying a 3-inch deck gun, but when Schwieger's crew lobbed a pair of hand grenades at the ship as a warning, the British crewmen carefully avoided their ship's weapon. At 8:20, a boarding party climbed onto the *Candidate*'s deck and an hour later returned to the *U-20* with her papers, log, and manifest. Schwieger gave the crew thirty minutes to abandon ship and, once they were clear, put a torpedo into the merchantman's side. The *Candidate* stubbornly refused to sink, and the Germans had to resort to using their deck gun on her. After firing a dozen rounds, the *U-20* backed away and watched the *Candidate* sink. A patrol boat arrived on the scene but wisely concentrated on picking up the crew of the *Candidate,* and the *U-20* in turn ignored the patrol boat. An hour and twenty minutes after the *U-20* had put the torpedo into her, the *Candidate* rolled over and sank.

Schwieger took the *U-20* down to periscope depth, and the submarine headed west. Just after noon, the U-boat surfaced to give chase to a White Star liner, but the ship dodged into a lingering fogbank, and the *U-20* lost sight of her. An hour later, the *Candidate*'s sister ship *Centurion* hove into view. Going back to periscope depth, Schwieger tracked the steamer, then, remembering the *Candidate*'s deck gun, decided to forgo a warning shot and promptly fired a torpedo into her port side. There were no injuries aboard the *Centurion,* and her crew hastily abandoned ship, though the freighter gave no indication that it was sinking. Schwieger fired a second torpedo at her, then watched, disgusted with the performance of his torpedoes, as it took the *Centurion* over two hours to go to the bottom.

Schwieger later noted his frustration with his torpedoes in his log, calling them "not so good." By 6:00 P.M., the fog closed in again, so thickly this time that visibility was down to thirty yards. Schwieger took the *U-20* down to twenty-four meters (eighty feet) and once more headed for the open sea, surfacing near the Conigbeg Lightship, spending the night on the surface and recharging his batteries.[9]

At 6:00 P.M. on May 6, Captain Turner was uncharacteristically socializing with the passengers. Charles Frohman had given a party in his cabin and invited the captain. Turner, who genuinely liked Frohman, was happy to accept the invitation and showed up in notably good spirits. Alfred Vanderbilt was there also, but in contrast to Turner, he was noticeably depressed; earlier that day, he had received a message that one of his lifelong friends, Fred

Davies, had died unexpectedly in New York. But perhaps in an ironic salute to the best theatrical traditions of his friend Frohman, Vanderbilt did appear.

At 7:00 P.M., a wireless message was brought to Frohman's cabin for Captain Turner. Excusing himself, Turner stepped outside the cabin to read it and saw that it came from the Admiralty. It read, "Submarines active off south coast of Ireland." Turner immediately left for the bridge. It wasn't much, but it was the first indication that there were U-boats at large in the war zone. Thinking it part of a longer message that was broken up, Turner asked that it be repeated. It came back the same as the first time: "Submarines active off south coast of Ireland."

At 8:30, another message came through, eventually to be repeated seven times that night. It read: "To all British ships. Take Liverpool pilot at bar and avoid all headlands. Pass harbours at full speed. Steer midchannel course. Submarines off Fastnet." Here was something a little more substantial. Fastnet, the rocky promontory at the westernmost tip of Ireland, with its great lighthouse, was the perfect spot for a submarine to lie in wait. Turner studied his charts and did some quick calculations. If his navigation was correct, the *Lusitania* would pass Fastnet early the next morning. If the weather stayed true to form for those waters at this time of year, he could expect fog, thick enough and extensive enough to be able to hide in. Turner ordered the ship's speed increased to eighteen knots and plotted a course that he believed would take him some twenty to twenty-five miles off the coastline, a far cry from the mile or so distance that he usually kept during peacetime.

Just as Turner had anticipated, when morning came on May 7, the fog was thick and heavy. He cut the *Lusitania's* speed back to fifteen knots again and ordered the ship's immense foghorn started up. With the Irish Sea and the St. George's Channel busier than Piccadilly Circus these days, Turner was more concerned with avoiding a collision than being attacked by a U-boat. After all, if visibility was near zero for him, it was near zero for the U-boats, too.[10]

In Queenstown, the SNO, Adm. Sir Charles Coke, was seriously worried. Four separate sightings of a German submarine had been reported the previous day, all within twenty-five miles of Queenstown. At 9:20 A.M., he received confirmation of the sinking of the *Candidate,* followed shortly by the news of the *Centurion.* He knew the *Lusitania* was due to pass through his patrol area that day, steaming past Queenstown sometime around 2:00 in the afternoon. The cruiser *Juno* was out on patrol, due back in port around 1:00 P.M. Coke conferring with Admiral Hood, who had remained ashore, about the possibility of having Juno assigned to escort the *Lusitania.* Hood explained that none of his four antiquated cruisers could offer any real protection for the *Lusitania,* so Coke cabled the Admiralty, reminding them of the loss of the two Harrison steamers and asking for advice on how to best protect the *Lusitania.* Less than

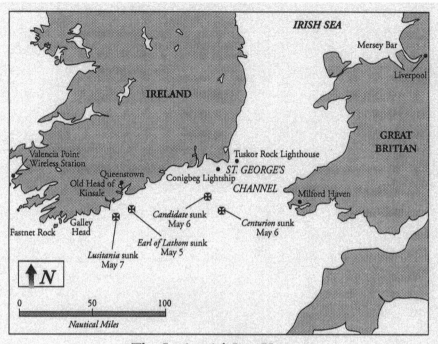

The *Lusitania's* Last Voyage

an hour later, the Admiralty sent out a message, addressed to all British ships: "Submarines active in southern part of Irish Channel, last heard of twenty miles south of the Conigbeg Light Vessel. Make sure *Lusitania* gets this."

Now Coke was really puzzled. The *Centurion* and the *Candidate* had been sunk nearer to Queenstown than to the Conigbeg Lightship, which was some fifty miles away. The Admiralty signal misplaced the U-boat completely. That the Admiralty gave the appearance of being worried about the *Lusitania* was shown by the insistent "Make sure *Lusitania* gets this," but the phrase "last heard of" did not convey that the information was nearly twenty-four hours old. It was almost as if a sort of creeping paralysis was taking hold at the Admiralty in Churchill's absence. Intelligence was being mishandled, and a frightening lack of initiative—or refusal to take it—was manifesting itself. No one took it upon himself to order the *Lusitania* to alter course or divert her into Queenstown. In Queenstown, Admiral Coke's hands were tied. He lacked the authority to divert the *Lusitania*, or even signal her that she was standing into danger. He could only watch and hope.[11]

Captain Turner estimated that the *Lusitania* had passed Fastnet sometime around 9:00 A.M., a little later than he had planned because he had been forced to reduce speed in the fog. The fog began clearing a little before noon, and land was just visible to port, a rocky bluff that Turner decided must be Brow Head. Yet it seemed to be only about 15 miles away, much less than the twenty miles he had planned on keeping off the Irish coastline. If it was Brow Head, it meant that the U-boat was far behind the *Lusitania*. According to the Admiralty, there was another one near the Conigbeg Lightship, still some 120 miles ahead, but no signs of danger in between.

Charles Lauriat got up a little before noon, and when he had dressed, he went down to the First Class Lounge to check the distance of the last twenty-four hours' run. It was 462 miles, the lowest yet. Disappointed that he had lost again, Lauriat went to lunch. He found himself sitting under a fan and caught in a cross breeze between the open portholes on both sides of the dining saloon. Lauriat asked a steward to do something about it. The fan was switched off, the portholes left open.[12]

At 12:50, Schwieger heard the sound of heavy screws almost directly overhead, and when they had passed, he surfaced to periscope depth. He saw an elderly British cruiser following a zigzagging course toward Queenstown, and though he tried to give chase, the cruiser, *Juno*, outpaced the *U-20* easily. *Juno* never saw the *U-20*, and when Schwieger was sure that she was safely out of range, he gave the order to surface.[13]

About the same time that the *U-20* encountered *Juno*, Captain Turner was handed another message. This one seemed even more reassuring: "Submarine five miles south of Cape Clear. Proceeding west when sighted at 10:00 A.M." Turner knew by now that he was well east of Cape Clear, so that submarine was safely behind him. It was the threat of encountering a U-boat somewhere in the entrance to the St. George's Channel that had him worried. After a few minutes' thought, Turner made up his mind: He would not stop for the pilot at the Bar of the Mersey River, but would steam straight into Liverpool at high tide. If there were submarines in the Irish Sea, stopping for any reason seemed to be an unreasonable risk.

But in order to do that, he needed to know exactly where he was. Already an error had crept into his navigation somewhere, and the *Lusitania* was closer to land than he had intended. If he were to take her up the St. George's Channel at night, he needed to fix his position to the yard, shooting a four-point bearing using a prominent landmark for his fix. He ordered the *Lusitania* course altered twenty degrees to port so he could get a little closer to the shore and make his fix all the more positive.[14]

Colonel House had been received by the King at half past noon. While they were lunching, the two men made small talk and exchanged anecdotes about mutual acquaintances. After lunch, the King took the Colonel into his study, where House proceeded to explain the details of President Wilson's "Freedom of the Seas" proposal, hoping that George V would endorse it. After hearing House out, the King stood in silence for a moment, looking through the windows of his study at the garden outside, all the flowers in riotous bloom and the kew birds singing lustily. As he fiddled with some papers lying on his desk, the King suddenly looked at House and asked, "Colonel, what will America do if the Germans sink the *Lusitania?*"[15]

Turner had his landmark now: He could see the promontory of the Old Head of Kinsale clearly. He was close enough inshore, about ten miles from the coast, to get a good bearing. Remembering the Admiralty's signal to steer a midchannel course, he decided that was close enough, and the *Lusitania* resumed her original course. What was necessary now was for the ship to maintain a constant course and speed for the next twenty minutes while Turner took the sightings necessary for a four-point bearing. Reminding the quartermaster and the Chief Officer of that, he began to take his sights. It was 1:50 P.M.[16]

Robert Timmins and his cabin mate, Ralph Moodie, had just finished lunch. The two men were British cotton dealers who worked in Gainesville, Texas, on their way to London on business. The trip across the Atlantic so far had been relaxing, and in that spirit, Timmins decided to order a second dish of ice cream for dessert. They joked about a Greek passenger who, the night before, had donned his lifebelt and went to sleep in one of the *Lusitania's* lifeboats. Both men thought the man's apprehension was hilarious. Archie Donald had taken a reprieve from his marathon bridge game and was having lunch with the Reverend and Mrs. Gwyer, along with Miss Lorna Pavey, a pretty young Red Cross volunteer that Archie seemed to have designs on.

Theodate Pope and Edwin Friend had just finished their lunch and decided to take a stroll along the promenade of B Deck. As they left the dining room, the passed the table where Lady Mackworth was seated, enjoying the company of two new friends, Dr. Fisher and Miss Conner. Dr. Fisher was teasing his sister-in-law about a remark she had made earlier when the ship was enveloped by fog. "It's been such a dull, dreary, stupid trip, I can't help hoping that we get some sort of thrill going up the channel."[17]

For Schwieger, the course change the ship he was watching had made was a godsend. His lookout had spotted her about twenty minutes earlier, but on a course and at a speed that would give the *U-20* no chance of catching her. Now that last course alteration would bring her right to him! Quickly he ordered the crew to action stations, and the *U-20* dove to periscope depth.

The torpedo tubes were quickly loaded as Schwieger began calling out ranges and bearings, watching the ship coming ever closer. She would be barely more than a half mile away when she crossed the *U-20*'s bow. This steamer was *big*, with smoke pouring out of three of her four funnels. His eyes glued to the periscope, Schwieger quickly confirmed that the torpedo tubes were loaded and ready, then waited for a few more seconds. Finally, he took a deep breath, then ordered, "*Los!*" ("Shoot!")

The *U-20* rocked slightly as the torpedo hissed out of its tube. The U-boat's log tells the tale with stark simplicity. "2:10 P.M. Pure bow shot at 700 meters range. (G-type torpedo with 3 meters depth adjustment.) Angle on the bow, ninety degrees, estimated speed 22 knots. Torpedo hits starboard side right below bridge."[18]

Much as Elbert Hubbard had accused the Kaiser of doing, Kapitan-Leutnant Schwieger had just lifted the lid off hell.

CHAPTER 9

The Day the Lusitania *Died*

THE TORPEDO WAS SPOTTED BY A NUMBER OF PEOPLE ABOARD THE *LUSITANIA* as it closed the last hundred yards to the ship's side. One of the first was young Leslie Morton, who had been stationed as an extra lookout in the bow of the ship. When he saw the white, bubbling streak of the torpedo's wake, he turned, cupped his hands together, and bawled up toward the bridge, "Torpedo coming on the starboard side!" At the same time that Morton was shouting his warning up to the bridge, Able Seaman Thomas Quinn spotted the torpedo from his post in the crow's nest and reached for the telephone to make his own report.

In almost that same instant, Florence Padley, who was sitting in a deck chair on B Deck just aft of midships overheard somebody say, "There's a porpoise!" She got up to take a look, then realized in horror how wrong the unknown observer was.

"That's no porpoise," she cried, "that's a torpedo!" She turned and ran to her cabin to get her lifebelt.

Not far from where Mrs. Padley had been sitting, Oliver Barnard was leaning nonchalantly against the ship's rail when an American woman strolled past, looked over the side, and then asked him in what he later recalled as an unbelievably casual tone of voice, "Is that a torpedo?" Barnard looked and suddenly found himself too heartsick to even speak—he watched the torpedo as it sped into the *Lusitania*'s side. Jay Brooks was standing near the second funnel when he, too, saw the white wake of the torpedo. He shouted out "Torpedo!" though he had no idea if his warning would do any good or if anyone would even hear it. Then he gripped the railing tightly, bracing himself for the explosion he knew was coming.

Standing on the starboard side of the bridge, Captain Turner had heard Morton's warning shout, followed an instant later by Second Officer Hefford calling out to him, "There's a torpedo coming, sir!" Turner stepped out onto the starboard bridge wing, looked down at the water, and saw the torpedo's wake rapidly approaching the side of the ship. It looked as if it would strike the *Lusitania* directly under where he was standing. Instinctively he stepped back a few paces as the torpedo closed those final yards and struck the *Lusitania*'s hull. It was 2:10 P.M.[1]

For a split second, nothing seemed to happen.

Then the warhead exploded, sending a shudder running the length of the ship that was felt by everyone on board. Curiously, the sound of the explosion didn't seem to carry very far, although it wasn't unusual for two people not very far apart to describe it very differently. To Carl Foss, the doctor from Helena, Montana, who had been finishing his lunch in the Second Class dining room on D Deck when the *Lusitania* was hit, the explosion sounded like "a big boom." To Dr. Moore, another physician sitting not far from Foss, it was a "muffled drumlike sound." Miss Barrett, who was finishing her lunch in the same dining room, described the sound as "the smashing of many dishes."

Lady Mackworth had just stepped into the elevator that would take her from the First Class Dining Saloon down to C Deck, where her cabin was. She felt the ship shudder but recalled the torpedo's explosion as nothing more than "a dull thud." Her father, D. A. Thomas, didn't think much of it at the time. Isaac Lehmann, the New York export broker, was sitting in the First Class Smoking Room when the torpedo hit. To him, it was like "a noise the boom of a cannon." Isaac Jackson, who was sitting in the same Smoking Room, described the sound in more destructive terms: "a rending, grinding sound rather than a sharp report." To George Kessler, the Canadian wine and whiskey magnate, the sound was rather dull. He thought it sounded like nothing more than "a thud against the side of the ship." Nevertheless, he knew instinctively what had happened and immediately began making his way to the Boat Deck.

Theodate Pope waxed poetic in her description—to her "the sound was like that of an arrow entering the canvas and straw of a target, magnified many thousand times." Ominously, she added, "I imagined I heard a dull explosion follow." She was not alone in thinking she heard a second explosion. Charles Lauriat, the Boston bookseller, had just stepped out onto the promenade deck when the torpedo hit, and his memory of that moment was vivid indeed: "Where I stood, the shock of the impact was not severe; it was a heavy, rather muffled sound, but the good ship trembled under the force of the blow; a second explosion quickly followed, but I do not think it was a second torpedo, for the sound was quite different; it was more like a boiler in the engine room."[2]

Captain Turner could have confirmed for Lauriat that there had indeed been a second explosion, although it had not come from the engine room or one of the boiler rooms. As the torpedo plunged into the *Lusitania*'s side, Turner had beaten a hasty retreat from his exposed position on the starboard bridge wing, a movement that certainly saved him from serious injury, possibly even saved his life. The torpedo struck the *Lusitania* at a point just a few feet aft of being directly under the bridge, and an enormous geyser of water and debris was thrown upward when the warhead exploded, wrecking both the bridge wing where Turner had been standing only seconds before and the nearby lifeboat No. 5 in a storm of water, twisted metal, torn gratings, wood splinters, and lumps of coal. The force of the explosion traveled the length of the *Lusitania*'s forward longitudinal bunker, springing its forward bulkhead, and forcing a huge cloud of smoke, coal dust, and white damp up through the ventilators on the Boat Deck, though in a few seconds the breeze created by the *Lusitania*'s eighteen-knot speed had blown this cloud away.

In these few seconds, Turner and everybody else on board felt the *Lusitania* give a sickening lurch to starboard and begin to list sharply. Turner knew exactly why: By chance, he had been looking directly at the fire/flooding indicator board when he felt as much as heard the rumble of a second explosion, this one coming from somewhere deep within the ship. The bows took a sharp dip into the water, the ship took on a list of almost fifteen degrees in a matter of seconds, and Turner watched in fear and fascination as the warning lights and indicators on the board seemed to, in his words, "go berserk for most of the forward compartments of the ship." Something had gone off inside the *Lusitania* like a gigantic bomb.

At that moment, Turner knew his ship was doomed. His duty now was to do everything he could to save the passengers and crew. His first concern was to determine how much damage had actually been done so that he might have an idea of how long the *Lusitania* could remain afloat. Turning to Third Officer Bestic, Turner told him to go below to the baggage room and try to assess the damage. The next problem was the tremendous headway the *Lusitania* still had. The momentum of a 33,000-ton ship making eighteen knots is enormous, even one that is listing fifteen degrees to starboard. Turner knew he had to get the people off the *Lusitania*, but trying to launch lifeboats while the ship was still going so fast was suicidal. There was no time to lose; Turner immediately rang the engine telegraph for full speed astern.

Down in the engine room, Assistant Third Engineer George Little heard the telegraph bells ring and the indicators swing over to "Full Astern." It didn't take much imagination on Little's part to realize what the captain was trying to do: Down there, the explosion had been no "muffled thud"—the whole engine room had reverberated with the detonation, and Little had felt the whole ship shake and begin listing. He and his men scrambled to disengage the forward turbines and engage the reverse set, shutting valves, opening others, ducting the steam from the boilers in new directions. But Little acted with too much haste and tried to bring the reverse turbines on line before the propellors and their shafts had stopped their forward motion. The inertia and momentum of spinning shafts and propellors was too great for the incoming flow of steam against the reverse turbines to overcome, and instead, the reverse turbines simply windmilled helplessly in the wrong direction. The incoming steam began to back up, building an enormous head of pressure in the main steam lines that the safety valves couldn't open quickly enough to relieve. Something had to give, and in despair, Little watched and listened as a succession of steam lines split and burst, then the safety valves opened, venting a cloud of steam that enveloped the *Lusitania*'s Boat Deck momentarily before the breeze of her own headway dissipated it. The available pressure dropped in seconds from 190 pounds per square inch to less than 50— nowhere near enough to spin the reverse turbines against the momentum of the propellor shafts; even in the best of conditions, it would have been barely enough to turn the turbines at all. Her speed barely reduced, the *Lusitania* continued to surge forward.

Up on the bridge, when Turner saw the steam bursting out of the safety valves, he knew what had happened. If he couldn't take the way off of his ship, then perhaps he could beach her on the Irish coast, so tantalizingly close. Turning to Quartermaster Johnston, he ordered the ship turned hard to port, hoping her momentum would carry the *Lusitania* to the shoreline. Johnston spun the wheel, but nothing happened—one of the steam lines that had ruptured was the line that provided power to the steering gear. The rudder couldn't be moved, and the ship's course couldn't be changed. There was nothing more Turner could do to try to save the *Lusitania*; all that was left now was to try to get the passengers and crew off the ship.[3]

Ten miles away, fifteen-year-old John Murphy was sitting on a stone wall near the Old Head of Kinsale lighthouse, out on the Head itself, watching the steamships pass, much like American boys his age would sit near a railroad track waiting for the express trains to come thundering by. He knew that the *Lusitania* was due to come by this afternoon, and he knew her on sight, so he was quite pleased when she came over the horizon, although he was disappointed because she was much farther out to sea than she normally would have been. As Murphy watched, the *Lusitania* changed course, then suddenly a huge column of water sprang up on her starboard side, the side opposite him. A few seconds later, he heard a dull, rumbling boom, then he saw the ship pitch forward and begin to heel over to starboard. Of all the sights he had seen over the years from his rocky perch, he had never seen anything like what was about to unfold before his disbelieving eyes.[4]

Eight hundred yards from his target, Kapitan-Leutnant Schwieger peered through his periscope and watched with satisfaction as the torpedo ran straight and true, striking the *Lusitania* almost directly under the first funnel. He carefully recorded what he saw next in his log:

> An unusually heavy detonation follows with a very big explosion cloud (far above the first funnel). In addition to the explosion of the torpedo there must have been a second explosion (boilers, coaldust or gunpowder). The superstructure above the point of impact and the upper bridge structure are torn apart and fire breaks out almost immediately around the bridge. The ship slows and begins to quickly heel over to starboard. At the same time her bows begin to dive under.

He continued to watch in morbid fascination as the *Lusitania* continued to roll over to starboard and briefly wondered if she would actually capsize. He couldn't believe that the single torpedo he had fired had caused so much damage.[5]

Charles Lauriat had found himself enveloped in that soot-filled cloud of steam that had burst onto the upper decks when the steam pipes ruptured. He had not only heard the torpedo explode, but he had also felt the ship react to the detonation. "You could feel the two separate motions very distinctly," he later recalled. "It seemed as if she were going down at once, but then stopped suddenly as if the sea had met the watertight bulkheads, and she seemed to right herself and even raise her bow a little." Noticing that the soot had ruined his suit, Lauriat briefly considered going down to his cabin to change, but then he noticed that the *Lusitania* was beginning to list even farther to starboard and this time showed no signs of righting herself. Lauriat changed his mind—there wouldn't be enough time to for him to change his clothes. But there were some important papers that he was loath to leave behind, and he wanted to get his lifebelt as well, so he turned and began to make his way back to his cabin.

He saw Elbert and Alice Hubbard standing near the railing and suggested that they had time to get to their cabin on B Deck and get their own lifebelts. Hubbard, who was standing with his arm around his wife, said nothing and gave no indication that he had even heard what Lauriat had said. Lauriat wasn't inclined to stand there and press the issue, so he hurried on toward his cabin, making his way down the strangely slanting passageways.

Like Lauriat, Lady Mackworth was alarmed by the sudden list. Leaving her father, D. A. Thomas, in the Dining Saloon, she made straight for her cabin, knowing she would find lifebelts for both of them there. Halfway down the passageway, she bumped into a stewardess, who was clinging to the handrail trying to keep her balance. The two women stood there for some seconds making polite apologies to each other, then suddenly realized that they were wasting valuable time and hurried on their way. Fetching her lifebelt and her father's, Lady Mackworth then made her way up the Boat Deck, hoping to find her father there. Catching sight of her friends Dr. Fisher and Dorothy Conner, she hurried over to them. In a quick aside to Dorothy, she said, "Well, I guess you've had your thrill!"

In truth there *was* something thrilling in those first few moments after the torpedo struck, before it became frighteningly clear that the ship was sinking an alarming rate. Many survivors later commented on the almost total absence of panic among their fellow passengers. The experience of the passengers in the Second Class Dining Room was typical. Everyone felt the two explosions, and the lights quickly went out. There were a few screams, but suddenly the commanding voices of H. L. Gwyer and Archibald Donald, a minister and a would-be soldier, rang out, assuring everyone that all was well. Almost instantly, the passengers began trooping out of the dining room as if they were, in Donald's words, a "regiment of soldiers." It was as if everyone had subconsciously expected the ship to be attacked, and now that it had happened, reflexes took over and people began to move toward the upper decks in a fairly orderly fashion. It was a scene that had parallels in First and Third Class as well.

There was one notable exception: When the torpedo hit the *Lusitania,* one young man bolted from the Second Class Dining Saloon in a mad dash for the upper decks. That was Robert Leith, the chief wireless operator on the ship. The Second Class dining room was at very nearly the aft end of the ship on D Deck, while the wireless office was in a deckhouse just behind the second funnel atop the Boat Deck, but Leith reached it in less than a minute. It only took a moment for him to get his set adjusted, then he began tapping out a desperate call for assistance: "SOS . . . SOS . . . MSU [the *Lusitania's* wireless call sign] . . . Come at once . . . Big List . . . Ten miles south of Old Kinsale Head . . . SOS . . . SOS . . . MSU." Over and over again he sent the same signal. Leith kept an eye on the power gauges as they fell to toward zero—the ship's power was failing fast. After a few more minutes of signaling, he knew he was sending from a dead key, switched over to his emergency batteries, then continued sending his plea for help.[6]

The *Lusitania* was going to need all the help she could get. Down in Boiler Room Number 1, Fireman Thomas Madden found himself in what seemed to be a fair approximation of hell. He had been standing between the two center boilers when the torpedo hit, and the concussion had thrown him hard to the deck plates. The noise left him and his mates deafened. But Madden didn't need to be able to hear to know that something was seriously wrong with the ship. He could feel through the deck plates that the great turbines had stopped, as had most of the machinery on the ship. The deck was tilting at an odd angle, and water was flooding the deck and rising rapidly. It seemed to be coming from the starboard side of the boiler room.

Steam began filling Boiler Room Number 1, and for a few moments, Madden was terrified at the prospect of one or more of the boilers exploding when the cold seawater reached them. But as the water continued to rise and no explosion came, he began searching for a way out. (Madden had no way of knowing it, but the sudden release of the safety valves when the torpedo exploded along with all of the ruptures in the steam lines meant that no head of steam could build up long enough to create an explosion—there were so many places for the steam to leak out as soon as it was created.)

The lights suddenly blinked out, and as he stumbled about in the dark, Madden bumped into Trimmer Fred Davis, who was, like Madden, deafened and stunned by the explosion. Together they made their way to the aft bulkhead and found one of the watertight doors, but it was jammed shut, and they had no way of opening it. As the water continued to rise around them, Madden and Davis struggled toward one of the escape ladders that led up to the Boat Deck. Madden knew exactly where he was and in a few seconds found the ladder, and the two men began climbing.

Just aft of where Madden was, in Boiler Room Number 2, the torpedo's explosion didn't seem as violent as it did in Boiler Room Number 1, but the second explosion knocked everyone off their feet. Trimmer Ian McDermott heard Chief Engineer Archibald Bryce shout that the watertight doors were jammed shut and that everyone should get topside as quickly as possible. Like many of his mates, McDermott made for the service elevator, but he didn't reach it in time. He watched it climb up the shaft, then the power failed, the lights went out, and tons of seawater began to pour into the boiler room from the open coal scuttles. The roar of the inrushing sea drowned out the cries of the men trapped in the elevator. There was nothing McDermott could do for them, so he began groping about in the dark, looking for one of the ladders that led up through the ventilation shafts to the upper decks. The water was nearly up to his waist and the whole ship was tilting crazily before he finally found it and began desperately climbing.[7]

The *U-20's* torpedo appeared to have done damage all out of proportion to its capabilities. The blast had opened the starboard longitudinal compartment to the sea, causing the initial list, and while the compartment was by no means watertight, owing to the number of poorly closed loading apertures and wide-open coal scuttles in the inner bulkhead, the *Lusitania* was heeling over much faster than she would have if the water were entering her hull only through those openings. Nor could the weight of water being absorbed by coal in the bunkers account for the list, since the bunkers were almost empty. Apparently, more compartments than just the longitudinal bunker were open to the sea, for in a little more than five minutes after the torpedo struck, the *Lusitania* had reached the critical point in her stability—twenty-six degrees of list—and gave no indication of stopping there.

Even more bewildering was that the ship was sinking—and sinking fast —by the head, but it was a longitudinal compartment that had been hit. That second explosion that came just seconds after the torpedo had detonated against the *Lusitania*'s hull had been what had mortally wounded the ship. Turner had watched the indicator board on the bridge "go berserk" forward of Boiler Room Number 1 immediately after that second explosion as something deep within the ship blew her bows apart.

What ever it was, it wasn't exploding boilers: Fireman Madden and Trimmers Davis and McDermott later recounted their survival in the first two boiler rooms and confirmed that none of the boilers in either room had exploded. It was not coal dust in the transverse bunker forward of Boiler Room Number 1, as that compartment hadn't been used as a coal bunker for over a year. Theoretically it could have been the five million rounds of rifle ammunition stored just ahead of that bunker; most likely it was the fifty-two tons of shrapnel shells going off in sympathetic detonation with the torpedo. Or it could have been something among some of the more questionable and unexplained consignments of cargo in that forward hold. Whatever it was that exploded, one thing was certain: It was powerful enough to guarantee the *Lusitania* a quick trip to the bottom of the St. George's Channel.

Up on the bridge, Quartermaster Johnston was calling out the number of degrees as the *Lusitania* continued to heel over. "T-w-e-n-t-y degrees to starboard, Captain!" At this point, Chief Officer Piper called out to Turner, "I'm going down to the fo'c'sle to help Hefford with the hatches—she's sinking fast by the bow, perhaps we can slow her down a bit!" Turner nodded, and Piper left the bridge. Turner didn't know that was the last he would ever see of Piper. Except for himself and Johnston, the bridge was empty; both men felt useless, but there was nothing more they could do now to save the ship.[8]

Robert Timmins never got to finish his second helping of ice cream. When the torpedo hit, he and Ralph Moodie went down to their cabins to get their lifebelts. Going up to the Boat Deck, they began helping two seamen lower a lifeboat that had about sixty people in it. Suddenly a steward appeared saying that orders had come down from the bridge to stop lowering any boats until the ship had slowed down. No sooner had he said this than the sailor manning the forward fall lost control and the front of the boat plunged down into the sea. Everyone aboard was pitched into the water. Very few came back up again.

This was what Turner had feared—that the mad momentum of the onrushing *Lusitania,* combined with the steadily increasing list, would make it impossible to safely load and launch the lifeboats. Turner went out on what was left of the starboard bridge wing and, in a calm, clear voice, began to reassure the passengers milling about at the forward end of the Boat Deck. He asked that the crew stop loading and lowering the lifeboats because of danger from the ship's excessive speed. He explained that despite the list, he believed the ship would remain afloat for at least a couple of hours, and that once the ship drifted to a stop, it would be a simple matter to launch all the boats on the starboard side. Together with the collapsibles, they would be enough to take care of everyone on board. By the time they were all launched, rescue vessels from nearby Queenstown would have arrived.

"What do you wish us to do?" one anxious woman called out from the crowd.

"Stay right where you are, Madam."

"Where do you get your information?"

"From the engine room, Madam. She'll be all right."

As if calling him a liar, the *Lusitania* suddenly groaned and lurched even farther over. A mad scramble started for the lifeboats, as all of the calm and order vanished in an instant. Lady Mackworth watched in horrified fascination as a mass of passengers from Third Class began surging up the staircases from below. As they pushed and shoved their way toward the lifeboats in terror, the strongest pushed their weaker companions aside or trampled them underfoot. Here and there a man and woman struggled forward arm in arm, but what struck Lady Mackworth was that there were no children among them. The children, she later decided, could not have long survived in such a crush.

The crew seemed to be paralyzed by indecision. Some obeyed Turner's order to delay launching; others instinctively began loading and launching some of the boats. The problem was that most of the crewmen available didn't know what they were doing. Lady Mackworth noticed one boat being lowered with so little coordination between the men working the falls at each end that the boat wound up with its bow almost touching the sea while its stern was still high in the air. Most of the people in the boat fell into the water, many of them not coming back up to the surface.

A big part of the problem was that there was an appalling lack of real sea-men, the Able Bodied Seamen who knew how to work and handle boats. Some were standing by the bridge awaiting orders; many more had been trapped in a freight elevator between decks when the power was lost, never to be seen again. Most of the remaining deck crew were simply "Ordinary Seamen," and Ordinary Seamen were simply that—ordinary, useful for swabbing decks and painting over rust, but with precious little practical knowledge of ships and the sea. The did their best, but in truth, it wasn't much.[9]

It was Third Officer Bestic who first learned that so many of the ship's crewmen had been lost. He had never reached the baggage room Captain Turner had told him to inspect: A handful of grimy, shocked sailors told him that almost everyone down there had been killed in the explosion, including dozens of the ship's Able Bodied Seamen. On hearing this, Bestic went back up on deck to his lifeboat station, Boat No. 10, which was halfway down the port side of ship, thinking that he might be of some use in launching boats from that side.

Port side was chaos from the beginning. The list had caused the boats slung in the davits to swing inboard, hard against the collapsibles stowed beneath them, often tearing their heavy canvas sides or breaking their iron stays. Before the boats could be lowered, they would have to be pushed over the railing and swung out from the side of the ship. These boats weighed over two tons each. It was only through a superhuman effort that Staff Captain Anderson and a group of seamen got Boat No. 2 lifted out of its blocks, but he and his men couldn't get it over the deck railing—the list kept causing the boat to swing inboard. At just this moment, Bestic came by, and Anderson thought of a solution for righting the ship: "Go to the bridge and tell them there to trim her with the port [ballast] tanks." Bestic relayed the order to Second Officer Hefford and returned just in time to see calamity overtake Boat No. 2.

The sailors seemed to lose their collective grip on the lifeboat, and it suddenly swung inboard, pinning several of the sailors as well as some passengers who had come forward, anticipating their chance to get into the boat, against the collapsible. The tangled mass of bodies and the two boats remained suspended for a moment, then began sliding down the deck toward the bow. Bestic and Anderson had barely been able to jump clear as Boat 2 swung inboard, and they were missed by inches only seconds later as the same thing happened to Boat 4.

Anderson, desperate not to have the scene repeated with Boat 6, tried to persuade the passengers to wait until the boat was swung out and over the railing and lowered past it before they tried to board it, but for every passenger that stepped back, another rushed forward into the boat. Anderson lost his tenuous control over the crowd, and in swift succession, Boats 6, 8, and 10 all went slithering down the deck to join the wreckage of Boats 2 and 4 below the bridge.

Anderson almost succeeded with No. 12. By this time, Anderson and the crewmen had somehow managed to get the boat over the railing and lowered far enough to allow the passengers to climb in. Then the boat was lowered down the side of the ship, bumping the two-inch-wide "snap-head" rivets that held the ship's plating together as the list kept causing the boat to want to scrape down the *Lusitania*'s side. Just as Anderson was shouting down to the boat's passengers to use oars to push the boat away from the ship's side, the boat's keel fouled on the C Deck railing. The man at the after fall lost his grip on it, and the fall ran through the blocks, dropping Boat 12's stern like a rock. Everyone in the boat was flung into the sea, then seconds later were crushed when the forward fall parted and dropped the boat onto them.

Sobered by the experience of Boat 12, Anderson, crew, and passengers all cooperated on launching Boat 14. It was eased over the side, quickly loaded and lowered, and had almost reached the water as the *Lusitania*'s bow struck the bottom of the St. George's Channel. A shuddering jar ran the length of the ship, and the men at both falls lost their hold. Fortunately, the remaining drop was short and the boat stayed upright, and the passengers began frantically pulling away from the sinking liner. A few moments later, Boat 16 was safely lowered as well.

The launching of Boat 18 was a tragedy compounded by stupidity. As the rising water advanced up the deck, a pushing, shoving mass of humanity surged toward the stern, threatening to sweep all before it. Anderson barely maintained order at No. 18 but managed to have the boat swung out over the railing, where it was quickly filled to capacity. The ship was sinking so fast now that Anderson decided not to try to lower the boat, but instructed the crewmen at both falls to be ready to cut them when the water reached the boat's keel. Another seaman stood by the snubbing chain, ready to knock it loose as the falls were cut.

That wasn't how Isaac Lehmann, a New York export broker, thought it should be done, and he decided to take matters into his own hands. Immediately after the torpedo hit, he had gone to his cabin to fetch his lifebelt and his revolver—clearly he expected the worst. When he returned on deck, he saw a seamen securing a line holding Boat 18 in place and demanded to know why.

"Captain's orders," the seaman replied.

"The hell with the captain," Lehmann roared, producing his revolver. "I'll shoot the first man who refuses to assist in launching this boat!" It was a foolish piece of bravado: The crewman meekly complied and knocked away the snubbing chain while passengers were still climbing into the boat. Loosed of its restraint, the boat swung inboard like a pendulum, crushing Lehmann's leg against the boat's gunwale. Stunned, Lehmann watched as the boat then crashed to the deck and slid into the waiting knot of passengers and crew, Staff Captain Anderson among them, dragging them down along the deck into the rising water. In agony, Lehmann waited for the sea to come up and wash him off the deck.

Boats 20 and 22 never left their davits and were taken to the bottom with the *Lusitania*. Clearly, if any lives were to be saved, it would have to be in the starboard lifeboats.[10]

Dr. Fisher had stood on the deck watching Boat 10 make its perilous descent, then walked over to the starboard side of the Boat Deck, where he found his friends Lady Mackworth and Dorothy Connor. The three of them stood for a moment watching the chaos unfolding before them, when Lady Mackworth turned to Dorothy and remarked, "I always thought a shipwreck was a well-organized affair."

"So did I, but I've learned a devil of a lot in the last five minutes."

Also being educated was D. A. Thomas, who at first "didn't think much" of the torpedoing, but now thought very much of it indeed. Arriving on the Boat Deck in search of his daughter, he couldn't see her, although she was less than a dozen yards away at the moment. What he did see was the ship continuing to lean over and the water less than 10 feet below where he stood at the A Deck railing. A woman a few feet away was perched on the rail and kept screaming over and over, "Let me jump! Let me jump!" No one was anywhere near her, and Thomas, exasperated, shouted, "Then for God's sake, jump!" She did, and he jumped a moment later, coming to the surface close by the woman, who seemed quite calm now.

All along the Boat Deck, lifeboats were being launched any way they could, as any semblance of order broke down completely. First Officer Jones and Senior Third Officer Lewis were supposed to be in charge of the boats, Lewis taking Boats 1 through 9, and Jones taking Boats 11 through 21, but despite their best efforts, most of the launchings were haphazard affairs. Often no attempt was made to release the falls of the lowered boats so that they could be used again; they were just hacked away with knives or in some cases axes before the boats, some filled to capacity, others with only a handful of people in them, began to pull away from the wreck. The collapsibles that were stored beneath the conventional boats, instead of being rigged in the empty falls and davits, were simply left to float off as best they could.

Elizabeth Duckworth experienced this confusion firsthand. She had been walking along C Deck with her friend, Alice Scott, and Alice's son, Arthur, when the torpedo hit, shaking the ship, in her words, "from stem to stern." Rushing forward into the Third Class section of C Deck, they could see the bow sinking quickly, the water washing up over winches, capstans, and cranes. Panic seized the two women, and they began climbing the foremast rigging. An officer (probably Chief Officer Piper) calmed them and talked them down, explaining that there was a lifeboat waiting to be lowered on the promenade deck. The two women and the little boy rushed back to the waiting boat.

As they approached the waiting boat, another officer called out, "Hurry, we can get the little boy in, but we can't get you in!"

"All right, get him in," Elizabeth replied, and Alice handed little Arthur over the railing. Then the two women made for the next boat farther along the deck. When they got there, that boat was full as well, but a sailor pointed to the very last boat along the deck, so they started out for that one.

Elizabeth and Alice reached the boast just as the crew was preparing to launch it. The falls were sticking in the blocks and wouldn't move, and after a few minutes, Elizabeth decided she'd had enough and got back out of the boat. No sooner had she done so than the crew got the falls worked loose and the snubbing chain released. The boat swung far out away from the ship, dropping almost everyone in it into the sea below. Horrified, Elizabeth watched as Alice Scott fell into the water but never came back up. Seconds later, the falls parted and the now-empty boat went crashing down on the heads of its former occupants. Shaken, Elizabeth began reciting the Twenty-third Psalm to comfort herself. She noticed a trio of Irish girls standing nearby, singing, "There Is a Green Hill Not Far Away" in choked, frightened voices.

With the starboard lifeboats, the list was creating exactly the opposite problem it had caused on the port side. Here, the boats wanted to swing away from the side of the ship, opening up a yawning gap between the railing and the gunwale of the lifeboat. The snubbing chains helped control this, but the boats still swung out a good six feet. While not insurmountable, the gap was a serious obstacle, since jumping it would be difficult for children or elderly passengers.[11]

One of the first boats to get away was Boat 1, its only occupants being two Able Bodied Seamen, J. C. Morton and a man named Brown. For some reason, the passengers had refused to enter the boat, and Morton futilely tried to persuade them to slide down the falls into the boat once it had reached the water. No sooner had Morton and Brown freed the falls than Boat 1 collided with Boat 3, which also held just two seamen, one of them Morton's younger brother, Leslie. Thinking that Boat 1 had been damaged, Brown and Morton clambered aboard No. 3 and began assisting passengers, who suddenly had no qualms about getting into the boat. The ship was sinking so fast that many of them simply stepped off the railing into the lifeboat just a few feet below. When No. 3 was nearly full, Morton and Brown cut the falls, but the hammer for knocking out the pin holding the snubbing chain in place couldn't be found. Try as he might, Morton couldn't loosen the chain, and the sinking liner began to pull the lifeboat under. The Morton brothers jumped clear and swam away from the wreck, while Boat 3, most of its occupants swept away as it was pulled under, went to the bottom with the *Lusitania*, still held fast by the snubbing chain.

Boat 5 had been crushed by the waterspout thrown up by the exploding torpedo and was a total loss. Boat 7 was quickly filled with passengers and lowered, but before the falls could be freed and the chain let go, the boat's own davits fouled it and dragged it under. Boats 9 and 11 were safely launched, though both were loaded to less than half their capacity, and rapidly pulled away from the wreck, fearful of being caught in an inescapable suction when the *Lusitania* went under. Once clear of the wreck, both boats began plucking swimmers from the water and were quickly filled.

Boat 13 made it safely into the water, while Boat 15 was literally loaded to the gunwales. Determined to save as many as possible, First Officer Jones squeezed eighty passengers into a boat designed to hold sixty-five, and by carefully directing the men at both sets of falls, got the boat away from the ship without incident. A few moments later, Jones found Boat 1 floating empty and undamaged, despite its collision with Boat 3, and he quickly transferred half of the people in his charge to No. 1. Both boats then stood by the sinking *Lusitania* to pick up more swimmers.

The steadily increasing forward slant of the deck made lowering the lifeboats more difficult with each passing minute. The ship was now down by the head at an angle of nearly forty-five degrees, and the list still continued to grow. The snubbing chains would hold the boats no more than six feet from the railing, but as soon as they were removed, the boats would swing out eight, ten, sometimes as much as twelve feet, bobbing back and forth like pendulums. The *Lusitania* was sinking faster than ever now, as the water began sweeping up the decks, the bridge submerged, the forward funnel awash, the list still growing until it seemed that she would fall right over on her side. And still she retained some of her original momentum.

It was this momentum that caused Boat 17 to be lost. Just as Boat 17 was being lowered, the *Lusitania's* bow struck the bottom of the sea, and the impact cause the whole ship to quiver from bow to stern. The crewmen working No. 17's falls lost their grip, and the boat dropped into the water, turning over as it fell. The hapless occupants were tossed into the sea, and then the boat landed on top of them. Very few were ever seen again.

Boat 19 was carefully loaded with some sixty passengers, and the men at the falls were careful to compensate for the tilting deck and lowered the boat on a more or less even keel. But the strain proved to be too much for the after fall, which parted with a sound like a gunshot, dropping the boat's stern. Fortunately, the boat was only a few feet above the water, and nearly everyone aboard was able to hold on while the forward end of the boat was lowered and the fall was quickly cut away. Boat 21 had nearly seventy people aboard when it was lowered and reached the water safely, those aboard it pulling hard to get away from the sinking ship.[12]

Up on the Boat Deck, in the wireless office, Robert Leith was still tapping out the distress signal, still calling for anyone who could hear him to come at once. By now the rhythmic tapping had become almost reflexive. He didn't mention anything about a submarine or the *Lusitania* being torpedoed: He didn't have to—a ship like the *Lusitania* doesn't suddenly start sinking in the middle of a lakelike sea without help. As he continued to signal, he found a little time to pray, for as he watched the water creeping ever closer, Leith was haunted by the knowledge that he had never learned how to swim. And still the list grew . . .[13]

Walther Schwieger brought the *U-20* closer to the *Lusitania*. Still submerged, he examined the wreck more closely through his periscope. Although he couldn't hear the cries for help or the din of the sinking liner, some sense of the awful spectacle before him impressed itself on his mind, for he recorded in his log:

> The ship was sinking with unbelievable rapidity. There was a terrible panic on her deck. Overcrowded lifeboats, fairly torn from their positions, dropped into the water, as desperate people ran helplessly up and down the decks. Men and women jumped into the water and tried to swim to empty overturned lifeboats. It was the most terrible sight I have ever seen. It was impossible for me to give any help: I could have saved only a handful.

Stepping back from the periscope, Schwieger gave the order for the *U-20* to dive to twenty meters and proceed on a course to the southeast. It wouldn't be long before rescue vessels began arriving on the scene, most likely with units of the Royal Navy among them, and he had no desire to be anywhere near this spot when they arrived. Besides, his work here was finished.[14]

What Schwieger had glimpsed was a measure of the frenzy that had overtaken the decks of the *Lusitania* as the lifeboats were being lowered. Though he used the word "panic," there was actually little real panic on board, but the chaos must have made it appear so. The noise was deafening: Hundreds of people shouting, both aboard the ship and in the water; the crash and crunch of lifeboats being launched and lost; the residual steam from the boilers venting through the safety valves on the Boat Deck; the moans and shrieks of the ship herself as she heeled over. All over the ship, dozens of little vignettes were being played out as the end approached.

Back toward the stern, a small group centered around Charles Frohman. Leaning as always on his cane, Frohman knew that he had little chance, in his rheumatic, arthritic condition, to get into a boat. Around him were Rita Jolivet, her brother-in-law George Vernon, and Captain A. J. Scott of the British Army. Scott had found a lifebelt for Frohman and eventually got him to put it on, but moments later, Frohman gave it away. "Why fear death?" he quipped, quoting from James Barrie's *Peter Pan*, "It's the most beautiful adventure in life!" Soon a big wave came rolling up the deck, sweeping them all away. Rita was the only one of the group to survive. Nearby, two of her friends, playwright Charles Klein and novelist Justus Miles Forman, were also washed away and drowned.

Theodate Pope and her companion, Edward Friend, chose not to wait and be swept off the ship. When the torpedo hit the *Lusitania*, Theodate and Friend had been walking along B Deck. Feeling the ship shake from the explosion, Friend cried out, "By Jove, they've got us!" Friend had rushed down to their cabins to get lifebelts for Theodate and himself, at the same time fetching Theodate's maid, Emily Robinson. Now the three of them stood by the B Deck railing preparing to jump into the water. Friend went first, Theodate followed, then Emily. As Theodate surfaced, she struck her head hard against something—she thought it was the underside of a lifeboat—and then she drifted away, half conscious. She never saw Emily or Friend again.

Matt Freeman was having a terrible time of it. Earlier, he had seriously injured his hand trying to free a lifeboat fall that had jammed in its davit. Madame De Page quickly bandaged it, though something about the beautiful Belgian doctor's demeanor told Freeman that she knew she was going to die. After the last boat had pulled away, he went to the stern and dove into the water, only to strike his head on a piece of wreckage. When he surfaced, he could feel blood running down his face, and the salt water stung the gash badly. Instinctively he began swimming away from the wreck, fearful of the suction he was sure would come when the *Lusitania* finally went under.

Two Third Class passengers, Mr. and Mrs. N. M. Pappadopoulo, decided not to take their chances with the lifeboats. Instead, they stood on the C Deck promenade and quickly stripped, then dived into the water and, with strong strokes, began swimming toward the Irish shore, ten miles away. S. L. B. Lines of Toronto wasn't quite as ambitious. He had seen his wife safely into a boat, then quickly took off his jacket and shoes and dove over the railing. Some-one—he never knew who—threw a lifebelt to him, and he managed to get it on while floating amid a mass of wreckage. A few minutes later, he was hauled aboard the same lifeboat his wife was in.[15]

The reactions of some people were simply inexplicable. Despite the list and the rapidly sinking decks, Charles Plamondon refused to put his family into a boat, despite the desperate entreaties of their steward, Edward Skay. Olive North, a young English girl, saw one woman arranging and rearranging her bags as if she were getting ready to disembark at Liverpool, while another woman told Olive she planned to go to her cabin and meet her fate in comfort. Olive was more determined than that. "No, I will at least make a fight for it," she told the woman.

Charles Jeffrey, an automobile manufacturer from Wisconsin, spotted his friend Patrick Jones standing on the starboard side of B Deck, braced against the rail, his arm wrapped around a stanchion. Jones was a reporter and photographer for the International News Service, and he was busily snapping pictures as quickly as he could press the shutter and wind the film on his camera. When Jeffrey shouted for Jones to get off the ship, the photographer declined, saying, "These will be the greatest pictures ever!" Jeffrey never saw Jones again.

There were others who faced their end with remarkable dignity. Father Basil Maturin, looking pale but keeping calm, gave absolution to anyone who asked. The time last anyone saw him, he was handing a baby into one of the lifeboats.

Surprisingly, probably the coolest man aboard the ship was one of the most unlikely. No one would have expected a millionaire playboy like Alfred Gwynne Vanderbilt to be a pillar of courage, but that was exactly what he had become. Dapper as always, he quickly set to, lending a hand wherever he could. At one point, Steward Robert Chisholm saw Vanderbilt calming a woman who had become hysterical. He gave his lifebelt to a Seattle nanny, Alice Middleton, and helped her put it on. He told his valet to find all the children he could, and shepherded them into the lifeboats. No one will ever know what it was that drove him that afternoon, but it can be truthfully said that, like Malcolm, the Thane of Cawdor, "nothing in his life so became him like the leaving of it." One of the last to see him alive was fifteen-year-old Virginia Bruce Loney. After she had dived into the water, Virginia turned back and looked toward the deck where her parents and Vanderbilt were standing side by side, gripping the railing hard to keep their balance. She had a curious premonition that she would never see any of them again. She was right.[16]

The *Lusitania's* distress signal had been picked up by the wireless station at the lighthouse on Old Kinsale Head and quickly relayed to Queenstown, where the word quickly spread, and every available vessel, naval and civilian, began to get ready to put to sea. About thirty-five miles southeast of the *Lusitania* the British tanker *Narragansett*, along with the Ellerman line's steamer *City of Exeter* and the Leyland line's *Etonian*, all picked up the SOS as well. The three ships were all within sight of one another, and after a quick conference by wireless between their captains, all three changed course and headed straight for the Old Head of Kinsale, figuring they would see the wreck itself as they got closer. Another ship, the *Swanmore*, of the Johnson Line, also picked up the *Lusitania*'s SOS, but her skipper decided that it had to be a hoax and was probably the product of a U-boat trying to lure unsuspecting ships into a trap. Instead of responding, he put the *Swanmore*'s helm over and returned to Liverpool.[17]

The end was only seconds away. As her structure flexed and bent from the dynamic forces working on her hull, the *Lusitania*'s interior bulkheads began to give way. The bulkhead between Boiler Rooms 2 and 3 collapsed, and the sudden inrush of seawater, washing over what was left of the fires in Number 3's boilers, built up enough steam pressure to blow the third funnel off its base. Accompanied by the sound of tearing metal and snapping stays, the funnel collapsed and fell into the sea. From all over the ship came bangs and thuds, creaks and groans as interior fixtures tore lose, windows and skylights shattered, and partitions gave way.

The *Lusitania* was almost gone, lying on her side, her starboard deckrails awash, the bridge submerged. Captain Turner and Quartermaster Johnston had both remained at their posts, as if reluctant to give them up. Johnston was swept from one side of the bridge to the other as the water rose and found himself in the midst of a maelstrom of stays, valve heads, ventilators, and guy wires as he drifted along the length of the wreck. Somehow he managed to avoid all of these obstacles and was soon picked up by a lifeboat.

Turner was determined to stay on the ship for as long as he could, but when the list became too steep and the bridge began to go under, he had scrambled out onto the port bridge wing and began climbing the signal halyards, believing that in doing so he was fulfilling his obligation to be the last man aboard. By this time, the slant of the decks and the rising sea had washed almost everybody off the wreck, but there was still a handful of passengers at the extreme stern, though Turner had no way of knowing they were there. Clinging to the rigging, Turner began contemplating a captain's worst nightmare: He was about to lose his ship. Despite what he believed were his best efforts, a single torpedo coming out of nowhere had reduced the 43,000-ton behemoth he commanded to a creaking, flaming wreck. He watched in dismay as a huge, rolling wave passed over the Boat Deck around the base of the funnels, engulfing the wireless shack and the vaulted roofs over the First Class Lounge and the First Class Smoking Room. As the *Lusitania* finally began to settle, her masts and rigging going under, Turner let go of the halyards and struck out for a section of timber he saw floating nearby. Wrapping his arms around it, he turned back just in time to watch what was left of the *Lusitania* disappear.

Charles Lauriat had been right—there had been enough time for him to go below to his cabin and get the important papers he'd left there. But he had cut it very close, and when he got back onto B Deck—no simple feat, given that the ship was slanting forward at a forty-five-degree angle and listing to starboard by all of that and more—all of the lifeboats were gone. He saw one boat, filled mainly with women, that had gotten tangled up in the stays of the second funnel, and now that immense structure, big enough to drive two motorcars through side by side, hulked over the boat, threatening to press down on it and crush it as the *Lusitania* sank. As Lauriat watched, the boat worked clear and pulled away from the wreck with only a few feet to spare. Lauriat jumped into the water, only feet below the B Deck railing, got caught in one of the abandoned lifeboat falls, fought his way free of it, and surfaced just in time to see the *Lusitania* go under.

With her bow submerged and already resting on the bottom, her stern nearly a hundred feet in the air, the four huge, bronze propellors motionless at last, gleaming in the sunlight, the *Lusitania* gave one last, great moan of tortured steel and then quickly slid under the water. There was no immense suction, no churning maelstrom—one instant she was there, the next she was gone. It was 2:28 P.M. From the moment the torpedo struck the *Lusitania* to the instant she disappeared, eighteen minutes had passed.[18]

CHAPTER 10

The Rescue

As the *Lusitania* went under, the maelstrom of irresistible suction that everyone had expected never materialized. Instead, almost its exact opposite occurred: With a terrifying hiss of escaping steam, a gout of smoke and soot burst up from the wreck, filled with countless small bits of wreckage. For nearly a minute after the ship disappeared, there was a continuous upwelling of deck chairs and cushions, wooden crates and packing boxes, benches, barrels, lumps of coal, balks of timber, gratings, bits and pieces of furniture and furnishings, even bodies. When the upheaval subsided, all that was left of the *Lusitania* was a swiftly dispersing mass of debris.

Not much of it was what Isaac Lehmann thought of as "useful" wreckage, pieces large enough to help support a man or a woman, like the oar he found himself clinging to. His right leg was still throbbing, and occasionally a moan of pain would escape his lips, adding to the chorus of cries around him, as people in the water began to call for help from the lifeboats scattered across the sea.

Many of the lifeboats had been launched half empty, and soon the people in them were setting to with a will, trying to pull swimmers out of the water. Here and there a struggle broke out between survivors fighting for possession of a plank or a keg large enough to support only one of them. Some people screamed for help, others simply lay back in the water and methodically chanted "Bo-at! Bo-at" over and over again. Sometimes one of the big wooden storage boxes that had held spare lifebelts floated by. Six feet long by three feet wide, they reminded some people of coffins, while in at least one case they actually saved two lives. A fireman, rapidly approaching exhaustion and having nothing to cling to, saw one of the boxes drift by. Catching hold of it, he began to climb in when he noticed that there was already a woman inside. He asked, "Got room for one more?" and the woman nodded; they spent the next two hours lying side by side, wet and miserable, before being picked up by a fishing boat.

Most of the collapsibles had floated free of the wreck, although many of them were damaged by the lifeboats as they had swung to and fro. A peculiarity of their design was that the sides and the seats had to be raised together, and in most cases, there were dozens of frantic swimmers clinging desperately to the folded sides of the collapsibles. Getting these people to let go of their sole means of support for even a few minutes was quite often impossible, so most of the collapsibles were never properly used.[1]

In the hands of determined men, however, a collapsible boat could be used to work wonders. Two young seamen, Leslie Morton and William Parry, had somehow managed to get the sides erected on a collapsible and soon were busy pulling more than fifty people out of the water. Working with a handful of survivors who volunteered to pull the oars, the two young men worked until sundown chasing calls for help, looking for an arm waving, transferring the people they rescued to other lifeboats or, as help began to arrive, to the fishing boats and little steamers that had sailed out of Queenstown in answer to the *Lusitania's* distress signal, then going back to look for still more survivors. Eventually Morton and Parry were personally congratulated by King George V for their heroism.

Robert Leith, who had sent the distress signal, had been swept from the wireless shack as the ship went under, still desperately tapping out his call for help. He eventually found one of the collapsibles, this one with its sides damaged but the keel intact, and using it like a raft, Leith and a handful of other survivors floated wordlessly, waiting for the rescue they could only hope was coming.

Matt Freeman was still having a bad time of it. After injuring his hand helping launch a lifeboat, then gashing his head open as he dove into the sea from the deck of the *Lusitania*, he eventually found himself struggling with a half dozen other men for a handhold on a barrel that could support only three or four of them. Giving it up, Freeman finally found an overturned lifeboat and joined a dozen other swimmers clinging to its keel. As the afternoon passed and the sun began to get lower in the sky, the temperature dropped and the water began to grow colder. One by one, the people clinging to the upturned boat began to slip off as their strength gave out, until by the time one of the fishing boats from Queenstown arrived, only Freeman and two others were left.

Lady Mackworth was clinging precariously to one end of a piece of wood, a man she didn't know gripping the other end. After a time, the man began to move toward her end of the board, and she told him in no uncertain terms to stay where he was. Startled, the man retreated to his end of the board, only later to lose his grip and drift away. Lady Mackworth kept her desperate hold on the board, although she began to feel drowsy, and soon her consciousness was slipping away as the water began to get colder and sapped the strength from her body.

Theodate Pope had the feeling that everything she was experiencing was just a nightmare and that she would wake from it soon. When she had dived from the ship, she had struck her head on something—she believed it was the keel of a lifeboat—and had floated amid the wreckage in a daze. At one point, a man tried to save himself by clinging to her; she was too tired to struggle, and the man let go after a few minutes, though Theodate never knew why. After a while, she found herself floating in the middle of a mass of wreckage along with several other survivors. She could hear in the distance a somewhat off-key rendition of "Tipperary," and she wondered what had become of Edward Friend and her maid, Emily—she didn't know that she would never see them again.

Others heard singing as well, although in this instance it was the old Scottish hymn "Abide with Me," followed by, of all things, "Nearer My God to Thee." The singers were four surviving members of the Royal Welsh Chorus who had found themselves reunited on an upturned boat. More than one listener recalled that it was the same group of singers who had performed "The Star Spangled Banner" on sailing day in New York and given several concerts during the crossing.

Professor Stoughton Holbourn had no idea if his young friend, twelve-year-old Avis Dolphin, had lived or died. After the *Lusitania* sank, Holbourn had been caught in the massive upsurge of wreckage from the sinking ship, but being a strong swimmer, he quickly pulled away from it. He saw an unconscious man floating nearby and took him in tow, hoping to reach a lifeboat. By the time he got to one, the man he was towing was dead, and Holbourn let him go. The lifeboat itself was overcrowded, and the petty officer in charge decided to transfer some of those aboard to another boat floating nearby, this one almost empty.

After about fifteen people had moved to the other boat, the petty officer then announced that his boat would pull for the shore, some ten miles distant. Quickly the boat began moving through the debris, human and otherwise, that was littering the water for nearly a mile in every direction now. Holbourn was appalled by the number of people he saw in the water who had been drowned because they had put their lifebelts on backward and, instead of having their heads supported out of the water, had them held beneath the surface instead.

One of the *Lusitania*'s surviving electricians, George Hutchinson, was struck by same sight. He tried helping several people in that predicament, although most of them refused, thinking he was simply trying to steal their lifebelts. One man Hutchinson tried working with was Alfred Vanderbilt, but the two men couldn't get the lifebelt adjusted properly, and soon they drifted apart. No one ever saw Vanderbilt again.[2]

Around 5:00, some of the more watchful survivors noticed a smudge of smoke to the southeast. Soon the smudge gave way to the sight of two steamers, coming hard, bearing straight for the spot where the survivors were waiting. Rescue, at last, seemed at hand. Suddenly, without any warning or even an indication that the survivors had been seen, the two ships veered off, still steaming at high speed, but away from the helpless mass of swimmers and the handful of lifeboats. Before long, they were out of sight.

The two ships had been the *Etonian* and *City of Exeter.* The *U-20* was still prowling around the area, and by sheer luck, Schwieger had positioned his submarine right across the track of the three ships rushing to answer the *Lusitania*'s distress call. Spotting the tanker *Narragansett,* he fired one of his two remaining torpedoes at her. It missed—Schwieger later reported that he thought the steering mechanism was faulty—but it passed close enough to the tanker to be spotted, and it gave her skipper quite a start. He decided that the *Lusitania*'s wireless signal had been a hoax, a trap set by an ambushing U-boat, and promptly altered course to the southwest, out into the open sea.

The *City of Exeter* and the *Etonian,* a few miles astern of the *Narragansett,* hadn't noticed the tanker change course, and they continued straight on until they were in sight of the survivors floating about in the water. It was just at this moment that Schwieger, possibly anticipating using his deck gun on one or both of the ships, surfaced between the two of them. The two captains were as startled as the captain of the *Narragansett* had been, and they promptly turned their ships around. Schwieger gave chase, but the *U-20* was no match for the fleeing freighters, and he soon broke off the pursuit and set course for Germany. His mischief in these waters was done; if the *Lusitania*'s survivors were to be rescued, their only hope would be the "mosquito fleet" of fishing boats and coasters that had put out from Queenstown.[3]

When word of the *Lusitania*'s distress call reached Queenstown, there was no debating what the response would be. Queenstown, whose name had originally been the Cove of Cork but had been changed when Queen Victoria had visited the picturesque little village in 1849, had been a seafaring town since time immemorial, and as news spread along the waterfront, every vessel that could be readied in a few minutes' notice put out to sea. This "mosquito fleet" consisted of twenty-five to thirty fishing smacks (no one ever actually counted), a quartet of naval patrol boats, and three elderly torpedo boats, along with a Greek coaster named the *Katerina* and a side-wheel tender, the *Flying Fish,* affectionately known as the "Galloping Goose."

Vice Admiral Coke had ordered the four ships of the Irish Coast Patrol that were moored at Queenstown to set out immediately—his flagship, the cruiser *Juno,* and the three light cruisers, *Isis, Sutlej,* and *Venus. Juno* was the first to sail, leaving her moorings at 3:00 P.M., but she didn't get far: She had barely rounded Roche's Point, five miles out of Queenstown Harbour, when she was recalled by Admiral Coke. The admiral had received a peremptory signal from the Admiralty in Whitehall that he was not to expose his warships to submarine attack under any circumstances. *Juno* put about and returned to Queenstown; the other three cruisers never left their docks.

It was twenty miles from Queenstown Harbour to the spot where the *Lusitania* sank, and the first boats of the rescue flotilla encountered a handful of lifeboats halfway there. The survivors in the boats had been pulling hard for Queenstown but were rapidly approaching exhaustion. A couple of the fishing boats stopped to pick them up, while the rest of the mosquito fleet continued onward. The sun was low on the horizon by the time the first res-cue vessels reached the survivors; by this time, they had drifted over several square miles of ocean, and while the lifeboats and collapsibles were fairly easy to see, spotting a swimmer or some poor soul clinging to a bit of wreckage was going to be difficult as daylight faded.[4]

The people in the boats did the best they could. Like Morton and Parry, Charles Lauriat and James Brooks, along with a pair of brawny seamen, were able to get the sides of a collapsible raised and the seats in place, and soon were dragging soaked, exhausted survivors out of the water. One of them was a Toronto man named McMurray, who had struck out from the ship intend-ing to swim to shore but found that his strength wasn't equal to the challenge. After resting aboard the collapsible for a few minutes, however, he proved to be a tower of strength at the oars.

At one point, Brooks helped pull a woman aboard who was badly bruised and cut, and had most of her clothing torn off. She was black from head to toe, and everyone thought she was African. In fact, she was Margaret Gwyer, the clergyman's wife. As the *Lusitania* had gone under, she had been swept inside one of the ship's huge funnels, only to be spat out seconds later, cov-ered with soot, as a gout of hot air welled up from deep inside the ship. She was so dark that when she was reunited with her husband a few hours later, at first he refused to believe it was her.

Lauriat heard a remarkably calm voice call out, "Won't you take me next?" Lauriat turned and saw, less than ten feet away, a young woman with her chin resting on a plank, apparently all that was holding her up. She was surrounded by debris that kept her from lifting her arms out of the water. She then added, "I can't swim, you know," and gave Lauriat what seemed to be an almost apologetic smile. It was then that Lauriat noticed, of all things, that she was calmly chewing a piece of gum.

It was not a simple situation, the men in the boat saw right away. To move the boat any closer to the woman might disturb the wreckage around her, injuring her or causing her to slip off the board that was holding her up. Lauriat volunteered to swim over to her. "That's not necessary," she replied, "just pass me an oar." Gingerly two men held an oar out to her, while she carefully worked her hands free, still chewing away on the gum. After a few minutes, she was pulled into the boat and quietly took a seat after thanking everyone. When they arrived at Queenstown some hours later, having been taken aboard the *Flying Fish,* Lauriat noticed that she was still chewing that piece of gum.

The *Flying Fish* also picked up a little convoy of lifeboats that had strung itself together. All told, there were 150 people aboard three lifeboats that were tied together bow to stern. When they pulled alongside the *Flying Fish,* the passengers and crewmen at the oars had been pulling in time to the strains of the "Blue Danube."

Elizabeth Duckworth's boat had set out for the Irish shore as soon as it was launched, Elizabeth taking her turn at the oars when she was needed, and so was one of the first ones encountered by the mosquito fleet, in this case by the trawler *The Peel 12.* As she climbed aboard the fishing boat, another lifeboat, this one with only three people in it, drifted by. One of the men in the lifeboat called out that the boat had been overloaded and almost capsized, and that several people had been pitched out when the boat had tipped. They were floating nearby, he said, but they needed help quickly. Could the men in the trawler spare anyone to help? The officer who had taken charge of Elizabeth's boat shook his head, calling back, "No, I can't spare anyone."

"You can spare me," she told the officer, then gathered up her skirts and jumped into the passing lifeboat and took her place at the oars. A few others followed her example, and in minutes the lifeboat was heading back to pick up its lost charges.

It took less than an hour for the rescue vessels to pick up all of the lifeboats and collapsibles. The lifeboats were brought on board whenever possible, since they could be salvaged, but the collapsibles were abandoned. They had done their job, but most of them were too badly damaged to be worth saving.[5]

Now the challenge for the rescuers was to find the people still adrift in the twilight. The survivors were exhausted—often too far gone in fatigue to even wave an arm or call out to an approaching boat. Many were actually unconscious; many more were, of course, already dead. It was difficult sometimes to tell one from the other—was the stiffness in a body's limbs fatigue or the onset of rigor mortis? Was the coolness of the skin due to being immersed so long in the water or because life had departed the body?

In some cases, the situation was obvious: A body floating face down was clearly dead, some because they had no lifebelts, others because they had put theirs on backward and had their heads held under the water instead of above it. Here and there, the sailors on the rescue boats tried to revive the bodies they plucked from the water, with varying degrees of success, for they weren't trained for that sort of work and had no special equipment. So usually they stacked the bodies together on the decks of their boats, hoping that when they returned to Queenstown, the doctors there might be able to do something for them.

And then there were the bodies of the children, over a hundred of them. Especially pathetic were those little ones who were too small to be able to wear one of the special small-size children's lifebelts. All too often these "babes in arms" were exactly that—held close to their mothers' bosoms, where they died together.

No one will ever know how many people who survived the sinking were lost in the rapidly dwindling twilight; unconscious, unable to even call for help, they went unseen by the sailors who desperately strained their eyes for some sign of life. Captain Turner was lucky—he was spotted when one of the last rays of sunlight glinted off the gold braid on the sleeves of his uniform jacket and was seen by a sailor on the tug *Bluebell*. Staff Captain Anderson's body was spotted the same way. Something similar happened to a woman who was floating alive but unconscious: The reflection of the setting sun off her diamond rings caught a sharp-eyed fisherman's attention.

Lady Mackworth, unconscious after spending nearly three hours in the water, was also pulled aboard the *Bluebell*. When she opened her eyes, the first thing she saw was the concerned face of one of the tug's sailors. Seeing her alive and awake, he broke into a grin and said, "You'll be all right now." She wondered what had become of her father.

Theodate Pope had been fished out of the water, unconscious like Lady Mackworth, and brought aboard the trawler *Julia*. The crew thought she was dead at first and laid her on the deck among the other bodies they had picked up. It wasn't until 10:30 that night that she regained consciousness, finding herself wrapped in a blanket, lying beside a small open-hearth fire. A friend of hers, Mrs. Theodore Naisch, had recognized her and, seeing that she was still breathing, persuaded the *Julia*'s crew to move her to the captain's tiny cabin. Close by, twelve-year-old Avis Dolphin lay wrapped in a steamer rug, huddled close to a stove.

Not far away, Lady Marguerite Allen, of Montreal, also lay wrapped in a steamer rug. Numbly she wondered what had happened to her thirteen-year-old twin daughters, Anna and Gwen. Holding hands, they had jumped from the deck of the *Lusitania* moments before the ship made her final plunge, but the girls had been swept away. Now Lady Allen had no idea where they were.

There were touching moments of humanity in the middle of all the tragedy. Fifteen-year-old Kathleen Kaye, a slip of a girl, was remembered by many for the way she comforted the distraught people aboard the lifeboat they shared, sometimes administering first aid, taking a turn at an oar without complaint. In another boat, Greta Nielson fell overboard. She didn't know how to swim and had no lifebelt on. John Welsh, one of the *Lusitania's* few surviving engineers, dove in the water after her and was able to bring her back to the boat. It marked the beginning of a romance, and one week later, Greta and John were married in Manchester, England.[6]

Darkness had fallen, and the flotilla of rescue vessels began to make their way back to Queenstown. Survivors were wrapped in blankets and steamer rugs, plied with hot coffee and tea, and the occasional shot of whiskey or brandy when it was available. On every boat that had a stove or hearth, it was stoked up until it glowed so that chilled limbs could be warmed and unconscious survivors revived.

Once the boats reached Queenstown, the survivors were helped ashore, many having to be carried by groups of sailors or on improvised stretchers. The American consul at Queenstown, Wesley Frost, hauntingly described their arrival:

> We saw the ghastly procession of these rescue ships as they landed the living and the dead that night under the flaring gas torches along the Queenstown waterfronts. The arrivals began soon after eight o'clock and continued at close intervals until about eleven o'clock. Ship after ship would come up out of the darkness and sometimes two or three could be just described awaiting their turns in the cloudy night to discharge bruised and shuddering women, crippled and half-clothed men and a few wide-eyed little children. . . . Women caught at our sleeves and begged desperately for word of their husbands, and men with choking efforts of matter of factness moved ceaselessly from group to group seeking a lost daughter or sister or even bride. Piles of corpses like cordwood began to appear among the paint kegs and coils of rope on the shadowy old wharves. Every voice in that great mixed assemblage was pitched in unconscious undertones, broken now and then by painful coughing fits or suppressed hysteria.

Three temporary morgues were set up, all of them working far into the night as more and more bodies were brought in, some by boats, others having been washed ashore.[7]

Because of the tourist trade, Queenstown had more hotels than would be normal for a town its size, and these were thrown open to the dazed and exhausted survivors. The owner of the largest hotel was a German, who wisely took the precaution of locking himself in a closet in his basement before the first survivors began to arrive. They didn't mind—they helped themselves to keys and made themselves as comfortable as they could under the circumstances. When the hotels were full, private homes were opened up, while people all over Queenstown began rummaging through closets and trunks to find clothing for the survivors, many of whom came ashore naked, or nearly so.

For many of the survivors, exhaustion was so deep that it would be days before they could stir from their beds. Lady Mackworth had been so weak that when the *Bluebell* tied up at the dock in Queenstown, she had to crawl down the gangway on her hands and knees. She found her father waiting there for her. It would be a week before Theodate Pope was strong enough to sit up in a chair in her hotel room, while Elizabeth Duckworth's health took months to recover.

For some of the survivors, though, there was no question of sleep, no matter how exhausted they were. They were looking for loved ones—husbands, wives, parents, children, brothers, and sisters. They haunted the waterfront, holding up lanterns and torches, looking at the faces of the bodies stacked there. They wandered through the morgues, lifting the corners of blankets, all too often moving on to the next body, dreading what they might find, dreading even more not finding who they sought. Their plight was best summed up by the actions of one shocked father who had lost two of his four children, who kept trudging through the morgues muttering, "Fifty percent! That is not too bad! Some fathers lost their whole families." In desperation, some began posting notices, pathetic in their hope, heartbreaking in their implications:

> *Lusitania*—missing baby: missing, a baby girl, 15 months old. Very fair curly hair and rosy complexion. In white woolen jersey and white woolen leggins. Tries to talk and walk. Name Betsy Bretherton. Please send any information to Miss Browne, Queens House, Queenstown.

The next day, and for several days afterward, more bodies were washed ashore or brought in by fishing boats. Every effort was made to identify them, although in some cases it was hopeless. J. J. Murphy, the Cunard agent in Queenstown, worked closely with Wesley Frost in providing updated lists of survivors and victims. As bodies were identified, next of kin were notified and instructions were requested for how the body was to be buried and where. Many were embalmed in Queenstown and sent off to the United States, Canada, or England for burial. Charles Frohman's funeral in Temple Emanu-El in New York was attended by nearly 10,000 people. When the bodies of Charles and Mary Plamondon were returned to Chicago, flags were half-masted all over the city. Dr. DePage came to take his wife, Marie, back to be buried in her beloved Belgium. In London, last rites were said amid great and solemn ceremony for Father Basil Maturin, whose his body had been found washed ashore at Ballycotton Bay.

Some of the victims were lovingly buried on Irish soil: In the churchyard of St. Mulrose there is a small headstone that marks the spot where Margaret McKenzie and her husband of eleven days, James Shineman, rest together for all time. Others wouldn't have even that consolation—Leslie Mason's body was brought ashore by one of the fishing boats returning to Queenstown, but her husband, Stuart, whom she had married two weeks before, was never found. All told, some 900 bodies were never recovered.

One hundred forty bodies were recovered but not identified, and for them there was a common burial in a mass grave outside of Queenstown. On Monday, May 10, they were brought to St. Colman's Cathedral in the center of Queenstown. Flags flew at half-mast, a military band played a series of solemn pieces and dirges, windows all over the city were either shuttered or hung with black crepe. The bodies had each been placed in a simple yellow pine coffin, with the coroner's identifying number chalked on the top of each one. A joint Protestant-Catholic service was held at the cathedral, and then a line of carts (there weren't enough hearses for all of the coffins) began to wind through Queenstown to Old Church Cemetery on the outskirts of the city where, the night before, British soldiers had dug a huge grave. One by one, the coffins were lowered into the grave and covered with earth. It was after dark before the last of the coffins was covered.

No one would ever know exactly who was in them, for while a few efforts would be made in months to come to identify some of the bodies, most would forever remain unknown. Among those never found or never identified were Alfred Vanderbilt; Justus Miles Forman, the novelist-playwright, whose only play, *The Hyphen,* in a cruel twist of fate, had its final performance in Boston the same day the *Lusitania* sank; Elbert and Alice Hubbard (one observer sadly remarked that "Kaiser Bill had won the last round"); George Vernon, Rita Jolivet's brother-in-law, whose despairing widow took her own life two months later. No one ever found Chief Officer Piper or Chief Engineer Bryce; Lady Allen's daughters, Anna and Gwen; the young engineer from the Isle of Man, Walter Scott Quarrie; or the INS photographer Patrick Jones. And for some, their names were never even recorded. Far too often, the records of those lost include the simple notation "*—and valet,*" "*—and maid,*" "*—and manservant.*"

When all the figures were totaled, of the 1,959 passengers and crew who had sailed aboard the *Lusitania* on her last voyage, 1,198 had died, 785 of them passengers. There had been 159 Americans on board, and 128 of them lost their lives. Out of 129 children, 94 perished. The deed was done, the tally made. Now the world held its breath, waiting for Great Britain and America to react.[8]

CHAPTER 11

The Outrage and Excuses

THE WORLD WAS AGHAST AT THE NEWS OF THE SINKING. THE *LUSITANIA* WAS not some obscure tanker or a merchantman that had been torpedoed by accident. She was arguably the most famous and in some ways the best-loved ship in the world. Her photograph had appeared at one time or another on the pages—usually the front page—of nearly every newspaper on both sides of the Atlantic. It would be impossible for Germany to claim that this was anything other than a deliberate act. How America would react to the sinking, and how Germany would explain it, riveted the attention of the chancelleries and foreign offices of the nations of the Central Powers and the Allies alike.

Word that the *Lusitania* had been torpedoed began spreading almost as soon as her first distress signals were picked up by the wireless stations at Kinsale and Valencia. Within hours, details began following, as the survivors began trickling into Queenstown. The Cunard agent there, J. J. Murphy, was conscientious about taking names and other personal information, as well as learning whatever details he could about the disaster. He made hourly reports to the Cunard offices in Liverpool and London, as well as to the company office in New York. Working with him was the American Consul, Wesley Frost, who was looking after the interests of the American passengers, both survivors and victims. Frost reported to the American State Department, meaning in this case Bryan and Lansing. In addition to forwarding lists of names of the living and the dead, Frost also found the time to take statements from as many of the American survivors as possible; eventually he collected thirty-five affidavits in all, sensing somehow that they might be useful to the men in Washington who were faced with the task of giving voice to America's reaction to the sinking.[1]

In Great Britain, the news of the *Lusitania's* destruction was a bitter blow to the entire nation, and especially to the Royal Navy, which, right or wrong, would be called to account for her loss. In Liverpool and London, small riots broke out as mobs savaged German-owned business—or even those with merely German-sounding names. Many naturalized British citizens of German birth were forced to seek police protection, as were some nationals of neutral countries who were mistaken for Germans in the hysteria. Several were accosted and beaten bloody in the streets of the British capital.

The British government didn't hesitate to exploit this anger, releasing highly exaggerated and colored accounts of new German atrocities in Belgium shortly after the news of the sinking was made public. The resulting perception of the "Barbarous Hun" spurred the British war effort as nothing had since autumn 1914. The ranks of the British Army were swelled by 150,000 new recruits—all of them volunteers; conscription wouldn't be introduced for another year—in the six weeks following the disaster, and production soared in Britain's munitions factories. The hardening of public opinion began to strengthen the hand of the faction within the government that clamored for "total victory" rather than a negotiated peace. It was an ominous sign.

Naturally all of this was reported to Washington by the American ambassador, Walter Page. Unfortunately, he couldn't resist adding his usual embellishments to his reports, allowing his Anglophilia and pro-Allied sentiments to sometimes cloud his perceptions. At one point, just days after the disaster, he wrote to the State Department affirming that "official [British] opinion is of course reticent. The freely expressed unofficial feeling is that the United States must declare war or forfeit European respect. So far as I know this opinion is universal."

Far from being universal, such an opinion was a rarity. The British government vastly preferred to have the United States as a ready and willing source of supply rather than a cobelligerent with her own war aims and strategies that might well run counter to the interests of the British Empire. President Wilson, with the perspective of 3,000 miles of distance, saw through such pronouncements, realizing that they reflected more of what Page wished circumstances to be rather than the way they actually were.[2]

It would be incorrect to say that the news of the *Lusitania's* destruction was greeted with rejoicing in Germany; rather, the prevailing mood was that of a job well done. The German press willingly promoted the official government justifications for the sinking: The ship had been a disguised auxiliary cruiser, mounting ten or twelve 6-inch guns; she had been ferrying a large body of Canadian troops across the Atlantic; and she was carrying a cargo of contraband, especially munitions and high explosives. If any of those charges were true, then Kapitan-Leutnant Schwieger and the crew of the *U-20* were to be commended—they had struck a blow for the Fatherland. An editorial in *Kolnische* (Cologne) *Volkszeitung* summed it up when it said, "With joyful pride we contemplate this latest deed of our navy"—harsh sounding in translation, but more like "Well done, lads!" than gloating. Otherwise, there was no overwhelming public reaction, despite Allied propaganda that the German people were all but dancing in the streets for joy at the news of the *Lusitania's* sinking.

There was one odd sidelight, though, to the announcement in Germany that a German submarine had sunk the *Lusitania*. A Munich metalsmith, Karl Goetz, had thought it absurd that Cunard and the British government had allowed the *Lusitania* to continue to make regular crossings of the Atlantic at a time when the U-boats were sinking ships at an alarming rate.

Goetz had already made a name for himself for creating commemorative, often satirical, medals and medallions for himself, his friends, and a select clientele. In this case, he quickly created a memorable one. On the obverse he showed a large, sinking ship of indeterminate type, crammed with guns and aeroplanes, while on the reverse, a long line of passengers queued up to purchase tickets from a Cunard office run by a Death's Head. To Goetz, the satire was unmistakable. He made forty-four copies.

One of them soon fell into British hands, and as a propaganda ploy, some 300,000 copies were struck in Great Britain and distributed to the public—an example, it was claimed, of Teutonic callousness that mocked the cruel loss of life on the *Lusitania*. Such was the fever pitch of British propaganda that the story was widely accepted, and to this day, otherwise reliable historians are convinced that all 300,000-odd medals were made in Germany.[3]

News of the disaster began to spread in the United States in midafternoon on May 7, as Murphy's cables reached Cunard's New York office. Cunard, remembering the hysteria and confusion caused by the White Star Line's stonewalling the news about the *Titanic* three years earlier, wisely admitted as soon as the information was confirmed that the *Lusitania* had been torpedoed and sunk, and methodically released any new information that came in. Soon the extra editions of all the New York newspapers hit the streets, and the story was quickly picked up by newspapers up and down the East Coast, followed by those further inland. By the end of the day, the word had spread from one end of the country to the other that the *Lusitania* had been sunk by a German U-boat. For the next six weeks, the *Lusitania* was *the* front-page story in every American daily.

At first the reporting was straightforward, as more news of the disaster became known, but within twenty-four hours, editorial comments began appearing. The strident clamor from the New York press for retribution against Germany, some editors going so far as to propose declaring war on Germany, was to be expected. So were reactions from public figures that had been urging America to get involved in the war—exemplified by former President Theodore Roosevelt when he declared the sinking to be "piracy on a vaster scale of murder than any old-time pirate ever practiced. . . . It seems inconceivable that we can refrain from taking action . . . we owe it to humanity . . . to our own national self-interest."

What was surprising was the reaction in parts of the United States that had been relatively indifferent to the war in Europe. The Richmond, Virginia, *Times-Dispatch* was blunt: "Germany surely must have gone mad. The torpedoing and sinking . . . evince a reckless disregard of the opinions of the world in general and of this country in particular." The Denver *Rocky Mountain News* declared, "Today humanity is aghast that such a thing . . . could be possible in the Twentieth Century." Perhaps the clearest indication of the mood of the American press—and the American people—came when the fiercely anti-British Chicago *Tribune* solemnly urged the nation to unanimously back whatever response President Wilson chose.

Nor could the New York press be ignored for being so extreme—it was too influential, and often within the stridency of its clamor there were telling points made against Germany's actions. There was more than a grain of truth in the harsh rhetoric of the New York *Nation* when it said: "The law of nations and the law of God have alike been trampled upon. . . . The torpedo that sank the *Lusitania* also sank Germany in the opinion of mankind . . . it is at once a crime and a monumental folly. . . . She has affronted the moral sense of the world and sacrificed her standing among the nations." The editorial cartoonists were especially harsh: In the New York *World,* a Roland Kirby cartoon depicted Kaiser Wilhelm turning away from the ghosts of children, who with outstretched arms were pleading for an answer to their question, "But why did you kill *Us?*" In the New York *Evening Sun,* Robert Carter sketched the Kaiser draping an Iron Cross around the neck of a snarling wolf, labeled "War on Helpless Shipping," while in the background a flag with *Lusitania* written on it sank beneath the waves; the caption had Wilhelm saying simply, "Brave work!" Nelson Harding's cartoon in the Brooklyn *Eagle* summed up the feelings of most Americans: In it an armor-clad hand held forth a sword dripping blood; from the sword hung a wreath tagged "Official German Sympathy."[4]

What was just as surprising to Germany was the condemnation by neutral powers that the destruction of the *Lusitania* provoked. One Danish newspaper announced, "When in the future the Germans venture to speak of their culture the answer will be, 'It does not exist: it committed suicide on May 7th, 1915.'" In Sweden, despite strong cultural and economic ties with Germany, the vast majority of the press denounced the sinking as barbaric—including publishing a statement by thirty of Sweden's leading scholars, educators, and scientists that protested the sinking as an act that suspended "all laws of humanity." In Switzerland, the reaction was predictably mixed: The German-speaking segment of the population generally—but not universally—condoned the sinking, while the French and Italian-speaking population roundly damned it. In South America, even in Argentina and Paraguay, countries with large German immigrant populations, the destruction of the *Lusitania* was soundly condemned—in part, no doubt, because the German submarine campaign posed a very real threat to those nations' not inconsiderable merchant marines. What was perhaps the most surprising was that not a single neutral power openly endorsed the deed as a legitimate act of war; a few suggested that Germany might have been justified by some particulars of international law, but the only applause the German Navy was hearing was coming from within Germany and Austria-Hungary.[5]

It was surprising to the Germans, because within three days of the sinking they had offered what to them seemed to be carefully reasoned and argued, if somewhat lengthy, justification, disguised as a note of apology, for destroying the *Lusitania*. In a diplomatic memorandum sent to the U.S. State Department, drafted by Foreign Minister von Jagow and endorsed by Chancellor Bethmann-Hollweg, the Imperial German government expressed its "deepest sympathy at the loss of American lives" on the *Lusitania,* but did not disavow the act; instead, the memorandum tried to shift the "responsibility" (the diplomatic word for "blame") onto the British. Their rationale was that the British blockade had illegally stopped the flow of food and raw materials into Germany, compelling the Germans to take what they termed "retaliatory measures" with their submarines. The document argued that because British merchant ships of all sizes were "generally armed with guns" and had "repeatedly tried to ram German submarines," they no longer deserved to be treated as ordinary merchant ships, subject to the search and seizure procedures of the Cruiser Rules.

Further justification was offered when the document alleged, with a fair measure of truth, that the *Lusitania* had repeatedly carried cargoes of munitions and that on her last voyage, she not only had 5,400 cases of rifle ammunition in her cargo hold, but almost all of the rest of her cargo was, by the British definition, contraband. The implication, of course, was that if the British could arbitrarily define what was and was not contraband to justify stopping and seizing ships on the high seas, the Germans could use those same definitions to justify the U-boats sinking British merchant ships—including the *Lusitania.*

The British, the document continued, despite having been warned repeatedly, both officially and unofficially, by the Germans that they were exposing the passengers—including neutrals—on their ships to destruction without warning if they continued to illegally transport munitions on passenger vessels, continued to do exactly that, while all the while assuring everyone that they were quite safe. The note regretted that the United States felt more inclined to trust "English promises" instead of heeding German warnings. In other words, it was the fault of the British for being so duplicitous, as well as the Americans for being so naive. The fact that it was a German U-boat that fired the torpedo that sank the *Lusitania* was reduced to incidental status. In short, the sinking was not only permissible under international law, it was justifiable *because* it was permissible.

It was a startling document, revealing as it did certain fundamentals about the character of the German government and the German people. By carefully cloaking the sinking of the *Lusitania* in a shroud of legality in order to justify it, the German government placed it in the same category as the execution of Belgian civilians and noncombatant hostages in occupied Belgium and France: a legal reprisal in response to the illegal actions of the Allies. This put the *Lusitania*'s destruction on the same level as the program of *Schrecklicheit,* though while "frightfulness" was by the Germans' own admission a policy that was formulated before the outbreak of the war, no one was suggesting that the sinking of the *Lusitania* had been planned in advance. What was clear was that it was condoned by the German government: As far as Berlin was concerned, it was legal, therefore it was permissible; because it was legal, it was moral.[6]

Yet there was something about that rationalization that didn't sit well with either President Wilson or, more importantly, the majority of the American public. Certainly Germany could argue with some justification that the U-boats had the right to sink cargo ships without warning, and that since most cargo vessels also had a few cabins for passengers, there was a certain degree of risk that those passengers took and accepted when they booked their passage. But to imply that the *Lusitania*—or any other passenger liner, for that matter—was nothing more than just another cargo ship, as the German note clearly did, strained the bounds of credulity for all but the most narrow-minded legalists. The *Lusitania*'s cargo holds could carry barely a tenth of the capacity of most merchantmen: It could scarcely be argued that the amount of cargo she could transport would critically affect the British war effort one way or the other—the 5 million rifle cartridges in her hold on her last voyage weren't even one day's expenditure for the British Army on the Western Front. Kapitan von Papen, the German naval attaché in Washington, simply made matters worse when, referring to the *Lusitania,* he remarked to the Washington press that it was "absolutely criminal" that Cunard should be carrying passengers on a ship that was a munitions transport. Legal hair-splitting notwithstanding, the *Lusitania* was a *passenger ship,* and the images of men, women, and small children fighting to save their lives as they stood on the decks of that sinking ship were too powerful in the minds of the American people for the sterile language of legalism to overcome.

It was impossible to believe that Kapitan-Leutnant Schwieger, despite later protests in Berlin to the contrary, didn't know the identity of the ship he was about to torpedo when he was tracking her through his periscope. By first acknowledging and then seeking to justify Schwieger's actions, the Imperial German government made it clear that it condoned the killing of innocent civilians at sea just as it had in Belgium. Berlin had blundered badly: No matter what Germany would be able to accomplish diplomatically, the sinking of the *Lusitania* was a mortal blow to German attempts at swaying American public opinion. After May 7, 1915, Germany had little hope of the Wilson Administration adopting a policy of strict neutrality and cutting off the supply of munitions to the British—the sympathies of the American people had swung sharply in favor of the British.

For months, the American public, with a few notable exceptions such as Teddy Roosevelt, had been content to let the Europeans settle their quarrels among themselves. To many Americans, the Great War was just the sort of (seemingly) dynastic squabble they or their ancestors had left Europe to avoid. All the same, there were large and vocal segments of American society that made their particular sympathies known: the pro-British Eastern establishment, most notably the business community, who were clamoring for the United States to do more than simply serve as Great Britain's warehouse and factory; and the large numbers of German-Americans living in the upper Midwest, who for obvious reasons had no wish to see the United States actively supporting the British war effort, and would have been quite pleased if somehow the United States and Germany had found themselves on the same side. The German-Americans presented their arguments in very simple terms: The passengers who lost their lives aboard the *Lusitania* had been warned and should have been aware of the risks they were taking by sailing on a British ship. They had made their choice and had suffered the consequences.[7]

For the pro-British community, this stance actually made their viewpoint more palatable to the rest of the American public, since it smacked too much of the German government's rather overwrought legalistic justification for the sinking. The majority of the American people were angry—they weren't clamoring for war, but they *were* outraged. They demanded that Germany be punished in some way for the destruction of the *Lusitania*; Germany must be made to understand that there was a limit to the patience of the American people, and consequently the American government. While America wasn't ready to go to war over the *Lusitania,* the mood of the American public was clear: If something similar happened again, Germany had better be prepared to fight. The American people looked to their President, Woodrow Wilson, to give voice to their anger.

This was the moment for which Wilson had been waiting; now he was at the center of the world stage. He now had a global forum to expound his principles, his humanitarian ideals, and his belief that America's neutrality granted her the moral high ground necessary to become the mediator in what was daily becoming a bloodier and more barbaric war. Instead, Wilson became a victim of the machinations of the people around him, but even more so of his own pusillanimity. Three days after the sinking of the *Lusitania,* the same day the German "apology" was delivered, he was in Philadelphia addressing 4,000 newly naturalized American citizens. Seeking to define the United States' unique position in relation to the warring powers, he said:

> The example of America must be a special example. The example of America must be the example not merely of peace because it will not fight, but because peace is the healing and elevating influence in the world and strife is not. There is such a thing as a man being too proud to fight. There is such a thing as a nation being so right that it does not need to convince others by force that it is right.

It was a terrible blunder, and Wilson realized it almost immediately. The phrase "too proud to fight" was immediately derided almost everywhere across the country; it became almost synonymous with cowardice in some circles. Later, rather lamely, he tried to expand on the idea: Might did not make right—surely the example of the *Lusitania* had proven that—and if the United States went to war with Germany and defeated Germany, what would that prove, save that Germany could be defeated and America could do it? But the damage had been done: Throughout history, there have been ideals and rights that men and women had believed were worth fighting and dying for—the United States had been founded by such people. But Wilson had created the impression that as far as he was concerned, and the United States as well, since he had been speaking as the President and so had been speaking for America, the protection of innocent civilians in wartime was not one of those ideals.

It was a mistake that would cost Wilson dearly, both in the immediate future and four years later, when he would argue in vain for his principles at the conference table that hammered out the Treaty of Versailles. What he had intended as a message of conciliation and high-minded moral certainty had been interpreted as a confession of weakness, and he had to counter that perception. Consequently, his first reaction was to respond to the German apology in very forceful terms—or rather more correctly, ignore the German note of May 10—and send a strongly worded protest to Germany about the destruction of the *Lusitania.*[8]

When Wilson's cabinet met on the morning of May 11, the first order of business was to formulate America's official reaction to the disaster. It was already becoming clear that the President's "too proud to fight" speech the night before was turning into an object of ridicule, and Wilson made it clear that he wanted to send a strongly worded note to the German government, expressing the anger of the American public over the sinking of the *Lusitania* and repeating his declaration that Germany would be held strictly accountable for any loss of American lives to actions by German U-boats, and demanding an apology for the sinking as well as the withdrawal of the submarines from the waters around Great Britain. It would be an opportunity for Wilson to recover some of the ground he had lost the night before. There was already a sizable minority in the cabinet who favored breaking off diplomatic relations with Germany as a protest—a sharp slap in the face to Germany in the diplomatic parlance of the day—and the Secretary of War, Lindley Garrison, was all for declaring war on Germany. Wilson made it very clear that there would be no severing of diplomatic ties and war was out of the question, but the note the United States sent to Germany had to be forceful.

Three hours' work resulted in a rough draft of the note that Wilson, betraying where sympathies lay, turned over to Lansing to finish. Lansing immediately closeted himself with Garrison and Joseph Tumulty, the President's private secretary, who was every bit as hawkish as Garrison. They finished the note shortly before dinner, and the President approved it that evening; it went out the next morning with instructions that it be delivered to the German Foreign Secretary the morning of May 13.

This was the first of what would be three diplomatic notes to Germany about the destruction of the *Lusitania*. It was in several ways a curious document. Drafted by Wilson, revised and polished by Lansing, it had been sent out over Bryan's signature—and his protests, as he had almost no influence over its contents. Part of what made it so curious is that the process resulted in a document that adequately or accurately reflected the views of none of the three men, not Wilson the staunch idealist, Bryan the ardent pacifist, or Lansing the ambitious hawk. Because it so studiously ignored the German note of May 10, from the beginning there was a certain air of unreality about this document.

It opened abruptly, without the usual polite phases that normally open such a document. Instead, it simply lumped the sinking of the *Lusitania* together with the sinking of the *Falaba* and torpedoing of the *Gullflight*, along with the attack on the *Cushing*, a small American steamer accidentally bombed but not sunk by a German aircraft on April 28. Collectively, these incidents were termed a "violation of American rights on the high seas," despite the fact that all four incidents were very different in nature and at least two of them were permissible under *anybody's* interpretation of the Cruiser Rules.

The note then proceeded through carefully worded passages that attempted to paint Germany into a diplomatic corner by referring to previous

German endorsements of international law, including the freedom of the seas. At one point, the note took on the tone of a schoolmaster lecturing to a slightly dense student, as it offered the German government the opportunity to declare that it did not "countenance or sanction" these incidents and to repudiate the U-boat campaign, "which will correct the unfortunate impressions which have been created and vindicate once more the position of that government with regard to the sacred freedom of the seas."

One startlingly presumptuous statement stands out: "Manifestly, submarines cannot be used against merchantmen, as the last few weeks have shown, without an inevitable violation of many sacred principles of justice and humanity." Bryan felt that in saying this, the President was going too far, as the Germans had manifestly demonstrated that the U-boats could indeed conduct an effective campaign according to the Cruiser Rules, but that British countermeasures had forced the submarine commanders into abandoning them. If the Germans were to be chastised for giving up on the Cruiser Rules, Bryan believed, the British should be taken equally to task for forcing them to do so. Lansing strongly disagreed. The British, he argued, had done what they had out of necessity—their actions were defensive. It was up to the Germans to find a way to continue to observe the Cruiser Rules despite the British countermeasures.

Wilson agreed with Lansing, although it was more likely out of dislike for Bryan than for the soundness of Lansing's arguments. In truth, there were several flaws in Lansing's position, most glaringly in the contents of the secret Admiralty orders the Germans had captured on the *Ben Cruachan.* If sinking a neutral ship without warning was barbaric and violated "many sacred principle of justice and humanity," what kind of interpretation could be placed on orders that read, "Survivors may be taken prisoner or shot, whichever is more convenient," or "White flags will be fired upon with promptitude"? Wilson, though, gave in to his pro-Allied sentiments, and Germany would be called to task, but no corresponding protests would be sent to the British.

It was a remarkable assumption of special American rights that was the heart of Wilson's note. He declared:

> American citizens act within their indisputable right in taking their ships and in traveling wherever their legitimate business calls them upon the high seas, and exercise those rights in what should be the well justified confidence that their lives will not be endangered by acts done in clear violation of universally acknowledged international obligations, and certainly in the confidence that their own government will sustain them in the exercise of their rights.

It was an unprecedented assertion. Obviously Americans had the right to take their own ships wherever they pleased, but the idea that they enjoyed some form of immunity from attack "wherever their legitimate business calls them upon the high seas" was preposterous. The Hague Convention of 1905 had established beyond debate that a neutral citizen sailing on a merchant ship belonging to a belligerent power did so at his or her own risk, that their neutral status gave them no special exemption or protection under those circumstances. Wilson was clearly trying to establish a preferential position for Americans traveling abroad and expected that Germany would accept his assertion as a *fait accompli*. It was little wonder that the German Foreign Minister, von Jagow, laughed derisively when he read it, commenting: "Right of free travel on the high seas in wartime? Why not demand the right of free travel on land across a battlefield?"

The tone of the entire note was arrogant and condescending—again the echoes of schoolmaster Wilson can be heard—and reflected Wilson's misplaced faith that his diplomatic pen could somehow blunt Germany's maritime sword. What is most startling is the undercurrent of belligerency in the note: There were nothing of the measured tones of warning that were found in the note of February 10. Instead, this note seemed to be telling the German government how America expected Germany to conduct its naval war, with the implication that America had the power and authority to compel Germany to do so if need arose. Certainly, the note resembled in many respects an ultimatum, in which Wilson was telling the German government, "Toe the line—or else!" but without informing the Germans of what exactly "or else" meant. In truth, it was a huge bluster, because America was in no position to dictate policy to anyone, an embarrassing truth Wilson knew all to well. Just the same, it played well to the American public, which may have been Wilson's intention all along. The *Baltimore Sun* declared that "it contains all the red blood that a red blooded nation can ask," and indeed, the nation on the whole seemed satisfied that Wilson had given voice to America's anger.[9]

The German government, though, called Wilson's bluff. It wasn't until May 28 that the German Foreign Ministry got around to replying to Wilson's note of protest, the delay itself a carefully studied insult, and with their response the Germans made it clear that they considered Wilson to be dealing from a position of weakness rather than the strength he assumed. The note opened reasonably enough, with an admission of responsibility on Germany's part for the attacks on the *Cushing* and the *Gullflight*, saying that they were not only regretted but unintentional. Offering to refer the incidents to a court of arbitration as provided for in the 1907 Hague Convention, Germany was willing to make reparations and pay damages for the lives lost on those two ships. In the case of the *Falaba*, the Germans were adamant: The ship had resisted, so the U-boat had every right under the Cruiser Rules to destroy her. It was unfortunate that the life of an American had been lost, but reiterating the point made in the May 10 "apology" in traveling on a belligerent power's ship, a neutral passenger accepted the risks involved. The tone of the note so far was reasonable and mild.

However, once the subject of *Lusitania* was brought up, the note became as condescending as Wilson's had been. Whether this was intentional is unknown, but certainly it was possible that von Jagow and Zimmermann had chosen to subtly mock Wilson and his imperious manner. In any case, Germany made it very clear that it had already expressed its "deep regret" to those neutral nations whose citizens had perished on the *Lusitania,* and that was as far as Germany was prepared to go. There were, the German note said, "certain important facts" which "may have escaped the attention" of the American government that fully justified the sinking of the *Lusitania.*

First, the *Lusitania* was a ship built with Admiralty funding and design expertise, and "expressly included in the navy list" annually published by the British Admiralty as an auxiliary cruiser. Second, the Imperial German government had learned that "practically all the more valuable English merchant vessels had been provided with guns, ammunition and other weapons, and reinforced with a crew specially practiced in manning guns." The note also asserted that when the *Lusitania* left New York on her last voyage, she "undoubtedly had guns on board which were mounted under decks and masked." The note also made reference to the secret Admiralty instructions requiring British merchant captains "not only to seek protection behind neutral flags and markings, but even when so disguised to attack German submarines by ramming them." Mention was also made of rewards (such as the ones given to the officers and crew of the *Thordis*) being offered to merchantmen who successfully attacked U-boats. Finally, the nature and contents of the *Lusitania*'s cargo were questioned, reference being specially made to 5,400 cases of rifle ammunition, and it was asserted that the destruction of such cargo was an act of national self-defense.

It was a document that was every bit as inflexible as Wilson's first note, but Bryan immediately saw a significant opportunity in one passage and quickly brought it to the President's attention. The offer to settle the question of damages and reparations for the attacks on the *Gullflight* and the *Cushing* before a court of arbitration opened the door for settling the dispute over the *Lusitania.* This would have been an opportunity for both sides to present their charges and counter charges, proofs, and defenses. Arbitration before an international court at the Hague offered a way for the United States and Germany to settle their differences by establishing the facts in their disputes without running the risk of one side pushing the other too far. It would not take long for Robert Lansing—realizing that if Secretary Bryan suggested arbitration and President Wilson accepted it, his own influence with Wilson would diminish dramatically—to put an end to the whole idea.

All the same, this note was in its own way as remarkable and dangerous in its tone as Wilson's note of protest to Germany had been. Certainly, both sides were being intransigent, both were utterly convinced that their views were legally and morally correct, and neither was allowing itself much room for maneuver. There was one significant difference, however: The Germans were arguing their case, however right or wrong, from established precedents within the body of international law, and with a certain degree of justification; Wilson was seeking to establish an entirely new precedent, for which there was no justification.[10]

This greatly disturbed William Jennings Bryan, who feared that a confrontation was developing between Germany and the United States, where both sides were clearly angry and gave every indication that they would only get angrier, and that might, given the language already being used in the diplomatic exchanges, flare up into open hostilities. Wilson wanted peace as much as Bryan did, but if he continued to insist on rights for Americans traveling abroad that existed for no other neutral nation's citizens—rights that Germany was certain to refuse to recognize—an open break between the two nations was inevitable, with a shooting war not far behind. Bryan saw that the only way that Germany could accede to Wilson's assertion that the neutral status of American citizens gave them immunity from attack no matter whether they were traveling on a belligerent's ships or not would be to abandon the U-boat campaign altogether. As the submarines were Germany's only means of striking back at the British blockade, it was inconceivable that they would do so. If Wilson insisted, then Germany would simply ignore him and continue to sink British ships with complete disregard for whatever neutrals were on board. Should that happen, America would have no choice but to declare war on Germany.

Bryan, knowing his influence with Wilson was waning, urged the President to be cautious in his reply to this note from Germany. The charges that the Germans brought against the British made it clear that Britain's hands were not entirely clean—if the contents of the British Admiralty orders were accurate, then the British had been systematically provoking the Germans into an incident like the attack on the *Lusitania.* It would do the United States no good, Bryan believed, to take Germany to task for not abiding by the Cruiser Rules while at the same time the British were doing their best to make a mockery of them. What was more, the special privileges that Wilson was asserting were Americans' rights would play right into the hands of the British, who could protect their munitions shipments from the United States to Great Britain behind a shield of American passengers. Germany could then claim, with considerable justification, that the United States was no longer maintaining her neutrality, and declare war.

What Bryan urged Wilson to do was take the time to learn all of the facts in the case of the sinking of the *Lusitania,* to determine if there was any merit to the German charges. That way, the American response could be direct, accurate, and irrefutable. He also advised Wilson to simultaneously send a strongly worded protest to Great Britain about the British blockade of Germany and the hardships it was already creating. It was pure hypocrisy, Bryan argued, for the United States to demand that the Germans cease using their U-boats when the British were allowed to continue the blockade that compelled the use of the submarines in the first place. The two problems were so closely related, Bryan believed, that to condemn one without condemning the other would threaten American neutrality. Either the Wilson Administration had to be openly pro-Allied or truly neutral; it could not have it both ways.

This annoyed Wilson, who didn't like to have his own shortcomings or those of his policies pointed out to him, especially by someone he personally disliked, most especially by the despised Bryan. It would be difficult to say which bothered him more—that Bryan was the person who saw Wilson's inconsistencies and pointed them out to him or that Bryan was right. Enamored of his own phrases and moral posturing, Wilson found reminders of hypocrisy disturbing, particularly when they were true. The break between Wilson and Bryan, already an open secret, began to yawn wider and wider, as Bryan discovered that he was virtually alone in the Cabinet in his desire to be fair and impartial in the *Lusitania* affair.

This was an opportunity Assistant Secretary of State Lansing, eager to upstage and replace Bryan, was quick to exploit. Playing on Wilson's dislike of and barely concealed contempt for Bryan, Lansing told the President that he believed the German reply to be deliberately sarcastic in tone and intended primarily to placate the German people, and that any alleged "secret Admiralty orders" to British merchant ships were forgeries. As to the allegations raised in the German note that had troubled Bryan, Lansing went so far as to say:

> I cannot bring myself to admit that the facts are pertinent and entitled to an investigation. The only question that might be considered as possible of investigation would be whether or not the *Lusitania* was an auxiliary of the Royal Navy, but that appears so manifestly contradicted by the presence of passengers on board and the vessel being on its regular trade route that it offers slender excuse for inquiry.

Lansing then went on to tell the president that the issue was, in his opinion, one of "rights, not facts," discrediting Bryan's attempt to learn the truth about the sinking of the *Lusitania*. Instead, he argued that the special rights Wilson arrogated to American citizens traveling on belligerent vessels in his first note were the key to the entire debate. He was on dangerous ground here, and he knew it: In Lansing's possession, unknown to either Bryan or Wilson, was a memorandum that had been written by the State Department's legal section on May 10—before Wilson began drafting his first note of protest to Germany—commenting on the legality of the sinking of the *Lusitania* under applicable international law. The memorandum presented six specific points of law that made it clear, from a legal standpoint, that Germany had been within her right to permit and then condone the *U-20*'s attack. It said:

1. Great Britain had obliterated any distinction between British war-ships and British merchant ships, including passenger liners, through Admiralty orders given to merchant captains beginning in September, 1914.

2. Because the *Lusitania* was subject to those orders, that would have been sufficient reason to legally justify the sinking.

3. Based on the *Lusitania*'s manifests for her last voyage, she had been carrying a cargo of contraband, including munitions, which would have arrived in Great Britain had she not been sunk.

4. No validity under international law could be found for any claim that the lives of American citizens were sacrosanct aboard a ship belonging to a belligerent power in wartime.

5. The vulnerability of neutrals aboard belligerents' ships had been recognized by Great Britain during the Russo-Japanese War in 1905, when the British government has published warnings, simi-lar to the German warnings that had appeared in American news-papers on May 1, cautioning British nationals against sailing on ships belonging to one or the other of the warring nations.

6. Cunard had knowingly violated several of the Navigation Laws and Neutrality Laws of the United States, most notably Section 8 of the Passenger Act of the Navigation Laws, by shipping muni-tions of any kind aboard the *Lusitania*.

Lansing had never made this memorandum available to either Bryan or Wilson, but instead buried it in his own files. While Wilson may have dis-liked Bryan intensely and resented the political compromises that had com-pelled him to name Bryan as Secretary of State, Wilson did respect Bryan's abilities as a lawyer. Had he known that the State Department had indepen-dently produced a sound legal basis for Bryan's demand that the U.S. govern-ment learn all the facts in the *Lusitania* case before making further protests to Germany, his response to Bryan would have been far different. As it was, he

dismissed Bryan's plea as nothing more than the bleating of the man's pacifism and, instead, embraced Lansing's position, since it coincided more
closely with his own leanings. The wedge Lansing had been trying to force
between Bryan and Wilson was now firmly in place. Ironically, it would be
Bryan who would drive it home.[11]

Wilson began drafting a second note, replying to the German message of
May 28, with assistance from Lansing—making it clear to everyone in his
administration where his sympathies lay. Bryan bluntly told the President that
he would not allow another provocative note to be sent to Berlin over his signature without a similar protest being made to Great Britain over the irregu-
larities in the Royal Navy's conduct of the blockade of Germany. He
demanded an investigation into the German allegations about the *Lusitania*
in particular and British conduct in the United States in general. He wrote to
Wilson pointing out the basic flaw in the administration's position—Wilson
was simply assuming, without any basis in fact but only on advice from Lansing, that the British were telling the truth and the Germans were lying. This
amounted to telling the Germans that they would have "to accept our [the
American] view of the law as applied to the facts as we state them." Bryan
was fully aware of Lansing's strong pro-Allied sympathies, as well as his Wall
Street connections, and believed that disregarding Germany's accusations
about the *Lusitania,* as well as the British blockade, as Lansing was urging the
President to do, only played into the hands of the pro-British factions in
American business and government. He genuinely feared that another inso-
lently worded note to Germany would lead to a break in diplomatic relations,
followed by a declaration of war by Germany—a war America wasn't ready
for, didn't need, and didn't want. He would resign before allowing that to
happen, taking his case to the American people, believing they would understand the need to impartially judge the German accusations, and that the
only way the United States could stay neutral was to act neutral.

Wilson, suddenly presented with a golden opportunity to rid himself of
the increasingly tiresome Bryan, accepted his resignation immediately when it
was presented on June 8, 1915. Most of Wilson's cabinet were relieved to see
Bryan go; because the President and the cabinet were all to a greater or lesser
degree pro-Allied, they believed Bryan to simply be pro-German; they
couldn't conceive of a middle ground, where his desire for America to be truly
neutral was genuine. Yet the issue wasn't just the *Lusitania*—Bryan had
opposed monetary loans to any of the warring powers, had tried to have
American citizens prohibited from traveling on ships that belonged to any of
the belligerents, and had championed freedom of the seas for Allied and Central Powers alike. He believed that the rigorous standards of neutrality could
and should be equally applied to all the warring powers—for Bryan, "neutral-

ity" was meant to protect American lives and American interests, not to be a convenient smokescreen for American businesses to hide behind while making huge profits from selling war materials.

What he had hoped to be his finest hour instead became Bryan's worst nightmare. The press, misunderstanding his motives as completely as Wilson had, labeled him a German sympathizer, and instead of speaking to crowded halls overflowing with indignant Americans determined to give voice to the demand to keep America out of the war, he addressed ever-dwindling audiences, found no space available in the papers for his articles and commentaries, and swiftly found himself diminished to a figure of ridicule, without influence or following.

Ironically, though Lansing immediately replaced Bryan as Secretary of State, it proved to be a hollow victory for him: He succeeded Bryan simply because there was no one else immediately available, rather than for recognition of his abilities. The very traits that he had cultivated to ingratiate himself to Wilson became reasons for Wilson to believe that he wasn't quite up to the task at hand. Lansing had been pliable, willing, ready to parrot Wilson on any position; yet Wilson began to suspect that Lansing was little more than a glorified legal clerk—certainly he had none of Bryan's moral fiber, and he seemed incapable of debating any view of the President's, even if only for the sake of clarification. He possessed a brilliant legal mind, but it was shallow and narrow; Wilson soon found that Lansing's highly legalistic mind lacked the subtlety required for statecraft. It was little wonder, then, that Wilson soon began to take more and more of the affairs of the State Department into his own hands, eventually relegating Lansing to the duties of a highly placed but relatively ineffectual messenger.

That Wilson may have been seeing this side of Lansing even before Bryan's resignation is strongly evidenced by the note the United States sent to Germany on June 9, 1915, in response to the German message of May 28. Described as "blunt but not bellicose," it had been drafted in its entirety by the President, although it was sent over Lansing's signature as Secretary of State *ad interim*. It was a verbose document, strangely lacking in the forcefulness of the first note Wilson had sent to the Germans. It wrangled over legalistic details without substantially addressing the disputes between the United States and Germany, leading Theodore Roosevelt to observe acidly that Wilson was "too proud to fight, but not too proud to write." More importantly, the German offer of mediation went completely unremarked, an offer that would not be repeated.

The most significant passage of the note was where Wilson "addressed" the German charges that the *Lusitania* had been armed, transporting troops, and carrying munitions. More correctly, he dismissed them:

> Of the facts alleged in Your Excellency's note, if true, the government of the United States would have been bound to take official cognizance. Performing its recognized duties as a neutral power and enforcing its national laws, it was its duty to see that the *Lusitania* was not armed for offensive action, that she was not serving as a transport, that she was not carrying cargo prohibited by the statutes of the United States, and if she was a naval vessel of Great Britain that she should not receive clearance as a merchantman. It performed this duty. It enforced its statutes with scrupulous vigilance through its regularly constituted officials and it is able to therefore assure the Imperial German Government that it has been misinformed. . . . If the Imperial German Government should deem itself to be in possession of convincing evidence that the officials of the Government of the United States did not perform those duties with thoroughness the Government of the United States sincerely hopes that it will submit that evidence for consideration.

Exactly as Bryan had feared he would do, Wilson essentially told the German government that the only version of the "facts" that he would admit to being true was the American version—Germany's claims and allegations, whether true or not, were irrelevant. Consciously or not, and Wilson never gave a hint one way or the other. In the stiffly formal language of early-twentieth-century diplomacy, the President told the Germans that they could either accept the American government's version of the *Lusitania* disaster and respond accordingly—that is, by ending the U-boat campaign—or else there was nothing more for the two nations to discuss.[12]

Von Jagow, the German Foreign Minister, and more especially his assistant, Zimmermann, were convinced by this reply that Wilson was really looking for a pretext for breaking off diplomatic relations with Germany and openly siding with the Allies, even if the United States stopped short of actually declaring war. It was an impression that would have important consequences. Because Wilson's note never mentioned Germany's proposal of arbitration, and because it left neither nation with any room for diplomatic maneuvering, it created an impasse that could not be broken without Germany or the United States losing a great deal of prestige. Von Jagow and Zimmermann, with the approval of Bethmann-Hollweg, decided that any further negotiations with the United States were pointless: As far as they were concerned, Wilson wanted the finer points of international law scrupulously observed whenever they were beneficial to the British, but was unwilling to acknowledge them whenever they worked to Germany's advantage. Berlin would continue to go through the diplomatic motions with Washington, but only in the hope of keeping the United States out of the war—there was no question now of America being truly neutral.

That was the thinking behind the second German note, written in reply to Wilson's message of June 10. The German reply was almost a month in coming, that in itself an indication of how fruitless the German government expected it to be. Delivered on July 8, 1915, the note reaffirmed Germany's dedication to Wilson's "principles of humanity" along with "freedom of the seas" for "peaceable trade." But the note sharply reminded the American government that the British blockade was making as much, if not more, of a shambles of those "principles" than were the German submarines, and it was because of the British blockade that Germany had been "obliged to adopt submarine warfare" in defense of her "national existence."

The note repeated that the German government refused to accept Wilson's assertion of special rights for Americans traveling abroad and that it was "unable to admit that United States citizens can protect an enemy ship" simply being aboard her. Germany, it said, "merely followed England's example when it declared part of the high seas an area of war," then, echoing von Jagow's earlier remark, it declared that "accidents suffered by neutrals on enemy ships" in such war zones were no different than accidents suffered by neutrals who entered a war zone on land.

In many ways, this second German note seems to have been written more for the German people than for the American government, as if the Germans were attempting to reassure themselves that they were in the right rather than persuade President Wilson and his cabinet of the legitimacy of Germany's actions. At one point, the note offered a scheme for the safe conduct of a limited number of American ships, painted in broad red, white, and blue stripes like gigantic oceangoing barber poles, sailing in prescribed shipping lanes through the German war zone on a predetermined schedule. The whole concept was so humiliating that there was no chance of its being accepted by the American government; it gives the impression that it was created for the sole purpose of being rejected, allowing Germany to adopt the posture of the aggrieved party whose efforts at compromise had been scorned.[13]

Wilson, of course, felt compelled to respond with yet another note, as if getting the final word was somehow significant. The same slightly condescending, lecturing tone of the previous two notes continued, as did the demands that the Germans admit that the destruction of the *Lusitania* was an illegal act, along with the repeated assertion of American rights. On one point, Wilson unexpectedly yielded, but it was too little too late: Having said in his first note that it was a "practical impossibility" for submarines to conform to the Cruiser Rules and other conventions of international law, Wilson now announced that he had decided the U-boats should be able to conduct some form of offensive against British merchant shipping "in substantial accord with the accepted practices of regulated warfare." What caused this sudden change was never explained, but any positive response it might have produced from the German government was immediately stifled by the declaration that followed. The United States, Wilson assured the Germans, would continue to contend for the freedom of the seas, "from whatever quarter violated, without compromise and at any cost," and any actions by German U-boats that violated American rights would be regarded as "deliberately unfriendly."

This note would be Wilson's last word on the *Lusitania*. Throughout the entire exchange, the president and the German Foreign Ministry were preoccupied with the question of the legality of the destruction of the *Lusitania* and the 1,200 lives that were lost with her, a point that for the Germans held great significance—if the sinking could be legally justified, then in their eyes there were no moral dilemmas involved. Wilson, for all of his self-proclaimed humanity and principles, had allowed himself to become drawn into the debate, reducing the moral indignation of the United States to a handful of constantly rephrased and reworded paragraphs in a series of dry diplomatic notes. He had become enamored with splitting legal hairs over the Cruiser Rules, arrogating nonexistent "rights" of preferential treatment to American citizens traveling abroad, and implying that force that he knew he did not possess would be used to back up the claims and assertions he was making, supposedly in the name of the American people.

The German government saw all this and decided they had the measure of Woodrow Wilson: He was all academic bluster and high-minded talk. The Kaiser himself reviewed Wilson's third note and commented on it. Calling it "immeasurably impertinent," he scribbled his own interpretation of Wilson's actions and attitudes across the bottom of the last page: "In tone and bearing this is about the most impudent note I have ever read since the Japanese note of August 15 last! [That note was an ultimatum demanding Germany cede the naval base at Tsing-tao to Japan] This ends with a direct threat!"

Wilson's attitude had led the Germans to believe that there was no point in trying to negotiate with him: He seemed to be more interested in delivering lectures than in finding a solution to a diplomatic crisis. His self-styled role as "The Great Arbitrator" would be seen as nothing more than posturing by the Germans, who had decided that the best they could hope for from the United States was nonbelligerence. For Germany, American neutrality was a thing of the past—the German government would reply to Wilson's third note, but only after more than six months had passed, and it did so in a manner that implied that the Foreign Ministry was simply tidying up loose ends in what had been a fruitless, even pointless, diplomatic exchange. The determination was made in Berlin that there was no sense in further antagonizing the Americans, but accommodation was no longer possible: Should another crisis break out between Germany and the United States, the Germans would seek other ways to neutralize American industrial might and military potential.

This was Wilson's greatest failure. In all of his quibbling and lecturing, his statements of "humanitarian principles," his attempts to coerce Germany into abandoning the U-boat campaign, his assertion of American "rights," he failed to give full voice to the outrage of the American people at the destruction of the *Lusitania*. While Americans may not have been ready to go to war over the *Lusitania*, they weren't willing to allow another such wanton act of destruction to go unpunished. If it happened again, there would be war between America and Germany. Because Wilson never tried to express this to the German government, the Germans believed that America's attention could always be diverted away from the Fatherland, that America's wrath could always be somehow blunted, that such a confrontation would never come. By being "too proud to fight," Wilson made the fighting inevitable.[14]

CHAPTER 12

The Inquiry

NO SOONER HAD THE NEWS OF THE SINKING OF THE *LUSITANIA* REACHED London than the question of "How?" began to be asked, both within the government and among the public. Certainly no one believed in the "unsinkable ship" anymore—the *Titanic* had cleansed even the Edwardians of that conceit—but for months, Parliament and the public alike had been assured that the *Lusitania's* great speed was her best protection, that she could outrun any U-boat Germany had and so needn't fear attack. No one was murmuring darkly about conspiracies, though questions would be asked about German agents and British subjects in the pay of the Kaiser, but clearly someone somewhere had failed to do his job properly. If it was necessary for heads to roll, so be it.

One of the more obvious targets for public wrath was the Admiralty, and within the Admiralty the First Lord, Winston Churchill. Churchill had always attracted admirers and detractors, but now he seemed to be a lightning rod for critics: With the Gallipoli campaign floundering badly and the Government rushing to wash its hands of it and lay the blame at Churchill's door, the catastrophe that had overtaken the *Lusitania* might well prove to be the last straw for his political allies and opponents alike.

Churchill had actually been away from the Admiralty on May 7; in his typical "finger-in-every-pie" fashion, he had been visiting the Western Front, meeting with the commander of the BEF, Field Marshal John French, and watching the British assault on the German positions along the Aubers Ridge in Belgium. Churchill and French were conniving to have French replace Lord Kitchener as Secretary of War, and Churchill harbored ambitions of being named French's successor as commander of the BEF. (It would have been a disaster for Britain and the Allies had they succeeded—while Kitchener had glaring flaws as Secretary of War, French was an utter incompetent. Churchill's backing of French's ambitions stemmed from his own desire for advancement and personal glory, coupled with a strong dislike for Kitchener —the two men had detested one another for nearly twenty years. Churchill thought Kitchener was a stuffy, narrow-minded martinet, while Kitchener believed Churchill was nothing more than a clever upstart with more ambition than talent.)

Churchill's staff was well aware that his absence from the Admiralty offices in Whitehall on May 7 would reflect badly on him, and quickly tried to contain the damage. Within hours of the sinking, the Director of the Trade Division, Capt. Richard Webb, cabled Churchill, saying that "political considerations indicate" a need for "an early public statement which doubtless you will want to formulate."

Certainly, it wasn't possible for Churchill to admit, however justifiable it may have been, that the *Lusitania* was one of the furthest things from his mind the first week of May 1915. His political enemies in Parliament would have had a field day with such an admission, and Asquith's refusal to accept responsibility for the Dardanelles fiasco was providing those enemies with enough ammunition for their attacks on the First Lord.

In the case of the Dardanelles campaign, never has the old adage "Victory has a thousand fathers—defeat is an orphan" been so apt. Even though a majority of the War Cabinet had approved the plans for the assault in February, and Churchill had repeatedly urged that the tempo of operating be speeded up, when the initial landings were stopped at the beaches and the casualty lists for the Australian and New Zealand troops began growing distressingly long, the same Cabinet ministers who had approved the operation began sidling away, making excuses. It had been Churchill's brainchild, they claimed, therefore it was his fault that it was a failure. Because the War Cabinet at the time kept no formal minutes of its meetings, Churchill had no proof that some of his loudest critics had at one time been some of the most enthusiastic supporters of the Gallipoli campaign. Likewise, he was unable to defend himself adequately in the House of Commons, as such a defense would have required that he reveal top-secret information, including the success of Room 40 in reading the German naval codes—and not even political survival could cause Churchill to do that.

By the morning of May 8, British newspapers were questioning how the U-boat had managed to be in the right place at the right time to intercept the *Lusitania,* why the big Cunarder hadn't been given an escort, and if it would have been possible to divert her away from the area where the submarine was operating. Depending on how they were put, answering these questions would have been either embarrassing or impossible for the First Lord.

The truth of the matter was that, under international law, the *Lusitania* was no different than the most humble tramp steamer—it could even be argued that in some ways the tramp steamer, with its far greater cargo capacity, was actually more valuable to Great Britain and her war effort than were the *Lusitania* and the lives she carried. Such rationalization sounds callous under any circumstances, but Churchill was fighting a war, and war calls for hard choices to be made.

That was not an explanation, Churchill realized, that the British public was willing to accept, nor would it have gone over well in Parliament. Likewise, now was not the time to delve into the niceties of international law and explain that an escort would have made the *Lusitania* an even more legitimate target for a submarine to attack. It didn't require Churchill's political acumen for certain individuals within the Admiralty to realize that it would be far easier for the public to believe, and for Parliament to accept, that sinister forces beyond the control of the Admiralty had been at work, delivering the *Lusitania* into the clutches of a waiting U-boat, than for them to comprehend the harsher realities of warfare or legalistic loopholes. Influencing the Court of Inquiry to reach such a conclusion would vastly simplify the task of diverting public and political attention away from the Admiralty and the Royal Navy.[1]

One of the first individuals to come to that realization and act on it was Capt. Richard Webb, Director of the Admiralty's Trade Division, and charged with the safety and protection of all British merchant ships at sea. Knowing that a call for a formal Court of Inquiry was inevitable, and fearing that the Royal Navy and the Admiralty might be held accountable for the loss of the *Lusitania,* Captain Webb began to take steps to shift official attention away from the Admiralty. After all the years that have passed, little is now known of the character of Captain Webb. Certainly his tenure as the Director of the Admiralty Trade Division leaves the distinct impression that he was a typical midlevel officer, busy commanding a desk in Whitehall—certainly there is little in his conduct during the Court of Inquiry, not to mention the ridiculous contents of the Admiralty Instructions and Advises, which he was responsible for, to indicate that he had ever spent much time at sea or in command of a ship of his own. Colin Simpson referred to him as "either a fool or a knave—or both." It's easier to believe that he was nothing more than a dedicated careerist, one of those individuals who never undertake any action, never make a decision, without first considering how it will affect their careers for good or ill. Clearly he had a large stake in seeing that as much blame as possible was deflected away from the Admiralty: His Division was responsible for tracking and protecting all British merchant shipping—including the *Lusitania.* It was possible that close official scrutiny of his department could reveal some shortcoming that, if corrected, might have prevented the *Lusitania* from being attacked, so he began to look for ways to deflect attention away from the Trade Division—and himself.

The request for a formal inquiry was made on May 15, but the actual legal inquiry process had begun on May 8, the day after the *Lusitania* sank. A handful of bodies had washed ashore at Kinsale, and the local coroner, John Horgan, was required under British law to hold a formal Coroner's Inquest into the cause of death. Horgan later left a detailed account of the proceedings in his autobiography. Convening a jury of twelve "humble and honest citizens—shopkeepers and fishermen," as he described them, Horgan began the hearing on the afternoon of May 8 and finished with testimony from Captain Turner on May 10. It was a straightforward, workmanlike inquest, with none of the attempts at sensation that certainly would have marked it had Horgan been seeking publicity, as later critics would allege.

Probably the most important piece of information to come out of the Kinsale inquest was when Captain Turner was asked why he had maintained a speed of only eighteen knots, even though the Lusitania was capable of doing twenty-one. Turner's response was simple and direct: "We were going at 18 knots for the purpose of arriving at the Liverpool Bar [on the morning of May 8] so we could go straight ahead without stopping. We wished to get there two or three hours before high water so we could go right in without stopping for a pilot." When he was asked if he had been instructed to do so, Turner replied that he had been told to by Cunard.

When questioned about the details of the sinking, Turner came very close to tears several times as he gave his answers. As Horgan told it, "Clad in a badly fitting old suit and still suffering from the strain of his experience, he looked, and was, a broken man." At the end of his testimony, Horgan recorded, Turner "bowed his head as he burst into tears."

One very strange incident occurred during the hearings. Apparently the Admiralty had gotten wind of Horgan's inquest and sent word via the Crown Counselor for Coke to put a stop to the proceedings. It was a very irregular move and very illegal. It's unclear who sent the order or why, although it has been suggested that Horgan was a Sinn Fein sympathizer, and it was suspected that he would use the hearing as an opportunity to embarrass the British government. What was obvious was that someone at the Admiralty was concerned about what information might be made public in the coroner's inquest and wanted to stop it. All the effort accomplished, however, was to make the Admiralty look slightly ridiculous. Even though Horgan had no love for the British, he had little sympathy for the Germans or their methods of waging war. Still, he was a son of Ireland, and he couldn't resist taking a well-timed swipe at the British when this opportunity presented itself. At one point in his report, commenting on the tardiness of the Crown Solicitor's arrival with the Admiralty orders, Horgan commented, "That august body [the Admiralty] were, however, as belated on this occasion as they had been in protecting the Lusitania from attack."

Horgan's remark is revealing in that it demonstrated the public perception of the Royal Navy's responsibility toward the Lusitania. Churchill's instincts had been right: People *were* going to ask why the *Lusitania* had been unescorted and unprotected. All the same, despite his criticism of the Royal Navy, Horgan issued his verdict in no uncertain terms:

> That the deceased died from prolonged immersion and exhaustion in the sea eight miles south south-west of the Old Head of Kinsale on Friday, May 7, 1915, owing to the sinking of RMS *Lusitania* by torpedoes fired without warning by a German submarine. We find that this appalling crime was contrary to international law and the conventions of civilized nations and we therefore charge the officers of said submarine and the Emperor and Government of Germany under whose orders they acted with the wilful and wholesale murder before the tribunal of the civilized world.

A Coroner's Inquest at Kinsale, Ireland, was not the same thing as a formal Court of Inquiry before the Wreck Commission of the Board of Trade. British law required that any ship of British registry lost at sea for any reason be investigated by a Royal Commission. Often these were small, low key affairs, sometimes lasting less than a day, especially when the ship lost was small or the loss of life negligent, but their purpose was always the same: to determine whether the loss of the vessel was due to a structural flaw or failure, negligence on the part of the master or owners, or some outside circumstance or event that the owners, officers, and crew had no control over. Whenever lives were lost, the inquiry was required to determine whether the ship in question had been properly equipped with lifesaving devices and if they had been employed properly.

A Court of Inquiry investigating the causes of the sinking *Lusitania* might have seemed little more than a formality, but this case had the very real potential to embarrass the British Admiralty and the British Government. It would hardly do for Great Britain to be adopting a public stance of aggrieved moral outrage, only to have it revealed that the Admiralty could have actually prevented the disaster from occurring. The Board of Trade Court of Inquiry, as constituted by its Royal Warrant (the Crown document defining the scope of the commission as well as its authority), was scheduled to begin sitting in session on June 13 and would consist of a president and four assessors. The assessors, chosen as much for their political reliability as for their distinguished credentials, were Adm. Sir Frederick Inglefield, KCB, and Lt.-Cmdr. H. J. Hearn, RN, who would advise the president of the commission on naval matters; representing the Merchant Marine were Capt. David Davies and Capt. John Spedding. Presiding overall, indeed, dominating the Court, would be the fearsome Lord Mersey, Commissioner of Wrecks and formerly President of the Probate, Divorce and Admiralty Division of the High Court. Though Mersey would have the "assistance" of the four assessors, Mersey's authority over the Court would be absolute: The areas of investigation, the witnesses called, the admissibility of evidence, and the final findings of the Court would all be determined by him.

Lord Mersey—John Charles Bigham, Baron Mersey of Toxteth (Lancashire)—had first come to prominence as a public figure in Great Britain in 1896, when he headed an inquiry into the notorious Jameson Raid, then gained worldwide recognition in 1912 when he presided over the Court of Inquiry into the wreck of the *Titanic*. From the first, he exhibited those characteristics that would come to be an inescapable part of any inquest Mersey conducted: He was autocratic, impatient, and not a little testy. Above all, he did not suffer fools gladly, and he was famous for the barbed rebukes he issued from the bench to witnesses or counsel that he considered were wasting the Court's time. (The transcript of the *Titanic* inquiry records how at one point, Alexander Carlisle related that he and Harold Sanderson of the White Star Line often merely rubber-stamped decisions made by their employers with the words, "Mr. Sanderson and I were more or less dummies." Mersey replied dryly, "That has a certain verisimilitude.") Off the bench, Mersey was a soft-spoken, mild-mannered man of good taste. He was well educated and thoroughly urbane. Politically he was a Liberal, and his company and conversation were much sought after in London social circles. It was to his lasting credit that he did not allow his political views to influence his role as Wreck Commissioner; at the same time, he was a patriot and was not about to let the Inquiry embarrass Great Britain.

Unknown to Mersey at the time, the process of the British system of justice was being subtly but seriously subverted in the name of national interest. Because the inquiry became the "official" record of what happened to the *Lusitania,* and thus the source of decades of myths and misinformation, a closer examination to discover how and why a distorted record of events has been handed down to posterity is called for.

The process began with Captain Webb, who was determined to make certain that Mersey was presented with a convenient scapegoat for the disaster in the form of Captain Turner, effectively deflecting attention away from Whitehall. As soon as the Royal Warrant for the Inquiry was issued, Webb began drafting a memorandum for submission to Lord Mersey. Its contents were highly prejudicial, but Mersey was not to know that. Webb began by carefully sifting through the Admiralty Instructions and Advises, editing the contents of some and deleting several others entirely. Then he cabled both the Senior Naval Officer in Liverpool, Admiral Stileman, and Sir Courtenay Bennet in New York to ask if Turner had been given any special instructions prior to his departure from either port. When Webb further queried Admiral Stileman if Captain Turner had received the Admiralty Instruction memorandum issued on April 16 that required the use of zigzagging as a method of reducing the chances of a submarine attack, Stileman replied that he had not, as the memorandum hadn't arrived in Liverpool until May 2.

Webb took the contents of the Advises and Instructions, ignored Stileman's reply that Turner had never received the zigzag order, and carefully edited and reworded the Advises and Instructions into a document that made Captain Turner appear to be incompetent at best, and in the pay of the Germans at worst. Throughout the paper, Webb was careful never to clarify the distinction between the Instructions, which required compliance, and the Advises, which, as their name implied, were purely advisory and held no legal status requiring a ship's captain to follow—or even read them. The impression he created was that compliance with *all* of the Instructions and Advises was compulsory. He also took pains to be sure that when he was quoting from one of them, he never clearly stated whether the directive in question was an Instruction or an Advise, so that anyone reading the memorandum would have no idea which, if any, of them a captain was required to obey.

Webb began by stating that the *Lusitania* had received specific instructions to pass all headlands at maximum speed, avoid her peacetime route, and steer a "mid-channel course." For emphasis, he added that Turner had been given direct orders to zigzag at the *Lusitania*'s maximum top speed of twenty-two knots. He then repeated the Advise that stated that "the greatest danger of submarine attack was in the vicinity of ports and prominent headlands"—again not bothering to clarify that this was an Advise—and put the *Lusitania*'s position when she was torpedoed at less than eight miles from the Old Head of Kinsale. He said:

> It will thus be seen that in addition to printed orders in the master's possession, he received definite warning that submarines were active off the Irish coast, and that he should avoid headlands and steer a mid-channel course.
>
> In spite of these warnings the vessel appears to have been almost exactly on the usual trade route, and so far as is known was torpedoed 8 miles off Old Head of Kinsale. The vessel was apparently on this normal course and was proceeding at a speed of 18 knots. The distance from the scene of the disaster is approximately 240 miles and, proceeding at 18 knots, the *Lusitania* would have arrived off the Bar [at the entrance to Liverpool Harbour] shortly before 4 A.M. on the morning of the 8th. This would have been making port at daybreak, which is in accordance with Admiralty Instructions and it appears to be the only instruction which the Master did carry out. On the morning of the 7th of May, the *Lusitania* could have crossed the Bar at anytime between 4 A.M. and 9:30 A.M. The Master, therefore, had five hours in hand, and

could have covered the distance of 90 miles without losing the tide.

He might therefore have steered a course well out of sight of the Irish coast, and moved in mid-channel, and still have arrived at Liverpool in time to get his tide, while not exceeding a speed of 18 knots. If he had taken the precaution of zigzagging, in accordance with the memo of April 16, he could have worked out a zigzag at, say, 22 knots, which would have given a distance made good equivalent to a speed of 18 knots assuming this is what he wanted.

Further, when he was approaching the Irish coast there was no need to come in to the land. It was within his power to raise steam for a higher speed, to have kept well out to sea, and to have made St. George's Channel on a northerly course after dark.

The Master, therefore, had several alternatives to the course and speed at which he should proceed through the dangerous area, in which, as he had been warned, submarines are active. Instead of this he proceeded along the usual trade route at a speed approximately three quarters of what he was able to get out of his vessel. He thus kept his valuable vessel for an unnecessary length of time in the area where she was most likely to be attacked, inviting disaster.

The document simply begs for an almost point-by-point rebuttal, for it would have a profound influence on the pending Board of Trade Inquiry. Several points are obviously false, but their context is also significant. Webb implies that Turner was aware of the presence of the *U-20* ahead of the *Lusitania*, referring indirectly to the two messages received by the *Lusitania* on the evening of May 6. The first, which Turner asked to have repeated, said simply, "Submarines active off the south coast of Ireland." It was so vague that Turner at first believed it to be incomplete. Forty minutes later came the signal to avoid harbors and headland and to steer a midchannel course—the signal didn't specify whether this was an order or simply precautionary advice. The message ended, "Submarines off Fastnet." At the time this signal was sent, the *U-20* had already sunk the *Candidate* and the *Centurion* off Kinsale Head, nearly 100 miles to the east of Fastnet—the Admiralty knew from positions of the U-boats on the Plot that when the signal was sent, no U-boats were near Fastnet.

The next day, May 7, at 11:25 A.M., the message was sent advising that "submarines were last heard of twenty miles south of the Connigbeg Light Ship," with the attachment "Make sure *Lusitania* gets this." Webb carefully avoided any indication that this information was over sixteen hours old when it was sent, time enough for a submarine to have traveled almost one hundred miles in any direction, and consequently practically useless. Instead, the impression he strove to create was that Turner was kept fully up-to-date on submarine activity in waters where the *Lusitania* was sailing and deliberately chose to ignore the Admiralty's warnings.

His comments and observations about the course that Captain Turner should have followed were pure poppycock. He emphasized Turner's preoccupation with making the high tide at the Bar of Liverpool Harbour, but ignored why it was a necessity, since the *Lusitania's* huge draft would allow her to cross the Bar only at high tide. He also grossly overestimated the time available to the *Lusitania* to take advantage of the high tide: if Captain Turner was determined to reach Liverpool at daybreak in accordance with the Admiralty instructions, then he had to do so between 4:30 A.M. and 6:00 A.M.—arriving any later would have meant entering the harbor in full daylight, making the ship a perfect target for any lurking U-boat. Not only that, but by 6:30, the tide would have begun to ebb to the point where entering the harbor would have become problematical; the last thing Turner would have wanted to do was take the chance of running the *Lusitania* aground, leaving her a sitting duck. Should he miss the high tide, Tuner would have been forced to spend twelve hours steaming up and down the St. George's Channel, practically begging to be attacked by the U-boats that the Admiralty led him to believe were active in those very waters.

Equally absurd, and at the same time equally deceptive, was Webb's assertion that the *Lusitania* should have adopted a zigzagging course, making up the extra miles the zigzags would have added to the distance the *Lusitania* had to travel by steaming at twenty-two knots. With the six boilers of Boiler Room Number 4 shut down, the best speed she could make was barely twenty-one knots, of which Captain Webb, as director of the Trade Division of the Admiralty, was well aware. The difference between the two speeds, just over one nautical mile per hour, may seem trivial, but given the time and distance the *Lusitania* had to travel from the point where Webb asserted that Turner should have begun zigzagging, it adds up to several hours additional steaming. This would have meant that had Turner ordered the *Lusitania* to begin to zigzag as she approached the Irish coast, she never would have made the morning tide on May 7, leaving her stranded in the St. George's Channel, with all the resultant danger that would have entailed.

The most preposterous of Webb's assertions, and the most clearly indicative of his desire to deceive the Court of Inquiry, was his assertion that Captain Turner could have brought the *Lusitania* up into the St. George's Channel at high speed without making a landfall first—*and doing so after dark*. Trying to take the *Lusitania* up the narrow, island-studded St. George's Channel at night, without first making a landfall to firmly fix her position, not only would have been negligent navigation on Turner's part, but such foolhardiness most likely would have cost him his Master's Ticket, as it would have violated Board of Trade regulations.

Webb was also misleading in his assertion that Captain Turner followed his usual peacetime route along the Irish coast rather than steering a mid-channel course as directed by the Admiralty. Here he was deliberately obfuscating: In peacetime, Turner was in the habit of bringing his ships within a mile or so of the Irish coastline, known the world over for its scenic beauty, so that his passengers could see and appreciate it. On the *Lusitania's* last voyage, she was nearly eleven miles from the Irish coast. Also, the term "mid-channel" as Webb used it was misleading. The St George's Channel begins just to the east of the area where the *U-20* torpedoed the *Lusitania*; to the west is the open Atlantic Ocean. There is no real channel at that point, and so no way for a midchannel course to be determined. At the same time, Webb drew attention to the Admiralty Instruction to avoid well-known headlands, then implied that Turner had disobeyed this order as well by bringing his ship as close as eight miles (in reality eleven miles) off the Old Kinsale Head, ignoring the fact that Turner's usual practice was to bring his ship in much closer than that. Admiral Coke had provided Webb with the *Lusitania's* actual position when she was torpedoed, as well as information about the close-inshore route that Turner had followed in peacetime. Webb's misstatements, consequently, can only be realistically viewed as deliberate falsehoods.

The completed memorandum, with its obvious attempt to shift any blame for the *Lusitania* disaster away from the Admiralty, and more specifically away from Captain Webb's department, was submitted to First Sea Lord Fisher on the morning of May 13. At the same time, a signal arrived from the Foreign Office, sent by Sir Cecil Spring-Rice, the British Ambassador to the United States. Spring-Rice was passing along a series of reports he had received from Sir Courtenay Bennet of several incidents of German infiltration of Cunard in New York, copies of which were included with Spring-Rice's message. Apparently Captain von Papen, the German military attaché to the German Embassy in Washington, had been successful in getting a number of German agents, as well as German-Americans with strong pro-German sympathies, introduced into the workforce at Cunard's Pier 54. There they had attempted to sabotage several cargoes bound for Great Britain, as well as tried to conceal explosive and incendiary devices on a number of British ships.

The timing of the arrival of the message from the Foreign Office was pure coincidence, but Webb made the most of it. Reading Spring-Rice's cable, Webb added it and Bennet's reports to his memorandum, creating the impression that they were interrelated, an impression he reinforced with an attached note that read:

1. The circumstances in connection with the loss of the *Lusitania* are so extraordinary that it is impossible to completely dissociate the disaster from the facts reported by Sir. C. Spring-Rice.

2. In taking the course he did, the Master of the *Lusitania* acted directly contrary to the written general instructions received from the Admiralty, and completely disregarded the telegraphic orders received from Queenstown during the hours immediately preceding the attack.

3. On the facts at present disclosed the Master appears to have displayed an almost inconceivable negligence, and one is forced to conclude that he is utterly incompetent or that he had been got at by the Germans. In considering this latter possibility it is not necessary to suppose that he had any conception of the loss of life which actually occurred—he may well have thought being close to the shore there would be ample time to run the ship onto a place of security before she foundered.[2]

First Sea Lord Fisher was to be the first to be taken in by Webb's duplicity. By May 1915, Fisher was desperately trying protect his beloved navy from a flurry of charges ranging from incompetence to inefficiency to ineptitude being leveled at it from all corners. He had been bitterly fighting with Churchill for three months over the continued transfer of heavy units from the Grand Fleet to the Dardanelles, where four battleships had already been lost. The public and press were giving voice to mounting disappointment that the great Trafalgar-like battle of annihilation with the Germans that they had come to expect hadn't yet been fought—the critics were loudly wondering what good, if any, the Royal Navy, was doing. The subtleties of the distant blockade, of imprisoning the High Seas Fleet in the North Sea while cutting off Germany's overseas supplies of food, were lost on the newspapers and public alike. The increasing number of ships being sunk by the U-boats only seemed to reinforce the popular perception of the Royal Navy's impotence, and now the *Lusitania* disaster simply added insult to injury. Webb's document appealed to the old seaman, who was quite unaware of how deceptive it was, as it made it appear quite likely that any blame for the disaster could be shifted away from the navy. After underlining Webb's assertion that Turner had been bought off by the Germans, Fisher wrote in the margin, "Fully concur. As the Cunard Company would not hire an incompetent man—the certainty is absolute that Captain Turner is not a fool but a knave." Further down the page he wrote, "I hope Captain Turner will be arrested immediately after the inquiry, whatever the finding may be."

Fisher finished his comments on Webb's memorandum with a suggestion to Churchill and to Sir William Graham Greene, Secretary to the Admiralty, with "I feel absolutely certain that Captain Turner of the *Lusitania* is a scoundrel and has been bribed. No seaman in his senses would have acted as he did. Ought not Lord Mersey get a hint?" The entire mass of papers then went to Churchill's desk, where the First Lord reviewed them on May 14.

Churchill had returned from France on May 10, after having watched the British assault on Aubers Ridge with Sir John French, and was almost immediately called before Parliament, where charges of the Admiralty's failure to protect the *Lusitania* were hurled from both benches. When he returned to Whitehall, he spent a considerable amount of time reviewing the *Gullflight* incident and the findings of the Admiralty inquiry into the affair. He then renewed his argument with Fisher over the deployment of ships to the Dardanelles, a debate that was becoming increasingly bitter. When the feuding spilled over into a Cabinet meeting that morning, his colleagues in the Cabinet began to regard him as something of a political liability.

When he finally got around to reviewing the packet of documents Webb had assembled, it didn't take long for Churchill to realize the political value of having Captain Turner made the scapegoat for the loss of the *Lusitania*. It's impossible to tell how much of Webb's fantasy he actually believed: Churchill was a formidable administrator and an original thinker, at times gifted with brilliant strategic insight, who wouldn't hesitate to argue with or even overrule senior admirals with whom he disagreed on the operations of the Royal Navy. But he was no seaman, and he knew it: On matters of seamanship he always deferred to his officers, a habit of which Webb was well aware. While he refused to endorse Fisher's prejudicial comment, "Ought not Lord Mersey get a hint?"—the political consequences of such a blatant attempt to subvert the judicial process were unimaginable—it was hardly surprising that, given the skill with which Webb had mixed fact and fantasy, Churchill endorsed his memorandum with the words: "I consider the Admiralty case against the Captain should be pressed before Lord Mersey by a skillful counsel, and that Captain Webb should attend as witness, if not employed as assessor: we shall pursue the Captain without check."[3]

The whole packet was then delivered to Lord Mersey, with a covering letter from Webb that noted: "I am directed by the Board of Admiralty to inform you that it is considered practically expedient that Captain Turner, the Master of the *Lusitania*, be most prominently blamed for the disaster." Fortunately for Captain Turner, Webb didn't know his man: It would take more than the wishes of the Admiralty to cause Lord Mersey to undermine the process of British justice, though it would be a close-run thing.

The Inquiry was held in the Central Buildings, Westminster, on June 15, 16, 17, and 19, and were then moved to the Westminster Palace Hotel on July 1, with one more session meeting there on July 17. There were seven hearings all told, four open to the public, two announced to the public but held in camera, and one unannounced to the public until after it had been adjourned. The Inquiry would seek answers to a series of questions drawn up by the Board of Trade, intended to determine exactly what circumstances and conditions caused the disaster and the consequent loss of life.

For "security reasons," the Board of Trade questions were submitted to an "intelligence advisory committee" set up by the Admiralty. Of the original forty questions mooted by the Board, nineteen were struck out by the committee, while the remaining twenty-one were carefully redrawn to avoid bringing to light any embarrassing information, as well as create the maximum prejudice against Captain Turner. The most glaring example was a three-part question that initially read:

1. Were any instructions received by the master of the *Lusitania* from the owners or the Admiralty before or during the voyage from New York as to the navigation and management of the vessel on the voyage in question?

2. If so, what were those instructions?

3. Did the master carry out those instructions?

The Admiralty committee removed the second part of the question, in effect forcing the wreck assessors to decide whether Captain Turner had followed orders without being allowed to know what those orders were.

Initially scheduled to appear before the Inquiry were twenty-five witnesses selected by the Board of Trade. Five of these witnesses came from the staff of either the Board of Trade or Cunard and were called on to give details of the ship's design and construction, passenger capacity, numbers and readiness of lifeboats, proof of British registry, and other formalities. The remaining twenty witnesses were all crew members. The Merchant Shipping Act of 1894 required all surviving crew of a foundered vessel to make a formal deposition as to what transpired as their ship was lost as soon as possible after the event. By May 28, all 289 surviving crew members had done so, and from these depositions, the selections were made as to which crewmen would testify. Also submitted to the Board of Trade were 135 "proofs" of passengers who wished to testify—that is, give sworn written statements to be submitted as evidence—as well as the thirty-five affidavits from American survivors collected by Wesley Frost, the United States' consul in Queenstown. Of the 135 proofs, the authors of five were invited to testify; Frost's affidavits were ignored completely.

The crew's depositions were remarkably repetitious, all beginning more or less the same way, with some minor variation on the text: "At the time of the sailing, the ship was in good order and well found. She was unarmed, having no weapons for offense or defense against an enemy and she had never carried such equipment. Boat drill was carried out before the vessel left

New York." Even before the first hearing, a disturbing intimation of false-hood was beginning to creep into the testimony being given to the Court: The boat drill had not been held before the *Lusitania* left New York, but on the third day of the crossing; and while the crew may have known whether or not the *Lusitania* was armed on her last voyage, they had no way of knowing with certainty whether or not she had ever been armed. Worse was to come.[4]

In examining the documentary evidence submitted to the Court before the hearings began, there is a sense that there was a deliberate attempt to steer the investigation away from specific aspects of the disaster by withholding or distorting information. For example, in all of the depositions taken, only the briefest mention was made in any of them of the fiasco of the port-side lifeboats, while none of the passengers that were called to appear before the Court made any mention of the port-side boats, the difficulties of launching the starboard lifeboats, or the chaos and ineptness among the crew. Just as studiously ignored were those depositions and proofs of crewmen and passengers that made any mention of two distinct explosions on board the *Lusitania*. Just who was responsible for this interference—and why—is impossible to determine, as is what they were hoping to accomplish, but the impression that someone was tampering with the evidence is very strong.

The Court assembled for the first time on June 15, 1915, at 10:30 A.M. in the Central Hall, Westminster, in London. Lord Mersey and the assessors sat on a raised dais at the front of the hall; to their left were the witness box and the benches reserved for the press. Before the dais stood the tables where the counsels for Cunard, Captain Turner, and the Board of Trade were to sit. Cunard and Turner were together represented by Butler Aspinall, K.C.; C. Laing, K.C.; and A. H. Maxwell. The Board of Trade had assembled a formidable battery of barristers, headed by the Solicitor-General, Sir Frederick Englefield (F. E.) Smith. He was assisted by the Attorney General, Sir Edward Henry Carson, while Messrs. P. J. Branson and S. M. Dunlop were the junior counsel. The Canadian government, various passengers, and the seamen's and trade unions were represented by legal counsels as well, but they had not been granted access to the witnesses or allowed to review the depositions or proofs. No one representing the American government was present.

As the proceedings opened, each of these representatives made application to appear on behalf of their clients. Mersey carefully heard each one out, ruled that they could put questions to the witnesses only through him, then firmly—almost rudely—brushed them aside, saying:

> I am not going to make anybody party to this Inquiry except those people who have been mentioned by Sir Edward Carson, namely the owners and the captain. Of course, it is understood that if at any time during the Inquiry I desire to clear the Court

and to take any part of the Inquiry in private, the gentlemen who
have spoken to me must retire.

Having for all practical purposes disposed of these claimants and whatever embarrassing questions they might have raised, Mersey then allowed Sir
Edward Carson to begin his opening remarks. Sir Edward began by citing the
details of the *Lusitania*'s design and construction, which was all fairly straightforward. He then addressed the German allegations that the liner carried a
concealed armament. "There was no such outfitting of the vessel as is alleged
and fancied or invented by the German government," he declared, "and your
Lordship will have the fullest evidence of that."

Carson then proceeded to call Alexander Galbraith, Cunard's assistant
superintendent engineer, to testify about details of the *Lusitania*'s construction, watertight bulkheads, compartmentation—and armament. Galbraith
could only answer Carson in the most general terms, as he was not as familiar
with the details of the ship as was Leonard Peskett, the *Lusitania*'s designer.
Peskett would have been called as a witness, but he had been stricken with
appendicitis in early May and hadn't yet recovered sufficiently to testify. What
was significant about Galbraith's answers was that he could neither confirm
nor deny the presence of any armament aboard the *Lusitania*—despite Carson's assurance to Lord Mersey of having "the fullest evidence" that no armament was present.

What made such an assurance on the part of Carson so surprising in the
first place was that none of the Board of Trade questions the Inquiry was investigating expressed or even implied that the presence or absence of any armament on the *Lusitania* had any bearing on the loss of the ship. Instead, they had
been formulated to determine whether Cunard or Captain Turner, together or
separately, was guilty of negligence that resulted in the ship's being attacked—
that is, if Turner's handling of the ship or his navigation were negligent, or if
any of Cunard's instructions to Turner caused him to become negligent. Carson's remarks were completely outside of the scope of the Inquiry, but interestingly, Lord Mersey, who was notorious for giving short shrift to those whom he
believed were wasting his time, did not call them out of order or superfluous.
Carson's statement highlighted the political overtones of the hearings. Categorical denial of the German accusations about the *Lusitania* would have a twofold
effect: First, it would place the burden of guilt for the sinking itself squarely on
the Germans; second, it would clear the Admiralty of any blame for the disaster. At least, as far as Lord Mersey was concerned, the Admiralty would be
cleared: If there was any guilt to be imparted on the British side, Mersey was
already sure the unfortunate Captain Turner would be the recipient.[5]

Equally remarkable was the rather cavalier manner with which questions
about the *Lusitania*'s cargo were quickly raised and then dismissed with simi-

lar speed. Carson, continuing his opening remarks, told the court that the *Lusitania* had been carrying "a general cargo bound for Liverpool." Carson again made reference to the German charges, specifically that the liner had been carrying a cargo of high explosives, and then, in rebuttal of that charge, quoted the note sent by the United States to Germany on June 9 (the note that had prompted Secretary of State Bryan's resignation), which read in part:

> Performing its recognized duty as a neutral power and enforcing its national laws, it was [the United States'] duty to see that the *Lusitania* was not armed for offensive action, that she was not serving as a transport, that she was not carrying a cargo prohibited by the statutes of the United States, and if she was a naval vessel of Great Britain that she should not receive clearance as a merchantman. It performed this duty. It enforced its statutes with scrupulous vigilance.

Carson then concluded, "Your Lordship will have the fullest evidence of that from the witnesses we will call in confirmation of what was said by the United States government." Again Carson used that term "the fullest evidence," and again that evidence was something less than complete. The full manifest of the *Lusitania*'s cargo was never entered into evidence; instead, a heavily edited version that combined parts of the sailing manifest and the supplementary manifest was submitted and identified as the true manifest by Alfred Booth, who was not cross-examined about it. In only one of the seven sessions of hearings was a witness called to testify as to the nature of the *Lusitania*'s cargo—and that was the secret session of July 17, which was not announced to the public until after it had adjourned. An instance of how the subject was neatly sidestepped occurred in Carson's initial cross-examination of Captain Turner; it would have actually been amusing had the implications not been so serious. He began by asking Turner, "Were you the master of the *Lusitania?*"

"I was."

"On the voyage from New York to Liverpool?"

"I was." Turner had immediately adopted the charactertic behavior of any seaman in a court of law—he answered the questions asked of him as briefly as possible and volunteered no additional information. It was an article of faith among sailors that lawyers, no matter who they worked for, were a seaman's worst enemy. Carson continued:

"You started the voyage on the first of May?"

"Yes."

"I will not go into the particulars of the crew and cargo because we know what it was. . . ."

Only one documentary reference to the *Lusitania*'s cargo came when Sir Edward read to the Court a letter from the Collector of Customs of the Port of New York, Dudley Malone, to Charles Sumner, the managing director of Cunard's office in New York. Curiously, perhaps significantly, the letter was not a sworn statement. It read:

> Dear Sir,
>
> I have your letter of June 1st, stating that you have received a cable from your Liverpool office as follows: "Send declaration of proper customs officials showing no description of cargo was loaded in violation American neutrality laws, particularly as regards passenger steamers." In reply to this inquiry I have to state that all the articles specified in the manifest of the Lusitania are permitted to be shipped on passenger vessels under the laws of the United States.

The Liverpool cable Malone quoted is intriguing. Even at first glance, it is obvious that the Cunard offices did not want a simple statement about the nature of the *Lusitania*'s cargo. Instead, it specifically asked for a declaration that the cargo, whatever it was, was not in violation of American neutrality laws. Given that Malone had allowed the enforcement of those laws to deteriorate to the legal equivalent of a sieve, it was hardly surprising that Malone so willingly complied.[6]

What is puzzling here is that Carson was once again raising an issue that was entirely outside of the scope of the Inquiry. The contents of the cargo, while they may have contributed to the actual destruction of the ship, could have in no way brought about the attack on the *Lusitania,* nor could it have caused Captain Turner to be negligent. But Carson, feeding the political fires that already surrounded the Inquiry, brought the subject to the fore, and Mersey, instead of dismissing the whole subject as irrelevant, let him pursue it.

Mishandling or misuse of evidence characterized most of the proceedings. In his opening address, Sir Edward indicated the torpedo's point of impact as being "between the third and fourth funnels. There is also evidence that a second torpedo was fired." While maintaining that the torpedo or torpedoes hit the liner amidships, Carson blithely ignored the fact that the *Lusitania* sank rapidly by the bow. The seven witnesses called to support Carson's statement only confused the issue further by stating that the torpedo hit:

"Forward of Number 1 funnel."

"A big volume of smoke came up between the third and fourth funnels."

"Number 1 funnel forward."

"I saw a wake between Number 2 and Number 3 funnel."

"Forward of Number 3 funnel."

"Between Numbers 2 and 3 funnels, and the second [torpedo] just under Number 3 funnel as far as I could judge from forward."

The seventy-two depositions and proofs stating that the torpedo struck just beneath or just forward of the bridge were carefully ignored, as were all of the statements that confirmed that there was only one torpedo that struck the ship. Three crewmen who stated that they had not seen the impact of the torpedo maintained that they did see the track of a second torpedo—each man claiming to have seen the wake coming from a different direction.

Carson spent considerable time and energy drawing attention to the reports that two torpedoes struck the *Lusitania*. That there had been two explosions on board the ship was already widely reported, both in the Great Britain and the United States: The idea of the second torpedo had surfaced as early as the day after the disaster. It was easy enough to believe, since most people found it difficult to accept that a single torpedo could have sent the *Lusitania* to the bottom—let alone cause her to sink as quickly as she did. Carson was, in essence, asking Mersey to officially endorse, on the flimsiest of evidence, that there had indeed been two torpedoes that struck the *Lusitania*.

That Mersey did so is hardly surprising, although his position can scarcely be envied. He was an honorable man being asked to preside over an inquest—in essence, a trial—that had its proceedings rigged and its evidence tampered with, of which Mersey was well aware, although to what degree, he had no idea—yet. Attitudes were rapidly starting to harden on both sides in the war, with sentiments beginning their slow turn away from the idea of the war being fought for national honor to that of its being fought for national survival. Neutral powers that could tip the balance between victory and defeat for one side or the other were being compelled by events to make choices. Between the German Army's ongoing campaign of *Schrecklicheit* in the occupied portions of Belgium and France on land, and the German Navy's ruthless conduct of the U-boat campaign at sea, Germany was making no friends among the neutral powers through her actions. Mersey was well aware that if information were to be revealed through his Inquiry that made Great Britain appear to be as ruthless or as callous as Germany—that high-explosive cargoes were being shipped on passenger liners; that the citizens of neutral countries were possibly being used as "shields" to protect British ships from submarine attack by their presence; that the Royal Navy, by accident or design, was deliberately exposing ships carrying neutrals to attack by German U-boats; that the crews of those passenger ships were so poorly trained and inexperienced that they presented a danger to their passengers in an emergency—then it would be all too easy for those neutral powers still struggling with their consciences over whether they should intervene in the Great War, and on which side, to simply decide not to intervene at all.[7]

Such thinking would explain how Mersey was able to justify how the Inquiry handled the fiasco of the lifeboats and the efforts of the crew to launch them. Unforgivably, considering Mersey's handling of safety issues in the *Titanic* inquiry, the tragedy of the port-side lifeboats received very short shrift. In what must be regarded as carefully rehearsed testimony, eighteen-year-old Leslie Morton stated that when he had gone to the port side, he had found no passengers or crewmen there, and no attempt was made to launch any of the boats from that side, as it was clearly impossible. Two passengers who testified recounted how they had seen both port-side boats and their occupants spilled into the water after being mishandled by the crew. One passenger stated she had entered a boat only to leave it at the request of Staff Captain Anderson. Third Officer Bestic, who had witnessed the whole port-side debacle from the start, was carefully led through his questioning so that the debacle of the port lifeboats was only briefly touched on. Although he admitted that none of the boats he was responsible for safely got away from the *Lusitania,* the entire subject, which Mersey would have relentlessly pursued had he been conducting this Inquiry with the same determination as he did that of the *Titanic,* was then immediately dropped and never brought up again. There were few survivors of the port-side carnage who could have contradicted Morton or added to Bestic's severely limited testimony, and none of them were called to testify.[8]

Not surprisingly, the most stinging criticism—and almost the only criticism—of the crew came from Captain Turner. When he was asked directly if he thought the crew had been proficient in the handling of the lifeboats, he was blunt: "No," he replied, "they were not." His chief counsel, Butler Aspinall, later tried to follow this point up by asking Turner why he really regarded the crew as inefficient. Aspinall put it to Turner this way:

"I want you to explain this a little. Is it your view that the modern ships, with their greasers and their stewards and their firemen, sometimes do not carry the old-fashioned sailor you knew in the days of your youth?"

"That is the idea."

"That is what you have in mind?" Aspinall persisted.

"That is it."

"You are an old-fashioned sailor-man?"

"That is right."

"And you prefer the man of your youth?"

"Yes," Turner replied, with some fire in his voice, "and I prefer him yet!"

Turner had reason for his asperity. Though not a sophisticated man by the standards of the pasty-faced, stoop-shouldered lawyers confronting him, he could see the direction the Board of Trade's case was taking, and that it was being carefully drawn so that the Court would have little or no choice but to place the blame for the disaster squarely on his shoulders. Turner's ordeal began weeks before the first hearing of the Court of Inquiry was held. Deserted by his wife, from whom he had been estranged since 1912, he was shunned in public, the victim of a whispering campaign in Liverpool that charged him with cowardice. The day the Inquiry began, as he was entering the Central Hall, a militant female walked up to him and handed him a white feather, a symbol of cowardice normally reserved for men who were thought to be avoiding military service on the Western Front.

That Turner was far from being at his best is undeniable, but it was utterly forgivable. The burden of having lost his ship and 1,200 lives entrusted to his care, the ordeal of spending nearly six hours immersed in the sea before being rescued, and the public vilification since the disaster had all taken a severe physical, mental, and moral toll on a man just turned sixty-three. Although he had no way of knowing it, the worst of what he would face during the Inquiry was yet to come. But so was his finest moment, when, with a single answer, he would turn the Inquiry around.

When he stepped into the witness box on June 17, he may well have begun to believe that he was a marked man, for this was to be one of the in-camera hearings, since secret documents would be produced as evidence during his cross-examination. Learning of this, Turner must have wondered whether he would ever have the opportunity to defend himself publicly, since the transcript of the day's testimony would be sealed, and he had no idea when it would be made public—if ever. Facing him were two of Britain's shrewdest lawyers, Smith and Carson, both of whom were determined to make Turner appear to be incompetent, negligent, or possibly even in the pay of the Germans. That he survived the ordeal is remarkable. That he survived it as well as he did was due to the skill of his lawyer, Butler Aspinall.

Turner's earlier interviews with various Board of Trade solicitors had been unhappy experiences for him. Told of Captain Webb's charges against him, he was denied legal counsel and then informed that he would not be allowed access to any of the Admiralty documents that Webb had used in preparing his memorandum to Lord Mersey. Turner knew that the *Lusitania*'s log and wireless log had been lost when the ship went down, so he had no way of presenting his position, course, and speed orders that would refute Webb's allegations. Turner also had no way of knowing that the signals and instructions that Webb had used in preparing his document contained signals he had never seen.

This was a weakness that Carson was quick to exploit when Turner took his place in the box. First Carson questioned him about the Admiralty Instructions and Advises. Earlier, Alfred Booth had testified that they were always issued to Cunard captains through the Senior Naval Officer in Liverpool, Admiral Stileman, not through the Cunard offices; a statement of Stileman's was on record that contradicted Booth on this point, but he was not called to testify to it, as the statement had been withheld from Turner's counsel. Turner maintained that all sailing instructions he received, regardless of their origin, came through the Cunard offices. The point is significant in that if the *Lusitania* had been lost because Turner had failed to obey an Admiralty Instruction, and he failed to obey it because he had never received it, the responsibility for the ship's loss would have fallen on Cunard, not Turner. The captain was about to be thrown to the wolves.

As he presented the successive Admiralty Instructions to Turner, Carson was careful to remind the captain of the date of each one, save for the last one, the Admiralty Instruction of April 16, which required ships to adopt a zigzagging course upon entering the German declared war zone. As each Instruction was handed to him, Turner was asked if he recalled reading it, and Turner readily admitted that he had. Then Carson handed him the April 16 Instruction, which was mandatory, but without specifying the date it was issued, and asked Turner if he had received it. Turner, believing that what he was reading was the Advise, which was voluntary, sent on February 10, which recommended taking evasive action by zigzagging after a U-boat had been sighted, said that he had. The language of the two were somewhat similar and Turner didn't realize he was reading a document he had never seen before. Carson moved in for the kill.

"Do you not see now," he asked smoothly, "that you really disobeyed a very important instruction?" Turner was confused, and when he didn't immediately reply, Butler Aspinall stepped in.

"You received this instruction?" he asked.

"Yes," Turner replied, though still unsure of what he had read.

"And you know of it?"

"Yes, I know of it."

"Now what do you understand it to mean?" It was clear that Aspinall had a sense of what was happening and what caused Turner's confusion. Turner thought for a moment, then carefully replied, "I understood it to mean that if I saw a submarine I was to clear out of its way."

"*If* you saw a submarine?"

"Yes, if there was one in sight."

Aspinall then tried to make Turner's thinking clear to the court: "If one was in sight, *then* you were to zigzag?"

"Yes."

"You may be wrong?"

Turner answered slowly, as if he, too, began to have an inkling of what had been done to him. "I *may* be wrong, but I certainly understand it that way."

"What caused you to alter your view?"

"Because it has been read over to me again; it seems a different language."

Although Lord Mersey failed to pick up on the point, Aspinall certainly smelled a rat. He had this exchange on the record now, so he could establish if need be that Turner was confident of all of the Instructions he had received *except* the one from April 16. Something wasn't right about that signal, which was a major link in the Board of Trade's case against Turner, and Aspinall was prepared to weaken it as much as possible. Meanwhile, Carson's questioning had turned to other matters.

Carson asked Turner why he had not ordered the boilers in Boiler Room Number 4 lit, so that he could increase his speed in order to be able to zigzag and still make the high tide at Liverpool. This bordered on the malicious, since Turner had neither the crewmen nor the coal to be able to fire up the extra boilers, and the decision to close down Boiler Room Number 4 was not Turner's, but had come from the chairman of the board of Cunard, Alfred Booth. He had done so at the urging of the Admiralty, which was unwilling to increase Cunard's operating subsidy and suggested closing one boiler room as an economic measure to make up for declining bookings as the war progressed. Turner replied that he didn't have enough crewmen to man all four boiler rooms, even though he knew that there were German submarines near Liverpool. This caught Mersey's attention. Recalling Captain Webb's implication that Turner had been collaborating with the Germans, he asked the captain how he knew about the submarines near Liverpool. Turner replied that it was common knowledge, and that he couldn't recall where or when he had heard it.

Cuttingly, Mersey responded, "It is not twelve months ago [i.e. before the war] I suppose?" Turner, who had no idea what Mersey was implying, said innocently, "No, my Lord, it was not that long."

Convinced now that he was dealing with little more than a seagoing buffoon who may well have been in the pay of the Germans, Mersey turned to the court and commented dryly, "You see? These answers are worth nothing when you test them. They are not worth much, anyway."

In his sarcasm, Mersey had no idea that he was about to be slapped down hard, and that he would bring it on himself. Carson, eager to press what he saw as an advantage, next asked Turner why he had brought the *Lusitania* to within ten miles of the Irish shore. "To get a fix," Turner replied, as if it were the most obvious thing in the world. He had just crossed the Atlantic Ocean, had made landfall in a fog, and needed to know exactly where his ship was if he were going to negotiate the entrance to the St. George's Channel and Liverpool Harbour without a pilot.

Mersey thought he saw another opening to demonstrate Turner's incompetence. Leaning forward, he asked the captain, "Do you mean to say you had no idea where you were?"

"I had an approximate idea, but I wanted to be sure," Turner said carefully.

"Why?" Mersey shot back.

Looking Mersey straight in the eye, and with some venom in his voice, Turner replied, "My Lord, I do *not* navigate a ship on guesswork!"

Mersey was brought up short by Turner's reply. Somehow that one sentence conveyed to him that Turner was neither incompetent nor had he been bought off by the Germans. Subdued, Mersey dismissed Turner from the witness box, then asked Butler Aspinall to approach the bench and comment on Turner's testimony. The dramatic shift in Mersey's attitude toward the captain was quite evident in the exchange between the two men.

Aspinall spoke first. "What I want to emphasize is this: that the captain was, undoubtedly, a bad witness, although he may be a very excellent navigator."

"No," Mersey responded quietly, "he was not a bad witness."

"Well, he was confused, my Lord."

"In my opinion at present he may have been a bad master during that voyage, but I think he was telling the truth."

"Yes." Aspinall nodded.

"And I think he is a truthful witness." Mersey paused for a moment, then continued. "I think he means to tell the truth. . . . In that sense he did not make a bad witness."

Aspinall replied, "I was going to submit that he was an honest man."

Mersey was hesitant as he answered. "I think he is . . . and I do not think Sir Edward or Sir Frederick have suggested anything to the contrary. . . . The impression the man made on me is—I came here prepared to consider his evidence very carefully, but the impression he has made on me is that he was quite straight and honest." Obviously, Mersey was beginning to suspect that the contents of Webb's memorandum were intended to do more than provide evidence for the Court.[9]

Aspinall then summed up his defense of Turner. He reiterated the precautions the captain had taken, including Turner's report on the faults he found when he took command of the *Lusitania* in March, along with reiterating his efforts to get them all corrected. Aspinall next went step by step over the details of Turner's course on the last voyage. He emphasized that Turner had carried out all of his instructions to the best of his knowledge, and attacked the idea that Turner should have brought the *Lusitania* into Liverpool at night without a landfall to check his position. Aspinall then got Mersey to agree that safety came before Admiralty Instructions. Finally, he produced a list of twenty-three ships that had been attacked or sunk in the same waters where the *Lusitania* was destroyed in the six weeks before the *Lusitania*'s last voyage. At this point, realizing how dangerous those waters were, all remaining doubts Mersey may have had about Turner vanished.[10]

The Solicitor General, Sir Frederick Englefield Smith, rose to deliver the closing address for the Board of Trade. Smith was an individual who was greatly impressed by himself and few others, and had a reputation, both in court and out, for his cynical, barbed commentary and dry, acerbic delivery that bordered on insolence, and often he and Lord Mersey had been well matched in the courtroom. As he faced Mersey this time, Smith knew that his usual attitude of smug superiority would not sit well with the Commissioner. So he began in what for him was a remarkably subdued manner, announcing that he had not been conducting a prosecution, but instead believed the case he was attempting to make would produce "some consideration which might or might not lead to an opposite conclusion to that Mr. Aspinall has contended." While trying to make his case, he concentrated on the signals sent to the *Lusitania,* which he contended would prove that Turner had been irresponsible in carrying out his instructions. In doing so, he walked into a trap unwittingly laid by Captain Webb: Anxious to produce as much damaging "evidence" against Captain Turner as possible, Webb had given Lord Mersey and the Solicitor General *differing* copies of the memorandum he had prepared. Smith began reading from his copy.

"On the 7th of May, a period when of course [the *Lusitania's*] attention had in the most pointed way directed to the fact that the general submarine menace had materialized at the particular point [south of Ireland]—on the 7th of May they received a message 'Submarine area should be avoided by keeping well off the land. . . .'"

Mersey interrupted him, asking, "Which telegram are you referring to?"

"The one of the 7th of May, my Lord."

"To whom?" Mersey was mystified at this point—he couldn't find the signal Smith was quoting.

"To all British vessels." Smith had no idea what was about to happen.

"Where is it referred to it in the evidence?" Mersey asked.

Here Smith referred to his copy of Webb's paper and gave Mersey the reference. This only confused Mersey further, who then asked, "Are you reading from the Admiralty memorandum?"

"Yes, my Lord."

"Would you tell me where it is?"

"If your Lordship will look at 'It has been ascertained that the following wireless messages were passed'—it is toward the end of the page—'on the 6th of May, the 7th of May and the 8th of May.'"

Mersey, still not finding it, asked again, "Are you reading from the memorandum headed *Lusitania?*"

"Yes, headed *Lusitania.*" Smith replied. Mersey handed his copy of Webb's memorandum to Smith and said simply, "Where is it?" After examining Lord Mersey's copy and comparing it to his, Smith looked up and said, "It is very curious, my Lord. I cannot explain it at all. Your Lordship's copy is not the same as mine oddly enough. I have a different document to the one Your Lordship has."

Aspinall was then asked if there was any reference to the wireless message Smith had been quoting in his papers and told Mersey there was none. Smith whiningly announced, "I have been working from it throughout the case!" Mersey glared at Smith, who lapsed into silence, and reached for Admiral Inglefield's copy of the log of the Admiralty wireless station at Valencia. Any Admiralty signals to the *Lusitania* would have been relayed through the Valencia station and logged there. Mersey compared his copy of Webb's memorandum with Smith's, and the two of them with the Valencia log. He found no trace of the message Smith had been quoting either in his papers or in the Valencia log—the message had never existed, but had been fabricated by Captain Webb in his effort to incriminate Captain Turner.

Mersey then summoned Sir Elis Cunliffe, who was the Board of Trade solicitor assigned to authenticate all documentary evidence, and asked him which set of signals was correct. Sir Ellis assured Mersey that the Valencia log was the master copy and correct, but could offer no explanation as to why the differences between Mersey's copy and Smith's copy of Webb's memorandum existed.

Realizing how precarious his position had suddenly become, Smith instantly assumed the defensive, lapsing back into his abrasive whine, declaring, "I must confess I do not want it. I think it is very unfair for me when it has not been put to the master"—referring to Inglefield's copy of the signals log—"and had not been produced into evidence to found any further comment on it." Inglefield's copy of the Valencia log showed Mersey not only that the message Smith had been quoting had never existed, but just how far Captain Webb's duplicity had gone, and gave an insight into why Webb had done it.

Smith finished his address rather lamely, and then Mersey, who took such a deception as a personal affront and believed Smith to be privy to it, addressed the Court. Wielding his words with the skill of a surgeon wielding a scalpel, Mersey cut into Smith: "Now I should like to ask a question. I shall have to deal with this point, and having regard to the form of the questions— I suppose the form has been carefully considered—it is possible for us to give a very short answer. 'Were any instructions received by the master of the *Lusitania* from the owners or the Admiralty before or during the voyage from New York as to the navigation or management of the vessel on the voyage in question?' You will observe, Mr. Solicitor, that the question does not ask 'and what were those instructions?' Therefore that question can be answered by a yes or no and I should like to know whether you think it wise that we should attempt to answer in detail. . . . I should like to know from you whether, as representing the Board of Trade, who propounded these questions and put these questions before us, what kind of answers you really wish to convey. I fancy—I do not know, because I saw a previous draft of the questions, and this draft does not, and this was the final draft, I came to the conclusion that those advising the Board of Trade purposely abstained from asking what the instructions were." Mersey had finally come to understand not only the reasons, but also the methods of Captain Webb's duplicity. Mersey adjourned the Court; he and his assessors would review the evidence and then meet to determine the verdict of the Inquiry and write the official report.[11]

Before that happened, a very curious interlude made its way into the proceedings. Both the Attorney General and the Solicitor General had decided to limit the number of passengers to be called as witnesses—that is, limit the number of witnesses over whom the government had little control and whose testimony could not be counted on to conform to the Board of Trade's wishes. Since the whole *Lusitania* affair was considered *sub judice* once the inquiry had been ordered, there was little worry that British passengers could go bearing tales to the British press, since the press was barred from publishing anything that speculated about the causes of the disaster while the investigation was under way. Unfortunately for Carson, Smith, and Lord Mersey, the same restrictions did not apply to non-British passengers. On June 22, Mersey was informed that one of the proofs submitted by one of the passengers alleged that the *Lusitania* had been carrying a cargo of munitions, some or all of which had been set off by the torpedo. The passenger was a Frenchman, Professor Joseph Marichal. Marichal's wife was English, which was why his statement was taken by the Board of Trade, but because he was French, it was promptly ignored. What couldn't be ignored was a similar statement Marichal filed with the French Foreign Ministry at the Quai d'Orsay in Paris. The British Ambassador to France learned that Marichal had filed his complaint—it was actually a request for damages—and informed the British Foreign Office. He was told to stonewall the Frenchman, but Professor Marichal was not to be put off. He threatened to publicize his statement and informed Cunard that he intended to take legal action unless he was compensated for his losses.

They were considerable. Marichal had been crossing on the *Lusitania* with his wife, who was expecting, their three children, and all of their belongings—they were returning home to Europe after having lived for a number of years in the United States. All of the family's possessions were lost with the ship, his wife miscarried the child after the sinking, and while the three children survived, the children and their parents were still not reunited. Marichal asked for £1,000 as compensation, enough to let him pay his bills, bring his family together, and find a home.

Lord Mersey's treatment of Professor Marichal was, simply put, abusive. He had closed the Inquiry on June 18, but reopened extempore proceedings on July 1 in the Westminster Palace Hotel. This was the hearing that was not publicized until after it had taken place. It was held in camera, with Professor

Marichal repeating his charges before Lord Mersey, that the torpedo that struck the *Lusitania* had hit her close enough to the forward hold to set off part or all of a cargo of high explosives she had been transporting illegally. Butler Aspinall asked the professor if he had earlier written Cunard demanding immediate compensation, threatening otherwise to "claim publicly and in doing so produce evidence which will certainly not be to the credit of Cunard or the Admiralty"? Marichal replied that he had, pointing out that the letter to Cunard was written *after* his proof had been submitted to the Board of Trade. Mersey then asked that if Marichal had received his compensation, would he have repeated his allegations in court? The professor said yes, he would. Mersey stared at the professor for a moment, then said simply, "I am sorry to have to say it, but I do say it—that I do not believe you."

Marichal replied that such a remark was a disgraceful way to treat a witness and stalked from the room. The next day, he wrote to Mersey, saying, "My impression is that you were exclusively bent on causing some sensation which would divert attention from very serious allegations against the Cunard Company. Had it not been so, it was clearly your duty if convinced I was untruthful under oath to have me prosecuted for perjury, and not to insult me." Calling Mersey's remark "despicable," he demanded an apology in Mersey's final report or he would continue his actions against Cunard. Mersey ignored the threat and never mentioned Professor Marichal or anything about the incident again.

But Marichal's remarks stung Mersey. Having been rebuked by Turner in court and accused of dereliction of his judicial duty in Marichal's letter, Mersey suddenly seemed to recall that he was charged by the Crown with conducting what was, in the final analysis, a court of law. That he hadn't done so and his court hadn't been such wounded Mersey deeply. Now the question for him was how to find a way to redress the wrongs done.[12]

For Professor Marichal, there was little that could be done. By ignoring him, the Inquiry marginalized his story and made him look faintly ridiculous. To pay him damages and admit to the possibility that his allegations were true invited a political nightmare that Mersey was unwilling to contemplate, let alone bring about. If there were secrets about the *Lusitania* and her cargo that the Admiralty wanted buried, let them stay buried. But Mersey was determined not to let himself be used as the means of making Captain Turner the scapegoat for the Admiralty's blunders, and he certainly was not going to let it be done to him by the likes of some scheming creature like Capt. Richard Webb.

Mersey called the four assessors together. He asked them to submit, in writing in a sealed envelope, their opinions as to whether the loss of the *Lusitania* was the fault of Captain Turner. Of the four, only Admiral Inglefield believed Turner was to blame, and because of the Admiral's close association with Captain Webb, Mersey rejected his opinion out of hand.

Infuriated, Inglefield went to the Secretary of the Admiralty, Sir William Graham Greene, and demanded that Turner stand before a court-martial. Greene offered Inglefield little comfort, however, for events had moved swiftly in Whitehall since May 14, when Webb's memorandum had been approved by Fisher and Churchill. On May 15, exhausted by his feud with the First Lord, Fisher resigned as First Sea Lord. Churchill himself resigned a week later, hounded out of office by his political enemies, who unfairly saddled him with the responsibility for the failures of the Dardanelles campaign. After rebuking Inglefield for his attempt at interfering in Admiralty proceedings, Sir William wrote Lord Mersey that after the departure of Churchill and Fisher, Captain Webb's memorandum no longer reflected the views of the Admiralty.

On July 17, Mersey issued the official report of the Inquiry. Undeniably, it was a masterpiece of political compromise, but it was far from the travesty of justice that it would have been had Mersey not become aware of the duplicity and manipulation of Captain Webb. Unfortunately for history, the findings of the Inquiry did leave much to be desired: In order to explain the second explosion aboard the *Lusitania,* Mersey had to accept that there was a second torpedo; testimony from credible witnesses had to be ignored lest the contraband nature of the *Lusitania*'s cargo be revealed; the extent of the conspiracy—for that is the only way the Admiralty's vendetta against Captain Turner can be described—to place the blame solely on Turner was never revealed. Mersey found no fault with the crew, nor did he have anything to say about how badly the lifeboats were mishandled. Concerning Turner, he compromised: "The advice given him [Turner], although meant for his most serious and careful consideration, was not intended to deprive him of the right to exercise his skilled judgement in the difficult questions that might arise from time to time in the navigation of his ship. His omission to follow the advice in all respects cannot fairly be attributed to negligence or incompetence. He exercised his judgement for the best. It was the judgement of a skilled and experienced man, and although others might have acted differently and perhaps more successfully he ought not in my opinion be blamed."

Mersey's final conclusion as to who was responsible for the destruction of the *Lusitania* was summed up in what would become the official British position for the next eighty-five years: "The whole blame for the cruel destruction of life in this catastrophe must rest solely with those who plotted and those who committed the crime."[13]

CHAPTER 13

The Aftermath

THE REPORT OF THE BOARD OF INQUIRY ON THE SINKING OF THE *LUSITANIA* was released on June 17, 1915, and the United States' third diplomatic note of protest was sent to Germany a month later, on July 21. Neither was the last word on the subject, although events would quickly intervene to drive the destruction of the *Lusitania* and the lives lost aboard her from the center of world attention. She was never forgotten, but she would never again command center stage. What had happened instead was that her destruction began a slow downward spiral for all the belligerents that would see "military necessity" and "national security" become excuses for almost every imaginable form of barbaric behavior.

For the United States, regardless of what later generations would be led to believe, the sinking of the *Lusitania* did not make war with Germany inevitable, despite President Wilson's belief that because of such acts a German victory in the Great War would "change the course of civilization and make America a military nation." He was convinced that the way to avoid such an outcome was not to lead America into the war on the side of the Allies but to stop it altogether. He continued to profess that impartiality on America's part was the only way to get both sides to listen to him—not realizing that neither side had any interest in seeing Wilson negotiate a peace settlement. Only a negotiated peace could last, he said, but a settlement forced on the vanquished by the victor "would be accepted in humiliation, under duress, at an intolerable sacrifice, and would be a sting, a resentment, a bitter memory upon which the terms of peace would rest, not permanently, but only as upon quicksand."

"A peace between equals" or a "peace without victory" was what he hoped to offer, but none of the belligerents were buying it—at least not from Wilson. As far as the Germans were concerned, his intransigence in the aftermath of the *Lusitania* disaster, especially his insistence on special status for Americans traveling abroad, simply proved what they had started to suspect in late 1914: that Wilson's sympathies actually lay with the Allies and that a "negotiated" peace would be one where Wilson simply brokered the Allies' terms, rather than one where the Allies imposed the terms themselves. As for the British, they had Wilson and the United States right where they wanted them—Britain had virtually unlimited access to American industry and financial resources, without the complications and compromises that would come from America being a belligerent.

Still, the unresolved question of responsibility for the *Lusitania* disaster gaped between America and Germany like an open wound, but instead of healing with time, with each passing week the wound seemed to grow larger: The problem was no longer just the *Lusitania*, it was the U-boat campaign itself. Kaiser Wilhelm seemed to have come to the realization that America could be pushed too far, and another outrage like the *Lusitania* disaster, however nicely cloaked in legality, would bring the United States into the war against Germany. Wilhelm also realized that this would happen not because of Wilson, but in spite of him, and so took steps to prevent such an occurrence: Orders went out to the U-boats to strictly observe the Cruiser Rules, and in any cases of doubt as to the identity of a target, to err on the side of caution and break off an attack. It was not long before the U-boats themselves gave lie to such assurances.

On August 19, the 16,000-ton White Star liner *Arabic* was sixty miles out of Liverpool, headed up around the north coast of Ireland bound for New York, when she was sighted by the *U-24,* commanded by Kapitan-Leutnant Rudolf Schneider. Knowing that the *Arabic* was an unarmed passenger ship, Schneider put a single torpedo into her anyway. She sank in a little over ten minutes, taking forty-four of her passengers and crew to the bottom with her, three of them Americans. What had already become, in the eyes of the world, a barbaric campaign was about to get even uglier.[1]

Later that same day, and not far from where the *Arabic* sank, the *U-27* stopped the steamer *Nicosian,* a 6,300-ton freighter carrying a consignment of mules for the British Army. Despite the fact that the *Nicosian*'s wireless operator had been frantically signaling for assistance almost as soon as the U-boat surfaced, the *U-27*'s skipper, Kapitan-Leutnant Bernhard Wegener, gave the passengers and crew of the *Nicosian* time to take to the ship's boats before attempting to sink her with his submarine's deck gun. While the *U-27* was merrily popping away at the *Nicosian,* a second ship, the *Barralong,* apparently another merchantman and clearly flying the American flag, was approaching. No one aboard the *U-27* paid her much attention, which was a fatal mistake: The *Barralong* was not the tramp steamer she seemed to be— she was a Q-ship.

Q-ships were specially modified decoys, designed to look like slow, timid freighters when in fact they were fast, heavily armed merchantmen, commissioned into the Royal Navy and crewed by navy regulars. They were fitted with hidden deck guns, and their holds were filled with buoyant cargoes, so that if they were torpedoed—which the Q-ships were expected to allow to happen in order to maintain their disguises—they wouldn't sink. Cruising in waters that were known to be popular with the U-boats, flying the flags of neutral nations, they invited attack. Whenever they were stopped by a U-boat, a carefully rehearsed charade immediately began, intended to lull the U-boat's crew into a sense of false security. A specially trained "panic party" would race up and down the decks, feigning terror and confusion, upsetting lifeboats, some of them falling overboard, while all the while Royal Navy gunners would be taking the range of the U-boat and carefully laying their concealed guns. At a prearranged signal, the false colors came down, the White Ensign run up to the masthead, and the false bulkheads concealing the guns were dropped. Before the astonished U-boat crew could react, the submarine would find itself sitting in the middle of a hail of well-aimed shellfire from the no longer helpless Q-ship.

The Q-ships were successful for a season, accounting for twenty-seven U-boats sunk, but on this date, the Q-ship's success would be far from unqualified. The crew of the *U-27* finally took notice of the *Barralong* just before she passed behind the *Nicosian,* which refused to sink, but seemed to regard her as no threat. But while the *Nicosian* was in between the *Barralong* and the *U-27,* the *Barralong*'s captain, Lt. Cdr. Geoffrey Herbert, hoisted the White Ensign of the Royal Navy, unmasked his hidden guns, and sailed out from behind the *Nicosian* ready to blow the *U-27* out of the water.

Herbert was in a foul mood—he believed that the *U-27* was the submarine that had sunk the *Arabic* earlier that day. In less than a minute, his ship's guns had hit the U-boat thirty-four times, literally blowing it to pieces. Somehow, Wegener and twelve of his men survived the holocaust and were pitched into the water as the shattered submarine sank. On Herbert's orders, the *Barralong*'s crew began shooting at the Germans in the water, killing Wegener and eight of his men. The four survivors scrambled aboard the now-deserted *Nicosian* for safety, but Herbert ordered a detachment of Royal Marines over to the crippled freighter, and one by one the four Germans were hunted down and clubbed to death.

The world learned of this atrocity when a handful of Americans who had been crewmen on the *Nicosian* protested to the American Embassy in London. When word of it reached Berlin, the German government promptly informed the British through neutral channels that it was "taken for granted" that Britain would "immediately take proceedings for murder" against the commander of the *Barralong* and his crew, demanding that the deed be punished "by a sentence of corresponding severity."

Britain's reply was a sarcastic acknowledgment of Germany's sudden recognition of the principles of civilized warfare, followed by a snarl that whatever the crew of the *Barralong* could be charged with, it was "negligible compared with the crimes which seem to have been deliberately committed by German officers and other ranks against combatants and non-combatants." What both sides seem to have realized and yet not fully comprehended was that a line had been crossed when Schwieger torpedoed the *Lusitania*, and going across that line again was becoming easier and easier all the time— atrocity fed atrocity, as each act of barbarism was justified by the one that had preceded it.

Even Robert Lansing described the *Barralong* incident as "shocking," while President Wilson, somewhat belatedly, began to realize that the Germans weren't alone in their ability to cast off the restraints of civilization in the name of military expediency: Germany may have shown the way, but that didn't make other nations less guilty for following. That the *U-27* incident was no fluke was demonstrated six weeks later when the *Barralong*, Geoffrey Herbert still in command, massacred the crew of the *U-41* after the U-boat had stopped the steamer *Urbino*. The *Urbino*'s first officer filed a formal protest with the Admiralty and the American State Department. Lansing did send a note of protest to Great Britain, but the Admiralty denied the incident ever occurred and awarded Herbert a Distinguished Service Cross.[2]

The second *Barralong* incident made Wilson extremely unhappy, and for a brief time, the attention—and growing hostility—of the American press and public was diverted away from the U-boats. Wilson, in particular, feared being labeled a hypocrite for his condemnation of German "barbarity" when the British were proving to be as bad, or worse. And while an accomplished hypocrite like Lansing could not have cared less about what people thought of him, it was politically inexpedient to continue to press the case against Germany when confronted with such British actions. Had the German Naval High Command been able to bring the U-boats to heel and avoid the loss of any more neutral ships or neutral lives, American neutrality could have been maintained, for there were pressures growing in Washington to take Great Britain to task once the Germans had been properly chastised.

Unlike the Kaiser, who could constitutionally ignore the Reichstag when he saw fit (which was often), Wilson was constitutionally accountable to Congress, and Congress was growing restless. Nothing had been said in the United States' diplomatic exchanges with Germany about the British blockade, or the continued seizure of neutral ships on the high seas by the Royal Navy, despite the urgings of William Jennings Bryan at the time. Now, belatedly, Congress realized that as long as America's attention had remained focused on the German submarines, the British Navy had been able to get away with quite a bit. Valuable cargoes were being impounded by the British, merchant ships were detained indefinitely, and intercepted mails and cables were yielding valuable commercial information to British interests.

Sadly, it wasn't a sense of impartiality or a desire to remain truly neutral, as had driven Bryan's efforts, but the losses being suffered by American businesses and the American economy that roused Congress's ire. Foreign trade actually began to decline, as the British blockade got increasingly tighter, and not even the dramatic increase in trade with Great Britain could counterbalance it—especially since many of the American companies that had done extensive business with Germany before the war were blacklisted by the British and now had no market. Adding insult to injury, American businesses and shipping companies were being forced to wait weeks or even months before seized cargoes were paid for or impounded ships released. The frustration of American businessmen began to make itself felt in Congress. Congressional leaders made it clear to Lansing that, once the U-boat issue was resolved with Germany, the State Department would be expected to start taking a more aggressive stance with Great Britain's conduct of the blockade.[3]

It never happened. For the next eighteen months, an endless succession of unarmed merchant and passenger ships were sunk by the U-boats, and the toll of American lives lost on them mounted, along with American anger at Germany. The next victim to follow the *Arabic* was another liner, the *Hesperian*, sunk on September 4 in direct defiance of the Kaiser's orders not to attack passenger liners. Thirty-two lives were lost; the submarine responsible was the *U-20*, still under the command of Walther Schwieger. In a macabre twist, the *Hesperian* was carrying one of the last victims of the *Lusitania* to be recovered and identified—an American—back to the United States for burial. Though Schwieger had no way of knowing the body was on board, to many Americans it seemed akin to salting an open wound.

And there were times when the Germans were their own worst enemy: Americans did not take kindly to the harangue the Kaiser gave the U.S. Ambassador on October 22. James W. Gerard did his best to hold his peace while Wilhelm first lectured him about American financial and material help for France and Britain, and then protested that "a number of submarines" had been built in the United States for the Royal Navy—when in fact none had— and were escorted to Great Britain by units of the American fleet. "America had better look out after this war," he declared. "I shall tolerate no nonsense from America."

Nor was the German cause helped by their continued terror tactics in the occupied portions of France and Belgium. On September 22, four French civilians were shot for helping French prisoners of war escape. Two weeks later, in an act that outraged the whole Western world, forty-nine-year-old

British nurse Edith Cavell was executed by firing squad for aiding the escape of captured British soldiers. *Schrecklicheit* was still the official German policy, reprisals the standard response to any show of defiance or resistance. The tactics of terror weren't confined to land, either: On November 7, 1915, the *U-38* stopped the Italian liner *Ancona* with the traditional warning shot across her bow. It was the only concession to the Cruiser Rules the submarine's captain, Max Valentiner, made that day. Once the *Ancona* had stopped, and while the terrified passengers and crew were frantically trying to take to the lifeboats, Valentiner began indiscriminately shelling the ship, hitting the hull, decks, and superstructure with little regard for the civilians aboard who were desperately trying to save their lives. The ship sank in less than an hour; 208 passengers and crew were killed, including 25 Americans.

The actions of commanders like Schwieger and Valentiner directly contravened the public declaration of the Kaiser that no more passenger ships were to be attacked, yet neither officer was disciplined for disobeying orders. This would give credence to the idea that the Kaiser's decree was meant more as a sop to public opinion, especially that of the Americans, than as official policy. The rot evidently had gone to the very top—or else had started there: Legality had replaced morality, and even the most cruel acts were acceptable as long as they were legally permissible. It appears that it never occurred to the Kaiser, his ministers, or his generals and admirals that while such actions might be acceptable to the German people, with their passion for legality and correctness, it was only serving to harden the hearts of the British and French, with whom they might some day have to negotiate a peace settlement, and alienating the Americans, who could provide the Allies with the manpower and industrial capacity to overwhelm Germany if they were provoked to war.[4]

As long as Germany was winning the war, though, such considerations were immaterial, and that Germany and her Austrian allies were winning was difficult to dispute. By the end of 1915, the Allies were standing on the defensive on the Western Front, having exhausted themselves in a series of failed offensives that had been intended to break through the German lines. In the East, the Russians were fighting hard, but lacking artillery, ammunition, even rifles for new recruits, they were falling back across the steppes as the Germans and Austrians attacked relentlessly. The evacuation of the Dardanelles began in December and would be finished within a month. The U-boats were sinking more and more ships each week—almost 400 Allied and neutral ships were sunk in 1915 by the German submarines, totaling over three-quarters of a million tons. In 1916, the losses almost tripled, while the British shipyards were barely able to keep pace with new construction.

The year 1915 ended with yet another disaster at sea: On December 30, the Peninsula and Orient steamer *Persia* was torpedoed by the *U-38*. The liner's boilers exploded within seconds of the torpedo's impact, killing most of the engineering crew, and the ship sank in a matter of minutes, taking 334 lives with her, one of them the American consul to Aden. When word of the sinking reached Paris, John Coolidge, a diplomat at the American embassy there, wrote a bitter commentary on Secretary of State Lansing, and by inference President Wilson, in his diary: "An American consul on his way to his post at Aden was on board, so probably Mr. Lansing will buy a new box of notepaper and get to work."[5]

Anti-American sentiment was growing in Germany, as Wilson's dithering was perceived as hypocrisy. One German paper declared:

> Frederick the Great was the first to recognize the Independence of the young Republic after it had won its freedom from the yoke of England, at the price of its very heart's blood through years of struggle. His successor, Wilhelm II, receives the gratitude of America in the form of hypocritical phrases and war supplies for his mortal enemies.

In another daily, a cartoon depicted Wilson releasing a dove, symbolizing peace, with one hand, while lavishing guns, ammunition, and supplies on the Allies with the other. A few days later, with timing that was probably not coincidental, a very belated response to President Wilson's third note of protest to the sinking of the *Lusitania* was delivered on February 16, 1916. It had been almost six months since Wilson had sent his note, and the German response was significant as much for what it did not say as for what it did.

The German reply began by repeating the same argument in justification of the U-boat campaign—that Germany had been forced into it because of the economic pressures created by the British blockade. It then went on to claim that out of respect for American sensibilities, Germany had already imposed restraints on her U-boats, a claim that was difficult to accept in light of the fate of the *Arabic,* the *Ancona,* and the *Persia.* The note also once more offered Germany's profound regret at the loss of American lives on the *Lusitania* and expressed a willingness to pay damages to the families of the American victims.

The German note read like the dull diplomatic exercise it was. Von Jagow knew full well that it would settle nothing, since six days before it was sent, Germany had announced that it would henceforth regard all armed British merchant ships as auxiliary cruisers, subject to being sunk without warning. Neutrals were warned that accidents could happen and that the safest way to avoid them was to simply avoid the waters around the British Isles. For all practical purposes, this amounted to unrestricted submarine warfare, and any ship anywhere was in danger of being sunk on sight.[6]

The U-boats weren't long in making the threat a reality: On March 24, the cross-Channel packet *Sussex,* an *unarmed* passenger steamer, was torpedoed by the *UB-29.* Though the ship remained afloat and was eventually towed safely to Boulogne, fifty lives were lost, including three more Americans. That same month, three Dutch ships—neutrals—were torpedoed and sunk without warning. On March 28, Germany made it official: The unrestricted submarine warfare that the February 10 announcement had implied was announced as fact. Any ship of any nationality, anywhere on the high seas, was liable to destruction without warning by the U-boats. American anger was growing into outrage. On March 26, an editorial in the *New York Herald* bluntly asked, "How many more Americans must be killed before America will declare war?" While war was the obvious solution only to the conservative establishment of the eastern United States, the conviction was growing across the country that the time for diplomatic notes, however sternly worded, had passed. Though the Royal Navy's interference with America's overseas trade might rouse the ire of American business interests, what the average American on the street grasped was that ordinary Americans had been killed by German submarines, simply because they happened to be traveling on British ships.

On April 8, the United States put Germany on notice. In a formal protest over the sinking of the *Sussex,* President Wilson's language was uncompromising:

> The commanders of the Imperial German Government's undersea vessels have carried on practices of such ruthless destruction which have made it more and more evident as the months have gone by that the Imperial German Government has found it impractical to put any such restraints upon them as it had hoped and promised to put.

If the Germans didn't call off the U-boats, the United States was prepared to act:

> Unless the Imperial German Government should now immediately declare and effect an abandonment of its present methods of submarine warfare against passenger and freight carrying vessels, the Government of the United States can have no choice but to sever diplomatic relations with the Central Empires altogether.

It didn't mean war, but it was close enough that Germany couldn't risk it. The German Chancellor, von Bethmann-Holweg, promptly assured the United States that the U-boats would strictly abide by the Cruiser Rules and that no attacks would be made on any passenger ships. The submarine commanders were informed in no uncertain terms that this time these orders were *not* to be disobeyed.

The commanders obeyed, and the number of sinkings dropped off dramatically, although the losses were still serious. The German Naval High Command chafed under the new restrictions, though: The British blockade was still in place, still as effective as ever, slowly strangling Germany, starving her into submission, and the High Seas Fleet still impotent as ever against it. The submarine had given Germany the chance to strike back, but hobbled by the need to abide by the Cruiser Rules, the U-boats could only hurt the British, not cripple them. To Admirals von Tirpitz, Scheer, and von Pohl, the situation was clear: The U-boats could win the war for Germany; the British blockade would surely lose it for her. Allowing the hypocritical Wilson and his "principles," along with the outdated restrictions of the Cruiser Rules, dictate how Germany would wage war was the height of folly.

Together the three admirals worked out an ambitious analysis of the U-boat campaign, correlating the tonnage of merchant shipping sunk with the numbers of U-boats at sea at any given time, along with the submarines lost to all causes. Then they projected what results they could expect if the U-boats were allowed to resume unrestricted submarine warfare, and the numbers of U-boats available were increased. Their conclusions were simple: If the U-boats were permitted to wage war on all shipping, no matter what flag a ship flew or what cargo it carried, they would be able to destroy enough tonnage, British and neutral alike, that British shipyards couldn't begin to replace the losses. The target number was 600,000 tons per month—if the U-boats could send that much shipping to the bottom of the sea for five straight months, Britain wouldn't have enough ships left to even import the food necessary to feed her people, let alone maintain her armies in the field. The possibility of America declaring war on Germany as a consequence was considered, but the admirals disregarded it: If the U-boats were successful, and there was every reason to believe they would succeed, the war would be over before the United States could ever effectively intervene. The arguments were persuasive, and the admirals went to the Kaiser in January 1917 to plead their case.[7]

The timing was shrewd, for the German army had been systematically inflicting a series of brutal defeats on the Allied Powers throughout 1916, so that as the new year opened, the German High Command was able to contemplate the possibility of a German victory. Russia's army was reeling back across the steppes, revolution beginning to tear at its ranks; the French Army had been decimated at Verdun, its morale dangerously near the breaking point, and now France depended on Great Britain to provide the larger part of the Allied effort on the Western Front, but the British suffered horrible casualties of their own at the Somme. Despite terrible losses, which in some cases exceeded those of the Allies, Germany still possessed tremendous manpower reserves, and Germany's government came to believe that they would be able to break Great Britain's ability to continue the war. The key to this strategy was, of course, the U-boats.

In truth, the Germans had no idea just how good a case it was: Great Britain was in worse condition than they imagined. Her dependence on American industry had grown and now was costing more than £2 million ($10 million) a day; her negotiable securities were almost exhausted, leaving only government credit to secure the loans necessary to continue to buy the munitions and supplies the British armies needed. The American Federal Reserve warned its member banks against making further unsecured loans to any belligerent, or renewing short-term loans that were soon due. Britain's back was brushing the wall: The harvest in the fall of 1916 hadn't been particularly good, forcing Britain to buy more of her food abroad; her finest troops already lay in Flanders' fields; she was running out of money. A year before, Britain had been content to use the United States as a source of supply but had no desire to see her become a belligerent. Now only America's entry into the war offered any hope for Britain, but President Wilson had just been reelected in November 1916 after campaigning under the slogan "He kept us out of war!" Once the Germans had restrained the U-boats in the spring of 1916 and no more American lives were lost, American anger toward Germany had abated somewhat. Certainly, there was still a smoldering resentment, but it wasn't enough to go to war over. The *Lusitania,* eighteen months on the bottom, was regarded as old news. Only a miracle could save the Allies.

The Germans themselves provided it. With the Kaiser's senior naval advisors—in particular, Admiral von Pohl, who commanded the U-boat fleet—unanimous in assuring him that unrestricted submarine warfare would sever Britain's lifelines with her empire and the United States, Wilhelm allowed himself to be persuaded that Britain's war effort would collapse for want of food, material, and manpower in a matter of weeks. Once that had been accomplished, with Britain unable to fight and Russia wracked by revolution, France would have no choice but to sue for peace—a peace Germany could dictate. His suspicion that America would fight if another outrage like the *Lusitania* disaster had never quite crystallized into a certainty, and on January 31, 1917, he finally approved of unrestricted submarine warfare, to begin February 1. The orders now to the U-boats were simple—sink any ship, of any type and any nationality, on sight.[8]

No one was more stunned by the German announcement than Woodrow Wilson. Resuming unrestricted submarine warfare was almost like a slap in the face—it was a personal affront. He was furious: Had the Germans forgotten that the cause of every dispute that had arisen between Germany and the United States during the war had been related to the U-boats? Had they forgotten that Wilson had threatened to break off diplomatic relations a year earlier when the Germans announced their first unrestricted U-boat campaign? The German announcement was tantamount to telling Wilson that they took neither him nor the United States seriously. Within forty-eight hours, Wilson ordered Count von Bernsdorff's passports returned to him, and all diplomatic ties with Germany were severed. It wasn't war, but it was close to it.

Yet even then it was difficult for Wilson to believe the Germans had gone that far. Going to Congress on February 3 to explain his decisions and his actions, Wilson remarked that "only overt acts on [the Germans'] part can make me believe it even now." Incredibly, the Germans weren't long in providing the most overt act imaginable.

The Germans are nothing if not thorough, and although the Kaiser and his ministers were convinced that Wilson's diplomatic break was merely bluster, they took precautions to guard against any effective American intervention in Europe. At the same time that Berlin informed Ambassador von Bernsdorff in Washington of the resumption of unrestricted U-boat warfare, instructions were being sent to Ambassador von Eckhardt, the Imperial German Minister in Mexico City. Playing on years of mutual suspicion and sporadic hostilities between Mexico and the United States, and in particular the intervention by U.S. Marines in Vera Cruz during the Mexican Revolution of 1914, as well as the punitive expedition against Pancho Villa, led by Gen. John J. Pershing, in northern Mexico in 1916, Germany sought a military alliance with the government of President Carranza. Von Eckhardt's brief was contained in a telegram that had been drafted and signed by the German Foreign Minister, Dr. Arthur Zimmermann, who had succeeded Gottlieb von Jagow in late 1916. The telegram read:

> WE INTEND TO BEGIN UNRESTRICTED SUBMARINE WARFARE ON THE FIRST OF FEBRUARY. WE SHALL ENDEAVOR IN SPITE OF THIS TO KEEP THE UNITED STATES NEUTRAL. IN THE EVENT OF THIS NOT SUCCEEDING, WE MAKE MEXICO A PROPOSAL OF ALLIANCE ON THE FOLLOWING BASIS: MAKE WAR TOGETHER, MAKE PEACE TOGETHER, GENEROUS FINANCIAL SUPPORT AND AN UNDERSTANDING ON OUR PART THAT MEXICO IS TO RECONQUER THE LOST TERRITORY IN TEXAS, NEW MEXICO, AND ARIZONA. THE SETTLEMENT IN DETAIL IS LEFT TO YOU.

YOU WILL INFORM THE PRESIDENT OF THE
ABOVE MOST SECRETLY AS SOON AS THE OUTBREAK
OF WAR WITH THE UNITED STATES IS CERTAIN AND
ADD THE SUGGESTION THAT HE SHOULD, ON HIS
OWN INITIATIVE, INVITE JAPAN TO IMMEDIATE AD-
HERENCE AND AT THE SAME TIME MEDIATE BE-
TWEEN JAPAN AND OURSELVES.

PLEASE CALL THE PRESIDENT'S ATTENTION TO
THE FACT THAT UNRESTRICTED EMPLOYMENT OF
OUR SUBMARINES NOW OFFERS THE PROSPECT OF
COMPELLING ENGLAND TO MAKE PEACE WITHIN A
FEW MONTHS. ACKNOWLEDGE RECEIPT.

ZIMMERMANN

The Germans had just played an ace that they believed could not be
trumped. By allying with Mexico, she would divert American troops that otherwise would have gone to France to fight Germans to America's southern
border to defend the American Southwest, at the same time making no new
manpower demands on her own resources. The U-boats would starve Britain
into submission, and France, left without allies but with a shattered army,
would clamor for peace. It was elegant, it was brilliant, it would be the greatest diplomatic masterstroke in German history.[9]

But if the Germans had played an ace, the British held the joker in the
deck—the code and cypher wizards in Room 40 at the Admiralty. The signal
from Zimmermann, which would be forever known as "the Zimmermann
telegram," was intercepted as it was sent by wireless and was given absolute
priority by the experts in Room 40. It was decoded within a matter of days,
and a copy of the telegram was presented to Ambassador Page in London,
who in turn delivered it to Wilson on February 24.

Now Wilson was confronted with an "overt act" of unprecedented enor-
mity. The situation was no longer a semiabstract debate over international law
and the rights of neutrals, nor was it a cause championed by a handful of East
Coast business interests and the newspapers they controlled. Nor was it even
a matter of ships sunk without warning and the American lives being lost
aboard them. This was an open, direct threat to the people and territorial
integrity of the United States. When the *New York Times* broke the story of
the Zimmermann telegram on March 1, 1917, it caused a nationwide sensation. The complacency, even indifference, that most Americans felt about the
Great War ended in an instant. For the first time since the war began, one of
the warring powers had threatened the United States openly and directly. The
Great War was no longer simply Europe's problem, or as the *Omaha World-*

Herald put it, "The issue shifts from Germany against Great Britain to Germany against the United States."

The change in the attitude of the American public was as profound as it was sudden. The threat was too real, too personal, to be ignored. Even the leading newspapers in the large German-American communities of the Midwest quickly came down on the side of unquestioned loyalty to the United States, depriving Germany of a large disruptive influence that she had counted on from her expatriate children. Led by the irrepressible Theodore Roosevelt, the groundswell clamor for the United States to join with the Allies in making war on Germany grew, until by March 20, Wilson felt compelled to call a cabinet meeting and sound out his advisors. Though some cabinet members like Josephus Daniels, were in tears, they were unanimous in their conviction that America had no choice but to declare war. The next day, Wilson called for Congress to meet in special session on April 2.

The night before Wilson was to address Congress and ask for a declaration of war against Germany, he sat up late with Frank Cobb, editor of the *New York World.* Wilson's hope for a "peace without victory" was shattered, his dream of arbitrating between the warring powers ruined. He could see no alternative to war now, although he believed he had tried every one available. With America in the war, freedom, tolerance, clear-headedness would all be lost. Cobb recalled that Wilson foresaw that "Germany would be beaten and beaten so badly that there would be a dictated peace, a victorious peace. . . . At the end of the war there will be no bystanders with sufficient power to influence the terms. The won't be any peace standards left to work with." Finally, as if still groping for a way out, Wilson declared, "If there is any alternative, for God's sake, let's take it!"[10]

As it was, at 8:30 the next evening, he rode to the Capitol in a light rain to face a joint session of Congress. He spoke for twenty-six minutes, in the careful tones of a university professor lecturing a hall of attentive students. "With a profound sense of the solemn and even tragical character of the step I am taking," he said, he asked Congress to "declare that recent course of the Imperial German Government to be in fact nothing less than war" against the United States and "formally accept the status of belligerent." Neutrality was impossible when faced with an "autocratic government backed by organized force which is controlled wholly by their will and not the will of the people." Wilson spoke of submarine warfare as outside the pale of international law and cited repeated acts of German sabotage in the United States, then finally offered the Zimmermann telegram as incontrovertible proof of Germany's hostile intent toward America.

Finally, the hushed listeners—Senators and Representatives, the Supreme Court and Cabinet, the Diplomatic Corps, and the invited guests in the gallery—heard that string of memorable phrases delivered as if his resolve were hardening, his determination mounting, with every word. With each phrase he seemed to realize—and so communicated to Congress and thence to the world—that principles can become mighty weapons, when wielded with determination and backed by men willing to use them. The German government, he said, was "the natural foe of liberty"; that, he made clear to everyone who was hearing or would read his words, was why America was adopting this course, because "the world must be made safe for democracy." It must be understood what America's aims were: "We have no selfish ends to serve. We desire no conquest, no dominion. We seek no indemnities for our-selves, no material compensation for the sacrifices we shall freely make. We are but one of the champions of the rights of mankind. We shall be satisfied when those rights have been made as secure as the faith and freedom of nations can make them.

"It is a fearful thing," he went on, "to lead this great peaceful people into war, into the most terrible and disastrous of all wars, civilization itself seeming to be in the balance. But the right is more precious than peace, and we shall fight for the things which we have always carried nearest our hearts." Those were simply summed up: "America is privileged to spend her blood and her might for the principles that gave her birth." He assured his audience with a benediction: "God helping her, she can do no other."

It was over; it was done. Five days later, Congress officially declared war on Imperial Germany and her allies. To the hard-pressed French and British, America's decision to take up the sword was greeted more by sighs of relief than by cheers. Russia had already known the first of two revolutions that would wrack her in 1917, and despite Premier Alexander Kerensky's pledge to continue to fight, there was no disguising that Russia's armies were collapsing. The French Army was caught up in the first waves of a mutiny that followed the bloody and futile Neville Offensive, which would leave her paralyzed for the remainder of the war. Britain was gearing up for what was to be her biggest—and hopefully last—offensive, trying to finally crack the Hinden-burg Line. Now it was only a question of holding on until the unimaginable resources and reserves of material and manpower at America's disposal could be mobilized and hurled at the Western Front. Germany was doomed. Though the war would drag on for another year and a half, the U-boats bringing Great Britain to teeter on the brink of defeat, the Germans had no hope of finding a way to counter the preponderance of strength that America at last gave the Allies.

Churchill would later wonder why, in his words, "the United States entered the Great War on April 6, 1917, and why they did not enter at any earlier moment? American ships had been sunk before by German submarines; as many American lives were lost in the *Lusitania* as in all the five American ships whose sinking immediately preceded the declaration of war." It is an interesting question, indeed. What was, in Barbara Tuchmans' memorable phrase, "the last drop that emptied [Wilson's] cup of neutrality?" F. E. Smith—by now Lord Birkenhead—acidly observed, though not without validity, that "the United States were in fact kicked into the war against the strong and almost frenzied efforts of President Wilson."

The answer, of course, is the Zimmermann telegram. For all of his principles and determination and neutrality and mediator's mentality, Wilson could not ignore such a blunt and direct threat to the United States. No other event posed such a grave and real threat to the nation embodied by the Constitution Wilson had sworn to defend. Here was no ambiguity, no legal hair splitting, no questions of definition or interpretation. Despite what later generations would be led to believe, the sinking of the *Lusitania* was not the incident that propelled America into the First World War. The United States had gone to war over naked German aggression against her, not because of the violations of international law by a handful of German U-boats. Just how far the events of May 7, 1915, were from Woodrow Wilson's mind when he asked Congress to declare war on Germany can be shown by one simple fact: In the entire course of his address, not once did he mention the *Lusitania*.[11]

CHAPTER 14

The Questions

WITH THE PASSING OF MORE THAN EIGHTY YEARS, THE DESTRUCTION OF THE *Lusitania* has lost little of its mystery. There are still a great many unanswered questions about how the *U-20* and the *Lusitania* came to be in the same stretch of the Irish Sea at the same time. Probably the most baffling are the questions that still linger over how and why the *Lusitania* sank so fast. Are there answers to these questions, and if there are, do the answers matter? Do they materially affect history's perception and interpretation of events leading up to May 7, 1915, and the disaster that overtook the *Lusitania* that sunny afternoon? And the most persistent and baffling question of all, was the *Lusitania* the victim of a conspiracy to have her sunk?

On several levels, these questions are all interrelated, and seeking answers to one invariably leads to looking for answers to the others. One question that persists in the face of overwhelming evidence is whether Germany was justified in sinking the *Lusitania.* From the moment word reached Berlin that the *U-20* was responsible for torpedoing and sinking the liner, the German government maintained that the sinking was justified for four reasons: that she was transporting Canadian troops to Great Britain; that she was carrying an illegal cargo of munitions; that she mounted guns in contravention of international law; and that the *Lusitania* was an auxiliary cruiser of the Royal Navy. It is a position that has not been altered by any German government to this day, despite all that has happened in the intervening years—a remarkable consistency for allegations that, according to Great Britain, reportedly had no basis in fact.

The first allegation is demonstrably untrue but was quite likely based on a misunderstanding. There *were* a number of Canadian officers returning to their units, as well as a large but undetermined number of young men on their way to enlist in the British Army aboard the *Lusitania,* but all of them were traveling at their own expense as private citizens, not in any official capacity. At the time, the British never made this distinction clear, while the officers' names that were recorded on the passenger lists included their ranks and units, a situation that could easily have created the impression that Canadian units were on board as well.

The truth of the second allegation is undeniable. Even before the *Lusitania* was sunk, a copy of her manifest showing nearly 5 million rounds of rifle ammunition and fifty-two tons of shrapnel shells were included in the cargo on her last voyage was on file with the Port Authority of New York. By any definition, this cargo constituted contraband and gave the Germans justification for intercepting her at the very least. That the rest of the cargo was, by British definition, contraband, and being shipped in violation of American neutrality laws, only further justified the cargo's destruction under the provisions of international law that both Germany and Great Britain accepted.[1]

But were there any guns? There is no conclusive evidence that the *Lusitania* ever mounted any armament, but there are tantalizing hints that she may have. It is known that she had magazines, shell hoists, and gun rings installed in August 1913. She sat in drydock in Liverpool for the first two months of the war while the Admiralty decided what to do with her, more than sufficient time for some of the guns she was designed to carry to have been mounted, especially since the mounting rings were already in place. It would have been impossible for a dozen 6-inch guns to be concealed on board the ship, especially since eight of them were planned to be mounted on C Deck, where they would have been visible to passengers of all three classes. On the other hand, a battery of four to six smaller guns might have been easier to conceal.

That this may actually have been done is a disturbingly real possibility. In 1961, a team of professional divers led by John Light conducted a series of exploratory dives on the *Lusitania* while the wreck was still in fairly good condition. One of the dives was specifically planned to explore one of the places where, according to the ship's plans, a gun was to have been mounted had the *Lusitania* been converted into an auxiliary cruiser. Working at a depth of over 275 feet, their time on the bottom was limited, but their dives were filled with revelations.

Light had found the wreck lying on her starboard side, in surprisingly good condition for having been on the bottom for over forty-five years. They found that the wreck had broken in two a little more than halfway back from the bow, just under the third funnel. Apparently the wreck broke when the *Lusitania*'s bow struck the bottom and her forward momentum was abruptly halted. The after half of the ship was mostly out of the water at that time, and unsupported, the stress of the sudden halt was more than the ship's structure was designed to take, and she broke.

The bow of the ship was a mess, twisted and bent at an unnatural angle. Partly due to the impact with the bottom, the odd position of the bow is more than vaguely reminiscent of the bow of the hospital ship *Britannic* (the ill-fated sister of the ill-fated *Titanic*), another ship that suffered an internal explosion and whose bow was almost severed by the blast.

Other details struck Light as odd. He found pieces of the ship's shell plating lying hundreds of yards from the wreck, with deformations that showed that the plates had been blown outward. Oddest of all was Light's discovery of evidence that someone had been cutting and blasting on the wreck. Light recalled looking all around at the wreck and the words forming almost involuntarily in his mind: "Someone has been here before." But who?

The answer might well have surprised him, for among the previous visitors had been no less than the Royal Navy. In 1946, the salvage ship *Reclaim* spent a week anchored above the wreck, though the Admiralty later denied she had ever been there. Crewmen who were aboard her at the time were forbidden to discuss the ship's activities under the penalties of the Official Secrets Act. Yet the *Reclaim* was there: The Coast Guard station at Old Kinsale Head recorded her presence. In 1954, the Southampton salvage firm of Risdon Beazley also spent several days diving on the wreck of the *Lusitania,* although they too deny having ever been there.

What Light discovered on his dive to explore the area of the wreck where a gun might possibly have been mounted was baffling. Arriving at the precise spot of the suspected gun mount, on C Deck abreast of the first funnel, he found that, in what should have been an unbroken expanse of superstructure, there was an opening in the side of the ship "some eight feet across, black and bottomless." Light and his diving companion, a lieutenant commander in the U.S. Navy, examined the opening carefully. To Light, it appeared that "some heavy object had dropped straight down [into the opening] *after* the ship had settled on its side. Maybe long after." Light also noted:

> The superstructure is made of light materials, and it looked as if something had just torn on through. And there were three steel cables leading into the hole that had sliced right into the surrounding metal. Maybe they were attached to whatever had fallen through. Maybe someone was trying to hoist that thing away and it broke loose.

Light and his companion decided to find out what "that thing" was and plunged down into the hole. Some 50 feet down, they came upon a tangled mass of wreckage. A long, cylindrical object was suddenly illuminated by their dive lights. Light described it as "a long, tapered object, slanting downward out of a mass of debris. I thought it was a gun." The lieutenant commander, who was closer to it than Light, was later categorical: "It was," he said simply, "a gun." Unfortunately, they had no time for further exploration—their air supply had reached the point where they had to return to the surface if they were to decompress properly. Technical problems kept Light and his divers from returning to that site on the wreck that year, and by the following summer, ownership rights had become so mired in legal entanglements that it would be more than twenty-five years before anyone would dive on the wreck of the *Lusitania* again.[2]

While not conclusive proof that the ship was armed, Light's discoveries cannot be easily dismissed, as he and his crew were all experienced divers, and the conclusion of an experienced naval officer that he saw a gun on board cannot simply be discounted as a case of mistaken identity or depth-induced hallucination. Light's observations about what he found on the wreck are of tremendous importance for another reason: He was able to examine the *Lusitania* while she was still in relatively good condition. By the time divers were able to return to the wreck, the ravages of the elements had begun to catch up to her.

That was in 1989, when Oceonics Limited, an American salvage company, dived extensively on the wreck. Over a six-week period, its divers brought up one of the *Lusitania's* screws, along with a variety of objects ranging from suspender belt clips, 6,000 silver-plated spoons, engine room machinery, Wedgewood crockery, a box of gold watch cases, a bathtub, several portholes and window frames, a bridge telegraph, and rolls of silent movie film, which were identified as *The Thief of Baghdad*. Because Oceonics' objective was salvage, the divers spent very little time examining the wreck for evidence that might have shed new light on the fate of the *Lusitania*.

The next exploration of the wreck took place in 1994, when amid a blaze of publicity, Dr. Robert Ballard led the same team that had discovered the wreck of the *Titanic* down to the *Lusitania*. What he found was a far different ship than the one John Light had explored. The intervening thirty-three years had not been kind to the wreck. Most of the superstructure had broken free of the hull and had slid down to the ocean floor, a tangled mass of wreckage and debris. There was no longer any sign of the opening Light had discovered—that section of the superstructure had simply ceased to exist in recognizable form. The four funnels, which were still present in 1961, had vanished, finally rusting away to nothing. The hull, which still appeared reasonably sound to Light, had begun to collapse, as the decks amidships began giving way and the weight of the heavy doubled shell plating caused her sides to collapse downward.

Even before the exploration of the wreck began, Ballard had announced what he was going to find. In an interview with Jim Brady in March 1993, he announced that proof that Winston Churchill had set up the ship was on the wreck. "The proof is down there," he claimed, "all you have to do is find it!"

If he really believed that, Ballard was sorely disappointed. What the expedition did claim to have found was no evidence of any kind of damage to the bow that would indicate an internal explosion in the cargo hold. Because the *Lusitania* lies on her starboard side, the spot where the torpedo hit her is inaccessible, as is most of the bow on that side. Ballard concluded, based on very flimsy evidence, that the detonation of the torpedo had caused coal dust in the forward transverse bunker to explode, blowing a large hole in the *Lusitania*'s side, which accounted for the rapidity of her sinking. Having concluded that, Ballard recanted his statement about Churchill's responsibility.[3]

John Light's experiences contradict him. One factor that gives Light's observations and conclusions particular credibility is that in 1961, hardly anyone cared about the *Lusitania,* what had happened to her, or how and why. Certainly Light never began his dives to the wreck with the hoopla and publicity with which Ballard surrounded his expedition, nor did he publicly announce what he would find on the wreck before he began diving on her. The most significant difference between the two men's experiences was that the ship was in far better condition when Light was diving on her: She was then still recognizably a ship; by 1994, she was rapidly becoming a pile of wreckage.

One problem with Dr. Ballard's assertion that coal dust in the transverse bunker exploded is that the deformation of the bow is not consistent with such a blast. The twisting and distortion caused by the bow's impact with the bottom and the hull pivoting on it as she continued to sink are readily apparent. But from a point roughly even with the cargo hold, the bow is distorted upward and away from the rest of the hull. The distortion almost exactly mirrors the pattern of damage done to the hospital ship *Britannic,* which had her bow nearly blown off by an internal explosion.

The wreck of the *Britannic* gives a further clue to the cause of the second explosion on the *Lusitania.* The *Britannic* either struck a mine—the most likely scenario—or was torpedoed by a U-boat whose commander later refused to take responsibility for sinking a hospital ship. Within seconds of the mine or torpedo detonating, a second explosion occurred. This blast was almost certainly a coal dust explosion. Even though the bunker that exploded was not a transverse bunker—that is, it didn't extend from one side of the ship to the other as the *Lusitania*'s forward bunker did—the explosion was powerful enough to blow a thirty-foot-diameter hole in *both* sides of the *Britannic*'s hull. The resulting structural damage almost ripped the Britannic's bow off, creating the unique deformation that was echoed in the damage to the *Lusitania.* On the *Lusitania,* however, where there should be significant damage to both sides of her hull from the blast if the second explosion had actually occurred in the bunker, there is no damage to the port side; there isn't even a visible distortion of the hull attributable to an internal explosion.

So with a coal dust explosion in the transverse bunker ruled out, the question then is what *did* explode aboard the *Lusitania?* The most likely candidate for the cause of the second blast is the shipment of fifty-two tons of 3-inch shrapnel shells listed on the manifest. Shrapnel shells contained a bursting charge that was significantly smaller than the charge of a comparable high-explosive round, but the total amount of the charges in the shipment of shrapnel shells would have easily equaled ten to twelve tons of explosives. When the warhead of the torpedo went off, the shock of the blast caused the shrapnel shells to blow up in sympathetic detonation. This would have been more than enough to blow a sizable hole in the *Lusitania's* bow, enough to account for Captain Turner's watching the fire and flooding indicator board "go berserk" for the forward part of the ship. It certainly would have been sufficient to cause flooding rapid enough to send her under in eighteen minutes. The damage and deformation of the bow during the sinking was severe, and a significant portion of the bow is inaccessible now that the wreck has deteriorated so badly, making isolating it and identifying that damage at this late date likely impossible.

At the same time, given the probability that the second explosion was caused by the shrapnel shells, there are still questions surrounding other parts of the *Lusitania's* cargo. There are several entries on both the sailing and supplemental manifests that don't make sense, hinting that a great portion of the *Lusitania's* cargo may not have been what it was said to be. Just what exactly *were* those 3,829 forty-pound "cheeses" listed on the manifest as being wrapped in burlap and packed in cardboard boxes? They were consigned to a box number in Liverpool, the box belonging to the Superintendent of the Royal Naval Experimental Establishment at Shoeburyness. In his book *The Lusitania,* author Colin Simpson infers that the "cheese" was in reality part of Du Pont's shipment of 600 tons of guncotton delivered to Cunard's Pier 54 on April 29, which then promptly disappeared within the next two days. He suggests that this guncotton was the part of the *Lusitania's* cargo that was set off by the torpedo's warhead. The problem with Simpson's scenario is one of scale: The total weight of the shipment of "cheese" approached eighty tons. If eighty tons of guncotton had exploded in the *Lusitania's* bow, the forward part of the ship wouldn't have flooded—it would have disintegrated!

At the same time, Simpson does raise a valid point by questioning exactly what that shipment of "cheese" actually was. Of all the shortages that the Royal Navy experienced during the war, a dearth of cheese was never known to be one of them. So the Superintendent of the Royal Naval Experimental Establishment was to be the recipient of eighty tons of—what? It's a question that will probably never be answered.

And what were those 329 bales of unprocessed furs? The consignee was Alfred Fraser, one of Captain Gaunt's most useful front men for shipping critical and priority cargoes to Great Britain. The furs were consigned to B. F.

Babcock and Company of Liverpool, a cotton dealer. The company records of Babcock show that they never dealt in furs and never did business with anyone named Alfred Fraser, not in 1915 nor in any other year. To conclude that the cheeses weren't cheeses and the furs weren't furs is inescapable; to speculate as to what they actually were is fruitless. Still, it's impossible not to believe that there was something very peculiar about the *Lusitania*'s cargo on her last voyage.[6]

One of the most disturbing questions that has lurked in the shadows of the *Lusitania* affair has centered around Robert Lansing. Was the Assistant Secretary of State a British agent or in the pay of the British government? Was Captain Gaunt more than just Lansing's friend—was he also his paymaster? Lansing worked hard to make certain that the sinking of the *Lusitania* remained an unresolved issue between the United States and Germany, diverting attention away from the effect the British blockade was having on American trade. Whenever Secretary of State Bryan advised moderation and arbitration to President Wilson, in an attempt to maintain the neutrality that Wilson claimed to so ardently embrace, Lansing would intervene, sometimes subtly, sometimes not, offering advice to Wilson that skewed American foreign policy away from neutrality and toward a pro-Allied position. All the while, Lansing maintained close financial ties with Wall Street, in particular with J. P. Morgan and Company, the bank that was handling the financial arrangements of the British purchasing missions in the United States. The dividends Morgan was paying on the profits from those transactions were making Lansing a wealthy man, while Captain Gaunt provided him with inside information that allowed Lansing to carefully invest in companies that were going to receive large orders from the British government, adding to Lansing's margin of profit. Certainly, the arrangement suited Lansing and his particularly perverse sense of values, of always doing what was best for Robert Lansing and the United States—in that order.

And yet, in a way, some of what Lansing gained turned to ashes. Having maneuvered and manipulated for almost two years to replace William Jennings Bryan as Secretary of State, no sooner had Lansing occupied Bryan's former office than he discovered that it was a hollow post. It was to be four months before he would be able to remove the word "acting" from his title of Secretary of State, and when he was confirmed in his position, he learned that it was not because he was the best qualified man for the post, but that no one who was better qualified wanted it.

President Wilson had decided to act as his own Secretary of State, reducing Lansing to little more than a glorified copy boy, diligently taking down his master's dictation. Why Wilson chose to take the responsibility for American foreign policy into his own hands has never been fully explained, although it soon became clear to those in the Cabinet that Wilson disliked Lansing as much as he had Bryan—possibly more. Certainly, Wilson acknowledged that Lansing was shallow: One thing that Wilson never lost sight of, in all the disputes and disagreements that ranged between Bryan and himself, was that Bryan was easily Wilson's intellectual equal. Lansing clearly was not. Perhaps the idealist in Wilson couldn't stomach the utterly self-serving nature of Lansing. Perhaps the hints of financial impropriety that haunted Lansing's career at the State Department caused Wilson to withhold his complete confidence. Whatever the reason, by the time the United States declared war on Germany, Lansing's influence over the President had become virtually nil. Lansing's marginalization was complete when Wilson left for France and the peace conference at Versailles. Robert Lansing remained behind in Washington, rubber stamping Woodrow Wilson's decisions.

Perhaps the greatest irony of all was the verdict of history. Posterity would remember William Jennings Bryan as one of the great visionaries of American politics. Robert Lansing became a footnote.

Of all the questions surrounding the sinking of the *Lusitania,* the most baffling and the most unanswerable is this: Was there a conspiracy within the British Admiralty to have the ship sunk? If the implication is that the details of her last voyage were manipulated in such a way that she was loaded with an explosive cargo, packed with innocent passengers, many of them Americans, and made to run afoul of the *U-20* so that her destruction could trigger a diplomatic crisis between Germany and the United States, the answer is an unqualified no. There were too many variables that were beyond the control of the Admiralty, the two most significant being the weather and the movements of the *U-20.* Had the patchy fog that the *U-20* encountered on May 6 persisted on May 7, it is entirely possible that the U-boat never would have seen the *Lusitania*; once the liner was past the submarine's position, there was no chance of her being caught. At the same time, the Admiralty had no way of knowing how long the *U-20* was to stay in any particular area: The *Lusitania* could have been ordered into a particular section of the St. George's Channel or the Irish Sea with the intent of having her encounter a U-boat, only to find that the submarine had moved elsewhere.

But if the question is asked, "Was there a conspiracy?" in the sense that circumstances were allowed or encouraged to develop in such a way that if a British passenger liner were to be intercepted by a U-boat, it would very likely be torpedoed without warning and a considerable number of lives would be lost as a result, then the answer is far less unequivocal. To say yes is to deny the element of chance an opportunity to work: It is entirely possible that the *Lusitania* met the *U-20* with no help from any outside influences. The nature of submarine warfare was that given the number of ships bound for Great

Britain, a certain number of them were going to encounter a submarine, and sooner or later one of them would be a passenger liner.

But there were actions that the Admiralty could have taken that would have increased the likelihood of that passenger liner encountering that submarine sooner rather than later, and if those actions were taken, then a justifiable charge of conspiracy, of creating and implementing a policy of "deliberate exposure," could be leveled at the Admiralty. Any such course of action would, of course, have to have originated with Winston Churchill—no one else in Whitehall possessed either the initiative or the authority to formulate and execute such a policy.

Churchill's observation that politics and strategy merge at the summit was not merely a statement of political philosophy, but a summation of how he perceived his role as First Lord. The Dardanelles campaign had been a military solution to a military and political problem; so was the blockade of Germany; likewise the decision to keep the Grand Fleet mobilized in the first days of August 1914. The U-boat war was fraught with military and political complications, and as Churchill's position as First Lord was a political appointment, he would have been failing his responsibilities if he neglected the political implications of the strategies he planned and employed. His seat in the War Cabinet simply reinforced that perception: The Cabinet was charged with the total responsibility of prosecuting Great Britain's war effort, military, economic, and political.

Sitting in the meetings of the War Cabinet certainly would have impressed on Churchill the importance of guaranteeing that Britain continued to be allowed access to American industry to supply her with munitions. He also would have been painfully aware that the blockade of Germany for which he was responsible was creating friction between the United States and Great Britain. And finally, he was all too well aware of the growing threat the U-boats posed to Britain's survival. That he should consider the possibility of such a drastic course of action as a solution to such a growing threat was inevitable—it was part of his job.

And it is known that Churchill did consider how to "precipitate a confrontation between the United States and Germany should an ocean liner be sunk with American passengers on board." The quote comes from the introduction to an Admiralty paper prepared on the subject by Cmdr. Joseph Kenworthy at the specific request of Churchill. The fact that the paper was prepared doesn't mean that such a policy was undertaken, or even under consideration, but it does show that Churchill regarded the idea seriously enough to have it examined in some depth.[5]

If the decision had been made to seek a confrontation between America and Germany, the key to its success would have been finding a way to provoke the Germans into such an attack. The U-boats were very careful to observe the Cruiser Rules in the first months of the war, with the result that there were very few lives lost, none of them American. If the submarines could be compelled to abandon the Cruiser Rules, that not unadmirable conduct would soon end. The program of arming merchant ships as a defensive measure against surface raiders presented an opportunity to do just that. Orders went out to the captains of all armed British merchant vessels, instructing them to use their deck guns to engage any U-boat that ordered them to stop or attempted to intercept them. This was augmented by the instructions to unarmed ships to attempt to ram any U-boat on sight.

While there was nothing wrong with making clear to British merchant ships that they were expected to defend themselves by whatever means was at hand—indeed, Churchill would have been negligent of his duties had he done any less—the First Lord cannot have been ignorant of the fact that the only reasonable German reaction would be for the U-boats to begin attacking without warning. The notorious orders to shoot prisoners and fire on white flags only added to the provocation.

The Germans obliged by reacting as they inevitably must have, by declaring a war zone around the British Isles and announcing that any British ship found in those waters was subject to destruction without warning. The stage was set for a great tragedy that would have to happen, sooner or later. The cryptographers of Room 40 made certain that it could happen sooner. By tracking from day to day the positions of all the U-boats at sea, they were able to brief the Operations Division on the movements and locations of the German submarines. From the details provided by the Plot of the position, course, and speed of every British and German ship at sea, the Operations personnel could determine which British ships, if any, were in danger of being intercepted by a U-boat. They could then warn the threatened ships away from the area where the U-boats were waiting—or if they so chose or were ordered, not warn the ships of the danger awaiting them.

It is known that this happened to the *Lusitania* on three separate occasions. On January 5, 1915, she was sighted and tracked in the Irish Sea by the *U-21*, which had already used all of its torpedoes. February 20 saw two ships torpedoed by the *U-30* within ten miles of the *Lusitania* as she was leaving Liverpool. Two weeks later, on March 6, the freighter *Bengrove* was entering the St. George's Channel at almost the same time as, and almost within sight of, the *Lusitania* when the *U-20* put a torpedo into the *Bengrove* that sent her to the bottom in minutes. On none of these three occasions was the *Lusitania* told beforehand that she was in the immediate vicinity of a German submarine, despite certain Admiralty knowledge that they were there.[6]

Obviously the Admiralty knew that the *U-20* was patrolling the entrance to the St. George's Channel on May 7, 1915, yet the signals being sent to the

Lusitania contained information that was always twelve, sixteen, sometimes twenty-four hours old. No effort was made to divert her into another port or direct her on a course that would have gone wide of the area where the *U-20* was claiming her victims. In other words, there were steps the Operations Division of the Admiralty could have taken to warn the *Lusitania* that she was standing into danger, but didn't. The question "Why not?" almost begs the answer "Because Operations was instructed not to." If that answer is true, the only reason can be because there *was* a conspiracy to have a British liner sunk by a German U-boat, with the resulting political and diplomatic furor working to Great Britain's advantage as worldwide censure fell upon the Germans' heads.

Was a conspiracy a possibility? Certainly. Was it a reality? That question can only be answered by the Admiralty files on the *Lusitania*. They are still classified Top Secret, more than half a century after the Official Secrets Act that covers them should have expired. . . .

There is one final question remaining to be asked about the *Lusitania* disaster, and that one does have an answer: What is the legacy of the day the *Lusitania* died? The answer unfortunately is not welcome, for all that it may be true. In deliberately blurring the distinction that existed between combatant and noncombatant, by trying to claim a military justification for the liner's destruction, Germany made it possible for that distinction to eventually be eliminated altogether. Eventually, any act of violence and excess done to civilians in the name of patriotism, national interest, or military necessity became not only acceptable but accepted practice. It was *Schrecklichkeit* ("frightfulness") carried to its terrible extreme, and it ushered in a century of violence and terror that would know no boundaries, no limitations.

What the *Lusitania* disaster did was highlight for all the world to see a peculiar flaw in the German character, a weakness that mistook legality for morality. The German campaign of *Schrecklichkeit* that had begun in 1914 against Belgian civilians who resisted the German invader was given full voice by the destruction of the *Lusitania*. For every act of terror and reprisal carried out against the civilian population of Belgium, the Germans had a legal justification to present to the world, as if the trappings of legality would be sufficient to excuse the murder of a six-week-old infant in her father's arms. The same legalistic minds tried to similarly justify the destruction of the *Lusitania,* claiming that the deaths of innocent men, women, and children on board a passenger liner were the results of a legitimate act of war.

There is no doubt that the British maneuvered, even manipulated to a large extent, the German government and navy, and in particular their U-boat campaign, until such an incident was almost inevitable. And yet it's hard to deny that the Germans were very willing accomplices. The terms of the declaration of a war zone around Great Britain by Germany in February 1915 implied that such an attack was likely, and that the Germans believed it to be the responsibility of other nations to see that it didn't happen—if a passenger ship ran afoul of a U-boat, it wasn't the submarine's fault; warnings had been issued. The German Naval High Command could have taken measures to prevent just such a tragedy, but didn't: Orders forbidding attacks by U-boats on passenger liners were issued only after the world was outraged by the *Lusitania* disaster, not before. As they had done with the atrocities in Belgium, the Germans repeatedly insisted to the world that they had been fully within their rights in sinking the *Lusitania*, and within their narrow interpretation of international law, they were.

But in a larger sense, the sinking of the *Lusitania* was an indefensible act of barbarism. What made it so—even more unjustifiable than any of the shootings, lootings, or burnings that were hallmarks of the German Army's occupation of Belgium—was its coldly methodical nature. It was not an act of retribution permitted under a policy, however reprehensible, carried out by combat troops against supposedly "peaceful" and "unarmed" civilians whom they believed had hurled a grenade into their midst, or sniped at them from the bell tower of a church. It was not the reaction of men who, in anger, lashed out at those they believed had harbored and encouraged their tormentors, a reaction that, while unforgivable, might at least be explained and understood. The German policy of *Schrecklicheit* was intended to crush any resistance by the civilian population in territories occupied by the German Army, but it was only to be implemented when resistance was offered, as a reaction and reprisal.

There was nothing of reprisal in the destruction of the *Lusitania*. Schwieger did not fire on her in self-defense, or to stop her from fleeing after she had been ordered to halt, or because he knew for certain that she was carrying an illegal cargo of munitions. While in the strictest sense, Schwieger was within his rights in torpedoing the *Lusitania* because of the contraband she carried, when he fired that torpedo at her, *he had no way of knowing that to be true*. In short, Schwieger torpedoed her because he *wanted* to.

It has been suggested that Schwieger mistook the *Lusitania* for one of the three big, four-funneled liners the Admiralty had requisitioned and was using as troopships, the *Mauretania, Aquitania,* or *Olympic;* his orders had specifically mentioned troopships leaving Liverpool, Bristol, and Dartmouth. Yet the *Lusitania* was *inbound* for Liverpool when she was sighted by the *U-20*. And it is difficult, if not impossible, to believe that during the entire time Schwieger had her in the sights of his periscope, he was unable to recognize the distinctive pattern of colors—black hull, white upperworks, black funnels—that all British merchant ships had been painted, in compliance with Admiralty instructions. Visibility was perfect, the *Lusitania* was little more than a half-mile away, and German optics were the finest in the world. There was no opportunity for mistaken identification.

The German government could have disavowed the sinking, repudiated and punished Schwieger, and in doing so avoided alienating the American government and, more importantly, the American people. Instead, the same arrogance that expected German ladies to step off of a sidewalk in order to let a German officer pass asserted itself in the repeated German claims that the sinking was entirely justified: A German officer, by definition, could not have exceeded his orders or committed an act contrary to the provisions of international law. To admit to such a possibility would imply that the German government itself was capable of such errors of judgment. Morality was not an issue: The sinking was legal, therefore it must have been moral. To the Germans, the legality of the destruction of the paltry amount of munitions the *Lusitania* carried, barely half a day's expenditure for the British Army, was of more importance than the morality of taking the lives of 1,200 people.

It was this refusal by the Germans to make the very real distinction between what was merely legal and what was truly moral that made the *Lusitania* affair a turning point in history. By destroying the *Lusitania* and claiming that destruction to be a legitimate act of war, the Germans forever blurred the line between combatant and noncombatant, and soon that line became obscured altogether as the rest of the world, with a dismaying alacrity, followed the German lead. The idea of total war, where there were no front lines and no distinction between the men and women who wore uniforms and those who did not, began with the sinking of the *Lusitania*. Civilian status was no longer any guarantee of protection from the worst of war's horrors, the front line no longer only where the soldiers fought.

The world changed the day the *Lusitania* died. It was not a sudden, radical, obviously dramatic change. Its full consequences would not become apparent until two generations had passed and a greater war than the one that witnessed her destruction had been fought. The disaster changed the course of history, not in the way that has been taught in textbooks for decades—the *Lusitania* was not the reason the United States declared war on Germany in 1917. When President Wilson addressed Congress, the *Lusitania* was to him just one more entry in a long catalog of atrocity and aggression by the Germans. Instead, the sinking of the *Lusitania* was the first long step down the road on which humanity would turn its back on the values of civilization, hard won and painfully built up over two millennia, only to be abandoned in a few short years in order to win a hollow victory in a war no one had wanted to start and everyone was desperate to end. Before the *Lusitania* was destroyed, a compromise peace might have been possible: Hatreds hadn't yet grown unmanageable, hearts had yet to harden to the point where negotiation was impossible. After the *Lusitania,* peace would come only when it was dictated by the victors, whomever they would be.

The legacy of the *Lusitania* disaster is one of human suffering. The men, women, and children traveling peacefully aboard the liner on the afternoon of May 7, 1915—all but a handful of them civilians—were treated no differently by the *U-20* than if they had all been wearing the uniform of the Royal Navy. Germany had served notice on the world that the dangers of war were no longer confined to those who served in the army or navy: Simply being a citizen of an enemy nation—or traveling on a passenger liner belonging to the enemy—was sufficient cause to make any man, woman, or child a legitimate target. It was an example the rest of the world soon followed. Eventually, but not slowly, that idea would take the form of French and Belgian civilians deported to Germany to serve as forced labor; of a starvation blockade by the British against Germany maintained after the Armistice to coerce the Germans into signing the Treaty of Versailles. It would grow into the bombing of Guernica during the Spanish Civil War and of Rotterdam and London in 1940. It would become the Rape of Nanking and the slaughter of uncounted thousands during the Japanese occupation of east Asia. It would become the mass deportation of slave workers in occupied countries in World War II, the fire bombings of Dresden, Hamburg, and Tokyo, and the atomic destruction of Hiroshima and Nagasaki. Eventually, the idea of total war would find its ultimate expression during the Cold War, when entire national populations were held hostage to nuclear threats. The legacy of the *Lusitania* became the ultimate expression of Winston Churchill's observation that "war, which had been cruel and glorious, had become cruel and sordid." Though it would take three-quarters of a century to come to full stature, it was a legacy that was inevitable from the moment the *U-20* fired that torpedo.

AUTHOR'S NOTE

THE *LUSITANIA* WAS A LONG TIME IN GESTATION. I HAVE ALWAYS HAD A STRONG interest in ships and the sea, so naturally my attention was drawn at an early age to the great liners of the early twentieth century and, of course, the two great disasters, the *Titanic* and the *Lusitania.* The *Titanic* became a lifelong fascination for me, which culminated in the publication of my first book, *"Unsinkable": The Full Story of RMS Titanic,* by Stackpole Books in 1998. The entire history of the *Titanic,* down to the most minute details, was an endless source of wonder for me, but while I was always very conscious of the need to place the *Titanic* disaster in its correct social and historical context, I was never much interested in exploring any significant historical impact the disaster may have had—if any at all.

In the case of the *Lusitania,* the precise opposite was true. While I could become as engrossed in a technical journal describing her turbines as I could one about the *Titanic*'s reciprocating engines, for some reason that I could never quite explain, the hold the *Lusitania* had over me was more because of the impact her destruction had on the history of the United States and the course of the First World War—or so I thought. The Great War being another source of endless interest to me, I suppose it was inevitable that my interest in the *Lusitania* take a turn in that direction. But the more I studied and learned, the more dissatisfied I became with the "conventional wisdom" I had been taught in my grade school, high school, and college classrooms—that the *Lusitania* disaster was a key event, if not *the* key event, in America's decision to enter the First World War on the side of the Allies. There was a question nagging at the back of my mind that I could never find a satisfactory answer to: If the sinking of the *Lusitania* was the event that propelled the United States into the war, *why did it take almost two years for America to make up her mind?*

I could never find a satisfactory answer within the confines of the conventional wisdom, therefore the conventional wisdom had to be wrong. That didn't make finding the right answer easy; it took more than twenty years for me to formulate what I could finally assert with confidence was a correct interpretation of the causes and effects of the events of May 7, 1915. *The Lusitania* can be said to have begun in discussions held over a period of two years, as an undergraduate student, with several history professors, most notably Dr. Paul G. Fried, of Hope College, Holland, Michigan, and Dr. Lynn Mapes, of then–Grand Valley State College, now Grand Valley State University, Allendale, Michigan. I was fortunate in that these two gentlemen had the greatest influence on my education and my thinking. Neither of them felt compelled to force their own interpretations on me; both of them encouraged me to think openly and freely. This book owes its origins to them—I owe them my gratitude.

As I've said before, any writer will readily acknowledge that good librarians and archivists are the people who make his or her work possible. Consequently, I want to acknowledge my debt to the staffs of several archives, libraries, and museums. The National Archives, Washington, D.C., contain the complete diplomatic correspondence of the United States, along with the private papers of Robert Lansing, and most invaluable, a complete transcript of the Mersey Investigation. The Bundesarchive in Coblenz, Germany, is the repository for much of the diplomatic correspondence of Imperial Germany, as well as the surviving logs of the warships of the High Seas Fleet. The British Public Records Office is the repository of all of the unclassified British Admiralty files from the Great War, along with copies of the transcript from the Mersey Inquiry and all of its exhibits. The staff were often worth their weight in gold in interpreting the sometimes rather turgid British "legalese" when my modern "American English" was not up to the demands of a 1915 lawyer's "English English."

I began my serious research at the Van Zoeren (now the Van Wylen) Library at Hope College in Holland, Michigan, and at the Grand Valley State College libraries in Allendale, Michigan. The staff, both faculty and student, on both campuses were embodied proof that the usefulness of a library is not always determined by its size, as they worked hard in locating old, out-of-print books and obscure periodicals through the Michigan University Library System. To all of them, from all those years ago, I will always be grateful.

I would be remiss if I failed to acknowledge my debt to the Mariners' Museum of Newport News and the National Maritime Museum in Philadelphia, along with Great Britain's National Maritime Museum in Greenwich, England: Between the three institutions, there is no equal anywhere in the world for the breadth and depth of resources or the accumulated knowledge of ships and the sea available to an historian. These museums are staffed by men and women who know ships and the sea, and so can give insights and perspectives on a subject that might otherwise escape an ordinary historian.

Alas, the great days of John Brown and Company, Shipbuilders, are but a memory, the firm's successor, John Brown Engineering, occupying a fraction of the banks of the Clyde that the great shipyard once covered when the *Lusitania* was built. But the staff were exemplary in their demonstrations of Scottish hospitality and helpfulness, leaving me to wonder where the phrase "dour Scot" ever originated.

I conducted a significant portion of my research in each of these institutions, and always I was received with consummate professionalism and courtesy by their staff, whether page, librarian, curator, or administrator. The faces and names often changed over the course of several years and many visits, so that now I can only dimly recall some of them, but to each and every one, I extend my genuine and sincere gratitude.

A special mention is deserved of certain individuals whose contributions to this work were so unique or so specific that they merit singling out: James Krogan, a naval architect and president of James S. Krogan & Co. of Miami, Florida, took time out from his work to explain the finer points of the *Lusitania*'s design and construction, as well as allowing me to take up an inordinate amount of his time discussing the details of the torpedo's impact and the likely origins and effects of the second explosion. Matthew McLean, a retired Bosun of the British Merchant Marine who now lives in Hollywood, Florida, offered advice that helped me avoid technical errors and provided insight into the life of a British merchant seaman that was invaluable. Harold Butler, of Davison, Michigan, a former Able Bodied Seaman in the American Merchant Marine (and, incidentally, my father), provided advice on nautical usage, terminology, and equipment. Trish Eachus, of Jacksonville, Florida, best friend and fellow author, read this book while it was still in manuscript form and offered her insights, comments, and criticisms about its content and readability. To all of them I offer my thanks, however inadequate the words may seem.

In every case, the people and institutions mentioned provided me with information or support—or both—of some kind, which makes me responsible for how I used it. If I have done so erroneously, the fault is entirely mine.

Facts about the *Lusitania*

Builder: John Brown and Company, Clydebank, Scotland

Length:

    Waterline: 755 feet

    Overall: 785 feet

Beam (width):   88 feet

Draft: 33 feet

Displacement:

    Standard: 33,395 tons

    Fully laden: 43,000 tons

Boilers: 25 (23 double ended, 2 single ended)

Machinery:

    4 propellor shafts, 4 sets of Parsons turbines, 2 sets per shaft,
    1 set (high-pressure) forward, 1 (low-pressure) reverse,
    per propellor shaft

Power output: 17,000 s.h.p. per shaft, total 68,000 s.h.p.

Designed speed: 24 knots

Achieved speed on trials: 25.75 knots

Highest attained speed: 25.88 knots

Launched: June 7, 1907

Lifeboats:

    As designed: 16 standard boats

    After April, 1912:   22 standard boats, 26 collapsibles

Taken from *Engineering*, special issue, August 1907.

Passenger accommodations:

First class	552 passengers
Second class	460 passengers
Third class	1,186 passengers

Crew:

Navigation:

Officers	9
Quartermasters	8
Boatswains	3
Carpenters and Joiners	3
Lamp-trimmer and Yeoman	2
Masters-at-arms	2
Marconi telegraphists	2
Seamen	40

Engineering:

Engineer Officers	33
Refrigerating Officers	3
Firemen	192
Trimmers	120
Greasers	21

Service:

Doctor	1
Purser	1
Assistant pursers	2
Chief Steward	1
Chief Steward's assistants	2
Chef	1
Barbers	2
Cooks and bakers	28
Matrons	2
Stewardesses	10
Mail sorters	7
Typists	2
Leading Stewards, barkeepers, etc.	50
Stewards	280

Total Crew	827

Passengers carried on last voyage: 1,257

Crew carried on last voyage: 702

Total persons on last voyage: 1,959

Passengers lost: 785

Crew lost: 413

Total lives lost: 1,198

The Cargo Carried on the *Lusitania*'s Last Voyage

This information is taken from the original sailing and supplemental manifests for the *Lusitania*'s last voyage. They are currently on file in the Franklin Delano Roosevelt Library in Hyde Park, New York. The originals run to twenty-five pages in length; for the sake of brevity, the cargo is listed by destination and type, but is not broken down by individual shipments. It will be of interest to note that over half of the cargo carried was, by British definition, contraband.

Destination	Consignment	Size	Insurance Value ($)
Liverpool			
	Beef, lbs.	342,165	30,995
	Sheet brass, lbs	260,000	49,565
	Cheese, lbs	217,157	33,334
	Bacon, lbs	185,040	18,502
	Copper, lbs	111,762	20,955
	Copper wire, lbs	58,465	11,000
	Butter, lbs	43,614	8,730
	Lard, lbs	40,003	4,000
	Staves, pkgs	2,351	200
	Ammunition, cases	1,271	47,624
	Confectionary, pkgs	655	2,823
	Canned meat, cases	485	1,373
	Furs, pkgs	349	119,220
	Canned vegetables, cases	248	744
	Dry goods, pkgs	238	19,036
	Oysters, bbls	205	1,025
	Military goods, pkgs	189	66,221

Destination	Consignment	Size	Insurance Value ($)
Liverpool (continued)			
	Aluminum mfrs., pkgs	144	6,000
	Copper mfrs., pkgs	138	21,000
	Salt, pkgs	100	125
	Brass mfrs., pkgs	95	6,036
	Cutlery, pkgs	63	10,492
	Bronze powder, cases	50	1,000
	Iron mfrs., pkgs	33	3,381
	Precious stones, pkgs	32	13,350
	Hardware, pkgs	31	742
	Leather, pkgs	30	16,870
	Lubricating oils, bbls	25	1,129
	Wire goods, pkgs	16	771
	Casings, pkgs	10	150
	Reclaimed rubber, pkgs	10	347
	Shoes, pkgs	10	726
	Tongues, pkgs	10	224
	Electrical material, pkgs	8	2,464
	Silverware, pkgs	8	700
	Steel and mfrs., pkgs	8	354
	Old rubber, pkgs	7	341
	Auto, vehicles, and parts, pkgs	5	616
	Brushes, pkgs	4	342
	Belting, pkgs	2	1,243
	Jewelry, pkgs	2	251
	Machinery, pkgs	2	1,386
	Notions, pkgs	2	974
	I.R. goods [?], pkgs	1	131
Bristol			
	Dental goods, pkgs	7	2,319
	Steel and mfrs., pkgs	4	331
Dublin			
	Engines and materials, pkgs	2	140

Destination	Consignment	Size	Insurance Value ($)
Glasgow			
	Notions, pkgs	1	479
Kobe			
	Liquid glue, pkgs	2	124
London			
	Cartridges and ammunition, cases	4,200	152,400
	Leather, cases	89	31,517
	Bronze powder, cases	16	887
	Printed matter, pkgs	14	147
	Dental goods, pkgs	10	3,962
	Books, pkgs	9	845
	Drugs, pkgs	8	458
	Motorcycles and parts, pkgs	8	1,650
	Machinery, pkgs	6	1,149
	Auto, vehicles, and parts, pkgs	4	340
	Electrical material, pkgs	4	3,200
	Machine patterns, pkgs	3	1,500
	Watch material, pkgs	2	2,489
	Electrical machinery, pkg	1	1,616
	Films, case	1	100
	Furs, pkg	1	750
	Optical goods, pkg	1	1,313
	Paintings, pkg	1	2,312
	Shoes, case	1	274
	Wool yarn, pkg	1	105
Manchester			
	Sewing machines and parts, pkgs	20	360

TOTAL INSURED VALUE OF CARGO	**$735,579**

NOTES

CHAPTER ONE

1. John Malcolm Brinnin, *The Sway of the Grand Saloon,* 316, 322–323, 325; Daniel Allen Butler, *"Unsinkable": The Full Story of RMS Titanic,* 7–8; Humphrey Jordan, *Mauretania,* 18.
2. Butler, 9.
3. Brinnin, 327–331; *Engineering,* special number, August 1907, 10–14.
4. Cunard Archive, Agreement with His Majesty's Government; *Engineering,* 14–15, 29–34; Colin Simpson, *The Lusitania,* 13–18.
5. *Engineering,* 30–41, 55–62; Cunard Archive, Agreement with His Majesty's Government, Instructions to the Master of *Lusitania* and *Mauretania*; Simpson, 18–20.
6. *Engineering,* 20–29.
7. Donald Barr Chidsey, *The Day They Sank the Lusitania,* 8–9.

CHAPTER TWO

1. Richard Compton-Hall, *Submarine Boats: The Beginnings of Undersea Warfare,* 35–41, 63–87; Edwyn A. Gray, *The U-Boat War,* 24–28; Drew Middleton, *Submarine: The Ultimate Naval Weapon, Its Past, Present, and Future,* 5–26.
2. Compton-Hall, 92–109, 126–135; Gray, 29–31.
3. Winston S. Churchill, *The World Crisis,* vol. 1, 11–13; Robert K. Massie, *Dreadnought,* 316–318.
4. William Manchester, *The Last Lion: Winston Churchill: Visions of Glory, 1874–1932,* vol. 1, 452–470; Massie, 154–170.
5. Manchester, 488–499; Massie, 187–199; Grand Admiral Alfred von Tirpitz, *My Memoirs,* 290–317.
6. Gray, 31–38; Edward Horton, *Submarine,* 73; von Tirpitz, 320–323.
7. Churchill, 193–195; Compton-Hall, 173–174, 178; Gray, 46–53; Charles F. Horne, ed., *The Great Events of the Great War,* vol. 3, 128–134; Horton, 140–148.
8. Churchill, 75–89; Manchester, 568–582.
9. David Kahn, *The Code Breakers,* 313–338; Barbara Tuchman, *The Zimmerman Telegram,* 32–39.

CHAPTER THREE

1. The course of events in the first two months of World War I, including the German policy of *Schrecklicheit,* have been written about so extensively that annoting them is superfluous. Probably the best overview of the beginning of the war is by John Keegan's *August 1914: Opening Moves,* while for the best detailed account, see Barbara Tuchman, *The Guns of August.* For the finest concise history of the war, see Martin Gilbert, *The First World War, a Complete History.*

2. Churchill, 297–311; Gilbert, 124–139; Alan Moorehead, *Gallipoli,* 18–76.
3. Churchill, 324–335, 352–387, 399–416, 434–446; Gilbert, 146–153; Moorehead, 118–157.
4. Thomas A. Bailey and Paul B. Ryan, *The Lusitania Disaster,* 28–30, 33–36, 40–44; Churchill, 417–426; Gray, 77–82; Simpson, 27–28.
5. Bailey and Ryan, 52–54, 55–58; Simpson, 74–75; *Papers Relating to the Foreign Relations of the United States, 1915, Supplement* (cited hereafter as *Foreign Relations, 1915, Supplement*), 189–190, 365–366, 370, 419–420.

CHAPTER FOUR

1. Manchester, chapters 2–11.
2. Churchill, 49–74; Manchester, 233–287; Massie, 567–611.
3. Churchill, 217–231; Massie, 311–338.
4. Compton-Hall, 26, 31, 129–130; Lord Fisher, *Memories and Records,* 518–522; Gray, 20, 39; A. J. Marder, *From the Dreadnought to Scapa Flow,* vol. I, 74.
5. Bailey and Ryan, 31–32; Marder, vol. II, 77–82.
6. Bailey and Ryan, 26–31; Churchill, 176–195; Robert Lansing, *My War Memoirs,* 218–219.
7. Bailey and Ryan, 21–25, 33–36, 40–46, 52–55; Simpson, 66–72; von Tirpitz, vol. 2, 141; *Papers Relating to the Foreign Relatons of the United States, 1916, Supplement,* (cited hereafter as *Foreign Relations, 1916, Supplement*) 97, 109, 117, 148–149; *Foreign Relations of the United States, the Lansing Papers* (cited hereafter as *Lansing Papers*), vol. 1, 358–360.
8. Bailey and Ryan, 53–55; Gray, 92; *Foreign Relations, 1915, Supplement,* 365–368; London *Times,* March 30, 1915.
9. Bailey and Ryan, 36–40; Ray S. Baker, *Woodrow Wilson, Life and Letters,* vol. 5, 248, 263; Churchill, 174, 356–358; *Foreign Relations, 1915, Supplement,* 98–100.
10. Bailey and Ryan, 41, 60, 62–63; Edwin Borchard and W. P. Lage, *Neutrality for the United States,* 220, 224, 351, 356; *Foreign Relations, 1915, Supplement,* 378–381; Gray, 98–100; *Literary Digest,* April 10, 1915, 789–791; Simpson, 107–109, 116, 119.
11. Simpson, 25.

CHAPTER FIVE

1. Butler, 33–35; Walter Lord, *The Good Years,* 49–72, 111–140, 255–270; Chidsey, 5–19; Barbara Tuchman, *The Proud Tower,* 245–247.
2. Chidsey, 16–18; Lord, 56–62; Edmund Morris, *The Rise of Theodore Roosevelt,* 28–32.
3. Baker, vol. 2, 116–131; vol. 3, 221–280; Paolo E. Coletta, *William Jennings Bryan, Progressive Politician and Moral Statesman, 1909–1915,* 187–199.
4. Bailey and Ryan, 98–99, Arthur S. Link, *Wilson: The Struggle for Neutrality,* 422.
5. Bailey and Ryan, 99; Coletta, 223–230; Churchill, 690–704; *Foreign Relations, 1915, Supplement,* 793–798; Horne, vol. 2, 170–189; Simpson, 47–49.
6. Bailey and Ryan, 31, 60, 77, 333; Baker, vol. 5, 186–187, 325; Lansing, 218–219; *Lansing Papers,* vol. 1, 378–379, 390; Carlton Savage, *Policy of the United States toward Maritime Commerce in War,* vol. 2, 303–304, 564; Simpson, 46–49, 50, 70, 108, 178.
7. Bailey and Ryan, 38, 60, 66, 87, 94, 242, 246, 314–315, 331–332; Baker, vol. 5, 247; *Foreign Relations, 1915, Supplement,* 98–100. 393–396; *Lansing Papers,* vol. 1, 462–463.
8. Simpson, 179–180.

CHAPTER SIX

1. Simpson, 39–41, 51, 59–61, 79, 99, 87–88, 105; State Department Archives 841.857. L97/74, *U.S. Statutes at Large, 60th Congress, 1907–09, vol. 35, pt. 1* (cited hereafter as *U.S. Statutes*). A remarkably complete accounting of the extent of British expenditures on munitions in World War I, the methods of payment, and the personalities involved are

extensively covered in Senator Nye's investigation of J. P. Morgan and Company during his committee's investigation of the business practices of the American munitons industry in 1936. The investigation is covered in two documents: *74th Congress, Second Session, Senate Report no. 994, 1936;* and *74th Congress, Second Session: Special Confidential Document Printed for the Use of the Special Senate Committee on the Investigation of the Munitions Industry, 1936.* Corresponding British records have never been made public.

2. Booth, Alfred and Booth, George. Correspondence in the corporate records of Booth and Company, London. George Booth to Alfred Booth, September 25, 1914; George Booth to Alfred Booth, October 4, 1914; Simpson, 10, 33–41, 56, 98.

3. Bailey and Ryan, 96–104, C. L. Droste and W. H. Tantum, *The Lusitania Case,* 15–18; Savage, vol. 2, 335–337; Simpson, 42–43, 51, 100, 162–163; *U.S. Statutes,* 1134.

4. Simpson, 55–57, 60, 90–91.

5. Bailey and Ryan, 54, 67; Droste and Tantum, 27–28; *Foreign Relations, 1915, Supplement,* 365–266, 368; Burton J. Hendrick, ed., *The Life and Letters of Walter Hines Page,* vol. 3, 320–325, 372–380; Charles Seymour, *The Intimate Papers of Colonel House,* vol. 1, 359–361, vol. 2, 431–432; Simpson, 57, 64, 75, 126–127.

6. Kahn, 301–340; Simpson, 57–59, 116–117.

CHAPTER SEVEN

1. Bailey and Ryan, 136–137, 184; *Proceedings at the Formal Investigation into the Circumstances Attending to the Foundering of the British Steamship "Lusitania"* (cited hereafter as Mersey Inquiry), 8–12; Simpson, 21–23, 31, 62, 66, 68–70.

2. Bailey and Ryan, 102–108; Savage, vol. 2, 336–337; Simpson, 90–91.

3. Bailey and Ryan, 17; Chidsey, 24–25; Cunard Archive, Business Records, 1914–1915; A. A. and Mary Hoehling, *The Last Voyage of the Lusitania,* 26–27; Simpson, 77–79.

4. Bailey and Ryan, 64–65; Chidsey, 24–26; Hoehling and Hoehling, 61–67; Simpson, 79–81.

5. Simpson, 87–89.

6. Details in this and subsequent chapters of the patrol of the *U-20* are taken from the log of the *U-20* in the Bundesarchiv, Coblenz, Germany. Bailey and Ryan, 114–127; Gray, 270; Hoehling and Hoehling, 13–16, 48, 49, 50–55, Fred T. Jane, *Jane's Fighting Ships, 1914,* 127.

7. Chidsey, 14–22; Hoehling and Hoehling, 21–25, 28, 31, 69, 73, 74, 226; Simpson, 99–100.

8. Bailey and Ryan, 74–77; Chidsey, 10–11; Hoehling and Hoehling, 33–34; *Lansing Papers,* vol. 1, 386, vol. 2, 46: George Viereck, *Spreading the Germs of Hate,* 64–65, Simpson, 81–83.

9. Both manifests for the *Lusitania's* last voyage, the Sailing Manifest and the Supplemental Manifest, are on file at the Franklin Delano Roosevelt Library, Hyde Park, New York, and are available for public inspection. Bailey and Ryan, 96–102; Hoehling and Hoehling, 27; Simpson, 95–99.

10. Chidsey, 12–13, 14–20, 48–52, 56–59; Hoehling and Hoehling, 28–30, 31, 36–40, 41–42, 57–59; Simpson, 101–105.

CHAPTER EIGHT

1. Hoehling and Hoehling, 61–69; Simpson, 80–81, 120–122.

2. Chidsey, 21–22, 48–50, 53; Hoehling and Hoehling, 68, 73–74, 75, 79–80.

3. Bailey and Ryan, 130–133; Chidsey, 54–55, Hoehling and Hoehling, 68, 82–83; National Archives, *Records of Department of State Relating to Internal Affairs of Great Britain, 1901–1929* (National Archives Microfilm) Microfilm Series M580, roll 197, frame 71, 525; *New York Times,* May 10, 1915; *New York Tribune,* May 10, 1915; Simpson, 20, 149–150.

4. Log of the *U-20;* Bailey and Ryan, 120–123; Gray, 175–176; Hoehling and Hoehling, 13–15, 50–54; Simpson, 85.

5. Bailey and Ryan, 176–179; 187–188; Kahn, 370–378; Simpson, 112–120.

6. Log of the *U-20*; Bailey and Ryan, 124; Hoehling and Hoehling, 80, 81; Simpson, 123, 131.

7. Seymour, vol. 1, 434–435; Simpson, 126–127.

8. Bailey and Ryan, 133–137, 215; Chidsey, 61–64, 66; Simpson, 120–122.

9. Log of the *U-20*; Bailey and Ryan, 124–126; Hoehling and Hoehling, 84; Simpson, 127–131.

10. Bailey and Ryan, 134–139; Chidsey, 61–64; Hoehling and Hoehling, 86–87, 90–94; Public Records Office (cited hereafter as PRO), Admiralty Files, ADM 137/1058, frames 28–29; Simpson, 131–132.

11. Bailey and Ryan, 173–175; PRO, ADM 53-45458, ADM 137/1058, frames 11–14.

12. Chidsey, 64–65; Hoehling and Hoehling, 72.

13. Log of the *U-20*.

14. Chidsey, 66; Hoehling and Hoehling, 91–93; Simpson, 133, 135–136.

15. Seymour, vol. 1, 439.

16. Hoehling and Hoehling, 94–98; Simpson, 138.

17. Chidsey, 64–65; Hoehling and Hoehling, 100–102.

18. Log of the *U-20*.

CHAPTER NINE

1. Chidsey, 68–69; Hoehling and Hoehling, 100–104.

2. Chidsey, 69–72, Hoehling and Hoehling, 107–110.

3. Bailey and Ryan, 163–165, Hoehling and Hoehling, 105–107; Simpson, 141–146, United States District Court, Southern District of New York, *Steamship Lusitania, petition of the Cunard Steamship Company for Limitation of Liability, before the Hon. Julius M. Mayer, U.S. District Judge,* (cited hereafter as Mayer Hearings), 410.

4. Chidsey, 73; Hoehling and Hoehling, 122.

5. Log of the *U-20*; Chidsey, 73–74.

6. Chidsey, 76, 79–80, 82; Wesley Frost, *German Submarine Warfare: A Study of Its Methods and Spirit,* 198–202; Hoehling and Hoehling, 109, 111–116, 118.

7. Hoehling and Hoehling, 126–130; Mersey Inquiry, 47; Simpson, 141.

8. Hoehling and Hoehling, 124–126; Simpson, 147.

9. Bailey and Ryan, 125, 205–206; Hoehling and Hoehling, 116, 125; Mersey Inquiry, 6–8; *New York Times,* November 21, 1915.

10. Bailey and Ryan, 150, 168, 171–173; Chidsey, 84–85, 89–90; Hoehling and Hoehling, 117, 205–206; Mayer Hearings, 262–272, 294–312; Mersey Inquiry, 6–7, 41, 49, 54–55, 68; Simpson, 151–154.

11. Hoehling and Hoehling, 113–115, 138; Simpson,155–156.

12. Chidsey, 84–89; Hoehling and Hoehling, 130–131; Mersey Inquiry, 170–180; Simpson, 155–157; *U.S. Statutes.*

13. Chidsey, 82–83; Hoehling and Hoehling, 158–159.

14. Log of the *U-20*.

15. Chidsey, 94–95; Hoehling and Hoehling, 149–150; 151–152, 154–155, 156, 157.

16. Chidsey, 96–97; Hoehling and Hoehling, 140, 146–147, 149, 153–154.

17. Log of the *U-20*; Chidsey, 81, 108–109; Hoehling and Hoehling, 119–120, 178, 200–201.

18. Chidsey, 89–90, 102–105; Hoehling and Hoehling, 160–164, 167–168, 170–173, 193–194.

CHAPTER TEN

1. Chidsey, 104–106; Hoehling and Hoehling, 128–129.
2. Bailey and Ryan, 171–175; Chidsey, 106–107, 113–115; Hoehling and Hoehling, 156, 175–177, 178, 179–181, 210, *Loss of the Steamship "Lusitania," REPORT of a formal investigation into the Circumstances Attending the Foundering on the 7th of May, 1915, of the British Steamship "Lusitania," of Liverpool, after Being Torpedoed off the Old Head of Kinsale, Ireland.* (cited hereafter as Mersey Report), 10.
3. Log of the *U-20*; Chidsey, 108–109; Hoehling and Hoehling, 201–202.
4. Bailey and Ryan, 174–175; Chidsey, 110–112; Frost, 209–212; Hoehling and Hoehling, 177–178, 207–208; PRO, ADM 53-45458, ADM 137/1058.
5. Chidsey, 114–116; Hoehling and Hoehling, 185–186, 202.
6. Chidsey, 117–120; Hoehling and Hoehling, 203–210.
7. Frost, 204–208.
8. Bailey and Ryan, 63, 193; Chidsey, 120, 121, 126–130; Hoehling and Hoehling, 215–219, 225–226, 227; Mersey Report, 12.

CHAPTER ELEVEN

1. Bailey and Ryan, 191, 192; Frost, 215; Hoehling and Hoehling, 218; Simpson, 158, 191.
2. Bailey and Ryan, 178, 226–228; *Foreign Relations, 1915, Supplement*, 385–386.
3. Bailey and Ryan, 86–87.
4. *Brooklyn Eagle*, May 10, 1915; *New York Nation*, May 9, 1915; *New York Evening Sun*, May 9, 1915; *New York World*, May 10, 1915; *Richmond Times-Dispatch*, May 9, 1915.
5. Droste and Tantum, 108; *Literary Digest*, May 22, 1915, 1206–1207.
6. *Foreign Relations*, 1915, *Supplement*, 385–394; *Lansing Papers*, vol. 1, 392, 395, 411.
7. Droste and Tantum, 130–131; Link, 377–378; C. C. Tansill, *America Goes to War*, 277.
8. Count Johann von Bernsdorff, *My Three Years in America*, 30, 56, 145; Link, 382; PRO, FO 115/1998, frame 30.
9. The complete text of the note is found in *Foreign Relations, 1915, Supplement*, 393–396; Baker, vol. 5, 350; *Foreign Relations, 1915, Supplement*, 99, 407–409; *Lansing Papers*, vol. 1, 413–414; Tansill, chapter 9.
10. The complete text of the German note is found in *Foreign Relations, 1915, Supplement*, 400–401; *Papers Relating to the Foreign Relations of the United States, 1914, Supplement* (cited hereafter as *Foreign Relations, 1914, Supplement*), 605–607, 612; *Foreign Relations, 1915, Supplement*, 119–120, 400–401, 406, 415, 419–422, 653; *Lansing Papers*, vol. 1, 436–437; *Literary Digest*, June 12, 1915, 1383.
11. *Lansing Papers*, vol. 1, 427, 436–437, 447–448; Link, 409; *Literary Digest*, June 12, 1915, 1383.
12. Text of the note is found in *Foreign Relations, 1915, Supplement*, 436–438; Coletta, chapter 12, "The Resignation"; Link, 422, 431, 434; PRO, FO 115-1997, frames 134, 138; Savage, vol. 1, 332–340.
13. Text of the note is found in *Foreign Relations, 1915, Supplement*, 463–466; Bernsdorff, 158; *Foreign Relations, 1915, Supplement*, 115; *Lansing Papers*, 163, 360; Link, 436–437.
14. Text of the note is found in *Foreign Relations, 1915, Supplement*, 480–482; Coletta, 330; *Foreign Relations, 1915, Supplement*, 171–172, 489; *Foreign Relations, 1916, Supplement*, 157; *Lansing Papers*, vol. 1, 492–493, 495, 503, 530–531; Link, 449, 454.

CHAPTER TWELVE

1. Bailey and Ryan, 180–183; *Parliamentary Debates* (Commons), 5th series, vol. 71, col. 1359–1363, 1963–1964, 2237–2238.
2. PRO, ADM 137/1058, frames 129–131; PRO, Board of Trade MT 9/1128.16308/1915. 9949.
3. Bailey and Ryan, 176–180; PRO ADM 137/1058, frames 129–131; Simpson, 165–172.

4. Bailey and Ryan, 199–202; Simpson, 188–194.

5. Mersey Inquiry, 6, 7–8, 11, 14–16, 46, 47.

6. Mersey Inquiry, 3–5, 14–15, 51–52; Simpson, 199–202.

7. Bailey and Ryan, 201–202, 220–222; Mersey Inquiry, 6, 46, 47, 66.

8. Bailey and Ryan, 205–207; Mersey Inquiry, 7–8, 51, 52, 63.

9. Droste and Tantum, 191–193; Mersey Inquiry, 16, 40; *Proceedings* in Camera *at the Formal Investigation into the Circumstances Attending the Foundering of the British Steamship "Lusitania"* (cited hereafter as Mersey Inquiry, *in Camera*), 3–5, 7–9, 10–11, 12, 14–15, 16, 21.

10. Bailey and Ryan, 213–214; Simpson, 215–217.

11. Mersey Inquiry *in Camera*, 23–24, 27, 31–33, 34; Simpson, 217–220.

12. Mersey Inquiry, 60–66.

13. Churchill, 475; Mersey Report, 12, 17–18, 21, 29; Simpson, 220–222.

CHAPTER THIRTEEN

1. Gilbert, 188, 191; Gray, 105, 110–112, 146; *New York Times,* September 2, 1915; Tansill, 365.

2. Bailey and Ryan, 22, 40, 51; Rear-Admiral Gordon Campbell, *My Mystery Ships,* 17–25, 73–80; *Foreign Relations, 1915, Supplement,* 527–529, 543, 577, 605–606; *Foreign Relations, 1916, Supplement,* 222; Gilbert, 188; Gray, 104–106; Simpson, 229–230.

3. *Foreign Relations, 1915, Supplement,* 576–577; *Lansing Papers,* vol. 1, 333; Simpson, 230–231.

4. Bailey and Ryan, 184; Gilbert, 191, 202–203, 205, 210; Gray, 109–110, 131–132.

5. Bailey and Ryan, 308–309; Gray, 132; Gilbert, 222; Philip J. Haythornewaite, *The World War One Sourcebook,* 49–53.

6. *Foreign Relations, 1916, Supplement,* 157, 171–172; *Lansing Papers,* vol. 1, 531, 593–594.

7. Churchill, 690–695; Gilbert, 302–304; Horne, vol. 5, 1–11.

8. Churchill, 697–698; Horne, vol. 5, xiv–xxiii; William Manchester, *The Arms of Krupp,* 278–292.

9. Churchill, 702; Gilbert, 312; Horne, vol. 5, 42–47; Tuchman, *The Zimmermann Telegram,* 51–69.

10. Horne, vol. 5; *New York Times,* March 1, 1917; Tansill, 399; Tuchman, *The Zimmermann Telegram,* 128–144.

11. The complete text of Wilson's address is in Horne, vol. 5, 107–117; Churchill, 698–703; Horne, 369–370, 410–412; Tuchman, *The Zimmermann Telegram,* 171–193.

CHAPTER FOURTEEN

1. The original manifests (Sailing Manifest and Supplementary Manifest) of the *Lusitania*'s last voyage can be found in the Franklin Delano Roosevelt Library, Hyde Park, New York. A copy can be found in the National Archives, Microfilm roll M580-197.

2. Kenneth MacLeish, "Was There a Gun?" *Sports Illustrated,* December 24, 1962, 37–47.

3. Robert Ballard, *Exploring the Lusitania,* 144–183, 191–195.

4. Simpson, 97–99.

5. Joseph M. Kenworthy, *Freedom of the Seas,* 211.

6. Simpson, 79–80.

Able Bodied Seaman. A special rating given to particular seamen onboard a merchant ship. Often abbreviated AB, an Able Bodied Seaman had to demonstrate extensive practical knowledge of a ship, its operations, and equipment to receive the rating.

aft. Referring to the rear or toward the rear of a ship.

after. Also used to refer toward the rear of the ship.

after deck. The section of upper deck aft of the superstructure.

amidships (midships). The general area of the center of the ship.

astern. In the direction of the rear of the ship, or, if in reference to a ship's motion, going backwards.

auxiliary cruiser. A large, fast passenger liner designed to allow the mounting of several medium caliber (4- to 6-inch) guns in wartime, permitting the ship to be used as a second-line cruiser to hunt enemy surface raiders.

battleship. A large, heavily armored warship, relatively slow, mounting large-caliber (11-inch bore or larger) guns. Designed to contest control of the sea with other navies, the battleship's traditional opponent was another battleship. (Sometimes called a dreadnought, after HMS *Dreadnought*, the prototype modern battleship.)

Bosun. A contraction of Boatswain (the term Boatswain is never used, except by landlubbers), the Bosun is the senior seaman on board a ship.

bow. The front of the ship.

bulkhead. A structural (i.e., load bearing) wall in a ship. A non-structural wall is called a partition.

collapsible. A now-obsolete form of lifeboat, with a rigid wooden keel and collapsing (folding) canvas sides held up by iron or steel stays. Collapsible boats were made redundant by the invention of inflatable life rafts.

condenser. A large machine that cools the steam that has passed through a ship's engines and condenses it back into water, so that live steam is not being vented from the ship. Alternatively the water can be fed into the boilers again.

cruiser. A medium- to large-sized warship, fast, lightly armored and usually mounting guns of 5- to 10-inch caliber. Cruisers were used to scout for the main battlefleet as well as patrol independently, hunting for enemy merchant ships.

davit. A curved arm that supports a lifeboat while it is being filled, raised, or lowered. The lifeboat's falls are connected to ten davits by means of pulleys.

destroyer. A small, light warship, very fast, mounting four to six small caliber (3- to 4-inch) guns, as well as an array of depth charges. Originally known as "torpedo boat destroyers," they were designed to screen a battlefleet from enemy torpedo boats, a task that evolved into hunting submarines, which gradually became their primary mission.

displacement. A measure of a ship's size, expressed by how many tons of water she displaces when she is afloat: In order for a ship to float, the amount of water she displaces must be greater than the actual weight of the ship.

double-ended boiler. A boiler having fireboxes (furnaces) at both ends.

fall. The lines by which lifeboats are raised and lowered.

fo'c'sle (forecastle). An ancient term used to denote the forward area of a ship in general, and often identifies the crew's quarters in that area.

fore. A shortened form of forward.

foredeck. A raised section of deck at the forward end of a ship.

forepeak. The forward-most compartment on a ship.

forward. Toward the front of a ship.

funnel. The nautical term for a smokestack—properly speaking, ships never have smokestacks, only funnels.

gangway. A large double-width doorway in the side of a ship's hull.

hawse pipe. An opening in the deck or hull of a ship through which mooring lines or anchor chains are passed through.

helm. A term used for the position at the ship's wheel where the Quartermaster stood on watch, controlling the ship's moment.

keel. The very bottom of the ship. Immensely strong, the keel is the main structural member of a ship's hull.

knot. A unit of speed and distance: A knot in speed is 1.15 land miles per hour; a knot in distance is 2,000 yards.

masthead light. A white light carried high up on a ship's mainmast, used along with sidelights to allow ships to determine each other's bearing, course, and speed at night.

ordinary seaman. A sailor on a merchant ship who had not qualified for any particular department or passed for his Able Bodied Seaman's rating; usually ordinary seamen were used for maintenance or other shipboard tasks that did not require specialized knowledge or experience.

port. The left side of a ship.

quartermaster. An Able Bodied Seaman who has been trained to "conn" (steer) a ship. This was an exacting position, as the QM had to be able to compensate for the immense inertia and momentum of the ship and control her movements as he responded to helm (steering) orders from the ship's officers.

reciprocating engine. A steam-driven engine with large pistons that are driven up and down by high-pressure steam, moving much like the pistons in an automobile motor, which turn the propeller by means of a crankshaft.

screw. Another term for a propeller.

single-ended boiler. A boiler having fireboxes (furnaces) at only one end.

starboard. The right side of a ship.

stay. A heavy cable used to support a funnel or mast.

steerage. A common term for Third Class, originally referring to the location of the Third Class accommodations, which were located in the most cramped and undesirable parts of the ship, often around the steering gear.

stern. The rear of a ship.

stoker. A member of the engineering crew responsible for shoveling coal into the boiler fireboxes, maintaining the level of the fire at its proper intensity, and keeping the firegrate clean of ashes and clinkers to allow a proper air draft across it.

superstructure. That part of the ship built on top of the hull, which is the actual load-bearing structure of the ship.

telegraph. A piece of equipment on a ship's bridge, usually made of brass (it resembled a large lollipop) that by a means of indicator dials and bells relayed speed and direction orders for the engines to the engine room.

trimmer. A member of the engineering crew responsible for shifting coal from the bunkers to the front of boilers, where it was shoveled into the fireboxes by the stokers. Trimmers also ensured that the coal remaining in the bunkers was evenly distributed and did not adversely affect the ship's trim, hence the name "trimmers."

turbine. A type of marine engine that consists of a large rotor covered with blades onto which steam is directed, causing the rotor to turn, which then turns the propeller by means of a shaft.

upper deck(s). The deck or decks that are exposed to the open air, i.e., there are no decks built above them.

Well Deck. A section of an upper deck that sits at a slightly lower level than the deck area fore and aft of it. Usually found between the superstructure and the fore or after decks.

wireless. A now-obsolete term for radio. Originally it was a shortened version of "wireless telegraphy," the original name for radio communication.

OFFICIAL SOURCES

Great Britain

Public Records Office (PRO)
Admiralty Files ADM 53-45458; ADM 137/1058
Board of Trade Files MT 9/1128.16308/1915.9949
Foreign Office Files FO 115/1998
Loss of the Steamship "Lusitania," REPORT of a Formal Investigation into the Circumstances Attending the Foundering on the 7th of May, 1915, of the British Steamship "Lusitania," of Liverpool, after Being Torpedoed off the Old Head of Kinsale, Ireland. (Mersey Report)
Parliamentary Debates, (Commons), 5th ser., vol. 71
Proceedings at the Formal Investigation into the Circumstances Attending the Foundering of the British Steamship "Lusitania." (Mersey Inquiry)
Proceedings in Camera *at the Formal Investigation into the Circumstances Attending the Foundering of the British Steamship "Lusitania."* (Mersey Inquiry, *in Camera*)

Corporate Archives
Booth and Company
    Booth, Alfred and Booth, George. *Correspondence.*
Cunard Archive
    Business Records, 1914–15
    Copy of Agreement with His Majesty's Government
    Instructions to the Master of *Lusitania* and *Mauretania*

Germany

Bundesarchiv, Coblenz
Log of the *U-20*

United States

Library of Congress, Manuscript Division
Bryan, William Jennings. *Private Papers.*
Morgan, J. P. *Private Papers.*

National Archives
Microfilm Roll Series M580-197, *Records of Department of State Relating to Internal Affairs of Great Britain, 1901–1929*
Papers Relating to the Foreign Relations of the United States, 1914, Supplement
Papers Relating to the Foreign Relations of the United States, 1915, Supplement
Papers Relating to the Foreign Relations of the United States, 1916, Supplement
Papers Relating to the Foreign Relations of the United States, the Lansing Papers
74th Congress, Second Session, Senate Report No. 994, 1936; and 74th Congress, Second Session: Special Confidential Document Printed for the Use of the Special Senate Committee on the Investigation of the Munitions Industry, 1936

State Department Archives 841.857.L97/74
U.S. Statutes at Large, 60th Congress, 1907–09, vol. 35, pt. 1

Federal Archives
United States District Court, Southern District of New York,
Steamship Lusitania, Petition of the Cunard Steamship Company for Limitation of Liability, before the Hon. Julius M. Mayer, U.S. District Judge

Other Archives
Franklin Delano Roosevelt Library, Hyde Park, New York

PUBLISHED SOURCES

Books

Bailey, Thomas A., and Paul B. Ryan. *The Lusitania Disaster.* New York: The Free Press, 1975.

Baker, Ray S. 5 vols. *Woodrow Wilson, Life and Letters.* Garden City, NY: Doubleday, Page and Company, 1935.

Ballard, Robert, with Spencer Dunmore. *Exploring the Lusitania.* New York: Madison Press,1995.

Bernsdorff, Count Johann von. *My Three Years in America.* New York: Eric Sutton, 1936.

Borchard, Edwin, and W. P. Lage. *Neutrality for the United States.* New Haven, CT: Thomas Ward, 1937.

Brinnin, John Malcolm. *The Sway of the Grand Saloon.* New York: Delacorte Press, 1971.

Butler, Daniel Allen. *"Unsinkable": The Full Story of RMS Titanic.* Mechanicsburg, PA: Stackpole, 1998.

Campbell, Rear-Admiral Gordon, VC. *My Mystery Ships.* London: Hodder and Stoughton, 1928.

Chidsey, Donald Barr. *The Day They Sank the Lusitania.* New York: Award Books, 1967.

Churchill, Winston S. *The World Crisis.* 6 vols. New York: Charles Scribner's Sons, 1926–31.

Coletta, Paolo E. *William Jennings Bryan, Progressive Politician and Moral Statesman, 1909–1915.* New York: John Day, 1969.

Compton-Hall, Richard. *Submarine Boats: The Beginnings of Undersea Warfare.* New York: Arco Publishing, 1984.

Droste, C. L., and W. H. Tantum. *The Lusitania Case.* Riverside, CT: 7C's Press, 1972.

Fisher, Lord. *Memories and Records.* London: Hodder and Stoughton, 1921.

Frost, Wesley. *German Submarine Warfare: A Study of Its Methods and Spirit.* New York: D. Appleton and Company, 1918.

Gilbert, Martin. *The First World War, a Complete History.* New York: Henry Holt and Company, 1994.

Gray, Edwyn A. *The U-Boat War, 1914–1918.* London: Leo Cooper, 1994.

Haythornewaite, Philip J. *The World War One Sourcebook.* London: Arms and Armour Press, 1992.

Hendrick, Burton J., ed. *The Life and Letters of Walter Hines Page.* 3 vols. Garden City, NY: Doubleday, Page and Company, 1922.

Hickey, Des, and Gus Smith. *Seven Days to Disaster.* New York: G. P. Putnam and Sons, 1987.

Hoehling, A. A., and Mary Hoehling. *The Last Voyage of the Lusitania.* New York: Henry Holt and Company, 1956.

Horne, Charles F., ed. *The Great Events of the Great War.* 7 vols. N.p.: The National Alumni, 1921.

Horton, Edward. *Submarine.* New York: Macmillan, 1963.

Jane, Fred T. *Jane's Fighting Ships, 1914.* London: Hodder and Stoughton, 1914.

Jordan, Humphrey. *Mauretania.* London: Hodder and Stoughton, 1937.

Kahn, David. *The Code Breakers.* New York: Macmillan and Company, 1967.

Keegan, John. *August 1914: Opening Moves.* New York: Ballantine, 1971.

Kenworthy, Joseph M. *Freedom of the Seas.* New York: Harcourt, Brace and Company, 1926.

Lansing, Robert. *My War Memoirs.* Indianapolis: University Press, 1935.

Link, Arthur S. *Wilson: The Struggle for Neutrality.* Princeton, NJ: Princeton University Press, 1960.

Lord, Walter. *The Good Years.* New York: Henry Holt and Company, 1957.

Manchester, William. *The Arms of Krupp.* Boston: Little, Brown and Company, 1968.

————. *The Last Lion, Winston Spencer Churchill: Visions of Glory, 1874–1932.* 2 vols. Boston: Little, Brown and Company, 1983.

Marder, A. J. *From the Dreadnought to Scapa Flow.* 4 vols. Oxford: Oxford University Press, 1964–70.

Massie, Robert K. *Dreadnought: Britain, Germany and the Coming of the Great War.* New York: Random House, 1991.

May, Ernest R. *The World War and American Isolation.* Cambridge, MA: Harvard University Press, 1959.

Middleton, Drew. *Submarine: The Ultimate Naval Weapon, Its Past, Present and Future.* Chicago: Playboy Press, 1976.

Millis, Walter. *Road to War, America, 1914–1917.* Boston: Houghton, Mifflin and Company, 1935.

Moorehead, Alan. *Gallipoli.* London: G. B. Harper, 1956.

Morris, Edmund. *The Rise of Theodore Roosevelt.* New York: Ballantine, 1988.

Paxon, Frederic L. *The Pre-war Years, 1913–1917.* Boston: Houghton, Mifflin Company, 1936.

Savage, Carlton. *Policy of the United States toward Maritime Commerce in War.* 2 vols. Washington, DC: Hutchinson, 1936.

Seymour, Charles. *The Intimate Papers of Colonel House.* 5 vols. Boston: Houghton, Mifflin Company, 1926.

Simpson, Colin. *The Lusitania.* Boston: Little, Brown and Company, 1972.

Tansill, C. C. *America Goes to War.* Boston: Houghton, Mifflin Company, 1938.

Tirpitz, Grand Admiral Alfred von. *My Memoirs.* New York: Hurst and Blackett, 1919.

Tuchman, Barbara. *The Guns of August.* New York: Macmillan and Company, 1962.

————. *The Proud Tower.* New York: Macmillan and Company, 1962.

————. *The Zimmerman Telegram.* New York: Macmillan and Company, 1958.

Viereck, George. *Spreading the Germs of Hate.* New York: Heinemann, 1930.

Periodicals

Engineering, special number, August 1907.

Literary Digest, April 10, 1915.

Literary Digest, May 22, 1915.

Literary Digest, June 12, 1915.

MacLeish, Kenneth. "Was There a Gun?" *Sports Illustrated* (December 24, 1962): 37–47.

Mayer, J. M. "Sinking of the *Lusitania*." *Current History Magazine of the New York Times* (October 8, 1918): 145–161.

_____ "Sinking of the *Lusitania*." *Independent* (May 17, 1915): 271–272.

_____ "Sinking of the *Lusitania*." *Living Age* (June 5, 1915): 629–630.

_____ "What Sank the *Lusitania?*" *Scientific American* (May 29, 1915): 488.

Newspapers

Boston American
Boston Globe
Brooklyn Eagle
Chicago Tribune
Detroit News
Detroit Free Press
Edinburgh Review
Glasgow Herald
Illustrated London News
London Daily Mail
London Morning Post
London Times
New York American
New York Herald
New York Nation
New York Sun
New York Times
New York Tribune
New York World
Richmond Times-Dispatch
Washington Evening Star
Washington Post

Aboukir, H.M.S., 27–29
Admiralty, British, 4–6, 109
  anti-submarine measures, 52–53, 66–68, 111–113
  blockade of Germany, 31, 37
  influences design of *Lusitania*, 7, 9–10
  instructions to merchant captains, 110, 207–209, 220–222
  interferes with Mersey Inquiry, 206–212, 224–225
  merchant ships armed by, 71–72
  mining, 68–69
  prewar attitude toward submarines, 22, 27
  strategy, 29–31, 61–62
  subsidizes construction of *Lusitania*, 6–7
Allen, Lady Marguerite, 173
Anderson, Staff Capt. John, 130, 156–157, 173
Arabic, R.M.S., 230,233
Aspinall, Butler, 214, 223, 225
Asquith, Prime Minister H. H., 58–59, 73, 88, 106, 202

BEF (British Expeditionary Force), 37– 38, 63
B. F. Babcock and Co., 250–251
Ballard, Dr. Robert, 248–249
Barnard, Oliver, 147
Barralong, H.M.S., 230, 231–232
Ben Cruachan, S.S., 53
Bennett, Sir Courtenay, 109, 206
Bestic, Third Officer Albert, 149, 156, 219
Bilbrough, George, 131
Bluebell (tug), 173
Booth, Alfred, 100, 112
Booth, George, 99–100, 110–111, 139

Bowen, Edward, 119
Britannic, H.M.H.S., 249
Brooks, James (Jay), 147, 171
Bryan, William Jennings, 122, 252
  character, 90, 92
  early career, 89–90
  relationship with Lansing, 92, 192–194
  relationship with Wilson, 194
  resigns, 194–195
  urges moderation in dealing with Germany, 90, 191–192
  views on U.S. neutrality, 90–91, 191–192
Bryce, Chief Engineer Archibald, 130, 156, 176

Campbell, Alexander, 124
Candidate, S.S., 140–141
Carson, Sir Edward Henry, 214, 215–216, 218–219, 220–222
Centurion, S.S., 141
Chisholm, Steward Robert, 163
Churchill, Winston, 29, 49, 61–64, 77, 139, 242–243, 248, 252–255, 258
  and Dardanelles campaign, 49–50
  and *Lusitania*, 77–78, 137–138
  and Mersey Inquiry, 212
  and U-boats, 65, 66–68, 70–72
  arms merchant ships, 71–72
  as First Lord of Admiralty, 58–60, 63–64
  early career of, 57–58
  forced from office, 228
  relationship with Admiral Fisher, 49, 56– 61, 201, 202
  strategic concepts, 73–75, 253–254
City of Exeter, S.S., 163, 170
Coke, Adm. Sir Charles, 142–143, 170
Connor, Miss Dorothy, 145, 152, 158

Cressy, H.M.S., 27–29
Cunard Steam Ship Company, Ltd., 4–7,
    10–11, 99, 109, 112, 114

Dardanelles (Gallipoli) Campaign, 49–52
    conceived by Churchill, 49–50
    early successes of, 50–51
    fails, 52, 262
    strategic importance, 49
Davis, Trimmer Fred, 153
DePage, Dr. Marie, 118, 162
Dolphin, Avis, 131, 173
Donald, Archibald, 131, 145
Dow, Capt. David "Paddy," 113
Duckworth, Elizabeth, 117, 131, 158–159,
    172

Earl of Lathom (schooner), 139
Etonian, S.S., 163, 170

Falaba, S.S., 56, 121
Fisher, Dr. Howard, 131, 145, 152, 158
Fisher, Adm. Sir John Arbuthnot, 49, 60
    as First Sea Lord, 49
    character and reputation, 60–61, 65–66
    interferes with Mersey Inquiry, 211–212
    relationship with Churchill, 49, 65
    resigns, 228
    views on submarine warfare, 66
Flying Fish (paddle steamer), 170, 172
Forman, Justus Miles, 124, 125, 162
Foss, Carl, 148
Fraser, Alfred, 98, 250–251
Freeman, Matt, 162, 168
Friend, Edwin, 118
Frohman, Charles, 124–125, 141–142, 175
Frost, Consul Wesley, 174

Gallipoli. *See* Dardanelles Campaign
Gaunt, Capt. Guy, 97–98, 112, 115
    intelligence operations, 110, 111
    purchase of munitions, 100–101
    relationship with Lansing, 97, 98, 251
    shipment of munitions, 112
Goetz, Karl, 181
German Army, 31, 43–45
    executes civilians in France and Belgium,
        43–44, 233–234
    policy of *Shrecklicheit*, 44, 184

German Foreign Office, 183–185, 190–191,
    197, 235
German Naval High Command, 25, 26, 29–
    30, 33, 52, 56, 63, 237, 256
George V, King, 140, 144–145, 168
Gullflight, S.S., 76–77, 188, 190
Gwyer, Rev. and Mrs. H. L., 132, 145, 156,
    171

Hall, Capt Reginald, 106
Hefford, Second Officer P., 147, 156
Hesperian, S.S., 233
Hogue, H.M.S., 27–29
Holbourn, Prof. Stoughton, 118, 131, 169
Holland, John Phillip, 19–21
Hood, Vice-Adm. Sir Horace, 115, 142
Horgan, Coroner John, 203–205
House, Col. Edward M., 105–106, 139–140,
    144–145
Hubbard, Elbert, 126–127, 175
Hutchinson, Electrician George, 169–170

Inglefield, Adm. Sir Frederick, 205, 227–
    228
Inverclyde, Lord, 4–5

Jeffery, Charles, 163
Johnston, Quartermaster Hugh R., 150, 154,
    164
Jolivet, Rita, 124
Jones, First Officer Arthur, 153
Juno, H.M.S., 144

Kay, Kathleen, 173–174
Kenworthy, Cdr. Joseph, 253
Kessler, George, 148
Klien, Charles, 124

Lansing, Robert, 232, 235
    character, 91–92, 93, 195, 251
    early career, 92–94
    financial arrangements, 92, 96, 101
    influence on Wilson, 192–194
    relationship with Bryan, 192–194
    relationship with Capt. Gaunt, 96, 97–
        98, 251
    relationship with Wilson, 92–93,
        251–252
    "strict accountability," 94–95

succeeds Bryan, 195
U.S. neutrality, 93–94, 193–194
Lauriat, Charles, 118, 132, 144, 148, 151, 164, 171–172
Lehmann, Isaac, 148, 157–158, 167
Leith, Robert, 152, 160, 168
Lewis, Senior Third Officer John, 123, 158
lifeboats, 133, 168
  attempts to launch, 156–158, 159–160
  loading, 158, 159, 160
  mishandled, 156–157, 158
  recovered, 171–174
Light, John, 246–250
  discoveries, 247–248
  explores wreck, 246–248
Little, Asst. Third Engineer George, 149
Loney, Mr. and Mrs. Allen, 118, 163
Loney, Virginia Bruce, 118, 163
Lusitania, S.S., 1, 14, 109, 120, 130, 179, 183, 184, 187, 190, 229, 239, 245, 254–255, 255–258,
  accommodations, 12–14
  captures Blue Ribband, 14
  construction, 14
  damage, 149, 153–154, 246–247
  design, 7–10
  explosions, 148–149, 153–154, 249–250
  last voyage, 129, 131, 140, 142, 144
  lifeboat drill, 133–134
  lifesaving equipment, 114–115
  loss of life, 176–177
  modifications, 78, 109, 110
  munitions carried, 123, 149, 185, 246
  peacetime career, 14–15
  powerplant, 8–9
  public outcry at sinking, 179–180, 181, 185
  salvage, 248
  sinks, 164–165, 167
  speed reduced, 112–113
  stability, 10
  survivors rescued, 171–174
  torpedoed, 147–149
  wartime career, 109
  wreck, 1, 246–7, 248, 249–250, 252

Mackworth, Margaret, Lady Rhondda, 124, 148, 151, 155, 158, 168–169, 173
Madden, Fireman Thomas, 152–153

Mahan, Capt. Alfred Thayer, 21–23, 24
Malone, Collector of Customs Dudley Field, 101–102
  allows false manifests, 102
  statement to Mersey Inquiry, 217
manifests, 101–102
  falsification of, 102, 111–112
  on *Lusitania*'s last voyage, 139,
Marichal, Prof. Joseph, 226–227
Mason, Mr. and Mrs. Stuart, 119, 176
Mauretania, S.S., 1, 7, 8, 11, 54, 256
McDermott, Trimmer Ian, 153
Mersey, Lord (Sir Charles Bigham), 205–206, 214, 215, 223–224, 225
  character, 206
  conduct of Inquiry, 206, 214–215, 217–218, 226–228
  political views, 206
  influenced by British Admiralty, 218
Mersey Inquiry, 205–206, 212–213, 214, 215, 218–219, 223, 226–228
  Admiralty interference, 213, 225–226, 228
  Captain Turner before, 219–223
  findings, 228
  political influences, 213, 218
  secret sessions, 213
  selection of witnesses, 217–218
  suppression of evidence, 213, 214, 217–218, 219,
Moodie, Ralph, 145, 154
Morgan, John Pierpont, 3, 4, 6
Morton, J. C., 159
Morton, Leslie, 118, 147, 168, 219
Murphy, John, 150
munitions, 101–102, 153
  U.S. regulations, 102–103

Narragansett, S.S., 163, 170
Nicosian, S.S., 230, 231–232
Nielson, Miss Greta, 174
North, Miss Olive, 162

Oliver, Vice-Adm. Henry

Padley, Florence, 118, 147
Page, Ambassador Walter Hines, 106, 139–140, 180
Pappadopoulo, Mr. and Mrs., 162

Parry, William, 168
Pathfinder, H.M.S., 27, 65
Peskett, Leonard, 7–8, 9–10, 77–78, 215
Piper, Chief Officer J. F., 153
Plamondon, Mr. and Mrs. Charles, 117, 162
Pope, Theodate, 118, 148, 162, 169, 173

Q-ships, 230–231
Queenstown (Cobh) 170–172, 173, 174,
    179
  rescue fleet, 170–171
  victims buried, 176
  survivors accommodated, 174–175
Quinn, Thomas, 147

Robinson, Emily, 162
Room 40, 32–33, 106, 107, 136, 202, 254
  deciphers German naval code, 32–33,
    107–108
  deciphers Zimmermann Telegram, 240
  monitors U-boat movements, 33, 108,
    120
Roosevelt, Theodore, 84–85, 87, 185
Royal Welsh Male Choir, 132–133, 169
Runciman, Walter, 74–75, 99–100

Schwieger, Kapitan-Leutnant Walther, 115,
    136, 144, 145–146, 184–185, 256–
    257
  attacks on merchant ships by, 136, 139,
    140–141, 170, 233
  character of, 115–116
  sinks the *Lusitania*, 145–146, 150–151
  wartime career of, 115–116, 233
Scott, Alice, and son Arthur, 131, 158–159
Shineman, Mr. and Mrs. James, 119, 176
Smith, Sir Frederick Englefield, 214, 223–
    225
Spring-Rice, Ambassador Sir Cecil, 210
Sussex, S.S., 236
Sumner, Charles P., 111–112, 113, 127
Swanmore, S.S., 163–164
submarines and submarine warfare, 17–27
  British concepts, 54–55, 26
  Cruiser Rules, 53–54
  early history, 17–19
  German concepts, 27, 55–56
  living conditions, 116–118, 134–136

merchant shipping vulnerable, 68, 70
prewar development, 21, 25–27
strategy, 237–238
tactics, 54–55, 70

Thomas, D. A., 124
Thresher, Leon C., 56
Turner, Capt. William, 141, 142, 143, 147,
    148–149, 155, 156, 164, 173, 204
  appears before Mersey Inquiry, 219–223
  attempts to save *Lusitania*, 149–150
  character of, 129
  navigation practices, 142, 143, 144, 145
  peacetime career of, 129–130
  survives sinking, 165, 173
  takes command of *Lusitania*, 113–114

U-9, 27–30
U-20, 115, 116, 144, 233, 254, 255
  attacks on merchant ships by, 136, 139,
    140–141, 170, 233, 245
  life aboard, 116–118, 134–136
  sinks *Lusitania*, 145–146, 150–151
  war patrol, 115, 119–120
U-27, 230, 231–232
U-28, 56
U-38, 234
U-41, 232
UB-29, 236
Urbino, S.S., 232

Valentiner, Kapitan-Leutnant Max, 234
Vanderbilt, Alfred Gwynne, 125, 126, 141–
    142, 163, 169–170
von Bethmann-Hollweg, Chancellor Theo-
    bald, 36, 183, 236
von Jagow, Foreign Minister Gottlieb,
    189–190, 196, 235
von Papen, Capt. Franz, 122, 184
  attitude toward Americans, 103
  character, 103
  intelligence operations, 103–104
  sabotage, 111
von Pohl, Adm Friedrich, 55, 237, 238
von Tirpitz, Adm. Alfred, 25, 54, 115

Webb, Captain Richard, 109, 110, 202
  evades responsibility, 209–210

interferes with Mersey Inquiry, 206–211, 212, 224, 225

Welsh, John, 174

Wilhelm II, Kaiser, 23, 24, 54, 223
  attempts to restrict submarine warfare, 230, 236–237
  authorizes unrestricted submarine warfare, 237, 238

Wilson, John, 131

Wilson, Woodrow, 85, 122, 229–230, 233–234, 235, 237, 238–239, 252, 257
  asks for declaration of war on Germany, 241–242
  character, 86

diplomatic exchanges with Germany, 94–95, 184–185, 186–189, 195–196, 197–198, 236
  early career, 86–87
  on U.S. neutrality, 87–89
  on submarine warfare, 95, 187–188, 238–239
  reacts to sinking, 184, 185–186
  "strict accountability," 94–95
  views self as "the Great Arbitrator," 94, 198–199

Zimmerman, Arthur, 189–190, 196, 239–240
  and "Zimmermann Telegram," 239–240, 243